# PRAISE FOR *THE AGILE ORGANIZATION*

This book offers a masterclass in translating the rhetoric of organizational 'agility' into a grounded, practical and most of all wise guide to both the strategy and implementation of agility. Linda Holbeche has few peers when it comes to writing about HR strategy and this book is another triumph.
**Stephen Bevan, Head, HR Research Development, Institute for Employment Studies**

Agility has to be at the heart of business thinking in a rapidly changing and uncertain world. This book provides an insightful and comprehensive look at what agility really means, from strategy and leadership, to culture, people, and processes.
**Peter Cheese, Chief Executive, CIPD**

This is a timely revision of this insightful book by Linda Holbeche. The book draws on multiple perspectives and case examples to support why and how organizations and individuals should invest in building an agile organization. A strong case is built for how agility, flexibility and resilience are all concepts that need to be given equal focus by organizational leaders; the reflective questions and checklists presented in each chapter clearly support this.
**Dr Christina Evans, Independent Career Coach and Educator**

With the post-pandemic shocks to our way of life and working, we now face a very uncertain geopolitical world economically, environmentally and to maintain peace. We now have to prepare ourselves for a future we cannot foresee. Agility, resilience and speed have become essential in our lives. Linda's latest book describes and illustrates ways forward for organizations and people to adapt to this ever-changing world. It is a 'must read' for leaders in all walks of life, to work with their people to prepare them to change and adapt to this new reality. It defines a new social contract between organizations and its people, including customers. Agility is no longer a buzz word it is a mindset we must all adopt.
**Roger Leek, Chair, Roffey Park Institute, formerly SVP, Global HR, Fujitsu**

This book clearly and eloquently checks all the boxes required to become change-able organization. It is comprehensive in breadth and useful with checklists on actions to make agility happen.
**Dave Ulrich, Rensis Likert Professor, Ross School of Business, University of Michigan, and Co-founder and Director, the RBL Group**

Highly recommended 'go to' guide on the agile organization and how to navigate the rapidly changing landscape to bring about meaningful transformation. The third edition brings more compelling practical insights and recommended actions to continue to be an invaluable resource for leaders, HR & OD practitioners and all those leading change. Already an essential reference and helpful guide for those in the NHS, this up-to-date contemporary edition will be greatly valued and relevant across all sectors and organizations. A must-read.
**Karen Dumain, National OD Lead, NHS England**

Linda very ably manages to demystify what agility means in practical terms through sharing of experiences of organizations who have been on this journey, making a compelling argument for a strong link between agility and resilience as a recipe for success. The practical tips and checklists in the book pave the way for professionals embarking on work in this area.
**Roshan Israni, Deputy CEO, University and Colleges Employers Association (UCEA)**

Linda's book provides a lucid guide for business leaders and HR practitioners alike in rapidly changing environments including pandemics, uncertain geopolitical landscapes, AI advancements and shifting worker expectations. Linda shows us how to stay ahead of the curve through organizational agility, achieved by engaged and resilient work cultures, more flexible people processes and innovation. A stimulating read.
**Mira Bacelj, Director, Human Resources, INTERPOL**

# The Agile Organization

*How to Build an Engaged, Innovative and Resilient Business*

THIRD EDITION

Linda Holbeche

First published in Great Britain and the United States in 2023 by Kogan Page Limited

| | | |
|---|---|---|
| 2nd Floor, 45 Gee Street | 8 W 38th Street, Suite 902 | 4737/23 Ansari Road |
| London | New York, NY 10018 | Daryaganj |
| EC1V 3RS | USA | New Delhi 110002 |
| United Kingdom | | India |
| www.koganpage.com | | |

Kogan Page books are printed on paper from sustainable forests.

**ISBNs**

Hardback    978 1 3986 0868 9
Paperback   978 1 3986 0866 5
Ebook       978 1 3986 0867 2

**British Library Cataloguing-in-Publication Data**

A CIP record for this book is available from the British Library.

**Library of Congress Control Number**

2023935992

Typeset by Integra Software Services, Pondicherry
Print production managed by Jellyfish
Printed and bound by CPI Group (UK) Ltd, Croydon CR0 4YY

# CONTENTS

# Introduction

Organizational agility is a hot topic these days – and is it any wonder? In a world undergoing continuous and multifaceted change, so fast-moving is the business landscape that organizations must adapt swiftly simply to survive. Organizational agility, or the ability to continuously adjust and adapt strategic direction in a core business, is increasingly considered *the* vital business success factor.

The term 'VUCA' is often used to describe the volatile, uncertain, complex and ambiguous world we now inhabit, with its turbulent financial and commodity markets and geopolitical instabilities. Financial turbulence has increased in intensity and persists longer than in the past.[1] The financial crisis that began in 2008 rendered many business models obsolete as organizations throughout the world were plunged into chaotic environments. Business cycles are now much shorter and high-velocity operating models are the order of the day. The COVID-19 pandemic accelerated the implementation of virtual working seemingly overnight. The war in Ukraine has jeopardized world peace as well as global supply lines. The days when traditional management models – such as strategic planning based on extrapolations from the past – were enough to keep organizations ahead of the curve seem long gone.

In a VUCA world no company consistently beats the market. Megatrends, such as demographics, digitization, connectivity, trade liberalization, global competition and business-model innovation, are leading to the emergence of new competitors and driving new ways of doing business. Organizations are also experiencing unpredictable consumer sentiment, increasing complexity, rising uncertainty, an overload of information and a lack of resources. Since 2020, against a backdrop of consumer activism, purpose in business has really taken off: people want to buy from ethical brands. The impacts of many of these trends are uncertain – but there are some common themes and multiple interdependences between the drivers, which suggest that their effects will be complex and enduring. This combination of factors is forcing many companies to rethink where future business success will come from since previous success is no guarantee of future prosperity.

The only certainty is that before long every organization will be challenged to change in ways for which there is no precedent and the old ways may no longer be the best ways. Innovation and the ability to change continuously and effectively will be key to survival and future prosperity. Pandemic lockdowns have accelerated the move towards remote and hybrid working. Many organizations are still working out their policies on the new 'workplace'. Of course, the alternative to business transformation is to stand still, Canute-like, in the face of the incoming tide of change, but that might not prove the wisest course. In other words, these profound changes in the global business environment require new ways of leading and managing organizations and fresh answers to the question: what do organizations have to do to survive and thrive in today's fast-moving, complex times?

That's what this book is about.

Essentially, I shall argue that if business leaders and people who work in organizations are to thrive in today's fluid landscape they must adopt agile practices and the mindsets that underpin them. I also maintain that agility is not a stand-alone capability; it must be complemented by organizational resilience, or the ability to learn and recover from significant setbacks. How organizations pursue agility impacts their resilience and their capacity to act. If agility is pursued purely as a cost-saving exercise, people are likely to feel treated as expendable costs and will be less likely to release their discretionary effort to make things happen for the organization. Thus the organization will be unlikely to achieve the beneficial 'value' outcomes of agility such as adaptability, speed, innovation and sustainability. Achieving the right balance of agility and resilience is essential to survival. This book proposes ways in which organizations and their stakeholders, especially the people who work for them, can attempt to have the best of all worlds.

## Who is the book for?

In writing a book it is usual to address one key audience. In the case of organizational agility, there are several audiences and these are the people I consider to be the key players in Agile. These include:

- Executives who act as sponsors of strategic change. They play a key role actually and symbolically in forging the way ahead. They need to develop their agile leadership abilities, which include knowing when to step away and let others get involved in decision making.

- Line managers are central to day-to-day operations and for many employees represent the reality of their relationship with the organization. They too need to play different roles in Agile, becoming coach and supporter to self-managed teams.

- Functional specialists in HR, Organization Development, Internal Communications, Marketing, Knowledge Management, Finance and IT all have roles to play in designing policies and strategies to support the development of more agile working practices, and must work together to produce well-integrated outcomes. I shall argue that HR and Organization Development (OD) specialists who understand the dynamics of change in organizational systems potentially have a significant contribution to make to their organization's sustainable success.

- The workforce itself, in all its component parts, including outsourced and contract workers. These are the eyes and ears of the organization, on the front line of discovery through their work with customers. They need to be willing to play a proactive role in agile execution and innovation.

- Finally, external stakeholders – boards, shareholders, communities – can only benefit when these internal stakeholders shift the paradigm and breathe life into the agile organization.

In some cases I have highlighted the specific roles of different key players – for instance through case study examples or whole chapters. I have included a checklist at the end of most chapters to help different audiences reflect on specific issues and to pinpoint how they might improve their organization's agility and resilience.

## How is the book organized?

This third edition builds on earlier editions of the book and incorporates some new material. The book sets out to answer a number of questions relating to organizational agility, such as:

- What makes an organization agile? Is agile something you do, or something you are?

- Where is the 'people bit' of agile?

- Is there such a thing as an 'agile culture'?

- How does continuous improvement differ from whole-system transformation? What kinds of structures enable agility?

- How can you develop organizational 'change-readiness', or increase 'dynamic capacity'?
- What is the system of change that leads to real transformation and what are the principles upon which this is based?
- What is the role of leadership in building organizational agility?

In framing answers to these questions I work through a model that I introduce in Chapter 2 outlining the 'what', 'why' and 'who' of organizational agility and resilience. In developing the model I have built on the work of various theorists to whom I am indebted. In particular I wish to credit the work of Dave Francis and Sandra Meredith, whose 2000 model originally inspired my thinking.[2] The remaining chapters of the book explore the 'how' of organizational resilience and agility.

## Chapter 1: Why go agile?

Here I set the context and outline the business case for organizational agility, working through a number of broad cultural, economic and environmental factors and megatrends such as digitization, which are leading to the development of new markets, businesses and channels and raising consumer expectations – at speed. While some might argue that the need for agility applies only to specific types of business, such as high-technology, I maintain that organizations of every sector and industry will be under increasing pressure to develop greater agility as these context effects grow more substantial. The after-effects of the COVID-19 pandemic and the uncertain geopolitical climate give the search for agility added impetus.

I define organizational agility and some of its related outcomes such as innovation. I consider what enables an organization to become more adaptable and resilient so that it can respond to a changing context more quickly and find ways to thrive in that new and challenging environment. I explore how many organizations are pursuing agility through cost-cutting, downsizing, offshoring or outsourcing non-core activities, working through networks of suppliers and 'partner' organizations. The connection between organizational resilience and the employment relationship between employers and employees is discussed. Implications for the skills and mindsets of people working in resiliently agile organizations are highlighted.

## Chapter 2: The resiliently agile organization

This is an overview of the resiliently agile model and related capabilities and routines. The model comprises four quadrants – agile strategizing, implementing, linkages and people practices. Central to the model is agile culture and people. The model's elements are explored in turn in later chapters of the book.

## Chapter 3: Agile strategizing

We discuss differences between conventional strategy making and the process of strategizing – in particular the importance of involving the people who will execute a strategy in its formulation. We draw lessons from long-lived, successful companies about the centrality of shared purpose and how this might be developed. We consider the role of top leadership in strategizing, and the skills involved, especially knowing where to go 'tight' and 'loose' with respect to control and enabling greater autonomy.

## Chapter 4: Agile linkages

Organizations increasingly pursue agility and flexibility by working across and beyond conventional boundaries of time and place. We discuss emergent flexible organization forms, including the rise of virtual working, and look at the skills implications. We examine some of the challenges of working in strategic alliances and partnerships, including their implications for managers, and consider what can help alliances to work effectively. We look at how one cooperative is able to successfully balance the global/local tension to achieve business success.

## Chapter 5: Designing for agility

Here we consider how digitization and the pursuit of customer-centricity are driving new ways of structuring work and organization. We consider some of the evolving ways of organizing for agility, including organizing around customer journeys. We consider a case of an HR team's customer-centric redesign from the outside in. We also compare a conventional versus agile design process. The chapter includes a case study illustrating a systemic approach to designing for agility.

## Chapter 6: Agile implementation

Closing the conventional gap between strategy formulation and implementation will require new ways of operating, new disciplines and the adoption of new routines and high-performance work practices, such as self-managed teams, so that innovation and speed become embedded capabilities in the new, agile 'business as usual'. We discuss lean methodology, agile project management disciplines and how to create an internal climate conducive to innovation. We consider the implications of these agile practices for the roles of line managers. We also look at work design for empowerment and the value of job crafting for individuals and groups.

## Chapter 7: Agile people processes

In this chapter we look in more detail at the 'people' aspects of agility; in particular some of the challenges of attracting and developing a flexible workforce – specifically those people deemed to be 'talent'. All too often these people challenges are addressed piecemeal, with separate, short-term solutions, and the temptation is to rush straight into action to 'fix' the problem. A more strategic approach is needed in order to equip organizations with the people they need now and for the future of work, so here we consider how approaches to strategic workforce planning, sourcing and recruitment, talent management, development approaches and succession planning can become more agile. We also consider approaches to developing customer-centric leaders.

## Chapter 8: Nurturing employee engagement and resilience

Simply having the 'right people' in the 'right' place at the 'right' time is not enough to ensure agility. People need to be willing to adapt to changing requirements and give their best in a sustainably resilient way. Here we consider the central link between employee engagement and employee performance, commitment and retention. We consider the roles played by executives, line managers, HR/Organization Development (OD) and employees themselves in creating a work context conducive to employee engagement. We also consider the links between employee engagement and wellbeing and how organizations can help to build employee resilience during times of change.

## Chapter 9: HR's role in building a high-performance work climate

In this chapter we look at some of the many ways in which the Human Resources function can contribute to building a culture of high performance and innovation. We consider flexible working and some of the challenges and opportunities of virtual and hybrid working. Here we focus in particular on how HR strategies relating to performance management, recognition, reward and benefits are changing to reflect context shifts and to support specific organizational strategies such as innovation. We also look at career resilience and how organizations can help employees to help themselves and access meaningful career opportunities.

## Chapter 10: Building a change-able culture

In this chapter we look at stimulating the development of a change-able culture, building a receptive organizational context for innovation, change and high performance. We look at what a 'change-able' context might look like, how to take stock of what may need to change and how to build a bottom-up social movement for change and improvement within organizations. We explore the role of leaders in culture change. We also look at the need to embed diversity and inclusion within organizations.

## Chapter 11: Agile leadership

The questions we consider in this chapter are what agile leadership is and how leadership can be built across organizations – not only by developing people and teams in 'formal' leadership roles but also by catalysing a culture of shared leadership and accountability at all levels. We look at the shifts taking place in leadership practice, including towards values-based leadership. We consider what these shifts mean for the skills and mindsets required of leaders – and how these can be developed. In particular we look at how leaders can build a culture of shared leadership – the bedrock of sustainable agility and renewal.

My aim is to demystify the theme of organizational agility and resilience and to offer some practical insights. I have therefore included checklists throughout the book and case study examples where possible to illustrate how some of the theory can be put into practice.

## ONLINE RESOURCES

*Access the full, informative additional content below for free by registering or signing in via* www.koganpage.com/the-agile-organization

Why are agility and resilience so elusive?

Examples of truly agile organizations are rare, while evidence of lack of agility abounds. Here we consider some of the reasons why that might be the case. We start by setting the search for agility in a historical context, looking at the changing nature of the 'white collar' employment relationship between employers and employees and the changing balance of power in that relationship. We then consider a range of structural and cultural practices that add to complexity and keep organizations anchored in the past. We also examine the new leadership mindsets and skill sets required for leading in fast-moving, ambiguous business environments. Finally, we look at some of the people 'push' factors for change, not least talent shortages and changing workforce demographics, which are driving a new focus on getting 'the people bit' right.

Change and transformation

Conventional planned change based on the idea that organizations are machines that can be 're-engineered' has a poor track record of success yet it remains a preferred management approach. Here we look at how 'planned' change can be effected in a way that achieves win-win outcomes for organizations and employees. We consider the move towards more agile change methods and the importance of getting stakeholders on board and involving people in the change process. We also look at how typical human responses to change can be anticipated and how people can be helped to manage their personal transition to the 'new'.

## Notes

1  Sullivan, J (2012) Talent Strategies for a Turbulent VUCA World – Shifting to an Adaptive Approach, *Ere.net*, ere.net/talent-strategies-for-a-turbulent-vuca-world-shifting-to-an-adaptive-approach/ (archived at https://perma.cc/4GV3-ADA4).

2  Francis, D and Meredith, S (2000) Journey towards agility: the agile wheel explored, *The TQM Magazine*, **12** (2), pp 137–43.

# 01

# Why go agile?

Until recently, notions of organizational agility may have been dismissed by some as a management fad. Yet the need for organizational agility has been growing for decades. Back in the 1990s Peter Drucker predicted that, against a backdrop of a possible fall of economic integration throughout the European Union and the increasing power of China, a new economic order would emerge based on a knowledge society in which information and communication technologies and advanced technologies would transform businesses and their operations. He argued that innovation and entrepreneurship, and the ability to work in partnership with other organizations, all elements of organizational agility, would make the difference between those organizations that survive and those that do not.

Drucker's predictions proved correct of course; yet he perhaps underestimated the degree of volatility that would follow. Before the COVID-19 pandemic, businesses were already under pressure from technological and other forces to manage change and make decisions more quickly than ever before. The pandemic has vastly intensified those needs. Never have companies of all sizes been under so much pressure to make their business models fit changing requirements.

Agility is an advanced management capability that allows leaders to innovate, exploit opportunities and achieve competitive advantage by making timely, effective and sustainable organization changes. Today the landscape of opportunities has dramatically changed and the need for some sort of agility for organizations in every sector has never been greater. The market turbulence of recent times has vividly highlighted the need for companies to anticipate and address pivotal events that affect their business. While planning for the unpredictable in a period of turbulence may seem impossible, many firms now recognize that the ability to work in complexity, innovate, flex and adapt at speed is critical for sustaining growth.

As Bart Schlatmann,[1] former Chief Operating Officer of ING Bank points out: 'Any organization can become agile, but agility is not a purpose in itself; it's the means to a broader purpose. The first question you have to ask yourself is, "Why agile? What's the broader purpose?" Make sure there is a clear and compelling reason that everyone recognizes, because you have to go all in – backed up by the entire leadership team – to make such a transformation a success.'

The challenge for leaders and managers is to define the role that organizational agility needs to play in an organization and ensure that essential agile capabilities, such as responsiveness, adaptability and resilience, are developed and used. This requires managers to deeply understand the concept of organizational agility, embrace relevant mindsets and decide how to use the potential benefits of organizational agility within a wider set of managerial priorities.[2]

In this chapter we consider:

- why organizational agility is important
- what organizational agility is about
- what is driving the need for agility
- why resilience is such a crucial counterbalance to agility.

## A context of disruption and fast change

Strategic agility is emerging as the essential capacity that organizations must possess if they are to adapt successfully to disruptive change. Today we are living in a new sociological, political and technocratic era characterized by periods of sharp, novel conditions that upset competitive dynamics, whether these are natural disasters or man-made crises.[3] Societies and businesses are being transformed in ways that cannot be predicted and outcomes are complex and harder to manage.

Disruption comes in many forms. The global political backdrop feels unstable as a confluence of trends unsettles the world order. Since the second edition of this book was published in 2018, we have seen political disruption across the globe, mass migration, resource scarcity, climate extremes; witnessed regime change in Afghanistan, the invasion of the Ukraine by Russia and experienced the global COVID-19 pandemic. The impact on economies is significant. Consequences include hugely increased fuel and food prices, disrupted supply lines and global inflationary pressures, food shortages, mass displacement and growing inequalities. International commitments made by many countries regarding climate change have gone into reverse as governments struggle to meet their energy needs.

The backdrop is ever more volatile thanks to debased political discourse that accentuates national and global divides. An increase in political populism across the globe has left democracy itself under threat, for instance when the Capitol, the seat of US democracy, was attacked by mobs protesting against the so-called 'steal' of the presidential election in 2020. In many cases political leaders harness the power of the media – social and otherwise – to distort the messy reality. Increasingly the line between truth and fantasy gets blurred, with significant consequences. Echo chambers within social media create seemingly unbridgeable chasms of misunderstanding between groups and peoples. In a politically adversarial context, notions of collaboration between nations and businesses may seem unrealistic.

As the 2022 UNDP Human Development report[4] points out, the backdrop of global resource scarcity is gloomy: 'Global crises have piled up: the global financial crisis, the ongoing global climate crisis and Covid19 pandemic, a looming global food crisis.' As a result, 'there is a nagging sense that whatever control we have over our lives is slipping away, that the norms and institutions we used to rely on for stability and prosperity are not up to the task of today's uncertainty complex'.

Not surprisingly pundits have dubbed this the 'Age of Anxiety'.

## The business case for agility

Arguably, for organizations as well as individuals the need for agility to weather the storm and thrive has never been greater. The executive community must navigate this global geopolitical and economic unrest, develop new ways forward for their businesses and attempt to attract and retain both customers and employees. In conditions of increasing turbulence, organizations need to be able to generate adaptive capacity and innovate. Even if the current turbulence settles down, it seems likely that underlying fluctuations in energy, labour, commodity and currency rates, the emergence of new and non-traditional competitors, and rising customer demands will continue to put pressure on traditional business and operating models for some time to come.

In the current challenging context new rules of the game are being invented; there will be some winners and many losers. Already we have seen that, without the attributes of agility, organizations are on the path to oblivion. The list of industries engulfed by complex strategic change grows longer every day and statistics on organizational decline are startling. Research conducted by the Deloitte Center for the Edge indicates that over the last 55 years the average company tenure on the S&P 500 has declined from 61 years to 18 years with many losing their leadership positions during that time. Entire ecosystems of industries as diverse as healthcare, aerospace, pharmaceuticals, energy, retailing, defence, advertising, financial services, retail and automotive have been radically transformed in the face of a variety of factors – political, cultural, economic, technological and demographic – that are forcing the pace of change. Research by the Center for Effective Organizations (CEO) describes such organizations as the 'thrashers'.

Success is nevertheless possible. CEO has found that a few large companies in every industry consistently outperform their peers over extended periods. These companies have proved able to anticipate and respond to events, solve problems and implement change better than the thrashers. And they maintain this performance edge despite significant business change in their competitive environments.[5]

What these survivor organizations have in common is agility. Agile organizations are better able to thrive in complex environments because they have developed the ability to spot business opportunities and threats early and to implement change quickly. Agile organizations create not only new products and services but also new business models and innovative ways to create value for a company. High-tech companies have been leading the way:

> As it stands, organisations like Netflix, Airbnb, Uber and of course Google have continued to experiment further into alternative structures and processes to encourage innovative ways for delivering work. Their aim is to ensure their people will take advantage of collaboration, build a fluid understanding of work, act intentionally about the lack of rigid hierarchy, experiment with quicker decision-making structures and processes, and promote the intelligent use of data, all with a view to engaging successfully with customers on a massive scale.[6]

Environmental and social issues have, rightly, become targets for responsible agency. Many agile consumer-facing corporations are starting to integrate more sustainable practices into their business models. They have found that in an environmentally conscious marketplace, sustainability can be good for business. At industry level, survivor organizations are responding to turbulence by entering broad-based alliances and consortia for acting on widely shared challenges, such as alleviating global warming, collaboratively strengthening global supply chains, speeding shared decision making through open-access information networks and setting industry standards. These are all ways of building adaptive capacity beyond a single organization.[7]

The returns on agility are significant. Agile companies exhibit superior business value relative to their industry groups.[8] Agile businesses have 29 per cent higher earnings per share, with net margins 20 per cent higher, return on assets 30 per cent higher and revenue growth 8 per cent higher than comparable businesses.[9] Not surprisingly, in a substantial 2009 study by the Economist Intelligence Unit the overwhelming majority of executives (88 per cent) cited agility as key to global success and 50 per cent of executives said that organizational agility is not only important but a key differentiator.[10] Despite 90 per cent of managers and executives being aware that their industries will be disrupted by digital trends to a great or moderate extent, a 2015 global survey conducted by *MIT Sloan Management Review* and Deloitte suggests that only 44 per cent of managers believe their organizations are adequately preparing for the disruptions to come.[11]

Given the changing context, the CEO argues that when the measure of high performance in business is profitability, as measured by shareholder return, this is impossible to sustain over the long term.[12] It proposes that return on assets (ROA) is a more meaningful proxy for profitability than either total shareholder return (TSR) or cumulative shareholder return and is a better indicator of management's effectiveness. This measure suggests that the management of agile companies takes a longer-term view and is more concerned about investing in value creation processes than attending solely to generating short-term shareholder value.

## Evolution of agility theory

First let's consider a brief account of where agility theories come from and what preceded them before looking further at what is driving the need for agility today.

Agility is a complex construct that can take multiple forms. Originally linked with Agile methods in software development, lean manufacturing, just-in-time supply chains and process improvement methodologies in the 1990s, agility theory is now informed by complexity science. 'Organizational agility' captures an organization's whole-system dynamic capability to adapt, develop and swiftly apply flexible, nimble, innovative, customer-centric products and services in the changing environment. Agility is not confined to high-tech or commercial enterprises.

These different theories reflect the times in which they emerged, though it could be argued that these intertwined social and business trends continue to influence people's thinking and expectations today.

## A global marketplace

Since the 1980s knowledge and service industries have become the main-spring of many Western economies. Industries such as financial services have been progressively deregulated to enable global competition. Today's marketplaces are ruthlessly competitive, in part because the dominant economic philosophy underpinning the global economy since the 1980s is neo-liberalism, or free-market thinking and practice. This thinking places shareholder value as the dominant goal of organizations, and related reward structures encourage short-term thinking from the top to bottom of organizations. Neo-liberal theory underpins mainstream management theory and practice widely taught in business schools. It has affected organ-izations of every sector, and also appears to have influenced societal values in the West. The globalized economy has increasingly operated along free-market lines, aided and abetted by the opening up of many previously protected markets. In the UK and US before the onset of the financial crash in 2008, consumerism – fuelled by easy access to cheap credit – led to wide-spread individual and public spending and debt. Deregulation enabled the proliferation of new financial products so complex and ultimately ill-founded that prior to the recession few people understood their nature. Early warning signs were ignored about what can happen when the pros-pect of huge bonuses drives ill-judged behaviour, as in the case of several 'rogue traders' whose reckless gambling brought their own employers' businesses to their knees.

### MANAGEMENT THEORY IN THE 1990s
In terms of management theory, processes became recognized as an impor-tant element of business success. A raft of approaches from manufacturing,

often described as 'Japanese management practices' – such as total quality management, continuous improvement, kaizen, business process re-engineering and lean methodologies – were increasingly adopted, usually by large organizations. Toyota was a leading exponent of such methods in the West. Putting the customer first became the rationale for 'delayering' organizations – making them flatter and more horizontal in terms of the customer process, removing many hierarchical management jobs that were often described as 'checkers checking checkers'. Limited amounts of outsourcing began in 'non-core' areas, enabled by technology and facilitated by the diminishing power of trade unions and lack of collective protections for employees.

### WHAT DID THIS MEAN FOR PEOPLE AND THE EMPLOYMENT RELATIONSHIP?

Increasingly common organizational downsizings started to undermine the white-collar notion of a 'job for life'. Given the fluidity of organizational environments, the old 'psychological contract' or employment 'deal' of job security and career progression in exchange for hard work and loyalty was becoming an expensive liability for employers who were now looking for more flexibility and cost-effectiveness with regard to the workforce. While people were regularly described as their organizations' 'greatest asset', they were increasingly treated as its greatest cost.

The emergent psychological contract (or 'new deal') implied that employees should no longer expect job security or career progression within the same company unless they were exceptional. Instead they should continuously upgrade their performance and skills to remain employable. Rather than looking for employee loyalty, employers now wanted commitment and flexibility from their employees. The assumptions behind the new employment relationship were unitarist: that the interests of business and those of employees were aligned, i.e. that what was good for the business was good for the people.

HR policies embedded these new approaches into the employment relationship. As performance management became more widespread, people's performance ratings became the justification for decisions about their continuing employment or promotion. The link between seniority (time served) and career and pay progression was largely disaggregated and performance-related pay was introduced in many sectors. The UK became the easiest country in Europe in which to hire and fire employees. What was good for the business was perhaps not always good for employees.

Many highly skilled white-collar workers felt disillusioned about the loss of the 'old deal' and, as the jobs market improved, now felt free to shop around, leading to medium labour flexibility. So much so that by the end of the 1990s business growth in some knowledge-based sectors, particularly consultancies, was being constrained by the lack of sufficient skilled people to do the work. Thus began what McKinsey dubbed the 'War for Talent', as employers vied with each other to attract and retain the best available 'talent'.

## The rise of agile

The arrival of the internet and other advanced technologies led to a huge increase in the scale and types of competition for organizations large and small, enabling even tiny enterprises based in developing countries to compete on a global scale. The concept of Agile arose in the late 1990s when an Agile movement came into being that was synonymous with the intensive use of IT and software development.

Agile began as a set of project management practices developed by a growing community of specialists in Utah who knew that conventional 'waterfall' types of project management for software development rarely worked in fast-moving contexts. Their Agile Manifesto set out four values that put the customer front and centre of the work and ushered in a different way of working:

- individuals and interactions over processes and tools
- working software over comprehensive documentation
- customer collaboration over contract negotiation
- responding to change over following a plan.

Agile methodologies include iterative project management methods, team-work including frequent communications, tools such as scrum and kanban boards or equivalent, customer involvement, lean tools and continuous improvement approaches. These are applied to develop many kinds of systems, including web-based applications, mobile applications and business intelligence systems, and increasingly to other aspects of organization such as culture change. While these processes can be important enablers, designing an organization for agility requires a focus on developing the core organization and leadership capabilities that enable the organization to make timely, effective and sustained organization changes that support long-term performance advantage.

In recent times it has been recognized that agility should be a whole-system capability in the face of extreme complexity. By the time discussion of the agile enterprise arose in the early 2000s, it was against a backdrop of widespread lack of trust in employers and, increasingly, institutions and their leaders in the wake of various corporate and other scandals. All too often agile applied to employment is linked with the 'gig' economy, which effectively turns workers into self-employed subcontractors to companies that operate as platforms. These workers typically lack collective bargaining power, receive low pay and lack any sort of job security.

A profusion of literature has been generated on the broader concept of organizational agility, much of it by consultancies, describing the shifts in mindset and practices required to run an agile organization. The wider definition of an agile organization is still being developed, but some of its key elements and attributes include speed, customer-centricity, teamwork, breaking down long-term challenges into short-term iterations, experimentation, innovation, co-creation, working across boundaries, learning from failure as well as success. This requires not only willingness to adopt new ways of working but potentially also a shift in culture, structure and mindsets. As was evident during pandemic lockdowns such transformations are possible and at speed with changes that were expected to take years happening in months, days or even hours. Based on this common experience, rather than reverting to old, familiar ways of operating we should be reimagining work and the workplace for the future when the context calls for new.

Some of the key capabilities of agility are as follows.

## Ability to adapt

While the metaphor of organizations as well-oiled machines that can control their destinies remains dominant in management thinking, it is increasingly replaced by the metaphor of organizations as complex adaptive systems that, like living organisms, naturally adapt to their context or they die. Evolution theory teaches us that organisms are naturally changing and adapting to their environments all the time, often in infinitesimal ways. They experiment, learn what works, find sources of nourishment and opportune contexts in which to grow. Applying the theory of evolution to organizations it is reasonable to assume that only the 'fittest' – those that can successfully respond to and learn from external events and adapt rapidly to their changing ecosystems – will survive and thrive into the future. Short feedback loops should ensure situational awareness so that organisms can pivot accordingly. This ability to adjust for fast improvement reflects the principle of agility. As Professor Ed Lawler III puts it, superior performance is possible only when there is a high degree of fit between the requirements of the environment and the capabilities of the firm. In today's increasingly turbulent environments, this fit is temporary at best. To remain successful, organizations must be able to change in a way that creates a new alignment when the environment changes; in other words they must be agile.[13]

## Ability to manage change

Many organizations struggle to manage change and appear ill-equipped to deal with major transformation, especially the kinds of change linked to what D'Aveni calls 'hyper-organization'.[14] The underlying logic of hyper-organization is to focus on staying slim, reducing costs and externalizing risks, stripping out unnecessary positions, outsourcing processes and people, ruthlessly pursuing greater efficiency while keeping up and improving performance levels.

As chief executives work to short-termist agendas and take drastic measures to minimize cost and maximize economic growth, managers consistently tend to pay more attention to the 'process' and 'technology' aspects of transformation than to the 'people' element, with often seriously limiting consequences for the organization and for people. More often than not, rather than creating the new ways forward needed for the organization, the way that change is managed can be so disruptive that it can tear the organization apart. When change results in organizational chaos, initiative overload and employee resistance, the gap between strategic intent and strategic implementation widens, slowing down progress still further.

The key question then is whether the 'natural' ability of human organization to change can be deliberately accelerated and optimized to benefit all concerned. Can organizations learn to become 'change-able' and adaptable? To some extent at least, yes. Reportedly, according to Darwin's *Origin of Species*, 'it is not the most intellectual of the species that survives; it is not the strongest that survives; but the species most adaptable to change'. As we discuss in Chapter 2, there are many ways to introduce positive change into the system even though direct benefits cannot be guaranteed. In later chapters we look at how various organizations are attempting to become more change-able.

## Speed

Given the rapid pace of technological development and growth of global competition, agility is the ability to move 'quickly, decisively, and effectively in anticipating, initiating and taking advantage of change'.[15] Almost every aspect of the business environment and business itself is being transformed by disruptive forces. As they pursue growth, in today's hyper-competitive technology-driven phase of globalization, organizations can expect extreme competitive and operating pressures. They need to move swiftly just to keep pace with developments, take advantage of opportunities or avert disaster. The days when major corporations could dominate markets and provide standardized products at inflated margins seem to be coming to an end.

Disruption and pace of change are two critical dimensions of turbulence that have increased in recent times, transforming the way we run organizations and live our lives. Each has unique implications and adaptive requirements that vary across organizations. With respect to pace, when product cycles are predictable fast change can be managed. McCann noted that the best-performing organizations in fast-paced environments move quickly to identify opportunities and avoid collisions.[16] Conversely, retaining competitive edge in the face of what Professor Clayton Christensen termed 'disruptive innovation' can be a real challenge.[17]

The term originally described how and why some changes in the technology sector (and now more widely in all business sectors) led, in a relatively short time, to a radical restructuring of the overall system. Just look at the UK retail sector, where a combination of tough trading conditions, reduced consumer spending and fierce competition from online retailers led to the closures of several well-known high street firms such as Woolworths, Comet and Focus. Christensen found that disruptive innovations in a given marketplace are often triggered by the arrival of new competitors who punctuate the existing equilibrium having spotted opportunities, usually aided by changes to a wider context. Thanks to globalization and technology, new competitors can emerge from anywhere and completely rewrite the laws of competition through innovation.

In the digital era everything is interconnected, with multiple accelerations both in terms of product development and execution. If the product road map takes longer than four to six weeks, a product (and company) is at a high risk of quickly becoming obsolete. Compare the fortunes of companies such as Eastman Kodak who appear to have waited too long before responding to marketplace developments, leaving them struggling to survive in a diminished form, with others such as Amazon, buffeted by the same challenging headwinds, that managed to reinvent itself from being a web-based bookseller to an online retail platform to a digital media powerhouse, then a leader in cloud computing. And this continual change has taken place without a performance crisis, demonstrating an ability to anticipate changes and adapt – instead of the reverse.

Agile organizations are able to react swiftly and decisively to sudden shifts in overall market conditions, the emergence of new competitors, and the arrival of new industry-changing technologies by developing a range of products that satisfy a range of customers. This requires a deep focus on customers, a proactive orientation towards change and the capacity for scanning, making sense of, and quickly acting on what is perceived in the environment. It is essential to pick out fast what matters and act accordingly. As noted by Horney, Pasmore and O'Shea, to succeed, 'leaders must make continuous shifts in people, process, technology, and structure. This requires flexibility and quickness in decision making,'[18] along with the capacity for moving resources wherever needed to support those actions.

## Innovation

As well as encapsulating the ability to adapt and thrive in fast-changing environments, agility is also defined as the ability to 'produce the right products in the right place at the right time at the right price'.[19] The consumer boom since the early 2000s continues apace and the consumer desire for novelty and stimulation is driving the quest for pace, quality and innovation as well as low cost. Consequently, it is no surprise that accelerated innovation now sits high on executive and board agendas in every sector. Innovation is what agile is all about. In highly dynamic environments, given the rapid spread of new software tools, organizations need innovation not only in products and services but also in functional processes. Companies that create an environment in which agile flourishes find that teams can produce innovations faster in both categories.[20]

In Christensen's 1997 book *The Innovator's Dilemma* he distinguished between 'sustaining innovation' (incremental or step changes in an existing order) and 'disruptive innovation' (major changes that ultimately transform an industry sector). So, while existing players in a given market might be better at sustaining innovation, it is usually new entrants who become the real winners at disruptive innovation. Compare for instance the fortunes of insurgents such as Apple with established firms such as Nokia. Nokia witnessed the Apple iPhone crush its global business, particularly at the high end of smartphones, which were by far the most lucrative segment of its business. Indeed, things are so fast-moving that manufacturers of high-end smartphones and tablets now fear that consumer demand for their gadgets may be slowing down due to market saturation.

In retailing consumers are looking for the latest products, choice, person-alization, quality and low cost. Innovation applies not only to product design but also to delivery mechanisms. Today shoppers can opt for online home deliveries or 'click and collect' services with goods ready for collection within hours at convenient points such as their local store. The business model involves cutting out the 'middle man' and shortening the supply chain. Of course, home delivery companies will not go without a fight and, partly in response to the spread of click and collect services, couriers are now making home deliveries every day of the week, thus pushing up costs to delivery companies. So the ability to keep abreast or ahead of customer demand – or better still, to create it – needs to be married with the ability to innovate technically and organizationally, and to plan and execute new courses of action that are cost-effective and fast. Agile working helps deliver products more quickly through practices such as two-week sprints. Standardization is needed but so too is empowerment; control is required but so too is innovation.

So, agile organizations that are able to 'successfully respond to and learn from external events, to innovate technically and organizationally, and to plan and execute new courses of action'[21] are better able to continually and successfully adapt to changing circumstances. Through technology the possibilities for innovation and new business opportunities seem endless. For instance, in April 2014 Google announced that it had bought a company called Titan Aerospace so that the internet's biggest giants are all now 'in' drones. Facebook/Meta had previously purchased a UK drone-maker called Ascenta, and Amazon is already working on the latest generation of its Prime Air drone. Drones are already in commercial opera-tion and, 'if you're a major multinational corporation, parcel deliverer, army or key emergency services provider and you haven't either invested in a drone manufacturer or at least trialled the things, you're in danger of looking hopelessly out of step'.[22]

## Does every organization need to be 'agile'?

Is agility a prerequisite for survival for every organization? After all, it could be argued that some organizations may endemically lack agility, and yet they remain successful. Consider universities, for instance. These long-lived elite institutions have been able to select the 'best' students and secure funding in a variety of ways, not least through endowments.

However, in today's globalized knowledge economy, higher education has become a major industry, rapidly expanding, highly competitive and marketized. Thanks to high tuition fees students (and their parents) are transformed into consumers, if not customers, of higher education establishments. The challenge for today's institutions is to differentiate themselves in an increasingly crowded global marketplace in order to attract the numbers of students and other sources of funding they depend upon. Thus, in a relatively short period of time, the dramatic shifts in the higher education landscape have significantly called into question the purpose and infrastructure of higher education, and have enabled new entrants and substitutes to compete, seize market share and put all but the most financially secure institutions under pressure to change their ways if they are to survive.

However, Agile methodology is not a universal formula. Some routine operations may work well as they are and just require continuous improvement. In contrast, Agile is key in conditions commonly found in software innovation, where customer preferences and solution options change frequently; the problem to be solved is complex; solutions are initially unknown, and product requirements will most likely change; the work can be modularized; close collaboration with end users (and rapid feedback from them) is feasible; and cross-functional creative teams will typically outperform command-and-control groups. Agile innovation also depends on having a cadre of eager participants. One of Agile's core principles is 'Build projects around motivated individuals. Give them the environment and support they need and trust them to get the job done.' These conditions exist for many product-development functions, marketing projects, strategic-planning activities, supply-chain challenges and resource-allocation decisions.[23] Increasingly the broader concept of agility informed by its cultural practices, values and customer-centricity is relevant to strategy and decision making, and organizational effectiveness.

That is why I argue that agility and its various components are essential for most, if not all organizations. At the very least, we need to change the way we think about change. I agree with Abrahamson that in a world where ongoing disruption can be envisaged as the norm, and change is therefore now a way of life rather than an exception, a useful way of thinking about today's context is to see it as one of 'dynamic stability'.[24] Such a mindset allows for change to be reframed as part of an evolutionary process, as the norm to be embraced positively, without major trauma, rather than a painful add-on to 'business as usual'. Such a perspective will also affect how we enact change, moving away from the kinds of reactive change management that result in radical disruption towards a cultural shift that readily embraces and stimulates change and innovation.

To achieve this shift, Abrahamson argues that a more modulated approach to change is required, what he calls 'pacing', in which major change initiatives are deliberately interspersed with 'carefully paced periods of smaller, organic change'.[25] After all, he suggests, although some change is management-led and occurs within a strategic framework, most change is really happening locally, almost imperceptibly in automatic, spontaneous and reflexive ways at individual and team levels. In later chapters, we explore how embracing change as dynamic stability may require a conscious mindset shift and active learning for employees and managers at all levels.

## Forces driving the need for agility

Let's look in a bit more detail at what is driving the need for agility. The drivers of discontinuous change are multiple – they include the broader politico-economic system implicit in Anglo-American neo-liberal forms of capitalism, global markets, political instability, demographics, technology, connectivity, sustainable developments, changing social attitudes, to name but a few – and their effect on business and organizational survival is intensifying. These forces are global in their scope and far-reaching in their impact, affecting not only the environment in which organizations operate but also redefining what they need to do in future to compete successfully. Public sector institutions too are under ever more intense pressure to produce excellent outcomes with decreased budgets. With tighter regulation, shifting public attitudes and growing demands for transparency in their practices and outcomes, even previously venerable institutions are coming under intense scrutiny.

As discussed earlier, even traditional institutions such as universities are not immune from neo-liberal free-market practices. Denneen and Dretler argue that over the past two decades the higher education sector has followed not 'Moore's Law' (i.e. the observation that over the history of computing hardware, the number of transistors on integrated circuits doubles approximately every two years) but what they call the 'Law of More': i.e. *more* and *bigger* are better.[26] Colleges have continuously built up campus facilities and increased campus spending, the numbers of programmes they offer and the size of the administration, hoping to raise their rankings and reputations. In such a competitive marketplace, the only outcome of this, these authors argue, is an increased debt risk.

*Technology*

With respect to disruption, technological advances are pressuring costs and prices much faster than in the past through increasingly connected supply chains, squeezing budgets and ever-tighter margins. Digital has enabled automation and hyper-personalization of consumer preferences. This is driving the need to improve operations, innovate, anticipate emerging trends and develop relevant skills. According to Gartner CFO surveys, digital competencies are key to driving enterprise digital growth. Black swan events such as the global COVID-19 pandemic highlight the need to build flexibility, agility and strategic thinking into planning, budgeting and forecasting activities – all core elements of adaptive capacity.[27]

Why is the digital age so disruptive? Whole industries, businesses and working practices are being rapidly transformed by the use and effects of technology. In its many forms – for instance Big Data, artificial intelligence (AI) and generative AI such as Chat GPT and Bard, the Internet of Things, automation, robotics and 3D printing – digitization is opening up vast new opportunities. For example, the digitization of texts, symbols, instructions, patterns, visual images and music allows huge data sets to be marshalled more efficiently than in the past. For the first time, in a 2013 IBM study CEOs identified technology – rather than market forces – as the biggest driver of change.[28] Again in 2014, CEOs ranked technology first, believing that the impact of emerging technologies on their organizations will be profound. A 2022 PwC CFO survey[29] found that a vast majority of CFOs are investing in technologies like clouds and analytics to drive growth.

Thanks to the transformations wrought by digitization, stakeholders including customers are developing very different expectations about how they want to receive services and products, and about their access to knowledge and information. Many economic activities that once depended on physical proximity and face-to-face encounters can now be conducted at a distance.

Digital has informed and amplified customer power that must be responded to: 'Yes, we do have a customer-centric movement going on – among customers… [they] are acting more empowered and emboldened and are continually upping their expectations of companies. More than just a "movement", this is a large rock rumbling downhill at increasing speed that imperils anything in its way.'[30]

In other words, organizations that want to be customer-centric must be agile, and vice versa. Customer-centricity begins with the belief that there is only one customer: the person who buys or uses your organization's services or products. Indeed, the customer experience is at the heart of agility. The Agile development process familiar to software engineers institutes a set of customer-focused management practices and values achieved through iterative and incremental development, in which requirements and solutions evolve through collaboration between self-organizing, cross-functional teams and their customers.[31]

The transformational impact of new or emerging science-based technologies has wider implications for the way businesses operate. Business models that have proved successful over time no longer are. Old legacy operating models tend to be very siloed. Increasingly work is carried out at the confluence of the digital, physical and social worlds. Digital business models can remove traditional operational constraints, reorder value chains and create new opportunities, whether for a digitally modified business, a new digital business or for digital globalization. Within organizations, hierarchies and jobs for life are being replaced by a knowledge-based network economy bristling with innovative online communication technologies, including mobile devices and cloud computing.

To take advantage of the technology for many CEOs the problem is not lack of investment but lack of execution. This is as much about culture and behavioural change as it is about process change, and the impact on workers can be challenging. Technology will replace some jobs and make others more complex. If new ways of working are presented as a means to produce efficiencies that potentially lead to job loss people feel they must work harder to keep their jobs. In inflationary times, industrial relations can disintegrate as workers strike to achieve pay rises to help them meet soaring costs of living.

Technology is also enabling social transformations in the way we live and work today, even redefining notions of 'work' and 'leisure'. Technology is enabling greater choice for employees and working lives are changing accordingly. Workforce expectations are changing fast, with the diminishing centrality of work in individuals' lives and a marked shift towards so-called 'independent' or non-linear careers, where people increasingly prefer to hold multiple jobs over the course of a career, to make lateral rather than upward moves.

During the pandemic, remote working became a necessity for many organizations and workers. Especially since the pandemic an increasing number of people now work from home at least part of each week, as flexible working options have expanded, aided by improved domestic access to high-speed broadband and the widespread availability of global devices. The OECD suggests that widespread teleworking may remain a permanent feature of the future working environment. However, many employers want workers back in the workplace.[32] On the other hand, now that huge numbers of employees in many industries have experienced remote and flexible work, some may be unwilling to go back to the way things were before. While some workers may long for the type of interactions that only an in-person workplace can provide, research by the communications firm Slack suggested that in 2022 only 15 per cent of UK workers wanted to be in the office full-time.[33]

In a period of full employment, offering flexible working is key to attracting and retaining talent. Many employees choose to leave employers who will not offer sufficient flexibility. The 'Great Resignation' is a real phenomenon. Some companies are becoming remote to keep existing staff happy and appeal to new recruits. This makes it critical to find out what employees want before making any long-term decisions about working patterns. In addition to flexible working, salary and progression, professional development and company culture are deciding factors for many people when weighing up opportunities. PwC created what they believe to be a new paradigm of work, by allowing its 55,000 US employees in 2021 to work from anywhere, a policy called 'Everyday flexibility'. The firm offers a range of formal flexible working options ranging from telecommuting to a compressed work week. Other companies are introducing four-day weeks or attempting hybrid working. Salesforce, regularly ranked a Great Place to Work, finds that actively listening and responding to people's needs and wants is vital. Teams are empowered to decide how, when and where they work. Work is shifting from a place we go to, to what we do. In an era when employees have Voice, the extent to which employers are willing to meet employee desires for flexibility will be a real test of whether the employment relationship will be win-win.

Looking ahead, work settings will need to become more agile, flexible, entrepreneurial, innovative and creative – and increasingly work will be about addressing adaptive challenges, the ones that AI and automation will struggle to deal with. Working patterns will become increasingly hybrid, with more remote supervisors, even though hybrid working models have yet to fully evolve. The overall impact of teleworking is ambiguous and carries risks especially for innovation and worker satisfaction and wellbeing, for instance in terms of 'hidden overtime'. The OECD recommends[34] that to minimize these risks policymakers and employers should ensure that tele-working remains a choice and is not 'overdone.' Connecting more diverse workforces will require a strong sense of common purpose and productivity will depend on high levels of employee engagement. Yet as technology disag-gregates jobs, careers and motivation may suffer. We know that mental ill-health is on the rise and that there are risks in replicating mistakes from the past when inventing new ways of working. To build agility we need a different set of strategies for addressing the complexities of managing performance and keeping employees engaged and well/healthy when teams are not working in the same place. Fairness and trust will be a central build-ing block of new employment relations.

## SOCIAL MEDIA

In a world in which relationships, business transactions, protest movements and even political uprisings are being enabled by social media, connectivity is the name of the game. Activism abounds for instance in movements around climate change, #MeToo and Black Lives Matter that are putting the ethics of business onto the agenda.

Social media are increasingly used by organizations for recruitment and vetting purposes. Where previously detailed company information was the privileged domain of the most senior management, today the use of social media for internal and external communication purposes reflects profound changes taking place in the ways in which employees expect to be managed and communicated with. Largely gone are the days when companies banned staff from using Facebook and other social networking sites for fear that they were wasting company time. Now many firms use social media for all company messaging, and many CEOs now regularly connect directly with their workforce through blogging, virtual conferencing and social media activities. In comparison with the speed with which messages are co-created and proliferated through the use of social media, conventional internal communications often seem slow and clunky.

In many organizations employees are encouraged to bring their own devices to work rather than the company providing them with hardware that will soon be obsolete. While saving company costs, such policies reflect the fact that companies can no longer control access to company data by employees. By implication, organizations must trust that employees will not abuse access to previously privileged company information but will instead help to promote their company brands through the use of such sites. So this democratization of access to information within organizations represents a potential shift of power bases within organizations, in which 'employees' are being reframed as 'customers' and 'partners'.

In the years ahead, rapid technological development will require organizations to continually review their provision in response to changing social attitudes of customers and staff in relation to the use of technology. After all, technology creates and stimulates new and empowered consumer behaviours, and social media provide accessible platforms for consumers to exercise their collective voice, and in so doing to demand innovative products, directly affect organizational reputations and stimulate change. To return to the example of the higher education (HE) sector, the development and proliferation via the internet of massive open online courses (MOOCs) allows individuals to download 'content' (i.e. lectures and whole courses from leading universities) free of charge. The market for such services is increasingly competitive and the 'customers' more demanding.

Of course MOOCs are not going to put universities out of business, but they do challenge a business model that assumes the institution holds a monopoly on high-quality content. Increasingly students (and their families) will choose universities that offer a high-quality university experience, with instant provision tailored to their learning and social needs, and for their success in helping students to achieve the desired outcomes of higher education, including qualifications and access to the first step on a career ladder.

Technological advance does of course have its shadow side. Some employers are increasingly seeking to use technology as a means of controlling their employees. For instance it has been widely reported that JP Morgan Chase is now tracking employees' onsite attendance through the keycard system in place at the company's buildings around the world and holding managers accountable for employees' presence in the office. Goldman Sachs has been reported to be monitoring how often employees are coming into the office. This has reportedly created an atmosphere of mistrust among the employee base, and frustration for managers.[35] As with the internet, the use of social media brings benefits and risks – of brand sabotage and cyberbullying for instance. There have been cases of teenagers committing suicide after viewing online content advocating self-harm that have highlighted the dangers of the unbridled use of unconstrained algorithms alongside the unwillingness of social media companies to block harmful content in order to protect the vulnerable.

AI in particular has been industrialized and quietly privatized, owned mainly by wealthy US and Chinese hi-tech companies. Advances in the industry include for instance text-to-image tools that allow anyone to enter a phrase and it will generate a range of original images, drawing on the vast array of images available via the internet. However, there is no regulation as yet to protect consumers against the use of such images for 'fake news', amplifying biases and widening social divisions. China is creating very effective facial recognition surveillance systems.[36]

## Capitalism in the spotlight

On a broader front, organizations reflect the societies in which they operate and vice versa. Neo-liberal free market philosophy has become deeply rooted in the public consciousness. Political philosopher Michael Sandel argues that since the early 1980s the UK has gone from *having* a market economy to *being* a market society.[37] A market society is a place where almost everything is up for sale, where market values dominate every aspect of life, from the private to the civic, driving up inequality as highlighted perhaps in the UK's Brexit vote.

Similarly, capitalism itself is under the spotlight in the wake of various infamous corporate and institutional scandals and the huge 'rewards for failure' granted to too many organizational chiefs. The values, accountabilities and morality of various politicians and corporate and institutional leaders have been called into question. Of course, it could be argued that, carried to an extreme, the neo-liberal pursuit of individual self-interest and placing shareholder value ahead of notions of community or public value was what gave rise to some of the unethical and reckless business practice that has been subsequently identified as a primary cause of the mainly Western economic crisis from 2008 onwards. There have been calls for stronger regulation and better governance as well as higher standards in public life. Company reputation is increasingly recognized as a firm's greatest asset and is easily destroyed by unethical practice.

Despite this, little appears to be changing in practice. It takes a major scandal to really spur businesses into action on ethical matters. An example of this can be seen in the 2012 garment factory fire in Bangladesh, which killed 112 workers producing goods for a variety of global brands. This raised public anger and put consumer pressure onto corporations to use their buying power to improve practice across their global supply chains.

Given the state of the global economy, with rising tensions in international relations, the deepening threat of climate change, and after a decade or more of unprecedented global economic and geopolitical uncertainty, the time seems right to question the seemingly inexorable flow of neo-liberalism with its extreme gaps between 'winners' and 'losers'. Resulting social divisions and the rapid rise of populism in many parts of the world are putting globalization into the spotlight, causing political, economic and social upheavals. At the time of writing the first edition of this book, the United Kingdom was firmly a member of the European Union; now Brexit has occurred with few visible gains and more social division.

Democracy too has become strained and free speech has become a bone of contention. Former President Trump's term in office ended in acrimony and disruption. David Marquand sees a wider issue: the fall of the public realm.[38] He argues that we are well advanced towards a state of genteel barbarism where the crisis is one of our moral economy as much as of our political economy. He sets out a framework for a new public philosophy founded on civic conscience and cooperation. In such a context, 'new' must genuinely result in 'different' and 'better'. Sandel calls for more collective reasoning around the value and meaning of our social practices.[39] Even some of the guru architects of neo-liberal management theory, such as Michael Porter,[40] now argue for a shift away from a primary focus on shareholder value towards 'shared value' as the principal aim of business.

For businesses the voices of consumer activists are an essential motivator today. Environmental Social Governance (ESG) concerns have come to the fore; it is no longer enough for an organization to be financially sustainable; it must also act purposefully and responsibly for the benefit of its customers, employees, its local communities and the environment. Many consumer-facing corporations are starting to integrate more sustainable practices into their business models. They have found that in an environmentally conscious marketplace sustainability can be good for business. According to 2021 research by EY,[41] sustainable organizations consistently beat their industry rivals on profitability metrics. This seems to be increasingly reflected in CEO attitudes. In its 25th annual CEO survey (2022),[42] PwC found that 'highly trusted companies are more likely to have made net-zero commitments and to have tied their CEO's compensation to non-financial outcomes, such as employee engagement scores and gender diversity in the workforce. Correlation is not causation, but at first blush, they suggest a relationship between trust and the ability to drive change' – a means of moving beyond short-term, 'it's the next leader's problem' thinking.'

This desire for more meaningful practice is evident among potential recruits, where 78 per cent of Generation Y are said to look at ethics, values and purpose before deciding which company to work for. Creating a culture of diversity and inclusion is more than simply a 'good' thing to do; it makes business sense. Such a culture can improve productivity, reduce staff turnover, drive better employee wellbeing and boost innovation. Purpose should be embedded throughout a company's structures, policies, processes and practices from diversity and inclusion to financial planning. Part of this involves empowering leaders and teams to make business decisions through the lens of purpose. So organizations must avoid 'greenwashing' because consumers and staff leave brands that don't take their stated commitments seriously and disappointed employees soon move on. To work best, sustainability initiatives should be distributed evenly across the value chain rather than siloed. This requires levels of collaboration that may be new for many organizations.

Healthcare provider BUPA has long sought to have an inclusive culture, starting with its 'Be You At BUPA' initiative,[43] a network that provides a representative voice and peer-to-peer support for colleagues while continuously driving employee-led inclusion. BUPA partners with ParalympicsGB to provide athletes with medical expertise and support to reach their peak performance in the lead-up to the 2024 Paralympic Games in Paris. For BUPA this advances its diversity and inclusion agenda and further enables it to be a customer-centric organization. This partnership will help BUPA evolve its products, services and customer touchpoints, supporting the diverse needs of customers.

Such partnerships become a channel through which organizational purpose is reaffirmed. It is not just customers that benefit from a purpose-driven company. In a competitive market, purpose can give employers the edge.

## Can competitive advantage be sustained?

In a turbulent context, even the very notion of sustainable competitive advantage becomes questionable – as firms such as Microsoft, Nokia and Blackberry bear witness. More than two in five CEOs in the 2015 IBM study now expect their next competitive threat to come from organizations outside their industries.[44] These new competitors are not just set to steal market share; they are upsetting whole industries, redefining how value is created and what constitutes value.

Some theorists argue that since the need to adapt is part of the evolutionary process, and if a company's competitive advantage is unlikely to be sustainable over the long term, what matters more is its ability to maintain evolutionary advantage over time. After all, old age, obsolescence or changing environmental conditions can cause previously healthy organisms to perish. Companies such as IBM increasingly talk of 'cognitive advantage' gained by those vanguard firms that are learning to optimize the partnership between cognitive computing, AI and humans. Yet insurgents can be just as vulnerable to change as existing players if they fall into the 'first-mover trap' (the belief that being first in the market creates a sustainable competitive advantage), one of seven 'misconceptions' in executive thinking identified by Rita Gunther McGrath.[45] Similarly a 2005 McKinsey study[46] found that the probability of market leaders being 'toppled' within five years stood at 30 per cent chance, over three times what it used to be a few decades before. All of this is putting pressure on leaders and boards to find new ways to run business in contexts where there are no easy answers and where recipes of success from the past may not be helpful.

The challenges posed by potential disruptors will require many existing players in a given market to respond in new and innovative ways. Traditional businesses in particular often struggle to get to grips with potential trends, opportunities and risks to their current business models, yet those that do are more likely to be in the driving seat of change, allowing for evolution rather than revolution. At least with human organizations there is the possibility that becoming aware increases leaders' choice about how to deal with the situation facing the organization. By way of example, a medium-sized UK distribution company specializing in supplying heating and plumbing products to the trade identified some of the following factors as driving change in its business:

- Government legislation, in particular tougher health and safety and climate change/environmental requirements. Only environmentally friendly boilers will sell in future, which means developing partnerships with new suppliers.

- In an e-commerce world with many customers ordering online, some customers will still prefer face-to-face interaction, so a variety of effective channels will be needed and these will need to be maximized, requiring different skill sets and approaches, shared client knowledge and integrated systems.

- The company is well known for its good relationships with customers. With an ageing traditional customer base a generational change will be needed among customers and staff to expand beyond this. The brand must be rapidly developed to appeal to newer, younger customers – keeping the best of the old alongside the new.

- Mobile technology, personalization and individual relevance mean that 'one size does *not* fit all' – speed of response and flexibility of offer will be required.

- Increasing demands by customers for transparency of pricing mean that margins are likely to be squeezed.

- With competitor consolidation in this mature business, the challenge is to leverage strengths in other areas and develop other partnerships.

In this case, the firm recognized that it needed to better understand its non-traditional yet growing potential customer bases and decided to invest in further market research. Having understood the needs of relevant customer segments, the firm decided to operate through multichannels to meet the more varied needs of tomorrow's mobile customers, trialling some channels ahead of others in order to test customer response. To supply more environmentally friendly products and services and potentially enhance its brand as prime supplier of such products would mean the firm revising its arrangements with long-standing suppliers, finding new sources who could meet requirements of quality, speed and price. Transparency on pricing would mean developing a variety of customer propositions offering greater choice and value and also a more win-win relationship with customers so that trust could be built and maintained. This in turn would require staff development so that branch employees' customer service skills could be taken to the next level.

For any organization, a useful starting point is to become aware of the trends that might most affect its current and proposed business and to work out what the specific risks and opportunities of different scenarios might represent for the business. We discuss this further in Chapter 3.

## Demographics

What of the future workforce? Changing workforce demographics are having a significant effect on organizations across industries and geographies. In the West the population is ageing and becoming much more ideologically and ethnically diverse, while in developing economies such as

China and India the population is younger, growing rapidly and gaining improved educational opportunities. Industries as diverse as utilities, oil and gas producers, retailing and hospitality, healthcare and the public sector are experiencing difficulties in sourcing new talent[47] and competition for talent remains fierce.

Companies face the challenge of attracting and retaining a productive workforce in the face of potentially shrinking labour pools and the increased mobility of the younger generations of employees. Currently organizations are also struggling to retain the people they need. The Great Resignation, also referred to as the Great Attrition, or the Great Reshuffling, is not a myth. Post-pandemic in many companies, increasing numbers of employees are retiring early, taking with them valuable knowledge and whose loss can place the organization at risk. Many workers are switching jobs and industries, moving from traditional to non-traditional roles, or starting their own businesses. Many who have left their previous jobs suffering from burnout and low pay have found a change of industry revitalizing. Some people are taking time out to attend to their personal lives or embarking on sabbaticals. Of course, with recession, the pendulum might swing back towards employers. However, at the projected pace of quitting, hiring and job creation, labour shortages in the West are likely to remain a challenge for some time.

At the same time, the application of automation and AI in the workplace is leading to an increasingly 'hourglass' workforce – with low-skilled work at the bottom, enhanced work at the top and a squeezed middle where roles disappear. The relative power in the employment relationship between employer and employee will determine what organizations offer their employees – or their 'employee value proposition'. For those at the top of the hourglass a wide range of new approaches to HR practices – often referred to as the Great Reset – is being designed to define, attract, recruit, motivate and develop 'talent' with growth mindsets.

It remains to be seen which of these (and other) influences will prove to be merely incremental 'sustaining innovations' and which will be 'game-changing' disruptive innovations. What seems increasingly clear is that, notwithstanding desires for fairness, there is unlikely to be 'one size that fits all'. So with a mix of employed and contractual roles, how do you build the agile and resilient workforce of the future? This has implications for how people are managed and led, the principles that govern the workplace and how roles are designed. Work itself must foster talent and organizations should aim to become a dynamic hub for the development of a diverse array of talent. We'll be looking at the implications of the pursuit of agility, resilience and innovation for the future of work, the workplace and workers later in this book.

## Resilience

Change is an inherent element of complex adaptive systems. As we have discussed, strategic agility is vital to any organization aspiring to address change that is continuous and relentless. Yet agility alone will not secure sustainable success.[48]

It is reasonable to assume that, in turbulent circumstances, organizations will not get things right all the time. There may be mistakes, some of them costly, so resilience is also about bouncing back from setbacks with speed and determination.[49] This is why, alongside agility, resilience (also termed organizational 'resiliency') is vital both for organizations and individuals. Among multiple definitions, resilience is the ability to respond to change that is severely disruptive and surprising;[50] the capacity to deploy different forms of strategic agility when confronted with the unexpected and to respond effectively to changing conditions.[51] It is the ability to recover effectively from setbacks and involves taking prompt, creative, situation-specific, robust and transformative actions to minimize the impact of powerful events that are not avoided or avoidable and that have the potential to jeopardize the organization's long-term survival.[52] Resilience helps minimize or avoid the damaging consequences of turbulence that impact profitability. An organization demonstrates resiliency when it experiences a severe, life-threatening setback but is able to reinvent itself around its core values.[53] At organizational level, this is about the robustness of systems; the capacity for resisting, absorbing and responding, even reinventing if required, in response to fast and/or disruptive change that cannot be avoided.[54]

Key resilience capabilities include 'anticipation'.

Resilient organizations are able to address pivotal events that affect their business because they are alert to, and anticipate, both internal and environmental changes, opportunities as well as challenges, and effectively respond to those changes using available resources in a timely, flexible, affordable and relevant manner. This 'detect and respond' capability is about active learning, proactivity and adaptive capability.

For a notable retailing success story, the John Lewis Partnership, a company founded in 1864, has remained in touch with its customers and ahead of the competition for over a century. It became the largest multichannel retailer in the UK in 2014 through its shrewd anticipation of changing customer preferences and the timely development of its online business ahead of the competition. At the same time, the brand is trusted because the firm delivers its promise to customers and staff while continuing to adapt to changing marketplace conditions. Its staff are trusted 'partners' of the firm and treated accordingly. Not surprisingly they are willing to 'go the extra mile' for the firm.

Agility and resilience are different but complementary capabilities that enable organizations to deal with the turbulent environments in which they operate.[55] In theory the pace of change can best be matched by building agility, while the disruptiveness of change is best matched by building resiliency. Different levels of resilience may result in different organizational outcomes. While modest levels should enable a firm to recover from disruptions and resume normal operations, high levels of resilience may place an organization ahead of its competition since it has learned to capitalize on environmental disruptions and is able to create new options and capabilities while undergoing a robust transformation in the face of adverse events. In this scenario, fast-paced markets are met with speedy product innovation, and severe setbacks are offset with robust response management. The challenge is gauging which of the two – agility and resilience – is needed most at any point in time. Clear, agreed-upon metrics and indicators of when agility and resiliency are being excessively pressured due to environmental conditions, for instance using gaming and simulations of a variety of extreme situations, along with taking every opportunity for honest debriefs of actual failures and poor performance, become important ways of identifying what is needed.

## Conclusion

Both strategic agility and resilience are prerequisites for organizations to thrive in a dynamic environment. Organizational agility – or the capacity for moving quickly, flexibly and decisively – needs to be complemented by resilience – or the ability to anticipate, initiate and take advantage of opportunities while aiming to avoid or recover from any negative consequences of change. These concepts share common roots and are built from complementary resources, skills and competencies. Together they enable firms to prepare for changing conditions, restore their vitality after traumatic setbacks and become even more effective as a result of the experience. Combined they represent an organization's adaptive capacity or its 'change-ability'.

While resilient organizations are nimble, flexible and agile, not all agile organizations are resilient.[56] Central to an organization's resilience capacity is its relationship with its workforce, and the extent to which the workforce feels 'engaged' or not with the organization and its fortunes. If agility is pursued purely from a cost-cutting perspective, and results in work intensification or job losses, it is probable that the employment relationship between employers and employees will suffer and trust will evaporate. How likely is it, then, that employees will wish to 'go the extra mile' for organizations that see them as costs to be cut or as commodities to be exploited? And while people are often described as a company's greatest asset, few businesses have a clear model of leadership that improves engagement, removes barriers to innovation and uncovers hidden strengths in people and the organization.

In a context where change is a key aspect of the business environment for the foreseeable future, organizations must become change-able. If change is to happen effectively, people at all levels need to embrace change; they need a desire for, a mindset oriented towards and a capability for (a way of acting upon) change. These can be developed to prepare individuals, groups and organizations for change, to render organizations more agile, more resilient and more responsive to change than they might previously have considered possible.

In practice this means that:

- *Everyone needs to be externally aware and alert,* willing to voice and allowed to act on such knowledge.
- *Products and services need to be innovated continuously* in order to meet the demands of the marketplace and customers.
- *Costs need to be kept low on all fronts,* tapping into the goodwill of local staff to implement cost-cutting initiatives while also innovating.
- *Organizations need to be flexible and adaptable* in roles, responsibilities and structures.
- *Key staff need to be able and willing to continuously develop themselves –* flexible sourcing and multiskilling.

- *Organizations need to aim for high engagement with staff* in order to tap into the discretionary effort of all their knowledge workers and create a win-win relationship.
- *Organizational culture needs to be highly adaptable, agile, organic* – with everyone, regardless of rank, willing and able to commit to the organization and contribute to its success.

Plenty of challenges exist, perhaps the greatest of which is assuming that agility and resilience are optional. For organizations and individuals that want to survive and thrive in today's fast-changing environment – they are not.

Of course, this is easier said than done – otherwise why are organizational agility and resilience so elusive? To explore the common obstacles to agility you will find a chapter online which examines these in more detail. The next chapter provides an overview of the routines and practices of organizational agility which we shall consider in more depth in later chapters.

---

CHECKLIST

What's happening in your context?

- What do you see as the role and purpose of your organization?
- Who are its key stakeholders?
- What trends are you seeing? What are the key waves that are shaping your environment, including work, workplace and workforce? What are the key opportunities and risks you foresee?
- What mechanisms does your organization have to identify and analyse emerging trends? How effectively are these trends acted upon and the necessary changes made?
- What is the basis of your company's reputation? Where is this at risk?
- Think about the speed and shape of change in your market or situation. Is change out of control? Is change predictable? Do you have the time and resource to make innovation bets?
- How well does your organization recover from setbacks?

# Notes

**1** McKinsey & Company (2017) *McKinsey Quarterly*, ING's agile transformation, www.mckinsey.com/industries/financial-services/our-insights/ings-agile-transformation (archived at https://perma.cc/2CVE-TPWE).

**2** *Deloitte Human Capital Trends 2016*, highlights the increasing importance of it, www2.deloitte.com/content/dam/Deloitte/global/Documents/HumanCapital/gx-dup-global-human-capital-trends-2016.pdf (archived at https://perma.cc/E3KG-J23B).

**3** Christensen, CM and Overdorf, M (2000) Meeting the challenge of disruptive change, *Harvard Business Review*, 78 (2), pp 67–76.

**4** UNDP. Human development report 2021/2022: Uncertain times, unsettled Lives: Shaping our future in a transforming world [EN/RU/ZH], September 2022, human-development-report-20212022-uncertain-times-unsettled-lives-shaping-our-future-transforming-world-enruzh.

**5** Williams, T, Worley, CM and Lawler, EE. The agility factor, *Strategy + Business*, 15 April 2013, www.strategy-business.com/article/00188?gko=6a0ba (archived at https://perma.cc/KP6B-W6EJ).

**6** Cheung-Judge, M-Y (2017) Future of organizations and implications for OD practitioners, *OD Practitioner*, 49 (1), pp 7–19.

**7** McCann, J, Selsky, J and Lee, J (2009) Building agility, resilience and performance in turbulent environments, *People and Strategy*, 32 (3), pp 44–51.

**8** Weill, P. IT portfolio management and IT savvy – Rethinking IT investments as a portfolio, MIT Sloan School of Management, Center for Information Systems Research (CISR), Summer Session, 14 June 2007. Research was conducted by MIT via the SeeIT/CISR survey of 629 firms – 329 of these firms are listed on US stock exchanges.

**9** Source: Business Agility Portfolios, MIT Sloan School, 2006.

**10** Economist Intelligence Unit (EIU) (2009) Organisational agility: How business can survive and thrive in turbulent times, Economist Intelligence Unit, www.emc.com/collateral/leadership/organisational-agility-230309.pdf (archived at https://perma.cc/GZT5-WZYU).

**11** Kane, GC, Palmer, G, Phillips, AN, Kiron, D and Buckley, N (2016) Aligning the organization for its digital future, *MIT Sloan Management Review* and Deloitte University Press, sloanreview.mit.edu/projects/aligning-for-digital-future/ (archived at https://perma.cc/6Z6P-PQWX).

**12** Williams, Worley and Lawler, ibid.

**13** Lawler, EE III (2008) Make human capital a source of competitive advantage, *Marshall School of Business Working Paper*, University of Southern California, ceo.usc.edu/make-human-capital-a-source-of-competitive-advantage/ (archived at https://perma.cc/A9HU-QU47).

**14**  D'Aveni, R (1994) *Hypercompetition: Managing the dynamics of strategic maneuvering*, Free Press, New York.

**15**  Jamrog J, Vickers, M and Bear, D (2006) Building and sustaining a culture that supports innovation, *Human Resource Planning*, **29** (3), pp 9–19.

**16**  McCann, Selsky and Lee, ibid.

**17**  Christensen, CM (1997) *The Innovator's Dilemma: When new technologies cause great firms to fail*, Harvard Business School Press, Boston.

**18**  Horney, N, Pasmore, W and O'Shea, T (2010) Leadership agility: A business imperative for a VUCA world, *People and Strategy* (HRPS), **33** (4), pp 34–42.

**19**  Roth, AV (1996) Achieving strategic agility through economies of knowledge, *Planning Review*, **24** (2), pp 30–36.

**20**  Rigby, D, Sutherland, J and Takeuchi, H (2016) Embracing Agile: How to master the process that's transforming management, *Harvard Business Review*, May.

**21**  Williams, Worley and Lawler, ibid.

**22**  Herriman, J. Game of Drones, *London Evening Standard*, 28 April 2014.

**23**  Rigby, Sutherland and Takeuchi, ibid.

**24**  Abrahamson, E (2000) Change without pain, *Harvard Business Review*, July, pp 75–79.

**25**  Ibid.

**26**  Denneen, J and Dretler, T (2012) The financially stable university, Bain & Company, www.bain.com/Images/BAIN_BRIEF_The_financially_sustainable_university.pdf (archived at https://perma.cc/W8EK-J4NA).

**27**  Gartner. These are the top CFO priorities for 2022, www.gartner.com/en/articles/these-are-the-top-cfo-priorities-for-2022 (archived at https://perma.cc/C5EY-G7MV).

**28**  IBM Institute for Business Value (2013) Reinventing the rules of engagement: CEO insights from the Global C-suite Study, www.ibm.com/blogs/ibm-training/reinventing-the-rules-of-engagement-ceo-insights/ (archived at https://perma.cc/DD2F-GA5J).

**29**  PwC. What's important to CFOs in 2022, www.pwc.com/us/en/library/cfo.html (archived at https://perma.cc/2DT3-D9PH).

**30**  Marsh, C, Sparrow, P and Hird, M (2010) Is customer centricity a movement or myth? Opening the debate for HR, Lancaster University Management School White Paper 10/03, www.lancaster.ac.uk/media/lancaster-university/content-assets/documents/lums/cphr/centricitymyth.pdf (archived at https://perma.cc/87RN-TVQP).

**31**  Denning, S (2013) Why agile can be a game changer for managing continuous innovation in many industries, *Strategy & Leadership*, **41** (2), pp 5–11.

**32**  OECD. Key policy responses from the OECD: Tackling coronavirus (Covid-19). Contributing to a global effort, 7 September 2020, www.oecd.org/coronavirus/policy-responses/productivity-gains-from-teleworking-in-the-post-covid-19-era-a5d52e99/ (archived at https://perma.cc/RG7B-2NRY).

**33**  Prescott, K. Taking up the Slack with home workers, *The Times*, 28 June 2022.

**34**  Ibid.

**35**  Oakes, K (2022) Culture fail of the month: JP Morgan Chase, *Culture Renovation*, culturerenovation.com/culture-fail-of-the-month-jp-morgan-chase/ (archived at https://perma.cc/32PV-CFP7); Thier, J. JPMorgan and Goldman Sachs are monitoring how often employees are coming into the office – but experts say that approach could backfire, *Fortune*, 7 May 2022, fortune.com/2022/05/07/companies-are-tracking-how-often-employees-are-coming-to-the-office/ (archived at https://perma.cc/6DHG-CNQB).

**36**  Fortson, D. The robot revolution is already here, *The Sunday Times*, 2 October 2022.

**37**  TED blog. The real price of market values: Why we shouldn't trust markets with our civic life: Michael Sandel at TEDGlobal 2013, log.ted.com/2013/06/14/the-real-price-of-market-values-michael-sandel-at-tedglobal-2013/.

**38**  Marquand, D (2014) *Mammon's Kingdom: An essay on Britain, now*, Penguin, London.

**39**  Cone Communications Survey.

**40**  Porter, ME and Kramer, MR (2011) Creating shared value, *Harvard Business Review*, January.

**41**  EY (2021) The CEO Imperative: Rebound to more sustainable growth, https://www.ey.com/en_uk/ceo/the-ceo-imperative-rebound-to-more-sustainable-growth (archived at https://perma.cc/VHL2-RGPV).

**42**  PwC's 25th Annual Global CEO Survey, Reimagining the outcomes that matter, 2022, www.pwc.com/gx/en/ceo-agenda/ceosurvey/2022.html (archived at https://perma.cc/G7G6-J67E); LinkedIn (2021) No need for the 9–5: How PwC successfully built a culture of work flexibility, www.linkedin.com/business/talent/blog/talent-engagement/how-pwc-successfully-built-culture-of-work-flexibility (archived at https://perma.cc/QJ3G-TX2J).

**43**  BUPA (2022) Building an inclusive workplace, www.bupa.com/news/stories-and-insights/2022/building-an-inclusive-workplace (archived at https://perma.cc/SH9C-PTEC).

**44**  IBM Institute for Business Value (2015) Redefining Boundaries: *Insights from the Global C-suite Study*, IBM.

**45**  Gunther McGrath, R (2013) Transient advantage, *Harvard Business Review*, June.

**46**  Defined as being in the top quintile by revenue in a given industry.

**47**  IBM Insitute for Business Value, Closing the Generational Divide, ibid.

**48**  Hamel, G and Valikangas, L (2003) The quest for resilience, *Harvard Business Review*, September, hbr.org/2003/09/the-quest-for-resilience/ar/1 (archived at https://perma.cc/FD3C-3BW7).

**49** Marcos, J and Macauley, S (2008) Organisational resilience: The key to anticipation, adaptation and recovery, Cranfield School of Management paper.

**50** McCann, JE (2004) Organizational effectiveness: changing concepts for changing environments, *Human Resource Planning Journal*, March, pp 42–50.

**51** Lengnick-Hall, CA and Beck, TE (2009) Resilience capacity and strategic agility: prerequisites for thriving in a dynamic environment, Working Paper series Wp# 0059MGT-199-2009, The University of Texas at San Antonio, College of Business.

**52** Heifetz, R, Grashow, A and Linsky, M (2009) *The Practice of Adaptive Leadership*, Harvard Business Press, Boston.

**53** Alpaslan, CM and Mitroff, II (2004) Bounded morality: The relationship between ethical orientation and crisis management, before and after 9/11, in *Current Topics in Management*, Vol. 6, ed MA Rahim, K Mackenzie and R Golembiewski, pp 13–43, JAI Press, Greenwich.

**54** McCann, J, Selsky, J and Lee, J (2009) Building agility, resilience and performance in turbulent environments, *HR People & Strategy*, **32** (3), pp 45–51.

**55** Weick, KE and Sutcliffe, KM (2007) *Managing the Unexpected: Resilient performance in an age of uncertainty*, 2nd edn, Jossey-Bass, San Francisco.

**56** Jamrog J, Vickers, M and Bear, D (2006) Building and sustaining a culture that supports innovation, *Human Resource Planning*, **29** (3), pp 9–19.

# 02

# The resiliently agile organization

In Chapter 1 we looked at some of the factors driving the need for agility and resilience and also considered some of the key aspects of organization that represent significant barriers. We have seen that agility's more recent roots are in software development and while the notion of the agile enterprise is a broader notion this is less well developed.

Adopting agility is a strategic choice and a wanted dimension of organizational effectiveness. Agile principles and practices should drive strategic change, sometimes redefining the essence of an organization. This has extensive implications for management practice and for organizational development. Leaders and managers need to understand where, when and how to embed appropriate agility, and how to create the conditions in which prudent and responsible opportunism can thrive.

I have argued that agility – the search for speed, innovation and adaptability – must be accompanied by resilience or 'bouncebackability' at organizational, team and individual levels. One without the other is not sustainable. After all, many organizations are using lean tools and Agile methods but are not changing the system as a whole, so things go on much as before without the significant shifts in culture required for sustainable change.

My goal in this chapter is to take a whole-system look at agility and resilience. We consider:

- the qualities, capabilities and routines of agile firms
- the resiliently agile model.

This model looks at organizational agility and resilience 'in the round'. This sets the tone for the rest of the book, since in later chapters we will explore in more detail what is involved in developing the key capabilities and routines that underpin the model and how these can be applied in practice.

Agility is a complex capability. It is not just one system but a set of structures, systems, processes, routines and behaviours – and how these fit together – that make up agile capability. For organizations to become resiliently agile will require not simply shifts in the tangible aspects of organization – for instance in structures – but also in the intangible aspects such as people's mindsets and skills, organizational cultures, philosophies, capabilities, routines and habits.

Taken together these should enhance an organization's latent agility and resilience.

## The qualities and capabilities of agile firms

The rare organizations that have agility and resilience embedded in their cultural DNA and have proved successful over time, such as WL Gore and Associates and Whole Foods Market, are thought to be best placed to succeed in a hyper-competitive environment. Such organizations have a strongly mutual ethic embracing the interests of employees as well as of the organization. As such examples make clear, being resiliently agile is not just what you do, it is what you are, or become; it is a state of being, the way your system works, which influences what you are capable of and what you do. So while Agile tools and processes are useful, the real enabler of agility and resilience is embodied in the people and culture of organizations.

The traits of an agile business include rapid decision making and execution, a high-performance culture, flexibility of management practices and resources, and organizational structures that support collaboration and learning. They have innovative business models, are consumer-oriented, digitally enabled, have greater vertical integration and more convergence of industries. They extend the depth and breadth of their offering to include external partners in development and distribution of products and services that extend across boundaries, often with both cooperation and competition among the partners. They incorporate digital and artificial intelligence deeply within the enterprise infrastructure. It is about thinking like a start-up, understanding the implications of technology for business growth, and creating the right human–IT dynamic. Enterprise agility reimagines an organization as a collection of high-performing teams, each with a clear purpose and the skills it needs.

Moreover, agile organizations are:

- Obsessed with providing customer value – prepared to put in significant effort to establish exactly what it is that their customers want, and then put those things first – they are *customer-centric*.
- Continuously adaptive, able to change ways of working in order to deliver optimum value to customers and to do so at a moment's notice – they are *behaviourally* resilient.
- Dynamically networked – at the centre of a number of interacting networks that enable the organization to gather knowledge and use expertise quickly and effectively – they are *context* resilient.
- Rigorously focused on new learning and creating value through knowledge – they are *cognitively* resilient powerhouses of innovation.
- Ruthlessly decisive – they must be prepared to dispose of parts of the organization that no longer add value.

Let us now consider some of the different aspects of organizational resilience – context, cognitive and behavioural – and how these play out in different situations.

## 'Bouncebackability'

As an open system, any organization is of course embedded in wider societal, industrial and political systems that influence the pace and spread of innovation. Through dynamic networks, organizations can gather knowledge and use expertise quickly to respond to adverse conditions and recover from misfortune, damage or a destabilizing perturbation in the environment that would otherwise destroy them. If crisis cannot be prevented, resilient organizations can bounce back from what has happened and turn crises into a source of strategic opportunity, thanks to their increase in learning and resilience capacity.[1] So the firm can withstand anything that comes along and has the means available for recovery and renewal next time if needed.

Traditionally, a major function of leaders is to solve problems, to intervene when dilemmas arise or when individuals differ on task-related activities. In disastrous situations strong crisis leadership and effective, speedy decision making are of the essence. The US Hancock Bank showed *context* resilience following the disaster of losing everything to Hurricane Katrina in 2005. The bank's leaders made some courageous decisions based on the bank's identity and purpose. Hancock reopened three days later, ahead of other banks, using IOUs – an extraordinary but effective solution to an extraordinary situation. Implicit therefore in the effective handling of crises is having the courage and the ability to evaluate strategies fast, make some tough calls and accelerate work programmes against organizational goals. The challenge for risk-averse leaders is to recognize when they have enough data to gain insight into possible ways forward, and to have the confidence to make decisions and take action.

## Learning as key to adaptation and innovation

Resilience is not just about getting through crises. It requires different leadership behaviours. Leaders of resilient organizations have the foresight and situation awareness to prevent potential crises from developing. They demonstrate *cognitive* resilience – the ability to notice shifts, work through unfamiliar situations and develop options on how to respond. Adaptive firms such as Apple, Google, 3M and Amazon are 'change-able'; they can adjust and learn better, faster and more economically than their peers, giving them an 'adaptive advantage'.[2] For cognitive resilience to flourish requires a learning climate where controlled experimentation and shared learning from successes and failures is encouraged. 'Fail fast' and 'Learn quickly' are common mantras in agile firms.

Pettigrew and colleagues used the phrase 'receptive context' to describe the degree to which a particular group or organization naturally takes on change and new ideas.[3] Organizations with a high receptive context are seen as 'ripe' for change; they quickly adopt innovative concepts in order to meet the challenges they experience. They focus rigorously on creating value through knowledge. Generative relationships between 'boundary workers', who act as environmental scanners, aid this process so ideas develop further and the observable outcomes are more than merely the sum of the parts. Change becomes a natural and inevitable part of organizational life so organizations can maintain effectiveness across a range of tasks, situations and conditions even while changing. Conversely, organizations with low receptive context might experience the same challenges and learn about the same innovations, but they lack the will or ability to implement the idea.

To build a receptive context Abrahamson recommends 'pacing' – interspersing major change efforts with small-scale changes at a more local level – so that key parts of the business are free to initiate where they add value.[4] This is not a pure Agile methodology, stripping away procedure and hierarchy just before the point of chaos, but rather a hybrid of change techniques. The aim is to empower and let change happen at a local level where it strategically makes sense, while taking advantage of standardization and lean methodologies where these are more appropriate.

### A LEARNING CLIMATE

If only leaders make all the decisions, this can stifle interdependency and adaptive mechanisms such as networks that can produce emergent change. Resilience requires that decision-making authority is shared, not just confined to those at the top. In common with 'learning organization' theories, resiliently agile organizations recognize that ideas and information can emerge from anyone, in any part of the system, at any time. Such organizations tend to have high levels of staff awareness and engagement and self-development opportunities for all. They look outside, embrace inter-company learning and are open to learning from others, including competitors. They also look inside, encouraging internal exchange so that departments see themselves as each other's customers. They have enabling structures, processes and patterns that support experimentation and allow great ideas to be turned into new products and services. For instance, IT is used for sharing knowledge and mutual awareness; reward approaches incentivize and reinforce learning.

In general, the most agile organizations tend to be entrepreneurial start-ups that initially act as powerhouses of innovation. Take any of the first-mover success stories from the computer and software industry – such as Hewlett-Packard and Microsoft. In their early days the founders and employees demonstrated common purpose, great skill and highly effective knowledge-sharing practices. As market shapers and leaders they forged the way ahead for whole industries to follow. It was typically only as they grew into large corporations that these pioneers formalized their processes and became so market dominant that they perhaps lost sight of the competition and were unable to keep up with changing client expectations or with competitors' innovations. The story of how Microsoft initially dismissed the development of the tablet by Apple as unimportant is a timely reminder of how easy it is to miss or dismiss emergent signals. So while agility may be part of an organization's DNA at the outset, it is important to watch out for and avoid the loss of learning, a precursor to rigidity.

## Flexibility and the employment relationship

Allied to adaptability is flexibility – the ability to employ multiple ways to succeed and craft a range of resource and capability alternatives and the capacity to move seamlessly between them.[5] This is about developing skills at aligning, realigning and mobilizing people and resources; taking resolute action and removing barriers to change; partnering and collaborating with others. To be flexible and responsive organizations need appropriately flexible roles, responsibilities and structures. In particular they need people with flexible mindsets and skill sets who are willing and able to adjust to what is now required of them.

Organizational agility and resilience depend largely on people's willingness to deploy their mental agility, skill sets, behaviours, resources and discretionary efforts on behalf of the firm. Agile firms therefore need a strong employment relationship built on trust and reciprocation. Today's 'white-collar' employment relationships tend to be based on the unitarist assumption that 'what is good for the business is good for the people'. Take flexible working arrangements for instance – these should give employees choice about where and when they work, but in some forms of flexible working post-recession, such as 'zero-hours' contracting, flexibility benefits only the employer. So workers lacking power in the employment relationship may find that what is good for the business is not so good for them. If the employment relationship becomes low-trust and employees become 'disengaged' from their organization, they are less likely to want to 'go the extra mile' to benefit the organization. What is needed is a more mutual employment relationship in which both the organization and its workforce can reap the rewards of agility.

## Routines: standardization and innovation

Major companies have traditionally understood that efficiency comes from routinizing the non-routine so that people can develop useful habits that drive their behaviour and allow them to fully deploy their resources under challenging conditions. Through practice they develop *behavioural* resilience – the routines that enable them to deal effectively with challenging situations. For example, the UK flying display team the Red Arrows practise their complex air manoeuvres daily until they become almost instinctual in response to any threat such as unexpected bad weather.

However, if organizational routines become set in stone, they keep the organization firmly anchored in the past. To gain adaptive advantage in a context of change requires a willingness to review and occasionally abandon the disciplines of conventional hierarchies and adopt new, more dynamic routines – a particular challenge in today's context of tighter governance, increased regulation and risk aversion.

So can routines be deliberately changed to increase agility? The answer is yes. In dynamically stable contexts (i.e. where stability and change are quite similar[6]), routines can evolve to contribute to the dynamic capability of firms.[7] They can also be consciously applied to improve:

- organizational adaptation[8]
- evolution[9]
- learning[10]
- flexibility[11]
- improvization and innovation.[12]

A cohesive sense of what a company believes (the genuine core values that contribute to cognitive resilience) is the foundation for developing day-to-day behaviours that translate intended strategies into new useful habits that lead to beneficial actions. So if organizational values lead to habits of investigation rather than assumption, or routines of collaboration rather than antagonism, and traditions of flexibility rather than rigidity, people are more likely to intuitively behave in ways that open the system and generate resilient responses.

Traditional management practice brings an over-focus on short-term performance based on metrics, key performance indicators (KPIs) and so on. This can lead to constraints that prevent the organization from being responsive. Now the move is away from siloed, static sets of operations towards more fluidity and boundaryless, networked structures to enable greater flexibility and innovation. Here the focus is on knowledge, trust, results.

Similarly, standardizing routines that cause ideas to proliferate, such as the practised behaviours for innovative problem solving, leads to heightened levels of inventiveness – or 'learned resourcefulness',[13] what Coutu calls 'ritualized ingenuity'.[14] So if people are in the habit of continuously scanning the market and have processes to speedily convert effective ideas into new products and business opportunities, they are better able to use whatever resources and opportunities are at hand to move the firm forward. This can lead to timing advantages allowing the firm to capitalize on rapid response opportunities, to do more with less, and to use all of its assets to full advantage.

Collins and Hansen describe how the development of the iPod was less the result of one person's brilliant idea than of a multi-step iterative process based upon empirical validation.[15] Paradoxically then, a system that supports innovation must both allow ideas to go forward in the absence of evidence, yet be steadfast in insisting on evidence of effectiveness for evaluation.[16] So the process of innovating becomes disciplined: 'The great task, rarely achieved, is to blend creative intensity with relentless discipline so as to amplify the creativity rather than destroy it. When you marry operating excellence with innovation, you multiply the value of your creativity.'[17]

Similarly leaders need to become clearer about when to control the innovation process 'tightly' and when they can be 'loose' so that people can exercise autonomy.[18] Loose elements allow for experimentation, essentially spreading the risk of change by simultaneous piloting of ideas or processes in different departments or geographic areas. Rather than providing solutions, leaders must frame the questions for employees to explore. However, this does mean that staff must be empowered to challenge and try new things and that they clearly understand their organization's purpose and the aim of initiative.

The Center for Effective Organizations identifies four routines in particular that distinguish the sustainably agile, high-performing organizations from what they call the 'thrashers'. These agile companies have the ability to *strategize* in dynamic ways, accurately *perceive* changes in their external environment, *test* possible responses and *implement* incremental and discontinuous changes in products, technology, operations, structures, systems and capabilities as a whole. To these I would add other key routines relating to how people will work together, such as *teaming* and *empowering*.

Clearly the appetite for new routines is there. For instance, an IBM study has found that executives are increasingly looking outside the organization to get new ideas rather than simply relying on internal formulae.[19] The deeper roots of the change towards 'open' innovation go back to the 1980s and 1990s when many global pharmaceutical companies began to look externally for product innovation. Today, almost half of the CEOs in the IBM study expect their organizations to source innovation from the outside – and are actively participating in open innovation networks. Seven out of ten CEOs of outperforming organizations are now intent on increasing their partner network in the pursuit of innovation. The ability to collaborate as trusted partners is therefore key.

Importantly, it is the whole system of routines, not the possession of one or two of them, that confers agility. It is this combination of qualities, capabilities and routines that underpins the resiliently agile model.

## The resiliently agile model

The model shown in Figure 2.1 outlines the component activities of organizational agility and resilience, which we shall explore in more detail in later chapters. It outlines some of the inputs – capabilities, resources and enablers, activities or interventions – required to build agility and resilience. It also details some of the outputs and effects – more broadly measured outcomes such as speed and innovation or results that may include immediate, intermediate and longer-term outcomes such as sustainable financial performance, positive organizational reputation, healthy employment relationship and so on. At the heart of the model are people and culture, which permeate all the quadrants.

### Quadrant 1: strategizing

Conventional strategy assumes that the future can be predicted but, in contexts exposed to the challenge of speed and complexity, predictability is unattainable. Instead, organizations need to develop strategic agility, defined by Doz and Kosonen as:

> The ability to continuously adjust and adapt strategic direction in core activities as a function of strategic ambitions and changing circumstances and create not just new products and services but also new business models and innovative ways to create value in complex and fast-changing conditions.[20]

What these authors call '*strategic sensitivity*' allows firms to accurately *perceive* changes in their external environment. This describes leaders' sharpness of perception and the intensity of their awareness and attention. Leaders with high levels of cognitive resilience have the capacity for high-quality 'intelligent' strategic thinking and dialogue that converts data into usable knowledge and are able to make and implement bold decisions fast. They demonstrate deep empathy with, and understanding of, customers and stakeholders.

FIGURE 2.1  Component activities of organizational agility and resilience

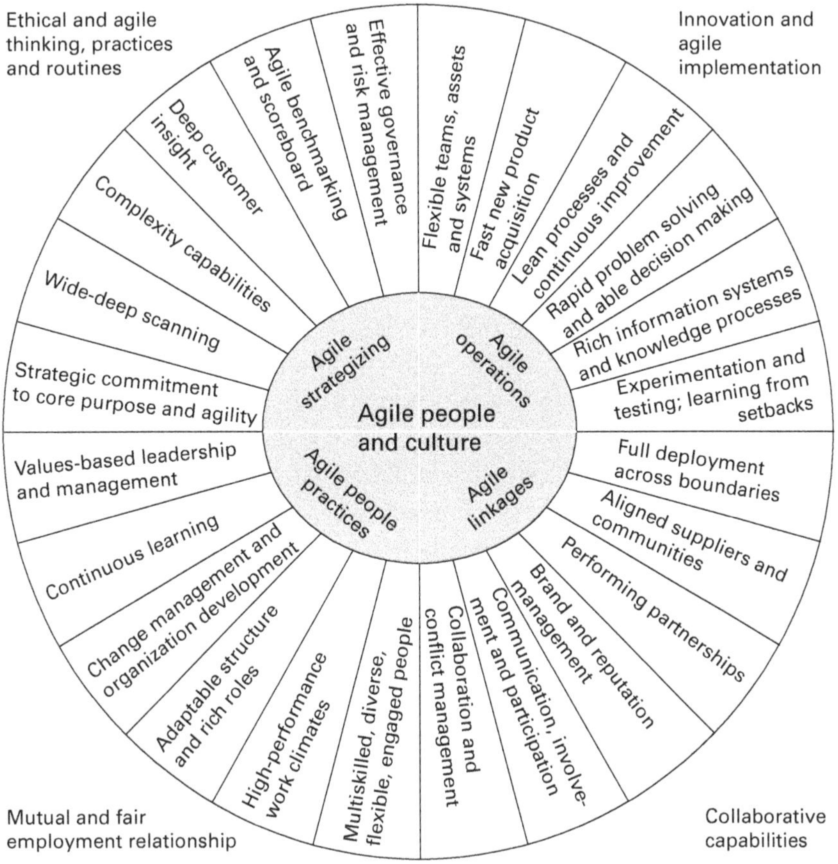

Ethical and agile
thinking, practices
and routines

Innovation and
agile
implementation

Agile benchmarking
and scoreboard

Effective governance
and risk management

Deep customer
insight

Complexity capabilities

Wide-deep scanning

Strategic commitment
to core purpose and agility

Values-based leadership
and management

Continuous learning

Change management and
organization development

Adaptable structure
and rich roles

High-performance
work climates

Multiskilled, diverse,
flexible, engaged people

Collaboration and
conflict management

Communication, involve-
ment and participation

Brand and reputation
management

Performing partnerships

Aligned suppliers and
communities

Full deployment
across boundaries

Experimentation and
testing; learning from
setbacks

Rich information systems
and knowledge processes

Rapid problem solving
and able decision making

Lean processes and
continuous improvement

Fast new product
acquisition

Flexible teams, assets
and systems

Agile
strategizing

Agile
operations

Agile people
and culture

Agile people
practices

Agile
linkages

Mutual and fair
employment relationship

Collaborative
capabilities

SOURCE © Linda Holbeche

## The shift to strategizing

Strategy is usually developed by those at the top and implemented by everyone else. The conventional strategic management cycle – *plan, do, check* and
*adapt* – often operates imperfectly and not surprisingly there is often a gap
between strategic intent (planning) and implementation (doing). In contrast,
agile strategizing is not confined to those at the top of organizations. Just as
living systems learn from their experiences, resiliently agile organizations
adopt a learning approach to strategy – where participation is encouraged
at all levels and strategy creation is a continuous process, rather than a one-
off going through the motions of developing an annual business plan then
getting on with 'business as usual'.

So strategizing involves a wider group of people in thinking and acting strategically. Everyone needs to be externally aware and 'savvy' – sensing changes in the environment, coping with ambiguity and taking mitigating action to avoid problems, or seizing latent opportunities, being willing to voice and being empowered to act on such knowledge. Given the dictum 'I own what I help to create', it makes sense to tap into the collective wisdom of employees and other stakeholders – to gather feedback and insight about customers and the changing marketplace, to develop ideas about what needs to change and explore the 'how' if not the 'what' of strategy. By being involved in collectively scanning the environment, people see the need for change and are usually more willing to play their part in making the changes required. Thus, unlike conventional approaches to strategy making, strategic agility becomes a shared, embedded capability and it becomes easier to close the conventional implementation gap, to some extent at least.

And there appears to be growing evidence that, thanks to the influence of information technology and social media, employees, especially Generation Y, increasingly expect to be involved in strategic development.[21] These expectations are likely to lead to a democratization of business model innovation in which more decentralized ideas generation and handling inside organizations can be used to integrate elements of the value chain in more flexible, but also often disruptive, ways. The task for top leadership is to build an inclusive community of leaders that taps into the collective intelligence of the workforce. As ideas evolve, leaders must provide constructive sense-making.

That's not to say that agile organizations lack strategic plans. Instead they focus planning on developing their core where they are the most strategically differentiated. A 2021 survey[22] by consulting firm Willis Towers Watson found that employees are twice as likely to stay in a purpose-driven organization. In agile organizations the obsession is providing customer value; continually developing new capabilities as a source of competitive advantage; being prepared to put in significant effort to establish exactly what it is that their customers want, and then putting those things first (see Table 2.1). As Peters and Waterman observed about the way 'excellent companies' interact with customers,[23] the most striking and consistent feature of agile organizations is their obsession with quality and service. Rather than being driven by technology or by a desire to be a low-cost producer, these 'excellent' companies are driven by the customer. They use strategies of service, quality and reliability to increase customer loyalty, long-term revenue and growth, in contrast to the short-term sales-oriented approach we see so often in companies. By focusing on their core and by deliberately developing deep customer insight in the context of emerging trends, agile organizations are able to adapt plans as the marketplace shifts, tailoring what they do to what is needed to grow the business.

TABLE 2.1  The shift to agile (1)

| Conventional strategy making | Agile strategizing |
| --- | --- |
| Annual process | Ongoing process |
| Focused on margins | Focused on customer |
| Innovate at the margins | Innovate at the core |
| Developed at the top | Top-down/bottom-up |
| Aim to increase productivity through controls | Aim to increase productivity collaboratively |
| Gap between strategy making and execution | Strategy making and execution are seamless |

We explore the mindset and skillset shifts required for strategic agility in Chapter 3.

But how can chaos be avoided? Leaders must also develop specific structures (also called system constraints) to serve as a counterbalance to randomness and anarchy. First, senior leaders need to create a strong identity for the organization so that clarity over organizational purpose or vision can act as a strategic compass and behavioural guardrail. Ethics and reputation become the system constraints within which investment and other decisions are made. Thus clear priorities can be set which help people to focus on the things that matter, enabling manageable workloads. In addition to shared purpose these structures include shared operating platforms and reward systems.[24] With respect to reward, recognition plays a key role in raising employee performance and engagement.[25] With respect to operating platforms, leaders must ensure that people can access high-quality and timely data and support the development of a culture conducive to learning and experimentation. Risk management becomes a meaningful enabler of innovation rather than a bureaucratic hurdle to be overcome. Agile methodology can then be applied – not only to projects – to ensure that the implementation of strategy can keep pace with changing requirements (see Table 2.2).

Thus a virtuous circle of high performance ensues – people gain 'line of sight' to the strategy, are aligned and enabled to perform, are more willing to offer their discretionary effort, receive feedback and encouragement and contribute ideas that move the organization forward.

TABLE 2.2  The shift to agile (2)

| Conventional strategy making | Resiliently agile strategizing |
| --- | --- |
| Based on forecasts | Based on wide-deep scanning and other (collective) intelligence |
| Pursuit of competitive advantage | Pursuit of multiple transient advantages |
| Commitment to shareholders | Commitment to stakeholders |
| Short term | Short and long term |
| Risk management restrains innovation | Risk management co-exists with innovation |
| Board scrutiny is light touch | Board scrutiny based on real understanding |
| Ethics occasionally sacrificed to commercial gain | Ethics always drive decision making |

## A unified top team

Top leadership – its role, capability and priorities – is one of the key factors influencing whether or not an organizational context is conducive to change and agility. To keep the organization functioning optimally at the edge of chaos the top team must be unified and coherent, and able to make bold decisions quickly without getting caught up in political power plays. Strategic agility therefore requires top-team commitment to agility, cabinet responsibility and collaboration. As we have discussed, this can be difficult to achieve because many top teams struggle to deal with today's complex and paradoxical conditions, and boards too may be highly risk averse and unwilling to endorse the degree of experimentation that may be required in agile strategy. Many top teams lack digital awareness and struggle to work out for their business the implications of digital transformation to increase agility – whether through AI, blockchain or automation. Yet without this commitment to agility at the top, the status quo will remain and Agile methods will be suboptimized. As a 2013 IBM report suggests,[26] leaders therefore need to be bold, dare to be open, embrace disruption and build shared value.

# Agile implementing

For agility there is little or no separation between strategy creation and implementation (as discussed above, and as we explore further in Chapters 3 to 6). That is largely because employees at all levels are aware of what the organization is aiming to do, what the challenges are and the part they can play in securing their organization's success. Agile implementation has two key elements:

- Agile operations to deliver strategic intent in the most effective way possible (discussed in Chapters 5 and 6)
- The process of change, an inevitable aspect of executing strategic intent (explored in the additional online content).

With respect to agile operations, the emphasis is on speed, efficiency and flexibility as well as on quality and innovation, with the customer as the central focus of all activity. Organizational assets and systems are designed to enhance flexibility, efficiency and speed so that there is resource fluidity,[27] or the internal capability to reconfigure business systems and redeploy resources rapidly. The focus is on teams and fewer hierarchical structures with a multiplicity of collaborations. Agile means reimagining the entire organization as a network of high-performing teams, each going after clear, end-to-end, business-oriented outcomes, and possessing all of the skills needed to deliver, such as a bank boosting the performance of customer journeys. We've seen a rapid acceleration towards these ways of tech-enabled working during the pandemic so that they have increasingly become the 'new normal'. Continuous improvement, lean tools and iterative Agile project management methodology are applied across operations and become part of the organization's culture, enabling continuous feedback, iterative adjustment to changing customer requirements and speedy and effective delivery.

## Agile innovation

In agile organizations 'business as usual' is always becoming 'business as new'. That is because they are learning organizations that are continually pushing boundaries of knowledge and skill through experimentation and testing. Rather than a stereotypical blame culture when mistakes are made, in agile organizations there is a culture of fast feedback and active learning – from setbacks as well as successes. Rich information systems and knowledge processes enable people to access the information they need to do their jobs and also to share ideas for delivering improved customer value. Change efforts are targeted on creating meaningful information flows and having the right people in place to analyse and interpret them (Table 2.3).

High-performance work practices are conducive to innovation, employee engagement and high levels of bounded employee autonomy. These include people working in small, non-hierarchical teams with a limited number of clearly defined goals that are achievable within a short period. Employees are empowered in day-to-day working life and there are ongoing opportunities for them to initiate and lead improvement and innovation in products, services and processes. Rapid problem solving and decision making at the right level are enabled by workplace practices such as self-organized team working, porous boundaries between internal organizational divisions and partner organizations, inclusive improvement and innovation teams, management–union partnerships, openness and transparency and distributed leadership.

TABLE 2.3  Agile innovation

| From | To |
| --- | --- |
| Innovation in limited 'pockets' | A culture of innovation |
| Individual ingenuity | Individual and group idea development |
| Risk averse | Open to risk |
| Haphazard implementation | Disciplined implementation |
| Reward for organization | Mutual benefits |

## The link between culture and performance

One of the principal debates around the concept of culture has focused on its potential link with a firm's performance. JB Barney in his resource-based view linked sustained superior financial performance to cultures that were valuable, rare and imperfectly imitable.[28] Kotter and Heskett observed that good performance was not only linked to the 'strength' of culture, but also to 'adaptability'.[29] Several authors have built in the idea of 'alignment',[30] or 'appropriateness' with its environment and competitive strategies.[31]

In organizational cultures that are supportive of high-performance working and agility, managers and leaders typically prioritize employee engagement. The highest-performing organizations in Bersin by Deloitte's top quartile on its Total Performance Index are inclusive and diverse;[32] they offer flexible, humanistic work environments, open offices and space to move.[33] Goals are reviewed monthly – in contrast to organizations in lower-performance quartiles, which do this once a year. Thus people learn quickly and can stop what is evidently not working and do something that does. Accountability and visibility result from Agile practices such as daily 'scrum' meetings, iterative testing and adjustment of products, and after-action reviews and improvements (see Chapter 5). Feedback is constant and employees set high standards for themselves and others.

At Netflix, former CEO Reed Hastings created a corporate culture based on his motto 'We Seek Excellence', which appears to attract and retain loyal, engaged and high-performing employees. Like Google, this company is highly selective about recruitment to ensure that new hires fit into its corporate culture. Employees are motivated to work there because they are treated with the utmost respect, paid good salaries and are given more responsibility and freedom for being valuable contributors to their team. Netflix management sets the expectations for employees to achieve results then trusts them to work the hours required to do the job. Management strives to create an environment where a key employee benefit is working with excellent colleagues; where every person is someone you can respect and learn from.

It is when all these practices come together within a system of mutually reinforcing practices that high performance becomes sustainable and the benefits for organizations and their stakeholders are really significant.

## Agile linkages

Disruptive innovation is leading to new, more flexible and interactive organizational forms, cultures, working arrangements and workplaces. Agile organization structures are less 'fixed' and more horizontal than conventional 'siloed' vertical structures, with permeable boundaries between functions, units and departments that allow for cooperation patterns and strategic collaboration to get established. Work is typically organized to ensure efficiency, effectiveness and collaboration, with strong, robust operations, process improvement and team working as embedded norms and clear, delegated decision-making authority at all levels. Such structures require high levels of self-management, accountability and willingness by individuals to keep on learning, developing and applying new skills. Management styles, communications processes, employment and development opportunities and reward structures reflect this. Relationships between the players involved are critically important to effective collaboration.

Agile structures have more permeable external boundaries too. Indeed, as we shall discuss in Chapter 4, the trend towards working collaboratively with partner organizations (often including competitors and outsourcers) is becoming widespread and may well accelerate as markets become ever more competitive. Organizations are dynamically connected externally via adaptable supply chains, open source, collaborative networks and strategic alliances. Within knowledge-intensive industries the networked organization is on the rise,[34] especially in mature industries such as pharmaceuticals where companies face the common challenge of building new markets as well as products. Partner relationships can also act as sensors for emergent environmental changes. Thus organizations can set out to exploit opportunities and build new markets with pooled resources and new working arrangements. Consequently, the resilience of organizations is also dependent on the health of partner organizations, the communities they serve and the individual resilience of their staff members.

To enable organizational linkages within and between organizations to work effectively and without damage to brand requires collaborative capabilities, innovation in roles and supportive structures. It also requires healthy employee relations – at individual and collective levels – including between trade unions and employers' organizations. Employee communications can play a key role in helping to build a flexible leadership culture in which people are informed, engaged, responsible and accountable at all levels.

Collaborative linkages between organizations can also enable freer movement across organizational boundaries for people in search of enhanced career opportunities. Employers usually consider such talent fluidity as a bad thing yet there are potentially positives to be gained. In US Ivy League universities, for instance, rather than being viewed as 'failures', outgoing employees are treated as alumni and future clients – and therefore valuable assets.[35] Those who leave can look forward to highly successful careers with long-lasting collaborative relationships with their former colleagues. Arguably many other types of organization could learn something from this higher education practice when they reflect on their own approach to talent management and career development.

Collaboration is also needed on a wider scale to address societal and other challenges. Within an organization's ecosystem, including society at large, suppliers and customer groups, there are increasing demands for flexible reactions from organizations to co-determine what happens in markets, cooperation networks and societies. In this interconnected and changing environment, no organization can stand apart from its communities any more.

Especially during and since the economic recession triggered in 2008 and also following the COVID-19 pandemic, the nature, role and ethics of business have come into question. Climate change has become a major driver of sustainable business initiatives. Consequently, no organization really wishes to be seen as 'greenwashing' – paying mere lip service to the notion of corporate social responsibility for environmental, social or governance matters (ESG). Indeed, a firm's reputation has become a vital business asset that can be irretrievably damaged if the firm becomes known to be an environmental polluter, for example, or exploiter of disadvantaged communities. And, as many high-profile cases have demonstrated, firms' reputations can be put as much at risk by the ways in which their suppliers conduct their business as by their own practices. Even apparently legal practices from an earlier era, such as the clever use of tax avoidance schemes to minimize payment of corporation and personal tax in their countries of operation, have damaged the reputations of a number of celebrities and global firms in various markets.

## Agile people practices

Both agility and resilience are needed if an organization is to have adaptive capacity or 'change-ability' in its cultural DNA.[36] As John Kotter points out, in a fast-moving context organizations need a dual operating system – the formal management system and a network of change agents, which requires more leadership more than just management.[37] It isn't just new leadership and management competencies that are needed to achieve change-ability; employee attitudes, behaviour and skills will also need to shift and stretch. Change-able staff are flexible and competent, multiskilled, 'engaged' and productive, willing and able to adapt to continuous change.

So in agile organizations people become centre stage – their passion, grasp, creativity, interactions and relationships shape the very future of our organizations. The importance of having the 'right' people, working in the 'right' ways, working on the 'right' things, is driving new employee-centric emphases in human resource strategies. To build a multiskilled workforce, instead of hiring new people with a narrow skill set to meet a temporary need, leading companies strengthen their existing employees with additional skills. They offer career and talent mobility, a modern learning environment where approaches to development are 'pull' rather than 'push'. Thus talent management strategy is a key tool in building a more agile and adaptable workforce capable of responding to new competitive threats and capitalizing on new opportunities.

Employee engagement is becoming a key area of focus, and the link between high performance and employee engagement has some face validity at least. The 'Engaging for Success' report highlights numerous studies that suggest that, when employees are engaged and empowered, they tend to be innovative, willing to share their ideas, more aligned around common objectives, more productive and accountable, more likely to be ambassadors and promoters of their employers' brands, and to have longer tenures than less engaged employees.[38] Therefore, by improving understanding of what drives employee engagement, organizations can be more effective at increasing it.

## Management and leadership needed

A number of reports have identified the growing importance of leadership and management in securing the future growth, productivity and competitiveness of firms. In the UK analysis by the UK Commission for Employment and Skills (UKCES) has shown that management skills are crucial to ensuring high-performance working, and best-practice management development can result in a 23 per cent increase in organizational performance.[39] The Business Benefits of Management and Leadership Development (February 2012), published by CMI in partnership with Penna found that 43 per cent of UK managers rate their own line manager as ineffective; and 93 per cent of respondents in a survey of 750 companies carried out by the Institute of Leadership and Management (ILM, 2021) reported that low levels of management skills were impacting on their business.[40] A report by Deloitte argues that the need to develop leaders at all levels is the number-one issue facing organizations around the world, yet only 13 per cent of respondents believe that their organization does an excellent job at developing leaders at all levels.

So there is a renewed focus on helping managers and leaders develop the skills and abilities they need to create high-performance climates that are conducive to workplace innovation. Executive team members need to spend more time together listening to signals and data from inside and out. They need to make fewer, bigger decisions that will provide clear purpose and priorities for the rest of the organization. More deliberate decision making at the top empowers the rest of the organization to move faster. Longer-term benefits accrue when managers support and enable staff, especially if staff members are more expert in their fields than their line managers. In particular, the leadership of networks demands new approaches to facilitation and empowerment practice that transcend earlier transactional and transformational theories of leadership.

## Conclusion

So, agility is a set of values and principles. Since agility inherently involves change, organizations need to be 'change-able', with the changing context reframed as 'dynamically stable'. Agile organizations learn to design and implement change programmes in such a way that change 'sticks' – for a while at least. But such a nirvana is not easily achieved within today's competitive contexts in which employees are often required to pay a high price for business success. So if organizations and their workforces are to thrive in changing times we must aim for a better balance between organizational and individual needs. We must seek to create work contexts characterized by trust, mutuality, growth and empowerment. That way, everyone wins.

The quest for business agility is driving changes to the ways firms are being managed and led and to the routines they must embrace if they wish to be resilient. The scale of change required will, of course, depend on the situation that an organization faces and its current capabilities. As we have discussed:

- Building an agile organization is not just about using Agile tools and methodology – it involves a *whole systems approach* to enhancing the qualities, capabilities, routines, resources and relationships needed to produce outputs that customers want over time.

- Leading and working in agile organizations requires *context, cognitive and behavioural resilience* at all levels – this is likely to require some significant shifts in mindsets and skill sets.

- *Culture can be more influential than strategy* in determining an organization's fortunes – and should receive relevant executive attention accordingly.

- In today's marketplace, *people, working alongside technology, are the source of production* – they must be partners in the process of organizational evolution and treated as such.

- Agility and resilience can be enhanced by 'tinkering' at the edges, but to be sustainable they must be built on *shared foundations of purpose, values and integrity*.

In short, a resiliently agile organization has:

- An organizational culture and structure that facilitates change within the context of the situation that it faces
- Staff who are willing and able to give of their best – in a sustainable way
- A learning mindset in the mainstream business and underlying lean and agile processes and routines to drive innovation.

As this *tour d'horizon* of resilient agility suggests, some organizations may be able to evolve gently towards agility, while for others, nothing short of a revolution will be necessary. In the coming chapters we work through each of the framework quadrants in turn, spending more time, as seems fitting, on the people and culture aspects of organizations. In the next chapter we look at the first quadrant: agile strategizing.

---

CHECKLIST

- **Strategizing**
  - How much commitment is there to agility in your organization?
  - Is there a clear vision in place? Does it have a supporting plan to deliver positive outcomes for stakeholders? To what extent are people aligned to the organization? Do they understand the strategy and how they contribute to it effectively through their daily work?
- **Implementing**
  - Do formal processes, procedures and systems connect? Do they support decision making and foster creativity and innovation? Do they enable people to perform and the organization to achieve its goals?
- **Structure**
  - How are tasks and people divided and authority distributed? How does this serve the delivery of the strategy and associated standards? Does it enable decision making, promote transparency and support organizational resilience and sustainability?

- **Linking**
  - How effective are partnerships? How well do people collaborate across silos?
- **Culture**
  - Do the core values and purpose act as guiding principles for the organization? Does the top team model behaviours congruent with these values? What gets valued and rewarded? To what extent is there trust and belief that people can make a difference?
- **People**
  - Is the capacity and capability in place to deliver the organization's goals? Are people empowered, engaged and able to fulfil their potential? Does the leadership style and the learning and development plan serve the ambitions of the organization and its people?

# Notes

1  Lengnick-Hall, CA and Beck, TE (2005) Adaptive fit versus robust transformation: how organizations respond to environmental change, *Journal of Management*, **31**, pp 738–57.
2  McCann, J, Selsky, J and Lee, J (2004) Building agility, resilience and performance in turbulent times, *People & Strategy*, **32** (3), pp 45–51.
3  Pettigrew, A, Ferlie, E and McKee, L (1992) Shaping strategic change: the case of the NHS in the 1980s, *Public Money & Management*, **12** (3), pp 27–31.
4  Abrahamson, E (1990) Change without pain, *Harvard Business Review*, July.
5  D'Aveni, R (1994) *Hypercompetition: The dynamics of strategic maneuvering*, Free Press, New York.
6  Teece, DG, Pisano, J and Shuen, A (1997) Dynamic capabilities and strategic management, *Strategic Management Journal*, **18**, pp 509–33.
7  Teece, DG and Pisano, J (1994) The dynamic capabilities of firms, *Industrial and Corporate Change*, **3**, pp 537–56.
8  Cyert, RM and March, JG (1963) *A Behavioral Theory of the Firm*, Prentice-Hall, Englewood Cliffs, New Jersey.
9  Miner, AS (1991) Organizational evolution and the social ecology of jobs, *American Sociological Review*, **56**, pp 772–85.
10  Feldman, MS (2000) Organizational routines as a source of continuous change, *Organization Science*, **11**, pp 611–29.

**11**  Adler, PS, Goldoftas, B and Levine, DI (1999) Flexibility versus efficiency? A case study of model change-overs in the Toyota production system, *Organization Science*, **10**, pp 43–68.

**12**  Miner, AS (1990) Structural evolution through idiosyncratic jobs, *Organization Science*, **1**, pp 195–210.

**13**  Rosenbaum, M and Jaffe, Y (1983) Learned helplessness: the role of individual differences in learned resourcefulness, *British Journal of Social Psychology*, **22**, pp 215–25.

**14**  Coutu, D (2002) How resiliency works, *Harvard Business Review*, 80 (5), pp 46–55.

**15**  Collins, J and Hansen, MT (2011) *Great By Choice: Uncertainty, chaos and luck – why some thrive despite them all*, HarperCollins, New York.

**16**  Plsek, P (2003) Complexity and the adoption of innovation in health care, conference on strategies to speed the diffusion of evidence-based innovations, 27–28 January, https://chess.wisc.edu/niatx/PDF/PIPublications/Plsek_2003_NIHCM.pdf (archived at https://perma.cc/59Y3-MAUL).

**17**  Collins and Hansen, ibid.

**18**  Lavie, D (2006) The competitive advantage of interconnected firms: an extension of the resource-based view, *Academy of Management Review*, **31**, pp 638–58.

**19**  IBM Institute for Business Value (2013) Reinventing the Rules of Engagement: CEO Insights from the Global C-suite Study.

**20**  Doz, Y and Kosonen, M (2007) *Fast Strategy*, Wharton School Publishing, Pennsylvania.

**21**  This view has been expressed by Booz Allen Hamilton, Boston Consulting Group and the McKinsey Global Institute.

**22**  Bremen, JM (2021) *Leading to the future, not the past*, Willis Towers Watson, https://www.wtwco.com/en-BE/insights/2021/07/leading-to-the-future-not-the-past (archived at https://perma.cc/6T3L-CPDG).

**23**  Peters, T and Waterman, RH Jr (2004) *In Search of Excellence: Lessons from America's best-run companies*, Profile Books, London.

**24**  Dyer, L and Ericksen, J (2009) Complexity-based agile enterprises: Putting self-organizing emergence to work, in A Wilkinson et al (eds) *The Sage Handbook of Human Resource Management*, Sage, London, pp 436–57.

**25**  High-Impact Performance Management: Five Best Practices to Make Recognition and Rewards Meaningful, Stacia Sherman Garr / Bersin & Associates, 2012.

**26**  IBM Institute for Business Value, ibid.

**27**  Doz and Kosonen, ibid.

**28**  Barney, JB (1986) Organizational culture: Can it be a source of sustained competitive advantage? *Academy of Management Review*, **11** (3), pp 656–65.

**29**  Kotter, JP and Heskett, L (1992) *Corporate Culture and Performance*, Free Press, New York.

**30**  Newman, KL and Nollen, SD (1996) Culture and congruence: The fit between management practices and national culture, *Journal of International Business Studies*, **27** (4), pp 735–79.

**31**  Goffee, R and Jones, G (2003) *The Character of a Corporation*, Profile Books, London.

**32**  High-Impact Performance Management: Using Goals to Focus the 21st Century Workforce, Stacia Sherman Garr / Bersin by Deloitte, 2014.

**33**  The Diversity & Inclusion Benchmarking Report, Bersin by Deloitte / Stacia Sherman Garr, March 2014.

**34**  Dyer, J and Nobeoka, K (2000) Creating and managing a high-performance knowledge-sharing network: The Toyota case, *Strategic Management Journal*, **21**, pp 345–67.

**35**  Kennie, T and Price, I (2012) *Disruptive Innovation and the Higher Education Ecosystem*, Stimulus paper, The Leadership Foundation for Higher Education.

**36**  Holbeche, LS (2005) *The High Performance Organization*, Butterworth-Heinemann, Oxford.

**37**  Kotter, JP (2012) Accelerate, *Harvard Business Review*, November.

**38**  MacLeod, D and Clarke, N (2009) *Engaging for Success: Enhancing performance through employee engagement*, London: BIS, www.engageforsuccess.org/wp-content/uploads/2015/08/file52215.pdf (archived at https://perma.cc/QN5K-XA7H).

**39**  Shury, J et al (2012) *UK Commission's Employer Perspectives Survey 2012: UK Results*, UKCES Evidence Report 64.

**40**  The Business Benefits of Management and Leadership Development (February 2012), published by CMI in partnership with Penna ILM (2021). Leading through challenging times.

# 03

# Agile strategizing

In this chapter we look at the first quadrant of the resiliently agile framework: strategizing. This is how top management teams establish an aspirational purpose, develop a widely shared strategy and manage the climate and commitment to execution. All decisions, including strategy, should flow from this purpose.[1]

In strategizing, the processes of strategy creation are no longer restricted to top management. To close the strategy implementation gap everyone needs to be aware of what the organization is aiming to achieve and have opportunities to play a part in shaping the future. Similarly, everyone needs to be capable of what the Center for Effective Organizations (CEO) calls 'perceiving' – the process of broadly, deeply and continuously monitoring the environment to sense changes and rapidly communicate these perceptions to decision makers who interpret and formulate appropriate responses.[2]

Strategizing is also an experimental process for the agile enterprise, in which individuals repeatedly generate ideas (exploration), identify ways to capitalize on ideas (exploitation), nimbly respond to environmental feedback (adaptation) and move on to the next idea (exit).[3] So while top leadership clearly has a key role to play in strategizing and perceiving, so too do others.

In this chapter we look at:

- the scale of the strategizing challenge – and lessons from long-lived organizations
- the role of top leadership in strategizing – and the skills involved
- getting others involved in the strategizing process.

## The scale of the challenge

Navigating a way forward for the business in today's fast-changing and ambiguous times can be challenging since cause and effect cannot be known in advance and things may or may not occur in the same way as they did in the past. As we have discussed, if organizations are to survive and thrive they must shift their business models – and their leadership skills – to become what Heifetz and Laurie call 'adaptive firms'.[4]

Strategy is about shaping the future. Innovation gives strategy new options for shaping a better future. Strategic innovation is about doing two things at once: focusing creativity on solving existing strategic problems and reacting to the new opportunities that insights, ideas and innovation make possible – both – at the same time.

Leaders need to be clear-sighted about where value is found and about the level of change required to enable the organization to survive and thrive. A business model describes the rationale of why and how an organization creates, delivers and captures value. It reflects the dominant performance logic that specifies how business is done, who the customers are and where the costs and profits are. This logic outlines how financial and non-financial resources flow through the organization, and the organizational capabilities required to achieve joined-up implementation of the business model.

The scale of business model transformation required will vary according to the organization and its specific situation. Laurie and Lynch argue that there are three strategically different situations that companies face when building on their current success – retaining, refining or changing their business model.[5] Each situation determines where innovation is most needed and the broad approach to organization design. In the first two cases, innovation is focused on both process and product. In the latter case, the organization needs to innovate its overall value proposition to the market. Innovation in the business model requires developments in the structure and/or the financial model of the business and so also includes strategic partnerships, shared services or alternative financing vehicles.[6]

Rita Gunther McGrath goes further, arguing that in today's context it is unrealistic of company leaders to assume that their firms can achieve sustainable competitive advantage (SCA).[7] Instead, she proposes that organizations should focus on achieving a series of transient advantages (TA) by launching new strategic initiatives again and again, and creating a portfolio of advantages that can be built quickly and abandoned just as quickly. So rather than working to a fixed business model, the pursuit of TA implies the organization must be able to run potentially multiple, experimental business models concurrently and be prepared to dispose of parts of itself that no longer add value. Nielsen and Lund identified five patterns by which companies can achieve scalability of business model.[8] The first pattern involved adding new distribution channels. The second entailed freeing the business from traditional capacity constraints. The third involved outsourcing capital investments to partners who, in effect, became participants in the business model. The fourth was to have customers and other partners assume multiple roles in the business model. The fifth pattern was to establish platform models in which even competitors may become customers.

To be resilient, organizations need to be ambidextrous – able to manage today's business efficiently, while also adapting to changes in the environment so that they are still around tomorrow.[9] The demands on an organization in its immediate task environment are always to some degree in conflict with the longer term (e.g. investment in the here and now versus future projects; differentiation versus low-cost production) so trade-offs need to be made. While these trade-offs can never be entirely contained, the most successful organizations reconcile them to a large degree and in so doing enhance their long-term competitiveness.

Given this level of complexity, how can leaders create strategies that provide sufficient clarity and avoid chaos? Looking back at companies that have survived successfully over time may provide some clues.

## Lessons from long-lived organizations

In a study of successful long-lived organizations, which he defined as 'living companies', Arie de Geus drew a sharp distinction between the purpose of living companies – to fulfil their potential and perpetuate themselves as ongoing communities – and that of 'economic companies', which are in business solely to produce wealth for a small group of individuals.[10] Long-lived companies have four essential traits in common: they are sensitive to their environment in order to learn and adapt; cohesive, with a strong sense of identity; tolerant of unconventional thinking and experimentation; and conservative in financial policy in order to retain the resources that allow for flexibility.

Similarly, Jim Collins and Jerry Porras studied long-lived 'visionary' companies such as Hewlett-Packard, 3M, Motorola, Procter & Gamble, Disney and Walmart.[11] They found that visionary companies had fewer charismatic visionary 'time teller' leaders and more 'clock builders' who focused on building a company that could prosper far beyond the tenure of any single leader and through multiple product life cycles. And in visionary companies, management tends to be home-grown, thus ensuring continuity and succession. Insiders maintain the core values and understand them in a way that outsiders usually cannot. Insiders also act as the most effective change agents who can stimulate change and progress.

Both studies emphasize the importance of being guided by a core ideology – strong values and a purpose beyond simply making money. This ideology provides a strong sense of identity and continuity that strengthens the organization in the face of change. Visionary leaders build a cult-like culture around their core ideologies. For instance, Walt Disney created an entire language to reinforce his company's ideology. At Disneyland employees are 'cast members'. Similarly, the Johnson & Johnson credo still guides employee behaviour decades after it was first developed.

Both studies also identified that, alongside a passionately held core ideology that provides stability and cohesion, there is a relentless drive for progress that stimulates change, innovation and renewal. So continuity and change co-exist. As Jim Collins points out: 'By being clear about their core values and guiding purpose – about what should not change – companies can feel liberated to experiment with everything else.'[12] And rather than seeing potential dilemmas and choices as problems to be solved, companies in both these studies recognized the importance of embracing a 'both-and' rather than an 'either/or' way of thinking.

In the current context, an interesting shift appears to be under way – according to a study by IBM – with regard to how some companies determine value.[13] Most conventional companies have 'an almost single-minded focus on "capturing" value solely for the benefit of the individual organization'. In contrast, the most successful organizations in the IBM study are interested in innovation that drives enhanced value for the widest group of stakeholders possible – customers, employees, partners and shareholders alike. Similarly, 'the purpose of any business or organization should be the creation of value in the form of contributions to sustainable widely shared prosperity, measured in terms of human flourishing and wellbeing', according to the UNDP Human Development report 2022.

So the routine primacy given to shareholder value in many businesses is starting to be challenged by the shifts taking place in the broader context and a new 'both-and' is perhaps emerging.

STRATEGIZING AND COMPLEXITY

This 'both-and' thinking is a key aspect of strategizing. Strategizing itself is consistent with complexity theory.

Despite the complexity and uncertainty of today's global environment, senior leaders are still expected to provide strategic leadership, defined as 'the ability to anticipate, envision, maintain flexibility and empower others to create strategic change as necessary'.[14] Most organizations approach strategy as if it were rational (i.e. assuming the future can be predicted and controlled). Leaders are expected to solve problems and make decisions. The shift taking place in how some leaders do that reflects the move away from the conventional top-down linear *predict* and *plan* approaches promoted by business schools towards *perceive* and *respond*.

The Cynefin framework developed by Dave Snowden, Cynthia Kurtz, Mary Boone[15] and others helps us think about the world of problems from a complexity perspective. This encourages decisions to be made based on circumstances and addresses the uncertainty of complex projects and systems. It begins by making a very important distinction – that between the known (or predictable) and the unknown (or unpredictable) realms. For each of these, different approaches are required.

The known world comprises two sub-domains:

*Simple*: this is the domain of known knowns. Cause and effect are generally clear and well established; patterns tend to repeat; events are consistent. Where there is every likelihood that the result will be predictable and will come out the same today as it did yesterday and also will tomorrow, best practices are very helpful. Routine mechanical or process issues also tend to fall into this domain.

*Complicated*: this is the domain of unknown knowns. Cause and effect relationships are knowable, although it may take expertise and analysis to sort out problems that are seen as arising when there is a gap between the outcomes sought and the actual results or state of the system. The job of the leader is to focus on the gap and the steps required to close it. There is often more than one right solution, but such problems are reasonably solvable and predictable. Many organizations act as though the vast majority of their problems fall into this domain and approach them accordingly – using gap analysis (where do we want to be, where are we now, how do we get from here to there) and measurement systems like

KPIs. Visions are described, strategic leverage points are identified, critical steps are listed and milestones are drawn up. Leaders take a 'mind the gap' approach.

On the unknown side, there is complexity, the domain of unknown unknowns and emergence. This represents a departure from mainstream systems thinking and is often referred to as 'new paradigm thinking'. Here the metaphor that best applies is evolution rather than engineering. In new paradigm thinking systems are considered dispositional (i.e. they are inclined to evolve in some directions and not in others). Cause and effect cannot be known in advance. Therefore, things may or may not occur in the same way as they did in the past; instead, simple rules (modulators) or 'managed serendipity' determine outcomes. In the complex domain, there are patterns in the overall system, but these may not be evident and individual events are not predictable. In new paradigm thinking, the approach involves looking for patterns and drawing on intuition to manage the evolutionary potential of the present. The emphasis shifts from conventional outcome measurement to assessing impact.[16]

In complexity leaders must mind the system and draw on intuition. Leaders must resist the temptation to narrow or solve too soon. Instead, facilitating the right conversations, experimentation and monitoring are more helpful, as is diversity of perspective. Leaders can set boundaries within which it is safe to try things out and learn as fast as possible – from both the successes and failures.

Whereas with complicated problems the leader's job is to sense, analyse and respond, in complex situations the leader's job is to probe, sense and respond and create the environment for patterns to emerge. That way leaders can focus on the critical few decisions that have the highest impact and pose the greatest risk, and ensure objectives and expectations are aligned.

So rather than taking a technical, singular view – defining some idealized future state and then attempting to close the gap by adopting a conventional problem-solving approach, looking for root causes and potential solutions – new paradigm thinking is relational and takes a holistic view. In complexity both-and applies: order and chaos need each other; ambiguity and paradox are inevitable challenges to be coped with. Change can be revolutionary and dramatic; strategy can be emergent and opportunistic, and diversity provides competitive advantage.

## Strategic leadership skills in complexity

Before we look in more detail at what this entails, let us consider the implications of today's complex challenges for leaders.

As we have discussed previously, given the level of business complexity in 21st-century environments, one of the main challenges is coping with ambiguity. Leaders must develop greater ease in working with paradox and trusting their instincts. The ability to gather information widely, decide what information to heed, what to ignore, and how to organize and communicate that which we judge to be important is becoming a core competence for leaders, according to Gardner.[17]

To help their companies succeed in what Prahalad and Krishnan call the 'new age of innovation', effective leaders look beyond the accepted, the norm, the known and the popular to what is necessary to thrive.[18] They do this with curiosity, courage, commitment, consummate attention, passion, resilience and dedication – and still bring people with them.[19]

Outstanding leaders now focus on finding the pathways through the contradictions and tensions within the firm, balancing uncomfortable, unpopular but necessary decisions with winning hearts and minds.[20]

The economic conditions and market challenges mean that decisions need to be made, and quickly. Complacency is one of the greatest dangers for any business and the challenge for leaders is to keep injecting urgency. Deciding not to do something is as important as acting. Adapting proactively and intelligently to situational changes requires sensing environmental shifts quickly, capturing insights about changes, interpreting their significance and responding effectively. Leaders need a global perspective, to understand their context and focus on critical volatilities and discontinuities.

In complexity, the task of leaders is to lead the development of vision and strategy. Much depends on how good a CEO is at motivating their team and generating the sort of excitement that leads people to do things in different ways. According to Bob Johansen, VUCA leaders energize the workforce by countering complexity with clarity, and uncertainty with understanding.[21] They interpret current reality and shape collective visions of the future through creativity and the development of the overall business vision and direction, setting a common objective that everyone strives to achieve and driving action to seize emerging opportunities. They help people to make sense of the volatility by working collaboratively and being excellent communicators who can connect with all levels of employees and ensure understanding. They translate organizational purpose and goals into action-able deliverables and empower employees at all levels to make decisions, ensuring that each person on the front line knows exactly what to do to achieve the goal.[22]

So leaders are faced with seemingly contradictory requirements: to achieve both strategic clarity and consistency *and* operational agility and resilience. Balancing conflicting demands requires a different management mindset, skill set and approach from those required to deliver a relatively 'simple' business model in relatively 'straightforward' scenarios. Some of the detect-able shifts in management emphasis are detailed in Table 3.1.

The mindset and practices needed for leading in complexity, and how to make changes in those contexts, are distinctly different from the mindset and practices needed in 'complicated' situations where the relationships between cause and effect can be revealed over time through analysis and therefore specific actions can be taken with some confidence of the outcome (and therefore certainty is of high value). In the complex space, because there is no knowable or 'right' solution, uncertainty, curiosity and openness are more useful. While there is no single right answer, there are also fewer wrong answers. This means that leaders must be comfortable with not knowing all the answers. In response to demands for enhanced transparency they must acknowledge their accountability for the performance of their

TABLE 3.1  A shifting emphasis

| From | To |
| --- | --- |
| Sensing and reacting | Anticipating, proacting, creating (e.g. new business models) |
| Business as usual | Agile business |
| Innovation in 'pockets' | System-wide innovation and continuous improvement |
| Customer service | Intense customer focus |
| Managing global supply chains | Managing global value creation |
| Efficiency | Efficiency and effectiveness |
| Employees as resources | Employees as partners |
| Engage and inspire | Enable and empower |
| Control of the agenda | Ride paradox and facilitate possibilities |
| Driving change | Building capability and capacity for change |
| Either/or | Both-and |

businesses. This can be very liberating for some leaders and also very frightening for others who believe that by not producing the 'solution' they lose one of the key means to control their organization and their people. As Johnston et al suggest, this can be quite an unsettling shift.[23]

A report by the Center for Creative Leadership notes that today's VUCA business environment requires leaders to be adaptable, open to change, and knowledgeable about their organization beyond their functional areas of expertise. They must develop deep self-insight into their strengths and weaknesses as leaders. Above all, leaders must be able to learn fast – because change is constant – and to possess more strategic, complex and adaptive critical-thinking abilities.[24] These skills and abilities are very different from the more technical or function-specific skills and abilities required of leaders in the past.

Roger Martin argues that to innovate and win, companies need design thinking. He says that we rely too much on analytical thinking as applied to innovation and organizational change.[25] He proposes doing experiments in an early stage of the process to test critical assumptions or components of the new idea/concept; then using the insights to adapt the design as a rapid, cost-effective form of de-risking. This form of thinking is rooted in how knowledge advances from one stage to another – from mystery (something we can't explain) to heuristic (a rule of thumb that guides us towards a solution) to algorithm (a predictable formula for producing an answer). Martin shows how leading companies such as Procter & Gamble, Cirque du Soleil, RIM and others use design thinking to push knowledge through the stages in ways that produce breakthrough innovations and competitive advantage. This is about experimenting and getting into feedback loops with the customer.[26] Similarly, instead of suggesting the 'solution', Cynefin advocates 'safe fail probes' and prototyping as a way of making sense in the complex domain: testing ideas/solutions, sensing the impact and responding to this by either amplifying the probe or suppressing it. Lightweight experiments and rapid prototyping such as this allow us to see and understand the landscape we are operating in so we can learn from what works and then adjust tactics.

As with all routines, these skills and competencies improve with experience and practice. For example, divergent thinking skills can be honed through scenario planning, brainstorming, devil's advocacy techniques and dialogue. Problem-solving techniques that rely on frequent iterations serve as catalysts for new ideas and increase the odds of success, simply because there are more options available for consideration. When applied routinely to solving problems, such techniques help leaders to know where to go 'tight' – i.e. with management specifying the parameters of the project, including the 'non-negotiables' and making the final decisions – and where the process is 'loose' so that people know where their contribution is invited and decisions can be made to best effect.

Of course, not every leader can lead effectively in paradoxical and ambiguous settings. Today the major leadership derailers include hesitancy to take necessary business risks, personal arrogance and insensitivity, politicking, controlling leadership style, and reluctance to tackle difficult people issues. So it is crucial for leaders to recognize their own strengths and limitations – and what their organization needs. When Google's founders, Sergey Brin and Larry Page, realized that Google was going to be a huge success they hired veteran Silicon Valley boss Eric Schmidt in 2001 to replace them as chief executive.[27] They recognized that just having a world-beating product and eager customers was not enough to secure sustainable success. They realized that even though they were brilliant at developing the product – the search engine – they lacked the ability to handle the business transformation required to take Google to the next level. Schmidt had the skills to turn Google from a promising start-up into a global giant. He was able to motivate workers and reshape departments and internal processes to ensure that Google could grow at a rapid pace. In other words, Schmidt had the rare skill to effect business transformation, to reshape the business and keep it performing while the company grew. It could be argued that every organization and CEO needs this mindset and skill set.

To provide the bold, sophisticated leadership that the 21st century demands, leaders must create a context for change, recognize and apply the new rules of the game, provide strategic clarity and build capacity to act. Yet they must remain flexible about how they get there. They also need a head for dealing with the risks that are an inherent part of innovation and change. Ideas such as 'control of the agenda' in the traditional sense must shift towards 'facilitating possibility'. Expressions such as 'driving change' must shift towards 'building capability and capacity for change'. Similarly, it is important to develop the ability for quickly deploying and then redeploying resources, talent and skills by learning to hedge bets and avoiding overcommitment. Agile leaders cross-train and frequently move people around to broaden the skill/knowledge base.

Above all, leaders need to be able to lead people through change and create convergence in contexts where the speed of change can be overwhelming. Relationships, integrity and the ability to build trust lie at the heart of this. As

Charles Tilley, chief executive of CIMA, points out: 'Business value goes beyond the numbers. A focus on relationships, in the context of the business model and how it creates sustainable value helps support better integrated thinking and decision making – leading to better governance, better performance management and better reporting: in short, better business.'[28]

## Leading the process of strategizing

A study by the Center for Effective Organizations (CEO) found that, in agile organizations, strategy has three explicit parts: a sense of shared purpose, a change-friendly identity that is nonetheless stable enough to ground the organization and a robust strategic intent that clarifies how the firm differentiates itself.[29]

### A sense of shared purpose

Firms foster a positive, constructive organizational identity through a strong sense of purpose, authentic core values and a genuine vision. First leaders need to define their business and its purpose. Purpose involves answering the question, 'Why does this organization exist?' According to the late Peter Drucker, the only valid definition of business purpose is to create a customer by offering value that captures the fancy of someone who is willing to pay to obtain something valuable. Therefore, the question, 'What is our business?' can only be answered by looking from the outside – at the customer and market – starting with the customer's reality, values and expectations.

Agile leaders create the strategic narrative that provides the rationale for change and helps people to see what success looks like.

A vision is a key element of this strategic narrative. The goal of a vision is to ensure that everyone is heading in the same direction to achieve the same outcome. Jim Collins and Jerry Porras, in their 1994 book *Built to Last: Successful habits of visionary companies,* used the term 'Big Hairy Audacious Goal' (BHAG) to define visionary goals that are more strategic and emotionally compelling. It should be possible to visualize your organization achieving its vision but not so easy for your organization to reach out and take hold of the vision straight away. It should provide a meaningful stretch that gives employees a reason to come to work, generates enthusiasm for what they do, and creates team spirit and a commitment to making it happen. Leaders use stories to empower, champion and celebrate change agents in the organization. And when leaders use positive language that implies capability, influence, competence, consistent core values and a clear sense of direction, they set the stage for constructive sense making.[30] For instance, NASA achieved its vision of 'landing a man on the moon and returning him safely to the Earth'.

It is about inspiring and engaging people, thinking about what motivates them and giving them the space to gain a higher sense of purpose, and localizing the message for teams so that they can make sense of their contribution to the larger organization. So it is important to check:

- Is the definition of the future simple, clear and compelling? (Your future should be defined and vividly described in terms of beliefs, behaviours and results.)

- Does everyone understand how they contribute to achieving the vision? Make sure every member of your team knows how they connect within the big picture. Being productive in ways that do not contribute to achieving the future vision wastes precious time and resources.

## A robust strategic intent: focus on the core

Agile organizations need to gain the advantages of operating at a global scale while also remaining responsive to customer needs and competitive actions on the ground. The organization's core is the heart of its strategic intent. Prahalad and Hamel identified the concept of core competencies – the complex combinations of skills, processes, resources, technologies and structures that together distinguish a firm and give advantage in terms of the company's ability to design, make, market, sell and deliver products and services of particular quality into defined markets.[31]

In any industry, there are three primary paths to competitive advantage: differentiation, low cost or structural advantage.[32] In today's marketplaces, strategic differentiation, focus and client alignment have become significantly more important than low cost or structural advantage. Without differentiation, companies may end up being in what is often referred to as the 'squeezed middle'. In pursuing a differentiation strategy the key to success is truly understanding your unique core and then focusing resources on it to create value.

The consistently highest-performing institutions in the Fortune 500 focus on the core where they are strongly distinctive and from which they derive their identity. This is where they invest the most and generate the greatest returns. By contrast, areas that are not core may be sources of weakness. Focusing on the core allows organizations to change at short notice, to build real-time capacity and potentially rapidly reconfigure the business portfolio. So, by focusing on the core leaders can build the characteristics that make their organizations stand out and set them ahead of the field.

## How does the process of strategizing work? Through dialogue

Ireland and Hitt argue that a more appropriate concept of strategic leadership in the 21st century is to move from the 'Great Leader' to the 'Great Groups' view of strategic leadership.[33] This means that everyone must have their say, in a non-hierarchical way, without the quieter people being drowned out by more vocal colleagues. This allows knowledge to be more readily shared and the results include outstanding financial performance, customer satisfaction, expanded knowledge bases, integrated communications with stakeholders, continuous process/people improvements and shared leadership.

Indeed, thanks to technology, knowledge is now a democratically available commodity. The Cluetrain Manifesto[34] suggests that employees are getting hyperlinked just as markets are. The ideal, according to these authors, is for the networked marketplace to be connected to the networked intranet so that full communication can exist between those within the marketplace and those within the company itself. Achieving this level of communication is hindered by the imposition of 'command and control' structures, but, ultimately, organizations will need to allow this level of communication to exist as the new marketplace will no longer respond to the mass-media 'voice' of the organization. Companies need to listen carefully to both. Mostly, leaders need to get out of the way so intra-networked employees can converse directly with inter-networked markets.[35]

Similarly, William Halal argues that because of hyperlinks and networks, organizations should develop internal markets for knowledge.[36] Indeed, he argues that the current era of knowledge will soon be superseded by the era of consciousness. This democratization of the knowledge workplace can be challenging for some leaders who have long been immersed in management hierarchies where important-sounding titles and reporting structures indicate power and encourage ego-driven behaviour. Yet when employees participate in strategizing, the familiar gap between strategy making and implementation starts to close as people come to understand why change is needed and have the chance to share collective intelligence and contribute their best ideas. Thus agility and resilience become intertwined in the process of direction setting.

Especially when change is needed, what matters is that dialogue takes place. Participation requires an open strategy process and heightened strategic awareness all round thanks to high-quality internal dialogue, through which employees can be actively involved in strategizing and where the main challenge for leaders is to help with collective sense making. Diversity of approach and thought is essential – getting people to view things from other people's points of view. This means leaders listening, understanding and acting upon what they hear. These capabilities enable information to flow more freely than ever throughout the organization as a human system. McKinsey has found that effective organizations seem to be transforming strategy development into an ongoing process of ad hoc, topic-specific leadership conversations and budget-reallocation meetings conducted periodically throughout the year.[37] Some organizations have instituted a more broadly democratic process that pulls in company-wide participation through social technology and game-based strategy development.

Many organizations bring together executives and graduate recruits to discuss business issues; recruits typically have energy and new ideas and may also have strong ideas about the values of the business. Some CEOs hold regional board meetings in different offices so that they can ask staff for feedback and discuss issues of concern. Organization Development (OD) specialists can help to facilitate large-scale gatherings that engage employees in dialogue about the organization's context challenges using methodologies such as Real-Time Strategic Change and Future Search.

When conflict occurs it is important, as Nancy Kline recommends, to get protagonists listening to each other, restating key points from each other's point of view and outlining areas of agreement.[38] For instance, in the early 2000s, a major UK newspaper publisher recognized that the advent of the internet and digital would have a significant impact on its business model of print journalism since consumers would expect to be able to download content on an ongoing basis and free of charge. The company wanted to get ahead of the curve and be seen as a market leader in this new way of providing information. Journalists were initially unconvinced and unwilling to embrace the new ways of working. Key to helping journalists see the need for change was getting them involved in discussion about the changing context and the adaptive challenge the firm was facing. A series of large-scale gatherings took place in which groups of journalists were provided with relevant context and business information and worked through the implications for the business. They identified a number of ways in which the new model could be made to work financially and became active partners with management in developing the new offering.

Some leaders may be concerned about opening up dialogue on all strategic matters for fear that this might slow down decision making. Here the rule of 'go slow to go fast' usually applies. Indeed, there will be many situations where it is inappropriate to involve people in the decision-making process. In such cases, careful signposting can help to avoid confusion about why people are not being consulted about some matters while they are about others.

## Identifying the challenges ahead

To help their organizations stay ahead in such challenging and volatile times CEOs need to anticipate what is coming next and identify the 'adaptive challenges' their organizations are likely to face. Without a crystal ball, how can leaders gain insight into the challenges ahead? Heifetz and Laurie use the analogy of a football coach, who 'gets on the balcony' from where they can see the whole pitch and watch the game in progress.[39] As they seek to create a more differentiated and financially sustainable organization, leaders need to 'get on the balcony' to perceive what is around the corner, look for new opportunities, spot the adaptive challenges and make the right moves.

## Wide-deep scanning

Getting onto the balcony requires wide-deep scanning of the changing business context, gathering intelligence from many sources to explore the 'big picture' issues facing the firm and its customers. How, then, do leaders 'get on the balcony'? Heifetz and Laurie describe how, when Lord Colin Marshall came to lead the loss-making British Airways in the 1980s, in looking into the nature of the threat posed by dissatisfied customers he and his team listened to the ideas and concerns of people inside and outside the organization.[40] They identified lack of trust by customers and employees as a key adaptive challenge for the organization; they recognized that competing values and norms were being played out within the executive team in dysfunctional ways that impaired the capacity of the rest of the company to collaborate. Marshall and his team held up a mirror to themselves, recognizing that they embodied the adaptive challenges facing the organization – and decided to address the situation. They created the vision of British Airways becoming the world's favourite airline. The leadership team set new standards for their own behaviour and started to model a new way of operating that built trust with employees and other stakeholders. They also held themselves to account.

Leaders should be asking themselves questions such as:

- Where do we see ourselves positioned today? Where would we like to be positioned in the future? How might we differentiate ourselves from other providers?
- What are we investing in, defending, innovating, personalizing? What are our inputs/outputs?
- How do we achieve international reach – multi-local or multinational?
- Is the core of our business strategy to respond quickly to change or are we about efficiency, driving down cost and eliminating waste wherever possible? Are we market following or shaping? (These different goals will bring different strategies, mindsets and cultures.)

In agile organizations employees too should be involved in wide-deep scanning. Accordingly, information flows both ways unfiltered. After all, it is not just the CEO and the executive team who have a perspective on what is crucial to the business – staff too should know what needs to be done to improve and grow the business and they will view it from a different angle. Moreover, what employees (especially Generation Y or millennials) increasingly want from their workplace is to be included, for the goals of the company to be tied to a vision, greater flexibility in scheduling and tasks, feedback and recognition.

Staff should be encouraged to be vigilant about the organization, its performance and potential problems. Leaders need to listen and learn. Heifetz and Laurie argue that rather than protecting people from outside threats, leaders should expose them to some of the uncertainties and external pressures for change. Foresight tools, such as scenario planning, facilitate future-orientated awareness and overcome pre-existing biases, simplifying complexity and reducing uncertainty with the aim of fostering faster and more effective decisions.[41] Such tools help people to make sense of emerging conditions. Managers and employees can be expected to gather intelligence from customers, regulators and other stakeholders via multiple touchpoints, structures and practices. As they work in groups on some of the challenges facing their organization, employees come to recognize the need for change, share ideas about what and how to change and become more committed to changing.

Scenario planning brings together decision makers with key stakeholders who generate insights through a workshop-type process as they explore the development of alternative futures.[42]

Scenario planning is increasingly used to help firms develop and refine strategic options in the light of potential context changes. For instance this could mean quickly exiting declining markets, using joint ventures, outsourcing extensively and creating global supply chains. It could mean redeploying resources to quickly counter or create advantage from them.[43] Once changes to the industry structure and the company's positioning are understood they can be assessed with respect to the organization's strategic intent, capabilities and risk appetite – as important or unimportant, opportunity or threat. Then more detailed mapping or modelling of strategic flows and processes can take place.

To build these practices into the fabric of their organization leaders need to work with staff to identify and unblock the systemic and practical barriers to great customer and business outcomes. By eliminating structural or cultural barriers that impede the flow of work, people, resources and ideas agile leaders close the 'implementation gap' and assure swift execution of strategy. It is important to create an action bias throughout the organization by setting clear priorities and deadlines and holding people responsible for meeting them. To avoid paralysis organizations should work on streamlining and clarifying roles and responsibilities in the decision-making process.

At Ohio State University strategic planning engages all members of its community.[44] The goal of the university is to be consistently recognized among the top 10 public comprehensive research universities in the world. To achieve this goal, every college and support unit – in collaboration with its constituents – has developed a strategic plan to prioritize objectives and guide decision making. Since all the strategic plans are founded in the overarching principles of Ohio State's vision, mission and values, the plans support and sustain each other. Their integrated nature is evidence of the commitment of the colleges and support units to a 'one university' ethic.

## Widening creative participation

Conventionally, creativity and thought leadership are confined to specialist research and development (R&D) teams, yet in agile organizations the creative contribution of a wider range of staff is tapped. To achieve transient advantages, and keep organizations fresh and ahead of the pack, a culture of innovation needs to be embedded throughout, both top-down and bottom-up. It is important to be clear where innovation is needed, and what type, and also be open to 'accidental' innovations that represent opportunities. Some new ideas may deliver results in the short term while others may require investment and deliver performance in the medium to long term. Sustaining innovations focus on making extensions and improvements to the existing business and functions. Disruptive innovations are new businesses that should be incubated and nurtured until they are ready to be commercialized and scaled.

Leaders need to invest in thought leadership, research and innovative models that also reduce risk, so it is important to bring together the right parties from the outset, including experts from around the business. Getting people thinking about a problem to be solved, or launching a new idea or concept for discussion can be a way of stimulating participation – employees can then help to shape and refine the initial idea.

Simple processes such as the following can help:

- Engage a team in brainstorming specific improvements related to a top strategic priority, problem, challenge or goal.
- Prioritize the top ideas as a team, without in-depth analysis.
- Every participant judges whether the best ideas are translated into the 'right' actions.
- Translate the top ideas into SMART (specific, measurable, achievable, realistic and timely) goals for ongoing tracking.
- Track progress as a management team, focusing intensely on supporting actions related to the goals and visibly recognizing the positive progress of the team.[45]

The key to building ownership is addressing the prioritization step as a group.

In some organizations, whole teams are charged with taking a refined idea further and developing an implementation blueprint; then sufficient resources are provided to aid implementation. In other cases, teams are themselves charged with discovering, so employees become the mainspring of new ideas. For instance, Oral-B wanted to find a way to create a unique selling proposition for its electric toothbrushes. The traditional approach is to brainstorm this in-house. Instead the firm took an unusual step and crowdsourced the challenge, using the eYeka platform.[46] In just 22 days Oral-B received 67 unique and innovative ideas from community members in 24 countries. Three won prizes. Using the eYeka community gave the firm a head start and helped them to anticipate some of the problems that needed to be considered in the development of the product; in particular, the importance of content, gamification, family interaction and socialization. Oral-B used the crowdsourced insights to develop an internet-connected brush that gathers data on the users' brushing techniques and notifies them when the head needs replacing.

## Focus intensely on the customer

Customers are at the heart of any business model. Without (profitable) customers, no company can survive for long. Galbraith describes customer-centricity as a fundamental paradigm shift – away from a bias where the organization and its agents operate on its own behalf in any transaction towards an 'outside-in' bias where meeting the needs of the users or purchasers of its products or services is paramount.[47] At the core of customer-centricity are four key principles:

- deep insight into the customer experience
- a focus on building relationships with customers to improve this experience and enhance loyalty (and thus retention)
- the gathering, interpretation and active use of customer data
- organizational agility to respond to insights from data and embed change.

Agile organizations remain strongly in touch with constantly changing customer needs; a customer-centric approach provides parameters for innovation, helps to create value and ensures flexibility.

### Outside-in thinking

The strength of an organization's customer focus tends to reflect its stage in the organizational life cycle (i.e. entrepreneurial, growth, maturity, decline, exit). At the entrepreneurial stage the focus is intensely on the customer, yet each subsequent stage of the life cycle gets further removed from this outside-in thinking. In the growth stage organizations tend to get into problem-solving mode as they deal with the challenges arising from initial undercapitalization. Typically, as organizations mature, they tend to develop inside-out thinking and lose touch with what customers really want.

Take the case of Kodak, a company founded in 1892 and that made photography available to the masses but had failed to adapt its business model to the development of digital photography, even though it had invented the technology. Kodak filed for Chapter 11 bankruptcy protection in January 2012. In contrast, Fujifilm, a firm whose roots are also in photographic film – an industry that declined with the advent of digital photography – took a different course, choosing to reflect on how it might apply its expertise to new markets. In September 2007 the firm launched a line of skincare products called Astalift based on technology it had developed for film.[48]

And while the good news is that Eastman Kodak emerged from bankruptcy protection in 2013 – slimmer, and with a new business plan, focused on packaging, graphic communications and functional printing – if the company is to thrive in this highly competitive market, company leaders will need to lead cultural change and find fresh ways of making business faster, easier and less expensive for its customers.

So organizations need to develop outside-in thinking and work back from the needs of the customer/end user when designing strategy, work and management processes. As Drucker pointed out, we must start with the customer's reality and expectations and understand what the customer thinks, fears, feels and hears. A key part of Colin Marshall's turnaround plan for British Airways in the 1980s was to build a culture of genuine customer service in which the customer was central. He instigated a pioneering training programme called 'Putting People First', in which every employee was invited to spend a day learning the airline's new mantra – understanding what real service meant to the customer – and meeting the man responsible. One of his key messages was about service recovery: 'The customer doesn't expect everything will go right all of the time – the big test is what you do when things go wrong.' Within a short time British Airways was able to fulfil its brand promise of an outstanding customer experience and did indeed become the world's favourite airline for a long period.

## Customer-centric HR

The shift towards agility and customer-centricity presents an opportunity for HR to embed its strategic value and relevance. A customer-centric approach to HR demands a shift away from an internal customer paradigm to reframe the relevance of HR in the context of improved value to the end-customer experience. Customer-centricity begins with the belief that there is only one customer: the person who buys or uses your organization's services or products. The people working within the organization are part of the system delivering an excellent experience to that customer. Your colleagues are not your customers (unless they genuinely are...).

However, this 'one customer' message can be controversial and confronting for 'internal customer' cultures, where HR has been positioned as serving the needs of internal clients. It can be argued that internal customer models reinforce structural divides, creating an unhelpful dynamic that distracts attention from the cross-business alignment required for collaboration in service of the end-customer needs, widening the gap between HR and the end customer, and drawing HR into an inward-facing role. It is important that this one-customer message is internalized by all 'back office' functions far away from the end customer, and HR can itself support this perceptual change through the delivery of engaging communication campaigns; workshops that help to draw a line of sight between the end user and internal roles; directing front-line opportunities and redesigning roles and processes (see Chapter 7).

While technology is a critical enabler of these principles, and in itself acts as a stimulus for change, becoming agile may require building (or acquiring) new capabilities, redesigning roles and organization, simplifying unnecessary bureaucracy and embedding new cultural norms to create a workforce that recognizes the importance of the customer and feels both capable and empowered to support them. This may require work to shift employee behaviours and attitudes, leadership perspectives, role descriptions and that broader area of *culture*: the legitimate arena of HR practice. HR expertise should be at the forefront of this work in four important areas: organization and work design; employee empowerment and engagement; leadership development; and performance management, which are addressed in this and other chapters. Although the challenge of becoming 'customer-centric' can feel unwieldy and complex, particularly in large, traditionally product-focused organizations, HR can lead change by adopting the experimental practices of more agile firms – work where you can, test and learn, fail fast and move forward.

So how can HR become more customer-centric? First, HR needs to understand what being a customer-centric organization really means, the forms it can take and the conditions that underpin it. Second, HR needs to collaborate closely with influential leaders (often the primary budget owners), and Operations/IT/Finance colleagues, working with Agile concepts to share and unpack models of work and create opportunities to take new designs forward. Third, HR must be an assertive expert contributor of HR and OD best practices that stimulate engagement and empowerment. Finally, HR must do this with a test-and-learn mindset – agile in itself – that learns from experimentation.

## Segmentation

In order to better understand and satisfy customers, companies usually group them into distinct segments with common needs, behaviours or other attributes. A business model may define one or several large or small customer segments, and a conscious decision should be made about which segments to serve and which segments to ignore. Once this decision is made, a business model and specific customer value propositions can be carefully designed around a strong understanding of target customer needs.

Customer-value propositions define why customers choose one company rather than another to meet a specific need. Each value proposition will consist of a selected bundle of products and/or services that provide benefits to a specific customer segment. Some may consist of existing products with modified or improved features; others will be innovative and represent a new or disruptive offer.

Organizations going agile must reimagine themselves around customer journeys, products and other axes of value creation.

Design, brand, status, newness, performance, usability and price are just some of the cocktail of criteria influencing customer choice. The challenge is to determine for what value each customer segment is willing to pay and the type of pricing mechanism chosen – fixed (predefined) or dynamic (where prices change according to market conditions such as buying airline or rail tickets) – can make a big difference in terms of revenues generated. Similarly, the nature of the customer relationship for each customer segment (e.g. self-service, automated services, online communities, dedicated personal service and so on) will strongly influence the overall customer experience and therefore sales and customer acquisition and retention.

## Co-creation and intelligent products

In today's creative times, concepts of mass customization, customer co-creation and open-source innovation have gained importance. Customers increasingly want a supplier relationship that gives them more individual choice and personalization. For instance, by involving child customers in building their toys means that few of the 'Build a Bear' toys are exactly the same. Companies such as Lego and Procter & Gamble recognized some time ago that involving customers in some of the R&D work that was previously carried out only by technical specialists would allow for customized products and services, as well as economies of scale, so producing lasting benefits.

The desire for co-creation is a reflection of changing social tastes and ultimately will alter the nature and viability of industries. Thanks to the digital revolution, new industries such as digital publishing have transformed the dynamics of knowledge creation and print publishing. Whereas content was previously produced and edited by expert professionals, today content can be produced and published directly through peer-to-peer networks via smartphones – no one edits the content; rather the audience democratically ranks and reviews in real time. The Apple iPod is an example of a product that taps into the growing desire of consumers to co-create their products and services. It essentially allows consumers to personalize their listening experiences by building playlists and assembling favourites, accessing them when and where they prefer. As a result, a whole generation of today's consumers now considers the fixed scheduling of mainstream television and radio channels as archaic. Similarly, social media have become a major vehicle for marketing and gathering market intelligence, often resulting in new or changed products and services. This active involvement of the customer in the development process changes the innovation dynamic. It is no longer a matter of companies managing a supply chain; to be agile, companies now need to connect with an entire low-capital-intensive consumer-to-supplier ecosystem – an enhanced network of units, suppliers, partners and consumers.

## Managing costs

Any organization needs to live within its means, concentrate on what matters most and transform itself for the future. To optimize a business model, leaders need to reduce the capital intensity of the business by managing costs and freeing up capital in non-core assets. Having a focused strategy allows you to define what you are going to invest in and articulate clearly what you are not going to do, so that you can avoid waste and distraction. The costs involved in operating a business model are likely to be found mainly in its key resources, activities and partnerships.

## Key resources

Key resources can be physical, financial, intellectual (for instance brands, customer databases, etc) and can be owned or leased by the company or acquired from key partners. In knowledge-intensive and creative industries human beings are crucial 'resources.' Leaders therefore need to invest in the social architecture required to attract and mobilize global talent. As we shall discuss in Chapter 7, this is likely to include clear values; investment in skills, training and development; clarity about performance, measurement and reward; and building collaborative and integrative capacity.

## Key activities and partnerships

Key activities are those required to create and offer a value proposition, reach markets, maintain customer relationships and earn revenues. These will vary according to the type of business model. For instance, in a company producing fast-moving consumer goods, key activities will include supply-chain management, production and problem solving. To enable these key activities, leaders need to ensure that the IT architecture is fit for purpose, with flexible systems, resilient business processes and focused measurement and analytics.

The challenge of keeping costs down can be addressed in many ways. Typically it means transitioning from multi-layered functional organizations into simpler forms, often with just three layers. In many cases, it makes little sense for a company to own all its resources or perform every activity by itself. Carrying out non-core activities through partnerships with suppliers or other third parties, for instance by outsourcing or sharing infrastructure, should provide economies of scale, reduce support and administrative costs, and increase flexibility by rapid scaling up/down. Organizations often embark on cost reduction by exploiting existing flexibilities and/or reducing work-force costs by delayering structures to remove unnecessary overheads. Some organizations seek productivity improvements by addressing absence rates, modifying pay, including overtime and increments, and also terms and conditions, including changing working hours, leave arrangements, sick pay and redundancy policies. Efficiencies can be achieved through back-office consolidation, process improvement, automation, delayering, changing the skills mix, various HR practices and processes, and flexibility in staff time or numbers. However, greater cost savings can probably be achieved by reducing complexity (arising from too many activities under way at the same time), fragmentation (e.g. through having conflicting data centres), redundancy and unnecessary hierarchy.

### Focus on value

In managing costs it is important to be clear whether the business model's cost structures are primarily cost-driven or value-driven, since this will affect the nature and extent of investment as well as the cost management required. Focusing on value – creating great products that customers will want and appreciate – requires a value-orientation mindset. By accelerating the route to quality and being willing to release products sooner, the organization can do less and achieve more. So leaders should be asking themselves: 'What capabilities and culture do we need in order to generate revenue faster?' If the goal is to become only medium responsive, then working with existing structures but aiming for continuous integration may be enough. However, a move to higher value-added – where responsiveness is key – may require significant investment and perhaps cultural and structural shifts, for instance, encouraging collaborative behaviours and developing team-based structures without silos.

## Benchmarking for agility

Agile organizations actively benchmark their key processes and capabilities against other agile organizations, regardless of sector (see Figure 3.1). They learn from but do not slavishly adopt other company practices unless they are directly relevant to their needs. Instead, they are prepared to find answers to questions such as: 'How can we serve our customers better, without incurring extra costs? What routines and approaches do the 'best in class' use? What can we learn from them?'

Areas to benchmark might include:

- specification and planning
- infrastructure design and microsystems
- measurement and oversight
- self-study and managing knowledge.

FIGURE 3.1  The benchmarking process

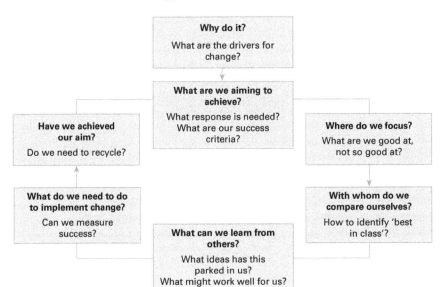

SOURCE © The Work Foundation

CEOs in some sectors are increasingly undertaking accompanied bench-marking visits to peer companies elsewhere in order to learn from each other. Reviewing what has been learned helps to pinpoint where change is needed and helps to answer the question: *How do I translate the measures and metrics we use to report performance in a way that is meaningful to the whole organization and its stakeholders?*

## Agile scoreboarding

Typically metrics revolve around the familiar cost, time and quality. The challenge, of course, is that many standard data-collection methods (e.g. employee surveys) can be very blunt instruments, partly because there are too many and they are not context-sensitive or dynamic enough and are mostly too linear to embrace agility and uncertainty. Consequently, many 'metrics' and forms of measurement are pursued at the expense of actual insight, and insight is not translated into meaningful behaviour.

The question of what constitutes success is under review following the financial crisis triggered in 2008, which exposed the systemic risks from malpractice (e.g. in the banking sector). In the context of agility and resil-ience, a new blend of organizational and individual 'indicators' is needed that takes account of the demands of a new generation of employees who want work to have more meaning and societal value. These might include metrics from categories such as customer satisfaction, employee engagement, climate indicators and operational performance.

Such indicators could enable employees to better understand and manage their own personal development, rather than measurement purely for the purpose of organizational performance management.

---

CASE STUDY
*ING – strategic proof points*

With a new CEO and a new global strategy ING was keen to ensure that the strategy was both understood and being adopted at local level. Accordingly, the Internal Communications (IC) team worked as part of an integrated multidisciplinary team with Corporate Strategy, HR, Branding and External Communications, with a shared goal to look beyond engagement with the strategy and to ensure adoption. IC led the co-creation of the CEO roadshow, which took place in many locations over an extended six-month period. This gave time for the team to adopt Agile methodology – to pause and accelerate, to take time out to listen, learn and adapt as they went along.

At the roadshows the CEO was able to meet local staff. He outlined the new global strategy, then invited each local CEO to present how local plans would be affected by the global strategy. This acted symbolically and practically as a catalyst for adoption. The IC team were able to spot in advance where there was a lack of resonance or a disconnect, since they had worked beforehand with local leaders to help them explore the implications of the global strategy for adoption in their context. Unlike in waterfall planning, where conflict usually becomes obvious only at the point of delivery, this pre-roadshow phase allowed potential conflict to be surfaced early and addressed quickly. By listening, watching and learning, the IC team were able to catch issues before they turned into crises. IC was also able to quickly bring back to the international team valuable insights about what was happening on the ground – and these were fed back into the process as appropriate.

Rather than using traditional campaign metrics to gauge how well adoption was going, the team looked at regular intervals for 'proof points' – in the forms of anecdotes, stories and other 'soft' evidence. From these they were able to formulate more meaningful 'hard' metrics. The global ING Communications Network continues to be instrumental in collecting and contextualizing these proof points to inform shifts in strategy and approach.[49]

---

## *A picture is worth a thousand words*

Of course, there are many ways to track progress towards a vision. The use of social media and other methods of capturing and analysing mass narratives via cloud technology may offer a way forward. Pictures are always more captivating than numbers or words – and a balanced scorecard,[50] modified to your company's needs, can help to articulate what you are aiming for and what return on agility looks like from a range of stakeholder perspectives. The balanced scorecard represented in Figure 3.2 highlights that this organization considers its responsibilities to its local communities alongside its other business drivers.

One major US corporation measures what it calls its corporate 'adaptive capacity' (AC).[51] It has worked with various researchers and consultants to build a way of monitoring and assessing the corporation's adaptive capacity at three levels – individual, team and organizational – along the lines of the balanced scorecard idea. It has termed this its 'AC dashboard'. In addition, it makes an annual assessment of the industry's adaptive capacity, especially to gain a more precise idea of how the corporation can and will endure in a crisis situation in the event of various types of major disruptions.

It also uses technology to track what is happening and turn all this information into knowledge. That is part of what drives the AC dashboard. New

FIGURE 3.2   A balanced scorecard

SOURCE © The Work Foundation

data mining and artificial intelligence applications – derived from software originally created to find patterns in overwhelming amounts of scientific data – help to make sense of all the information flowing through the organization. This allows it to respond to trends faster than most of the competitors, adding to its agility.

## Governance and risk management

In the wake of various corporate scandals and higher levels of regulation and scrutiny, new forms of risk have been identified and higher levels of accountability demanded of business leaders. In a resilient organization, leadership achieves a balance between risk taking and risk containment in order to ensure ongoing innovation as well as compliance.[52]

Executives are increasingly required to offer stakeholders much greater insight into the strategic imperatives of their organization and the value drivers underpinning business models. They need to demonstrate how strategy, governance, performance and prospects lead to the creation of value in the short, medium and long term. Increasingly, too, they are being held to account for the ways in which staff, customers and suppliers are treated, and also for the behaviours, values, standards, ethics and monitoring of their organization, its supply chain, its outputs and its impact on environmental and societal sustainability. Boards increasingly want to understand how critical 'resources' such as talent and future leaders are being sourced and developed, what the pipeline of intellectual property looks like and how this is being capitalized.

Boards also want to know what contingency plans are in place to ensure business continuity in case of various forms of disruption or sabotage. In theory, organizations using Agile practices should be perfectly suited to respond to shocks and crises such as the COVID-19 pandemic. They do this by embedding customer-centricity in their processes, delayering and empowering the organization, and bringing business and IT together, making reprioritization easier. For instance, in the US company just described, technology helps to build organizational resilience through 'strategic boundary management', which sometimes means trying to build smart firewalls where they are needed. In the case of disasters, boards also want to know that the business has strong business recovery plans. Businesses that come through major crises and disasters best are those that have thought through in advance how their people, operations and systems might be disrupted by a crisis and carry out disaster recovery exercises and rehearsals, running through as many 'what if' scenarios as possible.

The danger is that boards can become so concerned about risk that the vital spark of innovation can be smothered by over-detailed and bureaucratic risk-management procedures. To avoid this, in their search for new ideas and opportunities, boards and management teams need to define how much innovation they really want, and the risks involved in achieving the objective. For instance, is the organization trying to become market leading in a new technology category that carries high levels of uncertainty, or is innovation needed to help the organization make small-scale incremental moves, or both? By reviewing what the aim is, it is easier for executives and boards to appreciate the implications for both risk and reward and to equip the organization to innovate.

So to improve contingency planning and crisis-response capabilities, it is important to take simulations, role-playing and scenario planning seriously and make certain that the skills and competencies for handling surprises and crises are built.

When engaged in strategic (enterprise-wide) risk assessment, think about areas of most risk and exposure and develop plans to proactively manage each of them – focus on the higher-risk, under-managed relationships.

Learn to deal with the consequences of failed plans – 'take the hit' and react appropriately. This is about minimizing losses by avoiding escalation and learning from the process to anticipate it better the next time.

So leaders need to be asking themselves: 'How do we foster a climate that combines creativity *and* discipline – a culture in which sensible risk is encouraged?' This theme is explored further in Chapter 10. In Chapter 11 we consider how to equip leaders for complexity.

## Conclusion

In the current context there is no status quo. Stakeholders who believe that the need for change is a temporary phenomenon are in for an unpleasant surprise. Agility is defined by constant change, so the organization needs to have an appetite for change and the capability to enact it in a disciplined and structured way. So a key task for agile leaders is to build the organization's capacity to act – over the short, medium and long term:

- Closing the implementation gap requires *a strategizing approach*, building momentum for change by making decisions and *involving and enabling* the teams who will implement them.

- A *shared purpose* is key to providing clarity.
- In developing a shared competitive agenda and setting strategic priorities, focus on the core and on *desired outcomes for customers and other stakeholders* over the short and longer term.
- The ability to be *curious and inquiring* is crucial – fixing problems becomes secondary to a better understanding of how to work with them so that adjustments in the organizational system are better attuned to both the internal and external context.

The scale of the challenges being addressed is too great and organizations are too complex for changes to be restricted to certain corners – change needs to be organization-wide.

As new routines take root, instead of strategy making being a formulaic occasional process, strategizing becomes continuous and involves a wider constituency of stakeholders in activities such as wide-deep scanning, data gathering and analysis, testing, developing feedback loops and innovating. Scenarios can help to improve scanning and 'sense making' skills. Getting people to read broadly and explore new ideas together, build hypotheses and models about what is happening can help them to better manage uncertainty and ambiguity.

The case for workplace innovation is clear: it has a major impact on the organization's productivity, quality and competitiveness. To stimulate innovation we need stronger, more collaborative ways of working and a broad-based, systemic approach to generating and sharing insights and new ideas, including using internal and external networks. The onus is on top management for communication and sense making, on equipping employees with the tools to find, filter and focus the information they need so that they feel challenged to innovate, drive change and be accountable for outcomes, not just outputs.

The question is how to achieve innovation as part of 'business as usual'. While consistent 'no surprises' execution would be ideal, given the pace of change and the need for experimentation, people will not always get things right first time. It is not only the increase in external scrutiny that will determine whether or not people are willing to risk experimenting (and potentially failing) but also how the organization deals with the consequences of mistakes. So a blame culture kills innovation and staff morale while a learning culture enables it. Recognizing this means that leaders can be proactive and provide a light-touch risk infrastructure to assist experimentation and decision making at the right levels.

In the next chapter we look at how organizations navigate the ever more fluid business landscape by working in various forms of alliance.[53]

---

CHECKLIST

- Why does your company exist?
- Who are its customers?
- What are the key environmental factors that are likely to affect your organization in the medium and long term?
- What are the key drivers for change coming from within the business and organization?
- What possible future scenarios might result?
- What are the implications of these for your organization (factors to be capitalized/constrained)?
- How might this affect future demand for your products and services?
- How should you respond if you are to thrive or even just survive in this emerging reality?
- How are others (e.g. your competitors) responding?
- What is your vision for your organization's sector in 30 years?
- What will the most successful organizations be doing in 30 years that the others are not?
- In 15 years from now, what will have changed most in terms of for example your organization's context, customer base, production methods, supply chain, workforce…?
- Which aspect of your strategy is most critical to ensuring the future success of your organization?
- What are the key decisions that your organization faces currently?
- What mechanisms does your organization have to identify and analyse emerging trends? For instance, how do you systematically collect 'external' intelligence from your workforce? Who are the custodians who regularly scan and manage environmental challenges that you face?

- How effectively are these trends acted upon and the necessary changes made?

- What are the disciplines or critical success factors for you to succeed?

- What are the core competencies needed to accomplish your strategy/gain transient advantages?

- What culture do you need in order to accomplish your strategic goals?

- How much are employees involved in decision making? How much are their ideas invited, heard and responded to?

- How much are people expected to use their initiative to find customer-centred solutions?

- How well are good ideas/good practice disseminated?

- How well does your organization manage for diversity?

- Do people have clear parameters for experimentation? Do they know where innovation is needed?

- What aspects of organization and culture need to change?

- What are your current areas of focus?

- What will need to become key priorities?

- How will you address these priorities? What will you need to do?

- How can you and your organization become more forward thinking?

- What are the key implications of this analysis for people at company and local level?

# Notes

1  Basu, R and Green, SG (1997) Leader-member exchange and transformational leadership: An empirical examination of innovative behaviors in leader-member dyads, *Journal of Applied Social Psychology*, **27**, pp 477–99.

2  Worley, CG, Williams, TD and Lawler, EE (2014) *The Agility Factor: Building adaptable organizations for superior performance*, Jossey-Bass, San Francisco.

3  Ibid.

4  Heifetz, RA and Laurie, DL (2001) The work of leadership, *Harvard Business Review*, December.

5  Laurie, DL and Lynch, R (2007) Aligning HR to the CEO growth agenda, *Human Resource Planning*, **30** (4), pp 25–33.

**6** Marsh, C et al (2009) Integrated Organisation Design: The New Strategic Priority for HR Directors, White Paper 09/01, January, Centre for Evidence-based HR, University of Lancaster.

**7** Gunther McGrath, R (2013) *The End of Competitive Advantage: How to keep your strategy moving as fast as your business*, Harvard Business Review Press, Boston.

**8** Nielsen, C and Lund, M (2018) Building scalable business models, *MIT Sloan Management Review*, Winter, sloanreview.mit.edu/article/building-scalable-business-models/ (archived at https://perma.cc/HGK7-4XKE).

**9** Tushman, ML and O'Reilly, CA (1996) Ambidextrous organisations: Managing evolutionary and revolutionary change, *California Management Review*, **38** (4), pp 8–30.

**10** De Geus, AP (2002) *The Living Company: Habits for survival in a turbulent business environment*, Harvard Business School Press, Boston.

**11** Collins, J and Porras, J (2005) *Built to Last: Successful habits of visionary companies*, Random House Business, London.

**12** Collins, J (1995) Building companies to last, www.jimcollins.com/article_topics/articles/building-companies.html (archived at https://perma.cc/H8DT-GQ6Q).

**13** IBM Institute for Business Value (2013) Reinventing the rules of engagement: CEO insights from the global C-suite study.

**14** Hitt, MA et al (2002) Strategic entrepreneurship: Integrating entrepreneurial and strategic management perspectives, in MA Hitt et al (ed) *Strategic Entrepreneurship: Creating a new mindset*, Blackwell, Oxford, pp 1–16.

**15** Snowden, D.J. and Boone, M.E. (2007). A Leader's Framework for Decision Making, *Harvard Business Review*, November.

**16** Johnston, K., Coughlin, C. and Garvey Berger, J May 2014, Leading in Complexity, *Cultivating Leadership*, https://www.cultivatingleadership.com/site/uploads/Leading-in-Complexity-CC-JGB-KJ-2014-4.pdf (archived at https://perma.cc/3QMD-AUGJ)

**17** Gardner, H (2006) The synthesizing leader, HBR list: Breakthrough ideas for 2006, *Harvard Business Review*, **84** (2), pp 35–67.

**18** Prahalad, CK and Krishnan, MS (2008) *The New Age of Innovation: Driving co-created value through global networks*, McGraw-Hill Professional, New York.

**19** Fisher, JR Jr (2006) Leadership as great ideas, *Leadership Excellence*, **23** (2), p 14.

**20** Kakabadse, A (2015) The Success Formula: How Smart Leaders Deliver Outstanding Value, Bloomsbury Information, London.

**21** Johansen, R (2009) *Leaders Make the Future: Ten new leadership skills for an uncertain world*, Berrett-Koehler, San Francisco.

**22** Covey, S (2004) *The 8th Habit: From effectiveness to greatness*, Free Press, New York.

**23** Johnston, K, Coughlin, C and Garvey Berger, J. Leading in complexity, Cultivating Leadership, May 2014, www.cultivatingleadership.com/site/uploads/Leading-in-Complexity-CC-JGB-KJ-2014-4.pdf (archived at https://perma.cc/US2Q-KPL9).

**24** Petrie, N (2011) *Future Trends in Leadership Development*, Center for Creative Leadership White Paper Series.

**25** Martin, R (2009) *The Design of Business*, Harvard Business School Press, Boston.

**26** Ibid.

**27** Orton-Jones, C. Growth, innovation and business-transformation, *Raconteur*, 14 May 2014, p 3.

**28** Commentary on the launch of: The Tomorrow's Relationships: Unlocking value report. The Tomorrow Company in collaboration with the Chartered Institute of Management Accountants, the Chartered Institute of Personnel and Development, KPMG and Linklaters, n.d., www.kpmg.com/uk/en/issuesandinsights/articlespublications/newsreleases/pages/unlocking-value-in-relationships-is-key-to-success-in-business.aspx (archived at https://perma.cc/XWP2-FJXD).

**29** Williams, T, Worley, CM and Lawler, EE (2013) The agility factor, *Strategy + Business*, www.strategy-business.com/article/00188?gko=6a0ba (archived at https://perma.cc/G2D2-628C).

**30** Thomas, JB, Clark, SM and Gioia, DA (1993) Strategic sensemaking and organizational performance: Linkages among scanning, interpretation, action, and outcomes, *Academy of Management Journal*, **36** (2), pp 239–70.

**31** Prahalad, CK and Hamel, G (1990) The core competence of the corporation, *Harvard Business Review*, **68** (3), pp 79–91.

**32** Porter, ME (1996) What is strategy? *Harvard Business Review*, **74** (6), pp 61–81.

**33** Ireland, RD and Hitt, MA (2005) Achieving and maintaining strategic competitiveness in the 21st century: The role of strategic leadership, *Academy of Management Executive*, **19** (4), pp 65–77.

**34** Levine, R, Locke, C, Searls, D and Weinberger, D (2009) *The Cluetrain Manifesto*, Basic Books, New York.

**35** Ibid.

**36** Halal, WE (2021) *Beyond Knowledge: How technology is driving an age of consciousness*, Foresight Books, London.

**37** Bradley, C, Bryan, L and Smit, S (2012) Managing the strategy journey, *McKinsey Quarterly*, July.

**38** Kline, N (2002) *Time to Think: Listening to ignite the human mind*, Cassell, London.

**39** Heifetz, RA and Laurie, DL (2001) The work of leadership, *Harvard Business Review*, December.

**40** Ibid.

**41** Bootz, J (2010) Strategic foresight and organizational learning: A survey and critical analysis. *Technological Forecasting & Social Change*, 77, 1588–94.

**42** Ibid.

**43** Heifetz, R, Grashow, A and Linsky, M (2009) *The Practice of Adaptive Leadership: Tools and tactics for changing your organization and the world*, Harvard Business Press, Boston; Weick, K (2001) *Making Sense of the Organization*, Wiley, Chichester.

**44** Ohia State University. Unit-level strategic planning, n.d. oaa.osu.edu/strategicplanning.html (archived at https://perma.cc/QA35-2A9S).

**45** Kuppler, T, How to build culture muscle and improve engagement, ownership, and results, 11 August 2014, www.cultureuniversity.com/how-to-build-culture-muscle-and-improve-engagement-ownership-and-results/ (archived at https://perma.cc/2U7Q-3VAV).

**46** Orton-Jones, ibid.

**47** Galbraith, JR (2005) *Designing the Customer-Centric Organization: A guide to strategy, structure, and process*, Wiley, New York.

**48** Glenn, M (2009) *Organisational Agility: How business can survive and thrive in turbulent times*, The Economist Intelligence Unit, London.

**49** Kindly provided by Melcrum based on their research report *The Agile IC Function*, October 2014.

**50** Kaplan, RS and Norton, DP (1996) *The Balanced Scorecard: Translating strategy into action*, Harvard Business School Press, Boston.

**51** American Management Association (AMA) (2006) Agility and resilience in the face of continuous change: A global study of current trends and future possibilities 2006–2016, www.amanet.org/images/hri-agility06.pdf (archived at https://perma.cc/Q8C8-Y6PG).

**52** Bell, MA. The Five Principles of Organizational Resilience, *Gartner*, 7 January 2002, www.gartner.com/doc/351410/principles-organizational-resilience (archived at https://perma.cc/W3C2-TM9D).

**53** Dyer, L and Ericksen, J (2009) Complexity-based agile enterprises: Putting self-organizing emergence to work, in A Wilkinson et al (eds) *The Sage Handbook of Human Resource Management*, Sage, London, pp 436–57.

# 04

# Agile linkages

In this chapter we look at how agility crosses boundaries and explore some of the types of internal and external linkages being forged by organizations in pursuit of organizational agility, flexibility and resilience, and their consequence for organizational forms and ways of working. These flexible forms of organization cross multiple formerly fixed external and internal boundaries and require high degrees of collaboration. The growing interdependence of firms is evident in the myriad forms of collaborative arrangements between partner organizations, including many with competitors. As firms move from being vertically integrated to becoming more specialized they are contracting out non-core functions to outsourcers. So strategic alliances – some 'tight' linkages, some 'loose' – are transforming the business landscape. Combined, these factors necessitate proactive, innovative and flexible workforce management strategies.

We shall look at what working and managing in some of these more flexible arrangements means for the people involved. For managers and employees the challenge is to develop effectively the mindsets and capabilities – collaboration, empowerment and accountability – required to make these more flexible structures and cross-organization linkages work. People working within such alliances have to learn sophisticated skills relating to trust, relationship and team building, risk management and the ability to manage complexity. In particular we consider how to ensure that flexibility works for both the organization and its employees, and how collaborative capabilities, so essential to the success of these key linkages, can be built.

We shall consider:

- more flexible organizational forms including teams and outsourcing
- spanning leadership

- working in strategic alliances
- building an alliance culture
- cooperatives and linking capability.

## Crossing boundaries

The term 'flexibility' applies to the ways in which organizations structure themselves, the ways that organizations adjust their employment practices in reaction to changes in business circumstances, and also the ways that individuals organize their time, location and style of working. In many cases flexibility is achieved by crossing geographical, time, space and cultural boundaries – within and between groups, units and organizations. Many firms are linking with others in their ecosystem. To be successful these 'linkages' require a baseline of common understanding – shared goals, processes, budgets and also understanding of the 'other'.

Some of the ways in which boundaries are being crossed include the following.

### *Physical space: the mobile office*

Developing the 'flexible workplace' is usually driven both by the need to get employees out into the marketplace building business relationships – and winning business – and also to reduce costs of office accommodation. With mobile technology and the need for constant connections the requirement for costly travel and permanent real estate is coming into question. Satellite offices are an alternative form of flexible workplace. Such offices break up large, centralized facilities into a network of smaller workplaces that are often located closer to customers.

Small firms in particular are increasingly making use of 'hotelling' or shared-office options in which 'hotel' work spaces are furnished, equipped and supported with typical office services that can be hired by the hour, day or week instead of being permanently assigned. People using such facilities are typically supplied with mobile cabinets for personal storage, and a computer system routes phone calls and email as necessary. Hotels are often ideal places to meet with clients, collaborate and build relationships. They are also increasingly places for focused, intense work. Thus, hotels have become important 'third places', locations outside the home and office where people choose to get work done. Especially since the pandemic, many organizations are selling their mostly empty office space to realize savings.

In pursuit of ambidexterity, as discussed previously, organizations typically establish separately located units for exploratory activities, such as 'skunk works' that ensure that the needs of innovative businesses are protected rather than submerged within 'business as usual'. Such units can develop their own distinctive cultures and operating practices while having access to corporate resources. They must manage both organizational separation and linkages across units through a tightly integrated senior team.

And as we shall explore in Chapter 6, remote and hybrid working are throwing up new management challenges as well as opportunities.

### Integrated teams

Many of today's challenges are beyond the skills of any single disciplinary team to address effectively. Consequently, there is an increasing appetite for individuals and groups from different disciplines to work together on major projects, especially those involving strategic change, in order to produce more coherent outcomes. However, these expert communities may previously have operated in silos, so may not share the same approach to innovation or speak the same language, so may lack a common way to describe, negotiate and act on the issue in hand.

There are many cultural, structural and conceptual reasons for this, such as the different 'discourses' (i.e. language, artefacts, habits and conventions) of disciplines and functions such as HR, finance, management – which, while sharing commonalities, have some important differences. In particular, the discourse of finance seems far more powerful and dominant in organizations than that of HR. This may have hindered the development of an integrated understanding of how people are central to value creation and how, in turn, development of people should be central to business success.

To overcome these barriers to progress, setting an open innovation challenge or experiment can help to bring together people from different but relevant disciplines in a shared online space, to undertake a co-discovery process with those interested in the problem.

### Global teams

As never before, business success requires a global presence so organizations must communicate across cultures, geographies and time zones in order to meet the demands of global customers who want just-in-time delivery and 24-hour customer service. Thanks to a vast and sophisticated communication network, business, projects, tasks and jobs are being transferred to where knowledge is to be found in different locations. In today's global economy many workforces are multicultural. Global companies in particular seek to build diverse and geographically dispersed teams to reflect their markets and customers, to achieve lower fixed and variable costs abroad, to move development closer to the site of production or to establish development activities at local subsidiaries. Globally distributed customer service, production, sales, logistics and management functions are now commonplace. Virtual working too is on the increase among international teams as travel budgets shrink or become non-existent in these tough economic times. Above all, though, companies want access to professional skills and foreign resources.

The ability to share knowledge is vital to leveraging the benefits of cross-border innovation projects, and online communications should enable a swift response to the demands of the global market. The global workforce must be able to operate as a single, seamless team to service customers and maximize revenue streams, so managers and employees need to be capable of what Amy Edmondson calls *teaming* – the ability to coordinate and collaborate even without the benefit of stable team structures.[1] However, driving development activities and managing innovation processes across national borders is not always easy and there are many reasons why synergy is difficult to achieve. A Capgemini study found that typical challenges include poor leadership of cross-cultural innovation projects and a lack of communication or sharing of knowledge across national boundaries.[2] We shall consider later in this chapter how managing effectively at a distance can be achieved.

So managers and HR must source, connect with and coordinate a multicultural global workforce, often virtually. While there may not be a 'one size fits all' with respect to cultural leadership, embracing diversity in all its many forms is increasingly recognized as key to innovation and social justice. Cultural engagement is often the least developed dimension in intercultural encounters and at the same time it holds the key to how much people invest in improving the outcome of a situation. By working with the emotional dimension outside their comfort zones leaders can overcome the stumbling blocks and create business results.

## Outsourcing and offshoring

Outsourcing involves redeploying a firm's own personnel and organization assets to a third-party supplier to carry out 'non-core' work previously carried out by the organization. This form of subcontracting is often entered into on the assumption that efficiencies can be gained. Typical targets for outsourcing include catering, security, cleaning and facilities management, ICT, car park, payroll/HR services, warehousing and distribution, marketing, call centres (complaint handling, after-sales services), finance and accounting. The average manufacturer now outsources 70–80 per cent of its finished product.[3] Some outsourcing contracts are short term and transactional, intended to enable flexibility, while in other cases long-term contracts and even a full merger takes place.

Offshoring involves outsourcing assets and work processes to economies where the costs of labour are significantly lower than in developed economies. These are examples of what Swart, Purcell and Kinnie call the 'farming out model',[4] which is more of a reconfiguration of skills than a true integration of complementary skill sets.[5] These arrangements (or at least their contracts) are usually 'tightly' managed, and administering outsourced relationships effectively becomes a core competence in itself. Many companies that are lured by low-cost labour markets make decisions that satisfy short-term budget requirements but may face problems if they know little about domestic outsourcing and even less about offshore outsourcing.

This gives rise to the question: which assets are core and which are non-core? The answer is not always easy to give. For instance, many firms have outsourced to external agencies aspects of their HR processes such as recruitment only to recognize later that recruitment is a strategic process so have taken back responsibility in-house (in-sourced). Sometimes outsourced arrangements become more costly than the previously integrated models. Other typical problems include unsatisfactory delivery of services, uncooperative vendor behaviour and/or the competitive advantage to be gained from outsourcing no longer existing.[6]

### WORKFORCE IMPLICATIONS

When outsourcing decisions are being made, the needs of employees are often low down the pecking order of considerations. From a company viewpoint, if outsourcing brings financial benefits it is a logical move. However, for outsourced employees the deal may not be so good. Former employees of the firm may end up carrying out the same work as before but on reduced terms and conditions. They may find themselves competing for their jobs against employees from emerging markets, creating an environment of insecurity and limited commitment to the workplace.[7]

In such circumstances there no longer exists a supportive social contract between employer and employee. Many displaced employees end up feeling betrayal, anger at loss of benefits and changing working conditions and anxiety about changes at the new company. As they experience stress and uncertainty, many enter states of intellectual paralysis that result in productivity loss. The resulting emotional scars can even impact on those who are not outsourced, whose loyalty may decrease sharply as they wonder whether they will be next to be 'sold off'. Thus outsourcing can easily end up having a negative effect on motivation and on human performance and can result in intangible costs such as the loss of valuable knowledge.

On the other hand, outsourcing can also have a positive effect on some people. If the outsourced employees were previously ignored in their old firm, they may find that their skills are now considered valuable and there may be opportunity for career expansion and promotion. They may also have contact with a wider group of employees than before and have the chance to develop new skills. As Wayne Cascio points out, in contrast to a restructuring strategy that regards people as costs to be cut, a more responsible strategy focuses on people as assets to be developed.[8]

### Spanning or collaborative leadership

So working across boundaries is not straightforward. To support groups working across systems and developing engaging and collaborative ways of working requires spanning leadership, which is concerned with acquiring and disseminating resources external to a group. Today, many large organizations work across entire systems – such as in the health and defence industries, working with partners on common challenges. As David Chrislip points out: 'Collaboration needs a different kind of leadership; it needs leaders who can safeguard the process, facilitate interaction and patiently deal with high levels of frustration.'[9]

Leaders need to be able to think systemically and understand how the broader system works. They must look long term and be able to understand and work with different goals, cultures and business priorities from those of their own organization. They need to develop middle managers who act at the system interfaces. This may require a mindset shift for many leaders. Tarun Khanna argues that global companies will not succeed in unfamiliar markets unless they adapt – or even rebuild – their operating models and cultural assumptions.[10] In a global organization, mental models that are rooted in the HQ culture may lead to simplistic assumptions about how things work in different cultural contexts. The concept of 'contextual intelligence' is vital in developing talent. A culturally intelligent global leader lets go of habitual stereotyping, sees people as nuanced individuals and finds ways to focus on the business potential in the many differences in a diverse team. Therefore, being alert to what is needed, really listening and being prepared to adjust are key to stimulating real dialogue and mutual understanding. Englehardt and Simmons advocate the use of change strategies that recognize different stakeholder viewpoints of organizational effectiveness.[11] These stakeholder perspectives can then be reviewed within a consultation process as a means of consensus-building. And if conflict arises this can become the source of something new and better if partners are willing to embrace paradox and reconcile seeming differences in order to achieve their higher purpose.

## Working in alliances

Increasingly organizations are looking beyond their own boundaries and working with third parties and partner organizations in strategic alliances to be able to:

- Scale up and down rapidly by tapping into external resource networks.
- Achieve economies of scale in 'back office' operations while maintaining customer intimacy and responsiveness in the 'front office'.
- Grow without being constrained by bureaucracy.
- Access key skills.

Thus motivations for alliances fall broadly into the categories of achieving cost savings and/or going for growth and innovation. The organization's purpose in establishing alliances will determine the nature of form selected, how it operates and who benefits.

### What is a strategic alliance?

Strategic alliances come in all shapes and sizes that share some of the following distinguishing features identified in Roffey Park's research:[12]

- They are *strategic*, with partnering organizations bound together by a set of strategic intentions or goals for their alliance activity.

- The partnering organizations *exchange or share resources and assets* – these may take the form of physical assets such as shared facilities or less tangible assets such as marketing expertise, brand management, technical knowledge or process expertise.

- They result in some form of *joint activity*, where personnel from the partnering organizations interact and collaborate.

Strategic alliances are not just about major companies forming 'tight' connections through joint ventures (JVs). Collaboration can also occur through a variety of 'loose' forms, ranging from interactions between key individuals or joint teams through to a shared corporate entity. Joint activities may be precisely defined and highly structured, or they might be ad hoc and opportunistic.

A strategic alliance is widely understood to have the following common traits:

- Cooperation – two or more legally defined partners working together within a mutually defined area.

- Each partner aims to attain key strategic objectives through the alliance.

- Each partner has the option to withdraw if the alliance is not generating its expected benefits.

For instance, Microsoft has adopted a striking approach to collaboration to increase benefits to consumers. Users of Microsoft's Azure cloud computing platform can now also work on Oracle's rival service more easily, after a deal struck between the two companies.[13]

Most alliances fit somewhere along the continuum set out in Figure 4.1.

FIGURE 4.1  Alliances: a spectrum of integration

| Loose | | Tight | | Tight-loose |
|---|---|---|---|---|
| Informal | Contractual | | Shared entity | Entwined |
| Helping/learning | Outsourcing/supplier | | Joint venture | Multiple links |
| Allied, e.g. cross-selling | Franchising/ licensing | | Shared services | 'Networked organization' |

Virtual teams

SOURCE  Based on the Roffey Park study *Strategic Alliances: Getting the people bit right*

At the informal end of the spectrum, the growth of small firms is leading to numerous new networks for doing business. Self-employed people and 'micro firms' may lack many of the resources of a larger entity so join networks of like-minded peers to share business development opportunities, resources and learning opportunities. Similarly, consultants and clients are increasingly working collaboratively to solve the client's problem, share resources (including intellectual property) and do joint marketing of the (successful) outcome.

Contractual arrangements with third parties include franchising, licensing, outsourcing and offshoring and may ultimately include mergers and acquisitions. In between lie various alternative alliance arrangements such as partial ownership, relationships with preferred and trusted suppliers, multiple vendor contracts, joint ventures, consortia and shared services. For instance, in the UK public sector, institutions are increasingly developing pooled shared-service operations for HR and IT support as part of their new delivery models. Many employees will therefore experience working in alliances, some of which may be short-lived, while others may last for many years.

## Working in alliances: key features and challenges

Whatever their nature, the managerial and people challenges thrown up by strategic alliances are immense. At the heart of alliances is a willingness to dissolve boundaries, both between organizations and within people's minds, and to explore and learn from partners with different skills and ways of working.

### AMBIGUITY

Alliances operate on the basis of shared ownership/governance and involve ambiguous and complex lines of control and accountabilities. Unlike mergers, where ownership is clear and the 'new order' has been legally ratified and formally structured in the guise of a new corporate entity and management structure, alliances are more fluid, temporary and often more complex. They are therefore vulnerable and susceptible to problems, with employees often working under greater uncertainty than in more fixed organizational forms.

Alliances require an extra degree of commitment and cooperation from a wide range of individuals and groups of employees. An integral aspect of alliance governance, therefore, is constant bargaining, managing expectations, handling conflict and building consensus. Such a task requires business people to balance control with cooperation, to have a sense of where they should tightly manage an alliance and where they should retain only a light hold and allow synergies to emerge.

## POWER DYNAMICS

While the business drivers of a specific alliance may be clear, the power dynamics may be less apparent. Is this a partnership of equals or is one partner really driving the alliance? How do people within the partner organizations feel? Are they comfortable/uncomfortable? Are there disagreements between partners? Whatever the rationale for the alliance, it is likely that there will be a battle for hearts and minds, even at the stage of strategy formation and partner selection. In many cases, alliances emerge from strong relationships between key individuals and often continue even when their original purpose has been served – if the same individuals are involved. Conversely, alliances often fail, despite strong business drivers for collaboration, if one of the key individuals moves on or there is a falling out among the alliance champions.

Alliance partners inevitably have their own longer-term strategic goals and budget constraints so a degree of conflict is inherent in the relationship. Partners are understandably often coy about the 'hidden' benefits they hope for. For example, they may be planning to steal expertise from their partner, or potentially acquire the partner. Rather than hoping such conflict can be avoided, the aim should be to build the alliance around common ground and have good processes for resolving differences. The challenge is to build trust and cohesive ties and foster cooperation and innovation.

## CRITICAL SUCCESS FACTORS

No matter how effective the relationship between the deal makers, trust is usually underscored by clear contractual arrangements and role specifications. Johnson and Scholes identified the following critical success factors for joint ventures:

- proactive attitudes to commitment, trust and cultural sensitivity
- clear organizational arrangements
- the desire of all partners to achieve organizational learning from the alliance, rather than using partners to substitute for their lack of competences
- allowing the alliance to evolve and change rather than prescribing it too parochially from the outset
- efforts by partners to achieve strong interpersonal relationships, including bonding and flexibility to changing circumstances

- decentralization of decision making and sufficient autonomy from both corporate parents.[14]

Needs, aims, expectations, goals and outcomes should be explicitly expressed and agreed with the partner, including the importance of sharing information and knowledge. Areas of mutual competition also need to be made explicit so that agreed-upon ground rules can be developed about how to handle potential conflicts of interest. When the rules are clear, and there is joint commitment to them, the risk of misunderstanding diminishes.

### RELATIONSHIPS

The relationships between alliance partners are fundamental to the very concept of an 'alliance'. The trouble is that organizations do not have relationships with each other, only individuals do. So alliances are largely interpersonal phenomena, and effective personal relationships are central to the success or failure of an alliance.[15] If alliances fizzle out, it is often because key people have moved on and no one else forms a new, close relationship with the alliance partner.

Because alliance relationships can be full of uncertainty and tension, it seems doubly important that those involved in alliances form good and trusting relationships with each other as people. The more open-ended or informal the alliance, the more important the relationships, as there is no formal contract that binds the partners together. Both at the organizational and personal level, alliance players have to work hard at establishing cooperation and rapport, yet always remain mindful that an alliance is, at its core, a temporary business agreement between two separate commercial ventures with their own interests and priorities. It is as though the personal nature of the relationship allows people to deal better with the ambiguous and uncertain nature of the alliance.

Alliances present organizations and individuals with a new axis of collaboration and competition. As they move along this line, people will need to shed old certainties and embrace new ambiguities. Traditional control mechanisms, both formal and informal (reporting structures, pay systems, cultural norms) may be absent in alliances, requiring individuals and teams to exercise their own judgement and discretion about how to achieve the goals of the alliance. Cementing the alliance together, and filling the gaps where processes and structures do not exist, requires the personal commitment of individuals to make the alliance work. In alliances, people occupy centre stage.

Alliance partners need to understand each other's objectives and pursue 'win-win' solutions, which often involve compromise. If clear objectives have been set, alliance partners should then have criteria by which they will measure success. These high-level objectives need to be translated into clear short-term goals at team and individual level. A balance needs to be struck between formal management processes and the emerging 'spirit' of the alliance. Too much bureaucracy at an early stage signals lack of trust and stifles innovation, but unexpected synergy can occur if people remain open to new opportunities.

## KEY ROLES

There are many key roles in alliances but two of the most important are the '*champion*' and the '*alliance manager*'. Senior champions are vital at an early stage but also in sustaining corporate commitment to the alliance. The role of the alliance manager, which may appear under various titles, is a pivotal one in providing the 'glue' for the alliance. They are operationally responsible, working between partners and representing all interests.

The relationship with parent companies can be difficult to manage. Some parents are more controlling than others. In some cases the alliance manager has to spend more time reconciling differences in the parent company than taking care of alliance business. One manager described the ideal alliance manager as someone who genuinely understands a 'win-win' solution. The 'looser' the alliance, the less direct authority one has over the other partners – so influencing, negotiating and persuading without direct control are essential skills.

Are effective alliance managers born or made? Spekman et al suggest that highly successful line managers do not automatically make good alliance managers because they must 'wear a number of different hats... they must be facile with operational, strategic and policy level concerns and be able to move easily between these levels since each affects the alliance at one or more stages in its life cycle'.[16] They conclude that some skills can be taught, such as functional and managerial skills; others can be earned, such as credibility and respect, personal networks and even interpersonal skills such as tact, sensitivity and cross-cultural awareness. However, certain key competencies, such as 'virtual thinking, creativity, pragmatism, questioning, appear to be unteachable and are more to do with the fact that they think and see the world differently'.

Another key alliance role is that of the 'microbargainer'.[17] All kinds of microbargains are struck between employees on different sides of an alliance during their regular day-to-day and week-by-week interactions. These deal makers play an important role in facilitating the process of collaborative exchange, in protecting and preventing key skills from migrating to partners, and fully exploiting any learning opportunities.

'Gate keepers', on the other hand, monitor all kinds of knowledge transfers and have sole responsibility for granting partners access to the organization and its people and processes. Lang describes the important role of the 'boundary spanner' who 'helps to create and recreate the patterning of behaviours which themselves become the norms of the relationship'.[18] Individuals in these roles create and protect alliance boundaries and ensure that conversations take place between partners.

## Building an alliance culture

Alliances need to evolve their own cultures, which are often different from either of the parent cultures. In human terms, alliances involve cooperation, interdependence, mutual though different benefits and complexity. Some people who work in multiple alliances suggest that a more generic 'alliance culture' is evolving. This involves certain patterns of behaviour that alliance workers will use in different situations, such as unusually strong attention to positive relationships with others, manifest in careful manners, personal acts of kindness or generosity and attempts to solve problems amicably. Second, the 'culture' of the alliance is expressed on a day-to-day basis through the operating procedures used in the shared business activity, through attention to business goals and priorities, manifest in efficient use of meetings and goal setting.

### Behavioural ground rules

The concept of 'culture' can seem very abstract so how can this understanding of alliance relationships be converted into something that people can work with? As with virtual working, the simplest solution is to translate strategies for mediating difference and conflict and establishing trust into some behavioural form, for instance by establishing behavioural 'ground rules', which may be a more tangible device for discussing and agreeing how people will work together.

Senior managers have a key role to play in encouraging two-way communication. They need to be involved with the day-to-day operation to the point that they can keep their finger on the pulse of what is going on. Typically, at the start of an alliance, communication is top-down. Ideally, greater participation should be encouraged and bottom-up processes should be nurtured as soon as possible.

Processes for decision making are different in each alliance and are often difficult because of complex reporting lines and the need to achieve consensus between partners. The process for decision making must be agreed before the alliance is formalized. In a joint venture this may be easier where there is a major shareholder. Initially, decision making may be slow as too many people are involved in the process and it may take some time for sufficient trust to be built. Clarification is needed at the outset on which decisions need to be referred to the parents and which can be handled locally by the alliance manager. Decision-making processes themselves can be a source of competitive advantage and organizations can learn a lot about their partners by understanding their approach to problem solving.

## *Key skills and behaviours for effective alliance working*

Alliances could be said to represent agile working at its most fluid and ambiguous. Therefore, the skills required of employees and managers to make these organizational linkages work should equip all concerned to make a success of agile working. They include the following:

**Setting an open style of leadership (especially those in senior positions)** Alliance working seems to require a more informal and open personal style of leadership than the conventional model in large, hierarchical organizations. This is one way of showing that problems will not be hidden and that individuals are encouraged to use their own initiative to act. The open management style advocated for alliances is in line with a more general shift away from the 'command and control' behaviours, which are too slow to operate effectively, and towards those supportive of empowerment.

**Understanding your partner's needs** To work with another organization you have to really understand where it is coming from and show that you understand. Without this level of business and cultural understanding, negotiation and problem resolution are virtually impossible, so cultural agility is essential – sensitivity to other people's behaviour and the ability to modify one's own behaviour patterns when appropriate. Friendliness – the ability to develop warm interpersonal relationships quickly – is especially important.

**Goal focus** Each partner needs a clear view of what the alliance is for and how much resource it is worth. Because alliances can be ambiguous, people need to work harder to identify shared interim goals. They need broad business understanding – of their own and the partner's business and also the ability to see the alliance in a broad context. This may push strategic business understanding lower down the organizational hierarchy than is usually required.

**Managing differences and negotiating for success** Your needs and those of your partner will probably conflict. Alliance workers and managers need a repertoire of skills for managing conflicts large and small. By driving too hard a bargain you can make the alliance fail. The most successful alliance workers know when to stand firm and when to concede. This calls for patience and sometimes creativity as well as classic negotiating skills – the ability to solve difficult conflicts without damaging relationships.

Differences and tensions are bound to arise. Successful alliance working requires that these be raised and resolved with the minimum of damage to the underlying relationships. Keeping differences out in the open where they can be dealt with is better than letting trouble fester.

## Conflict and trust building

Inter-organizational conflict is built into most alliances because the organizations have different strategic and long-term goals. Moreover, trust is slow to grow and quick to be destroyed. Alliance partners can trust too much or too little for their own good.[19] The sharing of relevant information is critical to partners' ability to deliver their part of the alliance. Yet in high-tech and some of the more complex international manufacturing alliances, controlling competitive information becomes a very difficult area. Sensitive marketing information can be gleaned from local specification changes and, for organizations determined to learn, all information can be used to acquire intimate knowledge of a potential competitor's capabilities and markets. Changes to a more open culture are sometimes difficult to achieve for this reason and leave a residual suspicion. So absolute trust is not the ultimate goal but an environment is needed in which partners trust enough to avoid checking up on each other all the time.

Establishing and maintaining trust at a personal level is the key means of resolving potential conflicts. Exchange of information comes to symbolize the degree of trust between the partners. The more information is shared, the higher the level of trust. However, people also need to be clear as to which information they need to protect. Parkhe proposes some practical recipes for trust building such as avoiding surprises, open communication and frequent positive interactions between key people, followed by performance reviews to check behaviour.[20] Similarly, Axelrod emphasizes 'being nice' through playing fair and forgoing short-term gains in the interest of long-term benefits.[21] Lewis also suggests 'issue spotting', where alliance partners proactively raise potential issues, thereby reducing surprises and helping to build confidence that each partner is looking out for the other's interests.[22]

**Operational effectiveness** Work needs to be clearly managed, and processes are needed to ensure delivery within a complex and shifting environment. Good day-to-day work process is even more important in an alliance than in a conventional business. In building the skills of alliance workers, general teamwork processes and disciplines are useful, particularly for people working in project teams and cross-functional teams with divided loyalties. Adopting the disciplines of project management can be extremely helpful in bridging cultural differences and getting everyone to sign up to shared objectives, timescales, responsibilities and the need for regular progress review. It is often in the most informal alliances that such project management approaches increase effectiveness.

**Communication and information** Communication – both formal and informal – is critical in avoiding misunderstandings and in reinforcing trust. Communication needs to be open and honest, but alliance partners also need to judge what information they will share.

**Tolerance of ambiguity** Managing complexity – dealing with many issues and much information, especially for managers of alliance relationships – can be testing of both business and personal identity and allegiance. In particular, alliance workers require a high level of emotional resilience. They can feel they are giving a lot of emotional energy to the alliance, which their own organization may or may not see. Being patient and nice to everyone while driving for output uses a lot of personal energy. People need to find strategies for keeping themselves going, for getting support from others and not taking personally any periods of failure.

SKILLS FOR ALLIANCES, OR FOR LIFE?

These skills and behaviours have some striking similarities to what is being said more generally about skill change at work. The skills of cultural sensitivity and negotiation apply just as much across countries, work groups, functions and divisions as they do between alliance partners. Perhaps we should see alliance workers as the skill trendsetters of today. Employees should also see the chance of working in an alliance as an opportunity to learn ways of working that will stand them in good stead.

Individuals involved in alliances learn from their experience about how to take a wider view of business and how to deal with more complex personal relationships, although this is often a private experience, little discussed with others in their organization. Individual learning could be enhanced by building learning goals into alliance working for individuals and discussing learning more in performance reviews and team meetings. So attention should be given to building in processes for learning, sharing and protecting information.

Some HR teams are attempting to enhance organizational learning and mainstream alliance skills by documenting experiences from alliances to take forward into future partnerships. Others have compiled resource packs for alliance workers based on past experience. Learning can also be gained from a broader evaluation of alliances – what has worked well, what the problems were – to include a cultural evaluation as well as business outcomes.

## Strategic alliances: the innovation model

Increasingly the main motivation for entering strategic alliances is to enable growth and innovation. Digital working in particular is driving the requirement for increased collaboration for mutual benefits within and between companies, especially in sectors such as large-scale construction and car manufacture. In many cases, alliances are set up to achieve innovation that businesses could not achieve on their own. Here investment is made in combining unique skill sets in order to gain competitive advantage. Included in this category are 'tight' joint ventures to exploit a potential opportunity and the 'tight-loose' 'networked organization'.

### THE NETWORKED ORGANIZATION

Within knowledge-intensive industries the 'networked organization' is a loosely coupled configuration geared to building value for the network. The network or virtual structure is the most flexible and agile form of all. This consists of a small command unit that hires outside companies to serve as functional departments. It might, for instance, outsource manufacturing, call-centre operations and distribution. This keeps overheads down while allowing the company to hire only needed services. It can easily adapt to the marketplace by quickly adjusting its supplier network. Some loss of control is unavoidable since outside companies control processes. A partial solution lies in maintaining close contact with suppliers to ensure desirable outcomes. Such networks are often dominated by resource-rich firms. If the central firm's purpose is innovation it will connect with firms or other entities with diverse skill sets and engage with them in knowledge sharing and collaborative product development. In a network culture the shift that occurs is from 'my information is power' to one in which 'sharing is power'.

Some leading organizations are making considerable investment in developing an open innovation (OI) culture to enhance their internal corporate innovation capabilities. Open innovation management seeks to optimize the innovation inflows and outflows across the boundary that exists between an organization and its external innovation ecosystem, identifying and using ideas, technologies or innovations from parties external to an organization in order to create value. As organizations co-evolve and collaborate with others they need both access to knowledge and the ability to marshal resources quickly.

For example, both Unilever and GSK now have open innovation elements in over half of their R&D projects and are actively developing their open innovation processes to enable them to compete in complex global marketplaces. For Unilever, partnerships have become vital to delivery of what it calls its 'three big targets' – to help 1 billion people improve their health and wellbeing, to halve the environmental footprint of their products and to source 100 per cent of their agricultural products sustainably. The R&D strategy focuses efforts on innovation ecosystems led from Unilever's hubs. These include a science grid around the hubs (universities, etc), the wider science and technology community, strategic commercial partners (private) and ports in hotspots (public and private). Partnerships are already bearing fruit in terms of innovation and profitability and are considered indispensable for building future winning capabilities.

GSK is approaching open innovation from a multitude of directions that range from creating small, focused teams to soliciting ideas through the Innovation at GSK website that opened in 2007. GSK's global Open Innovation team invites people to submit their technologies or innovations to the company for review. It calls the process the 'Want – Find – Get' model. Its 'wants' innovations that will contribute to its growth. It 'finds' these 'wants' by building networks with innovators, then works with innovators to 'get' the technologies and develop consumer healthcare ideas and/or technology innovations from concept to delivery. Partnering with the UK government and Wellcome Trust provides another avenue to open innovation. Scientists from around the world are based at a GSK campus in Stevenage (UK) to create a global hub for the life-sciences industry, while benefiting from GSK's resources and facilities. Members include experts in R&D, marketing and business development located in R&D centres around the globe, innovation hubs that are open-space work environments that facilitate collaboration and foster creativity. As scientific peers, they act as liaison between the originator of the initial idea and the key individuals in GSK responsible for the assessment and development of the innovative idea or technology.

---

CASE STUDY

*Alliance Manchester Business School working in a creative alliance*

I am grateful to Ann Mahon, Professor of Health Leadership and Programme Director, Alliance Manchester Business School, University of Manchester, for this leadership development case study. This tells the story of how Alliance Manchester Business School, with the University of Birmingham as part of a KPMG-led creative alliance, worked with the UK's National Health Service (NHS) to create a leadership development programme that aimed to change the culture of the NHS.

Designing an innovative and impactful executive education programme through creative alliances

Today, the NHS is the world's fifth-largest employer, with 1.7 million workers in the United Kingdom; of these, 1.2 million are in England. However, there are also significant workforce challenges. Since 2010 there was an increase in all staff groupings, except management and backroom functions. There were also significant shortfalls in the nursing workforce, and the impact of Brexit on a system where 10 per cent of doctors, 5 per cent of nurses and many more care workers come from EU countries, remains uncertain.[23]

Moreover, in recent years, a series of high-profile scandals of failures of patient care have resulted in hostile media coverage and a loss of public confidence in the management and leadership of the NHS. In particular, the Francis reports investigating the poor patient care provided by the Mid-Staffordshire NHS Trust between 2005 and 2009 found that, although some specific individuals were responsible, the problems were systemic. Connections were made between failure of patient care and failures of leadership in all of the NHS organizations within the regional system from the board down.[24] Another major study of NHS leadership found that the dominant leadership style was pace-setting. This may explain some of the failures in leadership in Mid-Staffordshire because, although this style may reflect good intent, it has a negative impact on climate, stifling innovation, diminishing a sense of responsibility to the organization and reducing standards of care.[25] The challenge to change the culture of NHS management and leadership was profound.

Tinkering around the edges was not an option. The scale of the problem meant that leadership in the NHS required a fundamental review. The political climate was enabling – a coalition government was in power, austerity was not yet a reality of life and the NHS had just established a new Leadership Academy that had drive, ambition and passion to make a difference.

The creative alliance

It was against this background that in 2012 the NHS Leadership Academy asked for funding for a suite of leadership development programmes for all tiers of managers and leaders in the NHS.[26] This ambition, in terms of reach, impact and levels of funding was unprecedented. A call was issued for providers or consortia to work in partnership with the NHS Leadership Academy to design and deliver leadership development programmes. The call was not for a programme blueprint but rather for a provider or consortium that could respond at pace, at scale and co-produce a customized and innovative design.

Alliance Manchester Business School wanted to respond to this call, but not alone. Business schools are often criticized for failing to provide industry and public services with the skills and talents they need. There is both a *skills gap* and a *skills transfer gap*. Hall and Rowland's research into management education in the United Kingdom concluded that conventional syllabuses do not offer the opportunity for leaders to develop the agile leadership skills that organizations expect because curricula are characterized by an emphasis on content rather than process – an approach that is now neither desirable nor acceptable.[27] In addition to concerns about outdated pedagogy, business schools have also been described as being insular and exclusive. Unless they innovate, and become more flexible and agile, other providers will occupy their space.

The ability to collaborate with others is key. Currie, Davies and Ferlie make a plea to business schools to 'lower their walls' and work more collaboratively with other university departments if 'grand challenges' are to be addressed in a way that creates social value.[28] Such collaboration, however, needs to move beyond university partnerships if business schools are to maintain their market position as serious providers of executive education.[29]

In response to the invitation to tender issued by the NHS Leadership Academy at the end of 2012, KPMG convened a partnership that included Alliance Manchester Business School, the University of Birmingham, Harvard School of Public Health and others. All of the partners within the creative alliance had worked with at least one of the other partners before forming a consortium. The NHS Leadership Academy became a part of the creative alliance and a consortium was formed in February 2013. Expectations were high and there was a sense of urgency. The consortium itself had to be agile: it had just over eight months from being awarded the contract to recruiting its first intake to start the programme in October 2013.

## Creative alliancing in action

As a creative alliance, members of the consortium worked together on the tender writing process. A number of factors contributed to creating and maintaining this creative alliance. 'Our attention to understanding our respective individual and organizational values was one of the key factors and provided the foundations for establishing rapport, inclusion and working towards developing a set of shared consortium values. We did this during the formation of the consortium and throughout the tender-writing process. We spent many days working together, face to face or virtually, exploring design options and, perhaps more importantly, developing our shared values, trust and agreeing ways of working. Significant time was also invested in preparing for, and rehearsing, the two-day pitch. This time investment was important and intensive. It helped to produce a plausible, credible creative alliance and engendered personal and professional relationships based on trust, challenge and shared values.

There were challenges and tensions, exacerbated by pace, scale, expectations and our own collective values to make a difference and strive for excellence. For example, from a business school and university perspective, academics are used to designing and delivering their own educational modules and receiving challenge and critique from their academic colleagues, external examiners and other standard university quality assurance processes. In the model of co-creation adopted by the consortium, content and pedagogical approaches, although led by the universities, were created collaboratively with the NHS Leadership Academy and other members of the consortium. In addition, close project management added intensity to the process that was at times particularly challenging.

Through our shared vision, shared values and close working relationship with the NHS Leadership Academy we learned to be curious, responsive, challenging and flexible. We gained insight into our different organizational cultures, ways of working, constraints and freedoms, which allowed us to work well together, play to our respective strengths and respond with agility and pace within a tight and demanding time frame.'

The Anderson programme

The resulting MSc Healthcare Leadership, also known as the Anderson programme, is the product of this collaborative endeavour. This two-year national programme offers a dual award of an MSc degree and a senior leadership development award. Participants are drawn from different disciplines, professions and more than 500 NHS organizations. Key design challenges include how to achieve participant-centred learning, how to achieve impact beyond the individual and how to combine a leadership development programme with an academic programme.

The programme aims to develop key agile leadership attributes related to innovation, within an overarching framework that focuses on three key elements:

1  The generation of new ideas or demands from the client, customer, provider or consumer – the social context that precedes or triggers the innovation

2  The realization, or translation, of these demands into practice

3  The subsequent creation of value for the client or customer.

The programme design is underpinned by four core leadership principles and two golden threads that define the prevailing view of what high-quality leadership should be focusing on in the NHS (Table 4.1).

These principles and threads inform both the content and the pedagogy of the programme design and they evolved in the early stages of programme design and in consultation with patients and carers. The pedagogical approach is blended learning

TABLE 4.1  Principles and golden threads underpinning design

| Core leadership principles | Golden threads |
|---|---|
| • Making person-centred coordinated care happen | Focus on: |
| • Creating a culture for quality | • The patient experience |
| • Improving the quality of the patient experience | • Equality, diversity and inclusion |
| • Understanding self to improve the quality of care | |

with an emphasis on multidisciplinary and integrated content, experiential learning and a regard to both content and process. A key feature is the parity of esteem given to the experiential elements of the programme, compared with the academic elements. The blend also includes modules delivered via a virtual online campus and one-to-one and group tutorials.

Implementation

More than 2,500 participants have registered on the programme since it was launched in October 2013 and over 1,000 have graduated with the dual awards. Despite the programme's scale, a participant-centred and personalized relationship is achieved with participants through a tutor trio and a cohort model of delivery.

Value creation is assessed by drawing on internal evaluation and an independent evaluation conducted by Ipsos MORI, a leading UK market research company. There is some evidence of organizational impact but this is inhibited so far by the lack of engagement and organizational support from sponsors within typically very traditional contexts. The programme has had greatest impact at individual and team levels, and there is evidence of a strong positive impact on career progression and promotion. Effectively, participants have learned how to become agile leaders and are moving into positions where they can make positive change happen. They are applying their learning in their own contexts, building cohorts of fellow learners who are keen to enhance their learning agility and momentum for positive change.

So, as this case illustrates, business schools, working as part of a creative alliance, can offer innovation in the design and delivery of leadership development programmes that respond to increasing demands for customization, blended interventions and evidence of impact in true agile manner.

---

## Cooperatives and linking capability

Another form of alliance – cooperatives – differ substantially from publicly owned companies in their ownership structures and governance models. Cooperatives restrict ownership to their members and have participatory and democratic decision-making processes. In their efforts to internationalize in the global economy, cooperatives not only face a variety of problems that are common to all firms but also encounter specific challenges due to their particular value commitments, forms of incorporation and organizational structures that inhibit agility.

Strategic change in these organizations requires collaborative leadership involving constellations of actors playing distinct but tightly-knit roles. McKinsey research found the cooperative model to be particularly effective in creating organizational alignment. The fact that cooperatives adhere to a service-oriented mission (as opposed to public companies' mission of creating value for shareholders) tends to create a sense of higher purpose, which appeals to and mobilizes cooperative employees.[30] As a result, cooperative employees experience a strong sense of ownership of, and belonging to, their organization. This explains why cooperatives outperform publicly owned companies in customer-satisfaction surveys. On the other hand, McKinsey suggests three areas in which cooperatives need to improve their agility: making decisions, pursuing new opportunities, and sourcing and developing talent.

## Agility in decision making

One of the main strengths of cooperatives – their consensual and consultative decision-making processes – also contributes to one of their greatest weaknesses – delayed action due to healthy but lengthy debates that take place at multiple levels of the organization. Collaborative leadership is fragile and can easily disintegrate due to internal conflict.

To increase their responsiveness to changing conditions, cooperatives have to strike a balance between their democratic nature and executive agility. Leading cooperatives are finding three actions to be helpful: clearly distinguish the respective roles and responsibilities of executive officers and elected officials (such as board members); create more efficient processes for consulting with members on strategic direction; and improve performance-management systems that allow issues to be identified and acted on swiftly.

FrieslandCampina, the Dutch dairy cooperative, clarified the roles of executive and elected officials to remove bottlenecks from decision-making processes. To create a healthy distance between the cooperative democratic processes and the day-to-day rapid operating decisions required to compete effectively in the market the cooperative formed a separate operating company with its own board. The cooperative remained a full owner of the new operating company.

The Mondragon Corporation – a worker-federation cooperative in Spain that is involved in manufacturing, retail and financial services – pursues new business opportunities with agility. Founded in 1959, Mondragon is a federation of industrial co-operative associations with over 260 companies and subsidiaries. Although it remains closely tied to its place of origin, Spain's

Basque region, Mondragon now has a reach across 35 countries. This cooperative, whose slogan is 'humanity at work', was created to support employment for residents of the Basque region. Mondragon is, in its own words, 'created by and for people'. Mutuality is at its core: all employees have equal rights to vote and ownership; managing boards consist of a combination of employees from all levels of the organization; the highest managers earn no more than six times the lowest paid worker; distribution of 70 per cent of profits after taxes with decision-making taken through the General Assembly; no more than 20 per cent of workers can be temporary contractors; and re-allocating workers across co-operatives in the federation helps retain a skilled workforce.

Faced with increasing competitive threats that resulted from the liberalization of European markets in the early 1990s, Mondragon put in place three practices to increase its business innovation, productivity, and capacity to create jobs. First, it created R&D 'networks' dedicated to developing new products and services. These comprised 14 technology centers and R&D units specialized in fields relevant to Mondragon, such as lifting systems, packaging machines and thermoplastics. Second, it developed processes at all levels of the cooperative to encourage cross-functional and cross-business-unit innovation. For example, Mondragon has established three groups that specialize in cross-product initiatives. These groups convene employees from different divisions to explore new business ideas, which are eventually elevated to the coop-wide level for production and commercialization. These interdivision initiatives are made possible by clear coordination among top managers to ensure appropriate transfer of technology and know-how among divisions.

Finally, Mondragon put in place funding mechanisms to ensure the survival and success of new initiatives. The cooperative invests a minimum of 10 per cent of its gross profits into a 'development fund' that finances innovation, research and international business development. According to Mondragon, 21 per cent of its sales are from products that are less than five years old.

As cooperatives continue to grow and become large enterprises, organizational agility will increasingly determine their ability to competitively serve members in a fast-changing world.

Taken together, these mutual practices appear to have helped Mondragon to weather unfavourable economic conditions and foster resiliency. Improving their organizational agility while preserving their mission and principles is a fundamental organizational challenge of modern cooperatives. Through a combination of democratic principles, the values of solidarity, and strong competitiveness, Mondragon has simultaneously achieved both efficiency and equity and has become an alternative to the organizational and governance models of traditional capitalist firms.[31]

## Conclusion

Far more than in conventional structures with intact teams and command-and-control management styles, these more flexible organizational forms and working arrangements illustrate how agility can be made to work for both organizations and employees. They share many common challenges, not least building trust and managing ambiguity and conflict. At the same time successful collaborations are a fertile proving ground for new approaches and rapid skills development – and the opportunities they present to embrace new approaches should be grasped. In summary:

- The development of a shared vision and processes to share knowledge is vital, as are *processes to handle conflict and deal with ambiguity*.

- More flexible forms of organization call for more *sophisticated 'people' relationship skills* and working practices.

- People mediate the conflict and ambiguity between their organizations – so personal relationships make or break alliances.

- Trust is a vital component to the success of these arrangements. *Trust can be built* through honesty and providing the right support.

- Governance – *risks must be surfaced; mitigation strategies identified*; partners will need to hold each other to account within new governance arrangements.

- Employees act as a bridge between organizations – *they need to be empowered* to make decisions at local level.

- Operations – *clear, shared, short-term objectives*; project management disciplines; frequent communication and review; appropriate information sharing; processes for renegotiation and space for innovation.

Given the growth of these cross-boundary alliances, and the similarity of skills required for virtual, hybrid and alliance teamworking, organizations might consider whether such skills – perhaps called 'cross-boundary working' or 'working with partners' – should be mainstreamed into training and development for the majority of staff. Organizational learning can flow from more formal evaluations of the success of a business alliance, particularly when assessing the achievement of original targets by tracking business measures or key indicators, and also improved by more thorough review and documentation of learning experiences.

In the next chapter we shall continue to look at how internal organizational structures are becoming more agile and consider how to design for agility.

---

CHECKLIST

How well do your linkages work?

- To what extent does the current structure facilitate or impede flexible management of work processes/capabilities, functions, products, programmes, customers, geographies or partners?
- How much commitment is there to alliance working at the highest level?
- Where do your established HR practices facilitate or impede collaboration and integration?
- Are team members educated at the outset regarding possible cultural differences and barriers in communication?
- How much help do people receive in learning new skills and approaches? What are the processes for surfacing and handling conflict?
- How well are differences of approach managed?
- How effective is communication between parties?
- What is being learned from partnership working? How is this applied?

---

## Notes

**1** Christensen, K (2013) Thought leader interview: Amy Edmondson, *Rotman Magazine*, Winter, pp 10–15, www-2.rotman.utoronto.ca/rotmanmag/ThoughtLeader_Edmondson.pdf (archived at https://perma.cc/9NDU-FMR4).

**2** Miller, P et al (2012) Innovation leadership study: Managing innovation – an insider perspective, Capgemini Consulting, www.capgemini.com/resources/innovation-leadership-study-managing-innovation-an-insider-perspective (archived at https://perma.cc/6JU5-GBS3).

**3**  Corbett, MF (2004) *The Outsourcing Revolution: Why it makes sense and how to do it right*, Dearborn, Chicago.

**4**  Swart, J, Purcell, J and Kinnie, N (2005) Knowledge Work and New Organisational Forms: the HRM challenge, Working Paper series 205.06, University of Bath.

**5**  Dyer, J and Nobeoka, K (2000) Creating and managing a high-performance knowledge-sharing network: The Toyota case, *Strategic Management Journal*, **21**, pp 345–67.

**6**  Moran, J (1999) Outsourcing successful if bottom line improves, *Computing Canada*, **25** (34), pp 27–28.

**7**  Kakabadse, AP and Kakabadse, N (2000) Outsourcing: A paradigm shift, *Journal of Management Development*, **19** (8), pp 668–778.

**8**  Cascio, WF (2002) Strategies for responsible restructuring, *Academy of Management Perspectives*, **16** (3) pp 80–91.

**9**  Chrislip, DD (2002) *Collaborative Leadership Fieldbook: 25*, Jossey-Bass Leadership series, San Francisco.

**10**  Khanna, T (2014) Contextual intelligence, *Harvard Business Review*, **92** (9), September, pp 58–68.

**11**  Englehardt, CS and Simmons PR (2002) Organizational flexibility for a changing world, *Leadership & Organization Development Journal*, **23** (3), pp 113–21, p 49.

**12**  Garrow, V, Hirsh, W, Devine, M and Holbeche, L (2004) *Strategic Alliances: Getting the people bit right*, Roffey Park, Horsham.

**13**  Jones, C. Microsoft's willingness to work with others cements its dominance, Business, *The Times*, 18 October 2022.

**14**  Johnson, G and Scholes, K (1999) *Exploring Corporate Strategy*, 5th edn, Prentice Hall, Harlow.

**15**  Spekman, R et al (1996) Creating strategic alliances which endure, *Long Range Planning*, **29** (3) pp 346–57.

**16**  Ibid.

**17**  Hamel, G and Doz, Y (1998) *Alliance Advantage: The art of creating value through partnering*, Harvard Business School Press, Boston.

**18**  Lang, JW (1996) Strategic alliances between large and small high-tech firms (the small firm licensing option), *International Journal of Technology Management*, **12** (7/8), pp 796–807.

**19**  Parkhe, A (1998) Understanding trust in international alliances, *Journal of World Business*, **33** (3), pp 219–40.

**20**  Parkhe, A (1998) Building trust in international alliances, *Journal of World Business*, **33** (4), pp 417–37.

**21**  Axelrod, R (1984) *The Evolution of Cooperation*, Basic Books, New York.

**22**  Lewis, J (1989) *Partnerships for Profit*, Free Press, New York.

**23**  Kmietowicz, Z (2016) Brexit – not EU membership – threatens the NHS, 60 eminent doctors say, *British Medical Journal*, **353**, doi.org/10.1136/bmj.i3373 (archived at https://perma.cc/XZ2C-JJFZ).

**24**  Chambers, N et al (2017) Responses to Francis: Changes in board leadership and governance in acute hospitals in England since 2013, Department of Health, Policy Research Programme, PR-R11–0914–12–003; Francis, R (2013a) *Report of the Mid Staffordshire NHS Foundation Trust Public Inquiry*, 2013, www.gov.uk/government/publications/report-of-the-mid-staffordshire-nhs-foundation-trust-public-inquiry; (2013b) The Mid Staffordshire NHS Foundation Trust Public Enquiry: Press release; (2013c) Report of the Mid Staffordshire NHS Foundation Trust Public Inquiry: Executive summary.

**25**  Lynas, K (2015) The leadership response to the Francis report, *Future Hospital Journal*, **2** (3), pp 203–08.

**26**  European Federation for Management Development (EFMD) (2016) The NHS Leadership Academy and Alliance Manchester Business School: Cultural change on a national scale, *Global Focus*, **3** (10), pp 5–6.

**27**  Hall, RD and Rowland, CA (2016) Leadership development for managers in turbulent times, *Journal of Management Development*, **35** (8), pp 942–55, doi.org/10.1108/JMD-09-2015-0121 (archived at https://perma.cc/PHX7-W8SK).

**28**  Currie G, Davies J and Ferlie, E (2016) A call for university-based business schools to 'Lower Their Walls': Collaborating with other academic departments in pursuit of social value, *Academy of Management Learning and Education*, **15** (4), pp 742–55.

**29**  Lubeck, J, Cheng, BS, Myszkowski, G et al (2016) Future Trends in Business Education Executive Care, Unicon Research Report, Unicon.

**30**  Berube V, Grant, A and Mansour, T. How cooperatives grow, McKinsey Research, 2012, www.mckinsey.com/~/media/mckinsey/dotcom/client_service/Strategy/McKinsey%20on%20Cooperatives/PDFs/McK_on_Cooperatives-How_cooperatives_grow.ashx (archived at https://perma.cc/6UK5-LJEE).

**31**  Bérubé, V, Lamarre, E and Rutherford, S (2012) Improving cooperatives' agility, McKinsey Research, www.mckinsey.com/~/media/mckinsey/dotcom/client_service/Strategy/McKinsey%20on%20Cooperatives/PDFs/McK_on_Cooperatives-Improving_cooperatives_agility.ashx (archived at https://perma.cc/H3MX-CCAE).

# 05

# Designing for agility

Organization leaders know that their company's competitiveness depends on accelerated change implementation, innovation and agility. As discussed in Chapter 1, the digital revolution, often described as the 'fourth industrial revolution', is transforming the competitive landscape, with rapid shifts in customer behaviour that require an innovative response. As companies' value chains and business models undergo significant reinvention because of digital transformation, to remain successful, organizations must be able to change their designs to create a new alignment between the requirements of the environment and the capabilities of the firm. In today's increasingly turbulent environments, this fit is temporary at best, according to Professor Ed Lawler III.[1]

Organization design is a powerful tool to drive performance, increase flexibility, improve efficiency and service delivery to clients, and reduce costs. It is the art and science of managing polarities, with some aspects of design 'loose' while others are 'tight'.[2] During the COVID-19 pandemic organizations that embraced agility performed better than others, according to McKinsey research.[3] They were able to act swiftly by doubling down on value, taking a hard look at their company's real strengths – attracting customers, superior category management, great products and so on – and using them to design their agile units and teams.

In such a context, linear, conventional approaches to organization design that derive from general systems theory seem increasingly out of date. Not surprisingly, there is clearly a growing appetite for reimagining organizations and ways of working, as organizations adopt new models of business, operation and employment. Our conception of what is 'an organization' must evolve. New and more fluid approaches to designing organizations are required. Design is about far more than structures; to achieve agility it is vital that people are motivated and able to work in new ways so agility must be a whole-system capability. Senior managers who set business strategy and sponsor participation and design must embrace an agile mindset to realize the design's potential. HR and OD – the people professionals – often become involved in design work only once most of the structure and system decisions have been taken. In today's digital era, leaders require input from HR to ensure that new forms of design are fit for purpose and achieve new types of performance from a willing workforce.

In this chapter we shall consider some of the latest approaches to agile design and some of the ways in which HR can contribute to its effectiveness. We will look at:

- the need for more agile organization designs
- organizing around customer journeys
- redesigning HR from the outside in
- conventional and agile design processes.

We shall look at the implications of agility for work design in Chapter 6.

## The need for more agile organization designs

Organization design covers formal structures, processes and governance mechanisms, as well as the more informal networks and relationships that enable work to be done. Various systems models, such as the Galbraith Star Model™ (strategy, culture, structure, processes, rewards, technology, people and culture), highlight the importance of aligning all aspects of the system if a redesign is necessary. An agile organization design flows from strategy – the company's vision and mission as well as its long and short-term goals into structure – which defines core hierarchical units, and the lateral, cross-unit structural linkages that carry out important organizational processes. Processes are the flows of information and work through the organization. Vertical processes occur within core units and follow the hierarchical chain of the organization. Lateral processes operate across the units of the organization. These include management processes that determine the company's direction and allocate scarce resources, such as funds and talent, to different purposes and priorities and work processes that turn inputs into the value that is delivered to customers and other stakeholders.

An operating model describes the main pieces of organization required to support the business model – its business processes, technology approach, data, organizational structure, suppliers and partners, locations – and how they relate to each other. It represents the blueprint of standards and operating procedures that underpin the workings of the organization. To be agile these must be simplified, standardized and aligned in order to enable the firm to keep close to market changes, and to experiment and change tack as needed. This means that the entire system should be designed to enable people and machines to work together to deliver customer outcomes. Proactive learning, redesign and rapid implementation must become core organizational capabilities that are supported by the organization's design and operation.

## Aligning with strategy

Increasingly business strategies call for innovation. In a world of integrated networks, groundbreaking ICT innovations and rapidly changing customer preferences, new methods of solving problems have arisen that previously only specialist businesses could provide. ICT innovations enable robustly connected networks and knowledge sharing. Social machines are at the confluence of interactions between computers, data and humans – as is the case with Wikipedia – that allow communities to identify and solve their own problems, harnessing their skills and not relying on others. From a complexity perspective, eventually this enables self-organization and creates a network of swarming units in which patterns emerge. This augmented intelligence stands in contrast to traditional artificial intelligence, which is about making machines smarter.

Typically an innovation strategy is delivered through adaptable and flexible structures and systems that align with the strategies adopted, are sufficiently responsive to compete in complex competitive environments, and yet still maintain the reliability of control and efficiency of task management.[4] Innovation governance should ensure that there is a clear organizational structure for innovation, well-defined roles and responsibilities, effective decision-making processes and KPIs for innovation.[5]

Worley, Williams and Lawler propose that in an increasingly uncertain and unpredictable world management systems should be 'built to change'.[6] The 'agility' concept encompasses both adaptability and flexibility. Agile organizations are designed to be flexible and able to adapt swiftly as new competitive threats and opportunities are identified and must be responded to. Organizational adaptability focuses on how an organization's form, structure, and degree of formalization influence its ability to quickly adapt to its business environment.[7] Organizational flexibility represents an organization's capacity to adjust its internal structures and processes in a predetermined response to changes in the environment.[8] Speed of innovation without losing momentum is critical. Hierarchy must change as needed; so too must resources.[9] Stereotypically, the classic pyramid-shaped organization structure inside firms is giving way to more decentralized forms of internal organization that are generally flatter, leaner, less hierarchical and more flexible in nature than the traditional bureaucratic forms. Vertical structures must be complemented by strong lateral coordination mechanisms that provide the 'both/and' of scale and agility required to execute the business strategy.

Each organization needs to create a purpose-built design according to desired outcomes. Frameworks help business leaders to make choices that fit their context and strategic ambition. There are no right or wrong answers around organizational models, only choices that have strengths and limitations.[10]

## How great is the transformation required?

The path towards scaling up and mainstreaming agility beyond IT departments is long and winding. Years after Galbraith wrote about customer-centric organization design, agility was failing to take hold more generally.[11] US manufacturing took a different path, with some manufacturers continuing to pursue mass-production methods with increased emphasis on saving through economies of scale while other firms pursued 'lean' manufacturing that continued to focus on enhanced efficiency and cutting costs[12] – hardly conducive to innovation.

Yet, although structures are only one aspect of organization, they are symbolically and actually powerful in maintaining the status quo. Many organizations retain bureaucratic organization designs because of the benefits they derive, such as high degrees of management control, clear accountabilities, ease of planning and budgeting and risk management. Bureaucracy also has its downsides such as siloed behaviour, slow decision making, low empowerment or engagement, information shared on a 'need to know' basis resulting in risk aversion and little innovation. Traditional hierarchical structures – *simple, functional, product, divisional, geographic, etc* – affect behaviour. For example, a high degree of process separation leads to increased specialization but reduces cooperation and knowledge transfer between processes. A low degree of process separation increases knowledge transfer and cooperation but has a potentially negative effect on specialization. Therefore, designs need to be specific to the context and requirement.

A 2017 survey of 7,000 readers of *Harvard Business Review* by Hamel and Zanini found that bureaucracy is growing not shrinking, especially in large organizations.[13] Nearly two-thirds of respondents felt their organization had become more bureaucratic – more centralized, more rule-bound and more conservative – in recent years.

However, agility without some stability can lead to chaos. Therefore, rather than abandoning bureaucracy altogether, an appropriate degree of the right kind of (enabling) bureaucracy can help organizations to achieve the right blend of creative and efficient activity needed for long-term success and adaptability. Indeed, to enable rapid adaptation, a range of bureaucratic practices – resource allocation, goal setting, structure and other systems and processes – must be aligned to strategy, aligned to each other and subject to continuous improvement. In other words, the elements of enabling bureaucracy (functional formalization) that provide structure, procedures, division of labour and risk management can provide a stable foundation to enable rapid product and service development to flourish without chaos. And creating the right connections throughout the hierarchy and across functional boundaries enables the organization to create value.

## The ambidextrous organization

Redesigning whole organizations to align with business strategy presents many dilemmas so most organizations opt for a large element of the organization to focus on 'business as usual' while other pockets deliver the innovations. Different parts of the business may be pursuing different strategies and need different designs. This is the nature of ambidextrous organizations.

In earlier chapters we discussed the framework of organizational ambidexterity as a possible means of effectively bridging between agility and bureaucracy to achieve the best of both.[14] This describes the tension between *exploiting* current products, technologies and services and *exploring* new products, technologies and services, and allows organizations to do both.[15] For instance, in areas such as new product development, freedom to innovate is the critical need and the rallying cry should be autonomy, small teams and organizational agility. Other areas, however, where consistent outcomes are essential and where speed of execution comes from deploying common methods, best practices and enforced routines, may benefit from standardized approaches. The focus here should be on repeatability and efficiency.

Organizations can be designed to be ambidextrous – with some parts specifically organized for efficiency and optimization, and other parts for innovation, agility and networks; both will need to be co-lateral design systems that work together. Each requires speed in different areas, innovation versus execution, and achieves these results in different ways.

Ambidextrous organizations require four capabilities:[16]

1  **Optimization** – The focus is on the optimization of revenue performance through the Profit and Loss (P&L) performance network. This is needed at least in the short term so that the focus can be on both the optimization of revenue generation and innovation. An ambidextrous approach enables organizations to take both an offensive and a defensive position in the market.

2  **Shared services** – Functions should work together in an integrated way to add benefits to P&Ls. In the move towards greater agility, many organizations have adopted project-based management. Functional specialists should provide a 'home room' for projects, so that learning can be co-created and shared. If corporate functions such as HR and IT can be fluidly deployed as needed by strategic initiatives, rather than being housed within rigid departmental structures, teams can be formed and dissolved more rapidly to seize opportunities or respond to threats.

3  **An incubator** – Some form of innovation is happening in most organizations but typically not enough. The challenge is to increase organizational capability in digital innovation. The aim should be to experiment in order to produce a portfolio of innovations that include:

   o  *incremental–type* innovations that seek to improve the systems, products or services that already exist, making them better, faster, cheaper and ready to move to market

   o  *process* innovation – the implementation of new or significantly improved production or delivery methods

   o  *aggressive* innovation, where competitors try to outperform their rivals to grab a greater share of existing demand, usually through marginal changes in offering level and price

   o  *business model* innovation resulting in an entirely different type of company that competes not only on the value proposition of its offerings but aligns its profit formula, resources and processes to enhance that value proposition, capture new market segments and alienate competitors.

The incubator should have its own separate operating model; if the company's broader operating model is disrupted, things should be safe in the incubator.

4  **Building networks** – Hierarchy should be in the background, working in support mode towards the networks. The executive team are responsible overall for organizational decision making, though small two- or three-person nodes or subsets of the executive team can be attached to up to four networks. That way, if an issue emerges, executives can go into strategic choice alignment mode and put together a rapid design group to stress-test emerging options.

## Agile businesses organize around customer journeys

For agility, linking the customer with some sort of technology forces organizations to be more focused on organizing around customer segments, rather than thinking in conventional terms of organizing around products, geographies, etc. For instance, some organizations may be total platforms where the customer accesses the platform through an app that connects users while other parts of the organization are not associated with apps. As soon as you focus on the customer journey within its ecosystem of suppliers, competitors and stakeholder environment, the work system becomes the unit of analysis. If the customer is connected and involved in co-creating the product or service, the nature of decision making at the top changes and the middle management layer is potentially eliminated. Thus, in a real sense, customers co-create with the organization and help to shape the organization in a socio-technical system; as work changes, so too do the business model and work systems.

Systemic work design requires dedicated time and clear vision, driven by the needs of people rather than technology. Work systems must align around something that delivers better service, or care or other outcome for the customer. Since a significant amount of discontinuous change can be anticipated, the customer-centric focus should be not just on prevention of problems but on continuous experience improvement of core processes. IBM, for instance, adopted the front-back hybrid model, which addresses the need to develop a customer-centric unit and integrate it into the existing organization. Here the 'back' of the organization – including operations, R&D and supply chain – is structured for efficiency and operational excellence and the 'front end' for customer intimacy, responsiveness, customization and revenue growth. At operating level, technology enables decentralized decision making since more information is available. Workers with the appropriate analytical/digital ability are empowered to act, and continuous customer improvement becomes the norm and changes the value proposition.[17]

Typical structural features of technology-enabled customer-driven environments include:

- product-focused and designed around the customer journey
- non-standardized jobs and activities
- stretching roles and high-stakes work increasingly done in co-located units
- empowered employees; little direct supervision; high degrees of autonomy and accountability
- fluid, flat, team-based structures
- virtual teams or work groups
- integrator roles
- streamlined processes
- iterative project working
- boundaryless – can include partners, customers and suppliers
- flexible working practices
- high-trust working relationships
- self-management
- clear goals
- continuous feedback
- shared (and distributed) leadership
- enabled co-creation
- minimal formal rules
- upskilling and reskilling
- line managers as coach
- open communication networks.

The key requirement of customer-centric design is an 'outside-in' orientation to understand, and be responsive to, the customer experience; to act on data; and to embed change quickly. While there is no overall agile organization design, typically these have flat and lean team structures. Lateral teams are effective at driving performance and decision making and strong cross-organizational collaboration.

For such structures to be effective, empowerment and autonomy are key: process digitization must be matched by worker enablement and relevant performance management. This may require the redesign of the systems, functions, jobs, accountabilities and processes (see ING's example later) to allow for the use of discretion and decision making, and to minimize the handoffs or escalations required to meet customer needs. The teams that are central to value generation act as the core teams. They set the priorities that can help to accelerate value creation while other teams support this. Which teams are appropriate will depend on the organization's industry, situation and strategy. It is about matching force to need, getting the right people in the right roles and the right lateral processes to ensure coordination.

## The lateral organization

Lateral structural arrangements are required to ensure effective coordination. These consist of a decentralized structure in which groups and departments work together at the same organizational level to achieve a common goal, such as managing an entire customer process, rather than operating as separate and distinct entities. Lateral structural arrangements are typically incorporated into existing vertical reporting structures. This type of arrangement depends on having collaborative and informal relations between the groups involved and requires coordination and consultation, often achieved via a matrix. In today's digital economy a growing trend is towards a technology-enabled, team-based lateral organizational structure, similar to a traditional lateral structure, though carrying less management overhead. Without the need to climb a lengthy chain of command to receive approval for ideas or changes to the business model, teams can make the necessary changes to respond rapidly to different market conditions.

Lateral structures offer a number of advantages. For example, they foster a team mentality in which workers share information, which in turn creates a well-informed workforce capable of making quick decisions. They encourage open communication between workers in different departments and help to break down the barriers commonly associated with centralized organizational structures. However, among the disadvantages, complex matrix structures adopted by many global businesses often fail because they give too little consideration to how work is really done and they become unworkable in practice. For example, workers may experience conflicting loyalties when forced to report to managers from other departments; there may be duplication of activity and lack of oversight.

One of the most important factors to consider when developing a lateral structural arrangement is who will manage and plan interdepartmental interactions. Organization design expert Jay Galbraith advised that integration roles such as project managers, programme managers or product managers are vital to creating effective lateral relationships.[18] Effective governance procedures are needed, together with a simple performance measure that acts as a superordinate goal for the unit and assists in cross-functional trade-off decisions. As the lateral organization becomes more important, the role of the corporate centre becomes less about top-down control and more about making connections and defining the values and strong sense of purpose that can unite far-flung parts of the organization.

### Simplify: reduce complexity

Some form of matrix management seems inevitable to promote collaboration and manage resources, but it can also increase complexity and duplication. Agility can be increased by simplifying or removing unnecessary 'red tape'. GE, a company long admired for the way its approach to strategy, portfolio and talent interconnect in a strong HR culture, has been making breakthroughs in this area. Today, in line with an increasingly VUCA environment, GE aims to become an agile, customer-centric organization. GE's broad business strategy direction is growth through innovation. To deliver the strategy, employees need to collaborate, make quick and effective business decisions and provide customers with superior products and services. Simplification is a key operating principle. To enable this in GE has meant reducing bureaucracy and silos, introducing new ways of working, getting close to the customer, producing better, faster outcomes for customers and a new performance development approach (see Chapter 9).

GE's FastWorks platform, for creating products and bringing them to market, borrows a lot from Agile techniques. FastWorks is a successor in many ways to Six Sigma and consciously mimics the way that companies in Silicon Valley work. FastWorks is a rigorous process where a lot of time is spent on customer discovery to understand what clients really need and value. Lean start-up principles applied throughout the process include breaking down problems into solutions, which need to be understood and validated. Another lean start-up principle adopted by FastWorks is developing a Minimum Viable Product (or MVP), which is developing a prototype in the fastest and lowest-cost way. An MVP validates or invalidates one's assumptions or hypothesis. There is a focus on rapid and frequent experimentation, learning from the market, only funding projects that prove themselves, and acceptance and willingness to move on from failures. As Susan Peters, GE's head of human resources, points out, 'It is a really important element of what we're trying to do, which is to make a major shift of the company's culture towards simplification, towards better, faster outcomes for customers.'

## Redesigning HR from the outside in

The HR team in SNC-Lavalin's Atkins business in the UK and Europe region, previously led by HR Director Sharron Pamplin, gradually redesigned itself in a customer-focused way, working back from the end-user experience, in true agile manner. This puts a premium on effective communication and role-modelling for raising people's awareness of the need for change. In HR, as with other parts of the regional business, ongoing dialogue among all HR team members is made possible via the HR function's own regular global 'cadence' calls – video conference calls that bring the whole HR community together in one forum, which helps people understand the bigger picture and discuss their part of it. Similarly, the OneHRForum helps HR to develop shared understanding and purpose, and build trust. It provides an environment where people are genuinely empowered and willing to change.

In redesigning the people processes, staff involvement and co-creation were crucial. An Employee Journey mapping workshop took place involving staff from across the business to explore the key HR experience touchpoints along the employee journey from 'hire' to 'retire'. For example, when and how did people first know about the company? Was it attractive as an employer? How did they know what was available in terms of career opportunities? What did they experience in their first week? Was HR sufficiently focused on them?

By drawing on employees' actual experiences it was possible to identify how HR practices could be improved to create stronger links between employees and the company. For example, based on employee feedback about people's experience at the hiring stage, managers are now encouraged to interact with potential and newly appointed employees via LinkedIn before they join to make them feel welcome and well informed. This also fed into the development of a new employee value proposition that provides a bold and relevant voice on how the company aspires to be as an employer. Some practices that were previously considered countercultural, such as rehiring former employees, are now embraced – people are actively sought out, rehired and welcomed back as alumni with enhanced experience. By thinking about processes differently and asking, 'What value is this adding?' things are changing for the better. The Indian and UK HR teams worked together virtually to simplify the procedures required at the end of probation. Now managers are required to take action and report to HR only if there is a problem.

Work is also underway to develop a more long-term yet agile approach to succession planning and talent management. A job-families approach is being adopted, together with a strategic workforce planning initiative over a 12-year horizon called Workforce Futures 2030, with much of the initial focus on critical value generators. This strategic initiative, led by HR, is another example of staff involvement. The leadership team had framed the challenge (the problem to solve). They wanted to get to grips with what the future workforce might look like. Instead of taking the usual short-term reactive approach to resource planning, looking just a few months ahead, HR worked with leaders to think about what kinds of skills and capabilities would be required 10 years out. In particular, the leadership team wanted to understand what would be required to attract people in the early stages of their careers: Why would they join SNC-Lavalin's Atkins business? How will they work with the company – as employees or be connected to the firm in some other way? How will the business face up to the challenges that can be identified?

Two different employee groups from diverse business areas came together for separate one-day workshops to address this challenge. Participants ranged from senior and experienced staff members to graduates and apprentices. The workshops allowed people to explore the challenge imaginatively, using storytelling. The teams then worked on the challenge for six weeks and made various proposals to the leadership team, of which three were selected. These were sponsored by different senior leaders, with resources made available within the business.

Sharron Pamplin takes up the story: 'We've come a long way. The HR function is better able to change now. Team members are coming forward saying, "I've identified this problem – we need to change it."' Sharron's response is, 'Great – you all know this really well – what do you propose?' The team uses Agile methodologies such as 100-day sprints, pop-up projects, hackathons and 'lock downs', and involves their customers in the process.

In the business's UK and Europe region, different business groups are saying that HR is now working better, and they have brought on board colleagues who were not involved in the change process. As Sharron notes, 'We've seen an improvement in employee engagement and involvement at all levels. The Young Professional Awards for graduates and apprentices was introduced in 2017 as a means of giving high-profile recognition to people making a difference. One of the shortlisted apprentices actively disseminated knowledge, using One Note to track workplace and college learning. More widely, interesting practice is now shared via stories on Yammer and the company's website so is accessible to all.'

## Agile teams

To implement an agile operating model, new types of team 'structure' reduce the need for internal control and improve coordination. Team missions derived from strategy should be loosely coupled but tightly aligned; teams should be able to execute their missions with minimum dependencies. This also requires absolute clarity and transparency and buy-in from the people doing the work to embrace new ways of working.

Agile team structures should enable business advantage through continuous releases of new products by empowered and motivated teams. Spotify, for instance, releases new products before they are finalised in order for customer feedback to inform the improved design. Studies show group-work design enhancing team effectiveness and team innovation.[19] In technology-enabled work environments, cross-organizational 'scrum' teams can be pulled together to address specific issues and take responsibility for results they cannot deliver on their own.

However, the key element of the agile work system is multiple intact and self-managing agile teams which, unlike scrum teams, should be stable, organized around specific customer segments, and with the right blend of capabilities available in the mix. Since customers have data – this is sent to the cloud and refined data comes back – agile teams can analyse the volumes of data to pinpoint where and how they can improve the experience of customers. As teams make real-time decisions, things can change fast and for the better. Often teams are supported by specialist Agile coaches who can guide them through the relevant methodology as well as help with team dynamics. The lateral organization, which connects teams horizontally across internal organization boundaries and consists of well-designed cross-boundary teams, networks, functional processes and roles such as finance and HR. This is essential for achieving both agility and scale. These cross-boundary networks and connections don't happen by accident and need to be purposefully designed.[20]

Self-managing work teams have the freedom to make decisions about the division of labour, which has a direct impact on individual work design. Several studies suggest that the introduction of self-managing teams leads to greater job enrichment (e.g. job discretion, variety) among individual team members.[21] Work-group autonomy potentially provides greater opportunity for individual or team crafting of work designs that promotes team proactivity.[22] This way of organizing is not just for IT departments or for start-ups. In 2014 the US apparel retailer Zappos adopted 'holacracy',[23] a trademarked programme that represents an organic, self-managing structure in which formal job titles, managers and traditional hierarchies are abolished. Work is instead organized into either separate or overlapping circles in which collections of individuals collaborate in order to get the job done. Zappos uses self-steering teams in operations and call centres. There is no need for direct supervision by managers since, with continuous use of apps, management and the teams themselves can see how they are progressing and this data then feeds into the outcome-based performance management system. Staff are invited to join or leave according to their skill set. Staff lease their software, space and training from a budget they are given, then are left to get on with the job. Instead of having static job descriptions, individuals in a holacracy assume multiple roles, each associated with a purpose and domain, and accountabilities. Disciplined activity is necessary to realize positive outcomes. Essentially holacracy is a method of decentralized management and organizational governance, which claims to distribute authority and decision making through a holarchy.

That is not to say that leadership does not exist. Each project still has a leader who also acts as coach. Each circle has a project coordinator or lead who needs the key skills of a manager, i.e. good communication, the ability to inspire others and organizational skills. By implication, the nature of leadership required is less about managing people and more about visioning and empowering them to act. Leadership becomes a capability, not a person. Transparency is central to this way of operating since staff are held to account by their peers. The model is thus based on trust and win-win outcomes.

### Squads and tribes

Banks are under fierce pressure to cut costs and manage digital disruption. Some banks are embracing a variation on agile teamwork pioneered by

Spotify and Netflix. ANZ has overhauled the management structure of its Australian division. The new operational approach ('New Ways of Working') involves slashing bureaucracy and hierarchies to create instead multidisciplinary teams that should be able to respond to competitive threats much more quickly, improve the way the bank responds to customer needs, empower staff and improve productivity. The restructure aims to leave the division with 150 'agile' teams that will look more like start-ups than traditional parts of a large-scale bank. The changes should cut the time taken to roll out new products and make the bank more adaptable to disruptive shifts in technology, markets and regulation.

The stable backbone of iterative coordination consists, for example, of a 90-day priority-setting and resourcing cycle, a common culture, 'chapters' (i.e. groupings of employees with similar functional backgrounds) responsible for consistency, a longer-term vision for specific functional areas and agile leadership. When companies (such as ING, Spark and TDC) scale up to hundreds of teams, these enterprise-level elements of unity become extremely important.

Dutch-based ING Bank, once a traditional banking structure, with a conventional hierarchy, has embraced Agile principles across the organization over several years to build a fundamentally customer-centric organization.[24] Given the pace of change in customer expectations driven by the digital revolution, ING needed to stop thinking traditionally about product marketing and start understanding customer journeys in this new omni-channel environment. A radically new approach to organization was needed if speed, innovation and excellent customer outcomes were to become the norm.

ING's leaders believed it was important to start at the core. Accordingly, a team was set up comprising previously separate departments such as marketing, product management, channel management and IT development to consider agile ways of working. ING learned from pioneering organizations in other industries, such as Spotify, who have found that adopting iterative approaches to change, high levels of training, self-managing teams and empowerment produces better business results in ING's fast-changing business environment. As the COO, one of the change architects, describes it: 'We gave up traditional hierarchy, formal meetings, over-engineering, detailed planning, and excessive "input steering" in exchange for empowered teams, informal networks, and "output steering".'[25]

Agile structures and ways of working were introduced in 2015, initially for 3,500 staff members at group headquarters. The new structures, roles and team formations (tribes, squads and chapters) formalize customer-centricity and shared learning and minimize hindering bureaucracy. Squads are the basis of the agile organization. They comprise no more than nine people drawn from different functions; they are self-steering and autonomous and are dismantled as soon as their mission is over. A product owner is a squad member, not a leader, and is responsible for coordinating squad activities. Tribes are collections of squads with interconnected missions and include approximately 150 people who empower the tribe, lead to establish priorities and allocate budgets. An Agile coach helps individuals and squads to create high-performing teams. Chapters develop expertise and knowledge across the squads. Each chapter lead is responsible for one chapter and represents hierarchy for squad members, e.g. for performance management. Spotify uses a similar structure with loosely coupled but tightly aligned 'squads' encouraged to act as 'good citizens' with regard to sharing information.

## Setting up agile teams

Agile organizations require a learning mindset in the mainstream business and underlying lean and agile processes to support innovation. Agile project teams are part of the overall mix alongside operations teams. Among some of the pioneers of agile ways of working – such as Spotify and ING – teams, often called squads, combining developers, testers, data analysts, customer-journey specialists and user-interface designers, tended to work mainly on digital projects. But similar models have now been launched across the whole spectrum of business and technology. Retailers use squads built around specific product categories to drive volume and margin. Telecom providers ask squads to simplify products. Some companies are applying agile teamwork to transforming company culture.

### Design principles

Six design principles that underpin ethical work design and ensure people have line of sight to purpose include:

1  Create autonomous clusters of tasks.
   o  Tasks that have a high level of interdependence should be combined into one organizational cluster.
   o  In this way, the clusters created have optimal autonomy, thus preventing coordination cost, collaboration problems, and conflict.

   Such an approach has been pioneered by organizations such as Spotify, ING Bank, etc.[26]

**2** Create self-sufficient teams.

Four important aspects make a team empowered and self-sufficient:

- The team is assigned a semi-autonomous cluster of tasks (the first design principle).
- The team has the authority and responsibility to use the resources they need to perform the tasks allocated to them.
- The team needs to have both the information and the authority to solve problems and improve performance.
- The team has the skills and expertise among its members to perform the tasks required and solve the problems that impact its performance.
- Critical attributes for agile project teams include flexibility, adaptability, focus, a strong sense of purpose, viable processes.

**3** Manage the tensions between organizational units.

**4** Prevent redundant management layers.

**5** Create enough flexibility in the design to fit the context.

**6** Do not overdesign.[27]

The people who will thrive in agile teams may differ from those who enjoy traditional project working. For instance, stereotypically millennial workers will embrace agile approaches more readily than the traditional ones.

Teams will self-organize their work strategy, structure and collaboration paths to reflect the context. They may need guidance to do this well. Leaders of successful operations provide the right structures, processes, training and incentives to build a culture supportive of innovation and managed risk by, for example:

- establishing the set of values that underpin innovation efforts
- making decisions that define expectations
- setting goals that encourage and make it safe for others to innovate
- making decisions on innovation budgets
- adopting new measures of success and rewarding those who excel at them
- defining innovation governance responsibilities
- defining roles, key responsibilities of the main players and ways of working around the innovation process
- defining decision power lines and commitments on innovation.

And, in line with Galbraith's Star Model™, employees' coping ability is affected not only by space, structure and role but also by the unique culture of the company and the structure of top management – and the incentive system. Leaders stimulate innovation and creativity by encouraging and rewarding staff for using their knowledge in new ways to solve existing or emerging problems. Leaders must accept that, as new opportunities are developed in the process of trial and error, there will be some setbacks. Senior leaders must manage the tension between risk and mitigation; they must ensure that teams are clear as to what is expected of them and emphasize the outcomes that matter most to the organization's stakeholders – its shareholders, customers and others. By bounding experiments with agreed-upon criteria, and capturing learning, leaders can ensure that there is effective risk management of new ideas and that the company's capabilities are continuously improved. They must ensure that staff have the delegated authority required to make decisions related to their work, especially where their specific knowledge adds significant value.

Creating an agile environment has fundamental implications for managers and leaders, for the structuring of work and for the development of an increasingly self-managed team culture. While the idea of self-organizing teams has been around since the 1980s, the implications for the roles of line managers are only slowly emerging. At the very least, managers need to be versatile, able both to take direct control when appropriate and to be coach/ facilitator when it is not. A commitment to communication, training and change management is fundamental to success.

## Integrated functions

Some firms build integrative service delivery models with commissioning organizations, suppliers and other third parties working together. This means embedding agility in infrastructural disciplines such as IT, HR and Finance to support software-driven businesses. One of the world's leading universities carried out an overhaul of its administrative services. The intention was to design the organization for operational excellence that would enable the institution to be flexible and able to adapt to environmental challenges and opportunities. Over time many departments had built up their own systems and practices supported by dedicated administrative staff, but the complexity of the administrative environment made it very difficult to get work done, as the following quotations suggest:

- 'Our processes are complex: there are multiple approvals required for every sign-off.'

- 'Services are fragmented across multiple departments.'

- 'We have duplication of effort – departments across campus all figuring out how to do the same things.'

- 'Few processes are standardized: each department has their own way of doing POs.'

- 'There is not enough automation: many people still fill out time sheets with pen and paper.'

- 'Our incentives are misaligned – individuals optimize locally at the expense of the university.'

The challenge would be to simplify this complexity in order to: create an effective and efficient operating environment; create a financially sustainable future; instil a culture of continuous improvement and high performance over time with greater opportunities for professional growth.

---

CASE STUDY
*Example of how an integrated shared service was formed*

A single integrated shared service centre (SSC) was formed from four functional areas doing 'shareable work'– Research Administration, IT, HR, and Business and Financial Services. It was recognized that success is not just about technology implementation – it is about people and the use of technology and therefore requires both system and behavioural change. People would need to be equipped with the tools, methods, practices and mindsets to work in the new ways and integrate the new approach into day-to-day activities.

The move to the new site took place in waves, and units were given six months' advance notice to prepare for the move. As the transfer deadline approached, every month would bring fresh communications and milestones to ensure that the service and the people were on track to migrate to the SSC. Around 500 staff doing 50 per cent of the shareable work were reassigned. HR business partners remained close to their clients, in on-campus service centres.

Motivating employees to align their behaviour with the organization's strategy (strategic alignment) and give their best efforts (employee engagement) was a key challenge for senior leadership.[28] Many staff felt a sense of loss as the people and manual processes were replaced by technology and self-service. The new arrangements also increased the workload for faculty members who now had to input their own data. Indeed, once the SSC was up and running, the annual staff satisfaction survey indicated that many SSC staff missed being on campus and felt out of touch with the university's mission. Moreover, attitudes towards SSC staff changed when they were no longer based on campus.

To improve staff engagement, there was a deliberate and continuing focus on helping people feel connected. For instance, faculty started coming to the SSC to run lunchtime events. There were quarterly townhall meetings, streamed so that people could participate wherever they were based. An indicator of improving morale was that the annual staff picnic was now attended by more people than previously. On the whole staff remained very committed to the university's purpose, which proved a unifying rationale for embracing the change and producing the improved efficiencies and cost savings the organization was seeking.

## New organizational forms

New organizational forms are emerging, often in tech-led environments, which offer frameworks for building organizational environments geared for collaboration, innovation and continuous adaptation. Companies such as Wikipedia, Spotify, Nike, Google and Zappos are leading the way in creating collaborative, non-hierarchical ways of organizing that enable customer focus and collaboration. Rather than through fixed structures, work is delivered through networks of activities and teams of teams. Such company structures are built to be change-able, to enable agile working practices and improve productivity. They are resilient, with robust systems and learning approaches that emphasize fluidity of information flows between connected minds rather than top-down decision making.

More organic forms of design, such as networks, are highly flexible and adaptable and bring the potential for business advantage through continuous releases of innovations and optimal use of talent. Many of the tensions that can arise when attempting to scale up agility from team level include:

- tensions within traditional hierarchy
- inadequate resource or team leaders with the necessary skills
- lack of coordination/synchronization
- potential duplication/gaps
- risk of chaos.

Often the tensions arise from fear of loss or from risk to the individuals authorizing or required to support new arrangements.

Managers who associate agility with uncoordinated change, chaos and a loss of managerial control tend to micro-manage in a way that can seriously undermine the trust and empowerment required for agility. Embedding an outside-in orientation that maximizes customer value may require a reinvention of management roles, work practices, values and communications.[29] In more organic structures the manager's job is to optimize support for the team and to focus on capability building. Managers must keep sight of local optimization – and recognize the importance of teamwork, flexibility and agility – so must prevent silos from building up. Managers should also enable diversity and employee wellbeing.

Office-space design is being used to encourage innovative ways of working and to ensure that people take advantage of collaboration, build a fluid understanding of work and act intentionally. To promote personal reflection, rooms with ping-pong tables and bean bags are provided that offer chance to relax and reflect; collaborative labs, e.g. with a big white wall, enable idea sharing. Some firms provide smartphones and cloud-based collaboration tools that offer constant connectivity and erase the traditional 9–5 workday.

Other newer design types include:

- Flatarchy – Flatter structures allow employees from different levels to make decisions in the organization. An example of this type of structure is when an organization has an internal hub or innovation centre or 'skunk works'. The company lets employees pitch any new ideas that might help the company to grow. Examples include Google, 3M, Adobe, LinkedIn.

- Wirearchy (Jon Husband) – The emergent principle of wirearchy clarifies the dynamics of networked environments and brings the 'soft skills' of managing people and work into focus. Use is made of conceptually integrated methodologies and tools, such as organigraphs, strategy maps, strategy canvas, network analysis, sensemaking and other approaches emerging from this new set of conditions. These tools are all useful means of engaging in purposeful conversation about the 'why' and 'what' of grounding the theory of a business or organization and implementing the best ideas.

While many organizations want to innovate, some may consider such dynamic structures too risky and decide that a fully agile design is not right for them. Nevertheless, some of their structural principles – such as delegating power, joint decision making, staff being free to act and a shared sense of purpose – are key aspects of agility. As organizations become ever more decentralized, with greater customer involvement, and as more project-based people work independently and for more than one employer at a time, new models of organizing will continue to evolve, and the transformation of manager roles is likely to continue apace.

Let us now turn our attention to the process of organization redesign, comparing conventional and more agile ways of designing.

## Conventional process of redesign

Alignment around the business purpose is an essential feature of organizational design. Organization redesigns at macro (whole system) level concern business unit structures and reflect changing business models: how a firm goes to market, its products and customers, annual budgets and so on. Conventional design processes derive from general systems theory, which assumes design involves:

- linear, planned change
- primacy of design
- primacy of environment
- bureaucratic rules
- dynamic equilibrium.

While there are many ways to design an organization, most redesigns occur by mandate – top-down, with senior management sponsoring the process. Sometimes, a core design team is set up, chartered by senior management, to work with a small number of employees from a cross-section of the organization to analyse, redesign and develop implementation plans. However, there are many benefits to be gained, not least buy-in to the change, by actively involving a wider group of employees in the design process. A conference model could be used to involve large numbers of people from a cross-section of the organization participating in real-time analysis. This creates a movement of people mobilized for change, with groups working on meaningful design projects.

## Be clear about what the design should achieve

A traditional process of organization design involves stakeholder and environmental analyses (typically PESTLE) conducted to establish how the structure may fit their varying needs:

- What is the strategy (and is it clear enough to guide design)?
- What are the new strategic growth choices? These set the frame for decisions about organization.
- What changes in organizational performance, capabilities and competencies are required to carry out the strategy?

## Agree criteria

- What should the 'ideal' design accomplish, achieve or facilitate?
- What are the constraints or 'givens' in the new design?
- Are there existing structures the new design has to work within?
- Are there specific financial objectives the design has to achieve?

## Carry out diagnosis

When addressing a specific aspect of design, whatever problem/issue you identify, consider the key stakeholders in that issue, e.g. users/customers, employees, managers and local trade unions. They should be involved in organization design projects at the earliest opportunity. A comprehensive organizational assessment using the Star Model™ or other analytical framework as a template helps gather information from a cross-section of participants about the effectiveness of the current organization design. This should identify ineffective workflows, processes, structures and systems. The diagnosis should:

- relate to the desired outcomes (strategy, criteria and valued outcomes)
- identify needed competencies and capabilities
- focus on what the organization does well, as well as what is not working well (usually an in-depth process mapping analysis takes place to identify gaps and root causes)
- draw together, interpret and visualize the results with reference to a design framework and principles
- lead to agreement on the problem to solve.

Galbraith's 4Ds – dialogue, decisions, design and development – underpin stakeholder 'ownership' of the emerging design. This occurs from the start of the design process if the right stakeholders are involved as a network to deliberate on the solution to the problem.

## Macro design

The macro design session can last several days, depending on the size and complexity of the organization. Participants outline the 'ideal' organization, together with its ideal processes, structures and systems for the whole organization. They will streamline and simplify core processes, structures and reconfigure how business units, functions and teams organize around those processes.

For example when orienting work around core processes:

- Reconfigure how business units, departments, support groups and teams organize around those processes.
- Integrate all roles within self-organizing scrum teams; minimize project manager role.
- Work out implications for the kinds of management approaches required.
- Clarify governance arrangements.

In choosing a structure for your organization, consider its environment and strategic goals, and try to strike a balance between control and adaptability. Agile organizations often suffer from lack of synchronization. In enabling bureaucracies, rules and regulations can be helpful in enhancing the performance of an organization; standards are used to improve workers' capabilities and serve to transfer the best way of performing tasks, provide alignment between different jobs, and facilitate redesign of work processes. The challenge is to strike the right balance between Weick's[30] 'loose' form of coupling – where work is designed to be flexible and to enable improvization – and 'tight' coupling, often through centralization, which keeps people closely managed and decision making 'owned' within certain roles. Too much fixedness risks rigidity and tightly coupled systems tend to collapse when things go wrong.

While loose coupling can enable empowerment, too much flexibility makes decision-making difficult. To avoid this, Nike has centre-led design and brand marketing functions that act as integrators at the hub of an agile network of know-how. Some organizations have portfolio governance teams made up of cross-functional teams of leaders to approve investment incre-ments at the portfolio level of the organization.

## Plan to transition

In the micro design, identify all transition and implementation activities necessary to successfully embed the new design throughout the organiza-tion, for example:

- employee communication
- leadership training
- staffing changes that may need to happen before start-up begins
- team development – training people for empowerment
- limit turnover of key employees by actively communicating programme milestones and benefits at an individual and company level.

Tracking measures should be identified for the new design, which will be put in place at start-up (or sooner) on the journey to build the agile organiza-tion. These should be sequenced on a master implementation timeline. For each task or set of activities, include outline action plans.

## New design implementation

- New jobs and job changes are posted.
- Teams are co-located; new reporting relationships begin.
- Training and development.
- Resources are moved.
- Reward systems are adjusted.
- Coordination systems such as communication and information sharing are adjusted and improved.

## Embed and revisit

Ensure a review takes place:

- What are the success measures?
- Have we made progress?
- What have we learned?

While the general principles of conventional design are still valid, looking ahead, design processes are likely to change further.

## An agile design process

Increasingly organizations are being designed as platforms and networks. The organization design process must therefore involve the whole socio-technical system – the increasingly important relations between humans and machines – with the aim of joint optimization. Designing for agility increasingly draws on complexity theory(ies),[31] a perspective that primarily concerns itself with emergence of dynamic patterns, often at the edge of chaos.[32] From a perspective of complex adaptive systems, what one considers the 'organization' versus the 'edge' is actually an interconnected pattern of constantly changing dynamics.[33] Complex adaptive systems are subject to non-linear and iterative, agile change; they are self-organizing, have simple rules and give primacy to relationships and co-evolution.

To design an agile operating model, the organization's means of generating value for customers should be mapped in a series of value streams, against which the operating model is structured and relevant teams identified. It is important to look at the whole system and ask:

- What is driving change in the firm's environment and what are the strategic goals?
- Who are the key customer segments?
- How will digital transform the way work is delivered? Why structure this way?

It is also important to measure the organization's change readiness and assess management capability when selecting the proposed structure.

The 'backbone' in the form of technology, core processes and people to enable agility should be put in place and priorities identified for next steps. So, first, design the strategic architecture – the executive team and the layer below. Then the hierarchy below that must be redefined in relation to the business and operating model – the part of the organization that creates value for the customer.

Key capabilities should be identified. What new capabilities and behaviours will be needed to implement the strategy? What does this mean for jobs and skills? Since organizations will need to change strategy quickly, key organizational capabilities include the ability to rapidly modify execution and learn at high frequency (these should be among the key design criteria). Do staff have the appropriate resources and the right interfaces with other parts of the organization? What lateral processes can be put in place across the system to solve whatever gets in the way of performance? Are these structures appropriate to a fast-changing environment?' Thus, designs should enable the best ideas to move fast across brands, people to collaborate and the rapid integration of insights.

Hierarchy is still relevant even in the context of digital innovation. Senior management will still need to know what's driving competitive advantage and ensure that the organization is developing and advancing the right portfolio of activities. They need to ensure that the right teams are working on it, and pulling together the innovation picture. The top team will still need to ensure that productivity is on track and work out how and where to deploy resources. Governance will still need to be exercised.

### Designing from a socio-technical perspective

Critical to redesigning organizations is having a clear link between purpose – *why* we do what we do and *what* we do – the business mission and strategy focus. This provides the rationale for new ways of working – the *how* we organize ourselves to deliver outcomes for customers. Given that many people will be involved in the design process, a clear purpose, values and strategy are the glue that will enable all these multifunctional co-designers to coalesce around a common goal and clear criteria for success.

Process leaders write a definition statement/design brief that is called a 'product vision'. The focus of design needs to be human; technology is needed to make sense of data and help with the design but should not be the primary driver. Smart machines must be matched by smart co-workers to come up with new solutions for customers and competitiveness. If the company's competitive stance is defensive and over-controlling, how can people and organizations learn fast enough? In such a case, the nature of the socio-technical system change required involves a structure that can respond fast, learn and enable the firm to take both offensive and defensive strategic positions. The design applies to the whole organization and the emerging organization will be a team of teams – very dynamic.

The key design principles should derive from Agile – customer-centric, transparency, prototyping, iterations and review. Design tools such as stakeholder participation and organization-wide co-design – any large groups – and rapid prototyping can be used as an intact work system, not just an event. Design teams work on iterations, with the process leaders pulling those iterations into a steady state that includes a set of metrics. When the parts of the system that you are developing have a set of metrics, they can all produce to that set of metrics.

Engagement all around is vital – first between the agile team and the change management resource to ensure that the people side keeps up with the technical side. Engagement of senior leaders, both in support of the initiative and Agile as an approach, is critical. Finally, engaging impacted employees through consistent communication and celebrating success creates the necessary momentum to keep the effort progressing.

## Example of a socio-technical design process

American consultant Stu Winby orchestrated an organization design within a traditional US health-care system.[34] The aim was to use technology to improve patient care and enable patients with long-term chronic health needs to better manage their treatment at home. The process was broadly as follows:

**Research** – The patient journey and communication channels – emails, etc – were plotted to create an ecosystem map. This involved ethnographic data-gathering interviews and touchpoint analysis. Key gaps and duplications were identified through a variance analysis and an ideation map was developed to show what 'better' could look like from the perspective of patients.

**Design lab** – This was co-designed by all members of the team, including many patients and technology specialists. The focus was on how to eliminate problems identified by the research. The design resulted in the roles and responsibilities of different people in the ecosystem shifting. The people working on coding put together the software platform that brought the socio- and technical systems together.

**Prototyping** – The test phase – an app – changed the role of nurses and created new roles. This required changing the parent structure and led to centre transformation. Five pilots were trialled inside the organization to change to a team-based design for the work system. This trialling helped the organizers to understand what resistance might be anticipated and what was needed for people to accept the new technology and the prototype.

**Roll-out** – Once tested and working, the new practices were scaled across 70 centres, effectively becoming the new organization.

The following case study describes a systemic and profoundly human approach to increasing agility through organization design in one of the world's most respected design, engineering and project management consultancies.

---

CASE STUDY
*SNC-Lavalin's Atkins business*

I am grateful to Nick Roberts, previously President of Atkins, SNC-Lavalin's Engineering, Design and Project Management sector for kindly providing this case study on organization redesign within the UK and Europe region.

SNC-Lavalin's Atkins business is one of the world's most respected design, engineering and project management consultancies, employing some 18,300 people across the United Kingdom, North America, the Middle East, Asia Pacific and Europe. Together, SNC-Lavalin, a globally fully integrated professional services and project management company, and Atkins help their clients to plan, design and enable major capital projects, and provide expert consultancy that covers the full life cycle of projects.

Nick Roberts was President of SNC-Lavalin's Atkins business from January 2018. Prior to that he ran the Atkins business in the UK and Europe region. Nick was with the company for 20 years, holding several managing director positions across a variety of sectors.

During his time as UK and Europe CEO, Nick instituted substantial change at Atkins – both structural and, more specifically, cultural. Nick believed that change was necessary; that companies that stand still end up going backwards. Nick's concern was how to equip the business to survive and thrive in an increasingly volatile business environment. Change became more targeted, with a focus on improving operational efficiency – taking cost out, improving the efficiency of processes and signalling more efficient ways of working. However, Nick argues that focusing on efficiency alone is not sufficient to create a more agile organization. In fact, 'if you're not careful you can reinforce the old ways of doing things by increasing the efficiency of a moribund organization.'

The drive for a more strategic approach to change came principally from the market forces affecting the company's clients. Until the recent past, clients had been able to predict the shape and size of their capital programmes far in advance on a rolling five-year basis. 'We could foresee the spend, and so long as we discharged our work effectively, we had a successful business. However, now our clients – especially in the water and rail sectors – are changing in ways they can't control.' A bigger stretch was needed to build organizational agility – to create new ways of thinking and doing that would enable the Atkins business to anticipate and respond to change, meet client needs with speed and keep it ahead of its competitors.

Although Atkins was, and is, a very successful business, given the scale of change in the business environment, its ways of operating and social system were becoming difficult to work within. Nick was in a good position to gauge the scale of the change required since, as he points out: 'In many respects, I was a successful product of the old social system – with its strong vertical hierarchy, engineering/science discipline-centric culture, and self-determination as a leader. We had multiple P&Ls around, with smaller discipline-centric teams "owning" a client. These days, to serve our clients well, we need to be able to collaborate across disciplines/market boundaries, so the vertical boundaries were becoming a limiting factor and unfortunately the organization had become very inflexible. If teams needed to collaborate to meet the needs of clients, this could cause friction about who owned the client. So, if clients had lost their ability to predict, and we were not able to collaborate across boundaries, if we were not careful, we could start losing business.'

## Mobilizing people for change

To institute change on the scale Nick envisaged required widespread support and initially there was no burning platform for defining a new social system since the company was successful. The general view at the top was 'if it ain't broke, why fix it?' Moreover, the Atkins business operates globally, but its cultural heritage was British, warm and fuzzy, and many colleagues could not see the need for change. The shared assumption was that the organization would continue to be able to meet market expectations. Moreover, a high proportion of employees are engineers who are deeply invested in the purpose of the organization and geared towards solving complex problems – and are less likely to be motivated by the idea of driving business profits for shareholders.

   In Nick's view, this general lack of awareness of the need for a more agile approach was a risk factor. Nick's previous role had been with the US business where he was responsible for transforming an acquisition that had started to struggle. In that case, there was a clear burning platform that all could see. In the UK case, however, and in a larger organization, there was no perceived burning platform. What was needed was a much wider appreciation of the need for change and a willingness to embrace new ways of working. Therefore, Nick set out to create urgency – to motivate people to get things done: 'So when I became regional CEO, I saw my job as being to convince my most senior colleagues and the wider community of the need for change and for redefining the social system and the way we do business. What was valuable was that we started to create a language that change was required – we signalled this consistently. The first 18 months were difficult and it took a lot of effort to make people aware and for a lot of people to make the change.'

## Structuring the transition to agile

Nick aimed to engineer the whole organization in an adaptive way to create a seamless, frictionless way of operating and a highly connected organization. But to bring about the changes needed, Nick deliberately steered away from delegating change to a change leadership group: 'Intuition told me that a change delivery team would be rejected. People were likely to be passively aggressive towards a small change team and the change would be stopped dead. Instead, I wanted this to be about change for the people by the people. I worked with the adaptive leadership change approach (of Heifetz and Laurie).'[35]

Nick used structural change to create a very visible burning platform for a new social system. 'I know that structural change is rarely successful but in this case I believed I needed to radically disrupt the organization to enable collaboration. So, I had to completely reinvent the organization. I took down the vertical siloed model of 350 P+L "walls" and instituted a complete matrix – a common, consistent structure throughout the whole business. These were the first signals of ripping apart the horse-trading and creating a new social system.'

## Resistance to transitioning to agile

Of course, structural change of this nature and scale was deeply threatening to some executives, but agile leaders need to be ambidextrous: good at empowering others, but prepared to step up and be decisive when required. Nick tackled this resistance head-on, taking the view that he had to be 'bloody-minded' and insist that executives adopt the new approach because otherwise the change would fail.

Then the main resistance challenge came from the middle management levels: 'They could not believe that I, who had been successful within the old social system, was making such drastic changes. To make things happen, I had to be determined, courageous, obstreperous and bloody-minded.' However, as is often the case, where change can be challenging for some, for others it comes as a long-awaited, welcome liberation. As the new structures started to be implemented, much of the workforce came on board with the change and started to feel more empowered as a result. 'Within the first three months I knew we had a huge body of the organization below the top 500 who were pro-change.'

## Operating principles

Nick wanted the Atkins business to become a more sensing, feeling, self-healing organization. Yet, one of the common challenges of culture change is if the values and culture embedded in new organizational practices are potentially in conflict with a company's existing culture. Then the business needs to actively encourage behaviours that support its new objectives. This is not just a question of producing new wall posters about company values. To truly unlearn existing behavioural patterns there must be both a demand for new behaviour that builds on the desired values and an opportunity to practise it.

Thinking through how new management practices will – or will not – fit with the existing culture is an important first step in bringing about change. In Nick Roberts' case, he formed a team to work with people across the organization to define eight high-level operating principles that would act as behavioural 'guard rails' by which the business would hold itself accountable over coming years. These created the core vernacular on the new ways of 'how we operate around here'. For instance, one principle emphasizes that the health and safety of people is non-negotiable while others signal new directions, such as 'everyone is an equal partner and has an equal part to play'.

Though the principles needed some explanation in order for them to land, they have now been widely embraced and have become a central sign around which behavioural change is achievable. To bring the principles to life and make these changes happen, a short series of sprints (initially of 100 days) took place. As momentum for behaviour change grew, later sprints took just 10 days. By summer 2015, a more dynamic structure and a new behavioural social system that was more democratic for people were progressing well. All of this while the business continued to perform well.

## New ways of communicating

Agile communication is key to empowering people. To develop the sensing, feeling, self-healing aspects of the new social system required a different way of communicating from in the past – to be more intelligence-led and open in the way of sharing information.

Nick Roberts had been inspired by the shared leadership model and culture – 'team of teams' approach – of General Stanley A McChrystal, best known for his command of Joint Special Operations in Afghanistan in the mid-2000s. McChrystal believed that a purely vertical chain of command style of leadership and top-down 'cascade' forms of communication on a need-to-know basis were too slow to reach the troops in the field and were placing them at risk. Nick adapted the 'team of teams' communication approach by developing a regular 'cadence' call to share intelligence information as widely as possible, bottom-up as well as top-down. McChrystal's teams were able to use the intelligence to inform their actions on the ground. Establishing this platform brought all the high-level operating principles to life, in particular 'sharing knowledge is power', which puts a modern twist on the old adage that 'knowledge is power'. This resulted in a higher-tempo organization whose soldiers were empowered to use their initiative in hostile environments.

Nick believes that in a commercial setting such an approach is just as valuable. After all, the commercial environment is volatile and clients' needs are changing all the time. For Nick, the key to agility is building a connected organization that understands the mission but is not beholden to a hard-and-fast strategy when things are changing all the time. So, in the UK and Europe region, the top 300–400 people get together every month for the cadence call – a video conference to share client intelligence and new initiatives. On a weekly basis, Nick's managing directors hold an 'Operations and Intelligence' (O&I) call with 3,000 divisional and functional heads who, in turn, have similar calls with their hundreds of team members. In these calls, the intelligence and issues of the week are shared in a much quicker, more agile way than in the past. A Yammer feed runs alongside this, with people able to raise questions and get the answers they need on the call. The calls have also been helpful in connecting people. Since people can see each other on the video calls, they get to know one another, and who to contact for specific matters, wherever they are based. Thus, the social media system becomes the new social system.

So even in large and traditional organizations such as SNC-Lavalin's Atkins business, agility is possible. A combination of strong leadership vision and purpose, mobilizing people for change through new ways of communicating and increasing their awareness of the ways in which the business environment is changing, together with new organizational forms and a willingness to experiment, has enabled the rapid implementation of new ways of operating and the development of a more agile culture. In these and other ways, SNC-Lavalin's Atkins business has moved quickly in the direction of greater agility while also producing solid results, with a strong premium on its share price.

## Conclusion

As the SNC-Lavalin's Atkins business case illustrates, organizations can use design as a tool to create enabling bureaucracies and cultures that support agility and customer-centricity. There are many legitimate areas for HR to add value through its expertise, so the time is right for practitioners to embrace agility and customer-centricity. By collaborating with colleagues from marketing, sales or other external-facing functions that lead customer-experience projects, HR can use its expertise to enable empowerment, develop empowering leadership and fit-for-purpose performance management. In the process, HR gets closer to the end customer, improves its own practices, and increases its relevance and reputation.

Therefore, the agility design challenge for HR is to find the 'sweet spot' where value can be generated for the employee, for the customer and for the business. Creating truly agile, customer-centric organizations requires a partnership between technology, operations and people. Line managers too have key roles to play. As organizations move towards streamlined organizational structures, flatter management layers, the adoption of team-working processes and employee empowerment, line managers who 'own' people management all have a key role in building organizational agility. As organizations continue to evolve at pace in form and culture, bringing opportunities for those who embrace them, they need to explore various new possibilities for organization configuration, processes for getting work done and the redesigning of an organization's variables. This involves choices about work design, technology, people, rewards, coordination, information flow and layout.

Under the mechanistic assumptions of bureaucracy, partnership was not required because the role of each organization part was clear and complete. Under the increasingly fast-paced demands of customers and technology, that assumption is no longer valid, if it ever was.

In the next chapter we look at the work and management practices involved in implementing strategy.

---

CHECKLIST

What is the strategy? Is it clear enough to guide design? Is there a shared understanding of this strategy to guide coordinated activity across the business or functions?

- How does the current structure facilitate or impede work effectiveness/ strategy accomplishment?

- What design features are required to support the business logic?

- What is the core structure? What goes in the centre?

- What are the units at the next level down?

- Are there the right kinds of connections across units and/or with customers/ suppliers/partners to be able to effectively and efficiently make decisions, integrate work and resolve issues?

- Are the various parts of the organization well-linked through the information technology system?
- Does the right information get where it needs to be for empowerment and effective performance? Does information get shared across the organization? Where does this break down?
- Which major work processes/capabilities currently work well (or are integrated) and which need to be improved? Where does coordination/integration break down?
- What kinds of lateral roles/structures can be established to achieve integration/synchronization across your core units?
- What capabilities need to be built laterally into the organization?
- What cross-business teams and governance are needed?
- What should be leveraged?
- Where should entrepreneurial behaviour be encouraged?
- Is there a good process for developing people in new roles?
- Does the performance assessment process focus on the key individual and collective performances required?
- Is the firm developing the right leadership capability at all levels, as well as the lateral leadership capabilities required?
- Does the reward system motivate and reward required individual, team and business-unit performance?
- Is the reward system flexible enough for diversity of business units/work, yet also to foster the required inter-group collaboration?

# Notes

**1** Lawler, EE III, Mohrman, SA and Ledford, GE (1998) *Strategies for High Performance Organizations*, Center for Effective Organizations, San Francisco.
**2** Weick, KE (1979) The Social Psychology of Organizing, Second Edition, McGraw-Hill
**3** McKinsey. An operating model for the next normal: Lessons from agile organizations in the crisis, 25 June 2020, www.mckinsey.com/capabilities/people-and-organizational-performance/our-insights/an-operating-model-for-the-next-normal-lessons-from-agile-organizations-in-the-crisis (archived at https://perma.cc/PA5X-WZEW).

**4** Adler, PS and Borys, B (1996) Two types of bureaucracy: enabling and coercive, *Administrative Science Quarterly*, **41** (1), pp 61–89.

**5** Mangiofico, G (2013) Using trans-organizational development and complexity theory frameworks to establish a new early childhood education network, in C G Warley and P H Mirvis (eds) *Building Networks and Partnerships (Organizing for Sustainable Effectiveness, Volume 3)*, Emerald Group Publishing, Bingley, pp 35–63.

**6** Worley, CG, Williams, T and Lawler, EE III (2016) Creating management processes built for change, *MIT Sloan Management Review*, **58** (1), pp 77–82.

**7** Sherehiy, B, Karwowski, W and Layer, JK (2007) A review of enterprise agility: Concepts, frameworks, and attributes, *International Journal of Industrial Ergonomics*, **37** (5), pp 445–60.

**8** Dove, R (2001) *Response Ability: The language, structure, and culture of the agile enterprise*, Wiley, New York.

**9** Worley et al, ibid.

**10** Kates, A, Sinha, P and Pillans, G (2022) *Organization Design for Agility*, CRF, London.

**11** Galbraith, JR (2005) *Designing the Customer-Centric Organization: A guide to strategy, structure, and process*, Wiley, New York.

**12** Denning, S (2013) Why Agile can be a game changer for managing continuous innovation in many industries, *Strategy & Leadership*, **41** (2), pp 5–11, doi. org/10.1108/10878571311318187 (archived at https://perma.cc/HL8M-RHJ4).

**13** Hamel, G and Zanini, M. What we learned about bureaucracy from 7,000 HBR readers, *Harvard Business Review*, 10 August 2017, hbr.org/2017/08/what-we-learned-about-bureaucracy-from-7000-hbr-readers (archived at https://perma.cc/HR5F-7896).

**14** O'Reilly, CA and Tushman, ML (2013) Organizational ambidexterity: Past, present, future, *Academy of Management Perspectives*, **27** (4), pp 324–38.

**15** March, JG (1991) Exploration and exploitation in organizational learning, *Organization Science*, **2**, pp 71–87.

**16** Stu Winby in Parker, L (2016) Dialysis care: Out of clinics, into the home, *Silicon Valley Business Journal*, **34** (18), pp 4–5, stsroundtable.com/wp-content/uploads/2016/01/SatelliteHealthcare.Business-Journal.2016.pdf (archived at https://perma.cc/9U3P-FPBV).

**17** Parker, SK, Van den Broeck, A and Holman, D (2016) Work design influences: a synthesis of multilevel factors that affect the design of jobs, *Academy of Management Annals*, **11** (1), journals.aom.org/doi/10.5465/annals.2014.00 (archived at https://perma.cc/SCW3-ST2S)

**18** Galbraith, JR (1992) *The Business Unit of the Future*, CEO Publication G 92–3 (206), University of Southern California.

**19** Campion, MA, Papper, EM and Medsker, GJ (1996) Relations between work team characteristics and effectiveness: A replication and effectiveness, *Personnel Psychology*, **49** (2), pp 429–52; Xanthopoulou, D, Bakker, AB, Demerouti, E and Schaufeli, WB (2011)Work engagement and financial returns: A diary study on the role of job and personal resources, *Journal of Occupational and Organizational Psychology*, **82** (1); Hülsheger, UR, Anderson, N and Salgado, JF (2009) Team-level predictors of innovation at work: A comprehensive meta-analysis spanning three decades of research. *Journal of Applied Psychology*, **94** (5), pp 1128–45.

**20** Kates, RW, Travis, WR and Wilbanks, TJ (2012) Transformational adaptation when incremental adaptations to climate change are insufficient, *Proceedings of the National Academy of Sciences*, **109** (19), pp 7156–61.

**21** Axtell, C, Holman, D and Wall, T (2006) Promoting innovation: A change study, *Journal of Occupational and Organizational Psychology*, **79** (3), pp 509–16.

**22** Srikanth, K, Harvey, S and Peterson, R (2016) A dynamic perspective on diverse teams: Moving from the dual-process model to a dynamic coordination-based model of diverse team performance, *The Academy of Management Annals*, **10** (1), pp 453–93.

**23** Crush, P (2014) Managing without managers, *Edge Magazine*, May/June, pp 32–37.

**24** Mahadevan, D (2017) ING's agile transformation, *McKinsey Quarterly*, January, www.mckinsey.com/industries/financial-services/our-insights/ings-agile-transformation (archived at https://perma.cc/G78N-T7FF).

**25** Ibid.

**26** Thompson, JD (1967) *Organizations in Action: Social science bases of administrative theory*, McGraw-Hill, New York; Galbraith, JR and Kazanjian, RK (1986) Organizing to implement strategies of diversity and globalization: The role of matrix designs, *Human Resource Management*, **25**(1), p 37; de Sitter, LUJ, Friso den Hertog, F and Dankbaar, B (1997) From complex organizations with simple jobs to simple organizations with complex jobs, *Human Relations*, **50** (5); Puranam, P, Alexy, O and Reitzig, M (2014) What's 'new' about new forms of organizing, *The Academy of Management Review*, **39** (2), pp 162–80.

**27** Hackman, JR and Oldham, GR (1976) Motivation through the design of work: Test of a theory. *Organizational Behavior & Human Performance*, **16** (2), pp 250–79; Cherns, A (1987) Principles of sociotechnical design revisited, *Human Relations*, **40** (3), pp 153–62; Kuipers, H, Van Amelvoort, P and Kramer, E-H (2020) New ways of organizing: Alternatives to bureaucracy,: Acco, Leuven/Den Haag.

**28** Stallard, ML (2009) The force of connection: Boost employee engagement, productivity and innovation, *Developing HR Strategy*, Croner, Issue 29, November, pp 5–8.

**29** Denning, ibid.

**30** Weick, KE (1976) Educational organizations as loosely coupled systems, *Administrative Science Quarterly*, **21** (1), pp 1–19.

**31** Burnes, B (2005) Complexity theories and organizational change, *International Journal of Management Reviews*, **7** (2), pp 73–90.

**32** Beeson, I and Davis, C (2000) Emergence and accomplishment in organizational change, *Journal of Organizational Change Management*, **13** (2), pp 178–89; Haigh, C (2002) Using chaos theory: The implications for nursing, *Journal of Advanced Nursing*, **37** (5), pp 462–69.

**33** Gleick, J (1988) *Chaos: Making a New Science*, Penguin, London.

**34** Parker, L (2016) Dialysis care: Out of clinics, into the home, *Silicon Valley Business Journal*, **34** (18), pp 4–5, stsroundtable.com/wp-content/uploads/2017/08/Silicon-Valley-Business-Journal.pdf (archived at https://perma.cc/T9S4-283J).

**35** Heifetz, RA and Laurie, DL (2001) The work of leadership, *Harvard Business Review*, **79** (11), pp 131–40.

# 06

# Agile implementation

To improve performance in fast-moving times it is essential to quickly translate strategic intent into action. In Chapter 5 we looked at how the agile routines of strategizing and perceiving/sensing help to close the implementation gap by creating shared ownership of the organization's strategy. Boudreau argues that strategic plans should always be accompanied by execution plans and organizational goals that translate into actionable deliverables across four interrelated aspects of performance: market, culture, leadership and talent.[1] This involves making specific choices about the priorities, working practices and enabling mechanisms to achieve product breakthroughs and productivity improvements in a given context.

Operations are where the 'rubber hits the road'. If the pace of change were slower, organizations could evolve at a gentler pace. With change becoming continuous, change-ability should be embedded in the organization's operating model. This involves adapting structures, systems and work processes on an ongoing basis and clear and unambiguous performance goals and measures that support the business model.[2]

In this chapter we focus on some of the Agile processes involved in executing strategy and in creating new products and services at speed. Agile itself is a philosophy and a best-of-breed collection of methodologies, such as 'lean' used to develop and maintain software, that is now being more broadly applied to projects of other kinds. Indeed, Agile is being embraced by companies such as Phillips in order to become more entrepreneurial. Innovation becomes the new 'business as usual'. We shall look at how agile organizations *test* possible responses, and *implement* changes in their products, technology, operations, structures, systems and overall capabilities.

We therefore also consider some key features of a learning culture that is conducive to innovation:

- agile operations
- a culture conducive to innovation
- agile work practices
- project-based working
- experimenting – the routines of exploration and innovation
- designing work for agility and empowerment.

We look further at the process of change from the people perspective in the online resources.

## Agile operations

Agile organizations usually need to be 'ambidextrous',[3] aligned and efficient in their management of today's business demands as well as adaptive to changes in their environment.[4] Ambidexterity is achieved by balancing the routines of exploration and exploitation, which allow the organization to be creative and adaptable, while also delivering through more traditional, proven methods of business.[5] Working practices must be fit for purpose and agile, informed by Agile values. Developing agile operations requires new approaches to what Kevin Kelly describes generically as 'clockware' and 'swarmware'.[6] 'Clockware' refers to what is involved in operating the core production processes of the organization in such a way that they are planned, rational, standardized and controllable. In contrast 'swarmware' describes those management processes that explore new possibilities through experimentation, testing, autonomy, intuition and working at the edge of knowledge and experience. Both are needed – it is a question of balancing reason and intuition, planning and implementing.

As discussed, customers are at the heart of agility. The cultural emphasis is on being customer-intensive, iterative, enabling experimentation and innovation. This focuses the whole organization 'outside in' on meeting the needs of the users or purchasers of its products or services. By instituting iterative and incremental development guided by a set of customer-focused management practices and values, requirements and solutions evolve through collaboration between self-organizing, cross-functional teams and their customers.[7] In practice, this requires an organizational culture where sense making, decision making and action taking are tightly coupled, rapidly and repeatedly iterated, deeply embedded and widely distributed throughout the organization.

For the effective implementation of an operating model Dave Ulrich and colleagues propose that certain capabilities are essential – leadership, speed, learning, accountability and talent through leveraging human resources.[8] For an agile operating model I would add to this list: collaboration, customer responsiveness, strategic clarity, shared mindset/culture, efficiency and the attributes of robustness, resilience, responsiveness, flexibility, innovation and adaptation, identified by Alberts and Hayes.[9]

Worley and Mohrman[10] suggest the following key operating model ingredients of agile organizations:

- **Leaders who provide direction, coach and develop team capability – not command and control**
  - flat and lean structures
  - strong cross-organizational collaboration
  - lateral teams that are effective at driving performance and decision making
- **Clear accountabilities for business units, functions, teams and individuals**
  - whole-process focus with clear customer value
  - skills and knowledge to deliver customer value – without day-to-day management control
  - clear responsibilities and decision making
  - held accountable for results
  - leverages knowledge and resources across units
- **Mechanisms to learn and improve performance over time**
  - Share learning, experiment and test, benchmark and apply performance improvement methods
- **Organizational members who understand and are involved in the success of the business**
  - active involvement and participation
  - share in business success
  - know how their work contributes to business success
  - coordinate effectively with other business units.

Perhaps the most important aspect of an agile operating model is the 'swarm-ware' – a workforce that is actively involved in the success of the business. This requires a future-first, action-oriented mindset to replace a 'wait and see' approach as Deloitte points out: 'A more value-driven operating model that prioritizes agility and convenience for the customer involves everyone in delivering a particular value stream in multi-functional teams, rather than working in separate functions such as IT, marketing, etc. This allows the right people to be connected to the right information at the right time. Thus, they are empowered to make decisions at the coal face and can move more quickly in a very agile, digital way. This is about failing fast and sorting things out quickly, learning as we go.'[11]

If the workforce is skilled and motivated, working in agile ways and supported by the right processes and technology, appropriate HR policies and practices and effective management, it should be productive and innovative. So employee engagement should be integral to day-to-day management practice, rather than a stand-alone strategy. When people feel they are doing something that matters, they generally feel motivated and have a sense of achievement. Similarly, if employees have opportunities to develop their skills so that they can work more effectively, they can achieve more. When employees are encouraged and enabled to connect with other people in their organizations they form communities of like-minded individuals, who are willing to collaborate towards purposes that they share. When that happens, organizations are healthier, employees are more engaged and increased agility should lead to better productivity and business performance.

We shall return to exploring various aspects of the engagement-performance link in Chapter 8.

## A culture conducive to innovation

Resiliently agile organizations tend to have high degrees of behavioural resilience and can change the system completely in response to unpredictable external events. These include the practised actions, particular routines, resource configurations and interaction patterns that represent the firm's response to disruptive conditions. These behaviours are designed to both create and capitalize on a firm's flexibility. As an example: two remarkable pilots of the Second World War and innovators in aviation history – Eric 'Winkle' Brown and Jimmy Doolittle – both survived the war despite carrying out extraordinary aviation feats and facing extreme danger on many occasions. Both shared the characteristic of thorough preparation before any flight, checking every detail of the plane, routes, etc, so that when faced with the hazardous reality they could focus specifically and uniquely on what needed to be done in that particular context. These disciplined approaches, perhaps best reflected in the phrase 'practice makes perfect', are increasingly recognized as the mainspring not only of skill but also of innovation.

In response to the COVID-19 pandemic and the need for lockdowns, more-experienced agile organizations thrived because reprioritization comes naturally to them. Since teams were already experienced in using digital remote-collaboration tools, they were able to rapidly build an operating model that had everyone working from home. Many set up a series of structured events, or ceremonies, at the team level that allowed teams to keep their pace and rhythm, even if the priorities were changing quickly and team members were no longer co-located. They increased the frequency of these to ensure better communication within the team and created a virtual co-location to provide for regular social interactions. Outcome-based, digital and automated tracking systems gave them daily transparency on their performance.

However Agile tools alone won't work without a people-based culture that puts customer needs front and centre. If an organization's strategic intent is to achieve multiple transient advantages, then strong leadership and a culture conducive to innovation and learning are needed (i.e. where people share information, are open to other people's ideas and where the CEO is the 'owner' of the drive for innovation). Such a culture is customer-focused, entrepreneurial, productive and supportive of innovation. It is built on principles of organizational purpose, trust and accountability, a context in which staff are usually willing and empowered to experiment and innovate. It has a strong shared identity that glues the organization together and aligns individual, work group and enterprise goals as a continuum. Because, while creative thinking and adaptation are most obvious when an innovative idea is initially generated, further creative development and enhancement of the idea takes place during local implementation and as the idea spreads across the organization.[12]

## Agile work practices

Let us look now in a little more detail at some of the other elements of an agile operating model in support of a strategy of innovation.

## TECHNOLOGY/WORK PROCESSES

Among the 'clockware', technology is a key plank of an agile innovation strategy. A study by Harvard Analytic Services found that leading users take a more strategic and systematic approach than others and are aggressively making use of new technologies to pursue a very different, more growth-oriented set of priorities.[13] They place a far higher priority on innovation and faster time to market, while limited users place a higher priority on increasing productivity/efficiency and profitability. Leading users consider that, to gain competitive advantage, it is essential to develop more flexible business processes and technology infrastructures and to build stronger, more fluid connections among employees and with customers and suppliers.

## RICH INFORMATION SYSTEMS

The potential of new technology to be the source of communication and speedy production is evident as cloud computing, mobile devices and applications and social networking support new working practices. In many companies the use of iPads and tablets in the field has lowered costs and enabled better sales and customer service, and many companies are driving their businesses online. Agile organizations are built on an infrastructure of company-wide connectivity and information robustness. Rich information systems are those that provide people with access to the information and working knowledge they need to do their jobs. Alberts and Hayes in their book *Power to the Edge* propose that, to help individuals and organizational subunits make sense of fast-changing complex situations, there should be information 'pull' rather than broadcast information 'push', collaborative efforts rather than individual efforts, and information handled once rather than multiple times.[14] Virtual meeting tools support flexible and virtual business operations that cross functions, business units, geographies and time zones. Of course, when combinations of legacy systems do not speak with each other, or when companies involved in strategic partnerships use different IT systems, this can make doing the job very difficult. Especially in the case of mergers and acquisitions, a common platform is needed if the intended economies of scale are to be realized.

## KNOWLEDGE SHARING

Agile organizations rely on knowledge as a core resource that underpins all products and services and contributes towards organizational learning. Knowledge sharing is the formal and informal process of transferring information, skills or understanding between people and organizations. Technology can help companies to access and share knowledge across geographies, partnerships, time zones and supply chains, enabling and optimizing business potential. Focusing on customer outcomes, pilots and learning loops creates a management capability to adapt and rapidly respond to customer needs.

Research by the Agile Business Consortium found that:

- Informal discussions are the most common way of sharing knowledge within project teams and with company colleagues.
- Meetings are the most common way of sharing knowledge with the customer.
- Knowledge sharing is easier within project teams than with company colleagues or customers.
- Staff are motivated to share knowledge because they want to rather than because the company asks them to.
- The more Agile practices staff use, the easier they find knowledge sharing with team members.
- The more Agile practices staff use, the more frequently they share knowledge within teams and with customers.

To improve organizational knowledge sharing the Consortium suggests:

- Enable a knowledge sharing culture with flat management organization, trust, respect and rewards for sharing.
- Balance the use of technology, processes, expertise networks and physical space in knowledge sharing.
- Build on existing successful knowledge sharing networks, both official and unofficial.
- Create efficient and successful mechanisms for knowledge sharing beyond the team with management, peers and different specialists.[15]

Many firms set up centre-led hubs for critical capabilities, such as data and analytics, that teams can draw on, which enable companies to both build expertise and increase productivity by deploying resources flexibly. The hub provides a focus of deep expertise that liaises with experts within business units, who combine functional knowledge and business expertise to deliver required work packages (the spokes).

### A FRAMEWORK FOR KNOWLEDGE SHARING

Establishing a clear framework for knowledge sharing helps reduce the distance between executives and local staff. For instance, the CEO of Atlassian, an Australian software company, has instilled an open information culture that includes people as well as systems.[16] Workers are encouraged to 'put *information* out there' for others to consume rather than hoarding it in their private stores. Early in its corporate life cycle the firm developed its own 'corporate wiki' that was given the name 'Confluence' to represent the coming together of ideas. New staff members are instructed to use the wiki and, without the infrastructure for traditional 'document management', these staff members have little alternative but to 'buy into' the system. The very act of using a wiki, with its easy access to information and default 'open' nature of information, has led to a bottom-up democracy of information where information sharing is the norm and the wiki is a destination for lively discussion and debate.

A Capgemini study found that helpful practices include bringing together the most innovative employees into cross-functional innovation teams, in a new and different physical space, but without isolating them. It is important to establish performance measures, make things manageable and let the teams get on with it. Some companies prefer to ring-fence innovators in 'skunk-works', which describes a group within an organization given a high degree of autonomy and unhampered by bureaucracy, tasked with working on advanced projects. For example, in 2011 Walmart established @WalmartLabs, an 'idea incubator', as part of its growing e-commerce division in Silicon Valley – far removed from the company's headquarters in Bentonville, Arkansas.[17] The group's innovations, including a unified company-wide e-commerce platform, helped Walmart to increase online revenues by 30 per cent in 2013, outpacing Amazon's rate of growth.

## Agile work planning

Doing the right work starts with widespread ideas generation around business problems and potential innovations, focusing on desired outcomes for customers and organizational results. Risk and value-driven mechanisms should be used to decide which ideas to work on. Success should be defined in outcome-based terms rather than by output, describing the difference the results will make to the intended recipient, striking a balance between daily activity and the long-range view. A structure of standards can be developed based on what is happening when the outcome is being successfully achieved.

At product level, clearly stated goals, objectives and performance indicators provide a focus for the team's work. Key Result Areas or KRAs, also called Key Performance Areas (KPAs) refer to general areas of outcomes or outputs for which a role, or a combination of roles, is responsible. These are the areas within the organization where an individual, group or team, is logically responsible or accountable for the results. These inform management decisions about ways to allocate resources and deliver services. They also help individuals to clarify their roles, set individual and team goals, focus on results, prioritize activities and make value-added decisions.

Lean and Agile programmes of work then ensure that initiatives are delivered around planned business outcomes. There is ongoing measurement of how well the intended outcomes are being achieved, with feedback loops to inform decisions about when goals might need to be adjusted. Programme management is required to ensure that multiple streams of work deliver organizational benefits.

Continually reviewing current requirements with the future in mind enables a deeper understanding of the longer-term workforce requirements. The goal should be to pick optimal responsibilities for individuals based on their capabilities and current organizational needs. Tools for tracking organizational performance and health give leaders a sense of how quickly and effectively things are happening and where to pay more attention.[18] Also, information management becomes much simpler and more accurate.

During the COVID-19 pandemic, agile methods helped organizations to speed up their work and adapt to new industry landscapes, for instance by (re)examining their priorities and setting objectives and key results (OKRs). The weekly and daily rhythm of Agile teams worked well in remote settings. Thus, companies were able to respond to changing customer needs with high variety and quality, low cost and very fast throughput times.

## Lean execution processes

Agile methods integrate planning with execution, allowing an organization to create a working mindset that helps a team respond effectively to changing requirements. Operations typically use standardized processes and systems to achieve operational excellence and cost-efficiency. For organizations aspiring to be agile, the challenge is to standardize flexibility: to develop flexible assets, processes and systems that will continue to provide operational excellence and cost-efficiency – and also free up capacity for innovation.

Increasingly, organizations are embracing *lean thinking*. The core idea is to maximize customer value while minimizing waste in all its forms with the

ultimate goal being to provide excellent value to the customer through a
perfect value-creation process. To accomplish this, the focus of management
must shift from optimizing separate technologies towards an integrated
approach, optimizing the flow of products and services through entire value
streams that flow horizontally across technologies, assets and departments
to customers. Continuous improvement eliminates waste along entire value
streams, instead of at isolated points, creating processes that need less
human effort, less space, less capital and less time to make products and
services at far less cost and with fewer defects, as compared with traditional
business systems. 'Japanese' production strategies such as *just in time* (JIT)
strive to reduce in-process inventory and associated carrying costs. To meet
JIT objectives, the process relies on signals (or kanban) between different
points in a given process, which tell production when to make the next part.
Manufacturing firms such as Toyota that adopted these methods from the
1980s ended up raising productivity significantly (through the elimination
of waste).

As an NHS report in 2020 commented, the urgent demands of the
pandemic forced through many improvements in how NHS organizations
operated. The report urged:

> We need to hold on to this different way of doing things and strip away the
> unnecessary bureaucracy, reporting and regulation that for too long has stifled
> the service. We need everyone to embrace a culture that empowers local leaders
> and clinicians to lead, giving them the ability to make good decisions for the
> communities and partnerships they serve.[19]

Lightweight methodologies include 'scrum': 'a flexible, holistic product development strategy where a development team works as a unit to reach a
common goal'.[20] Although Deming's plan–do–check–act cycle is encompassed
in this system, Agile challenges assumptions of the traditional, sequential
approach to product development. It enables teams to self-organize by encouraging physical co-location or close online collaboration of all team members,
as well as daily face-to-face communication among all team members and
disciplines in the project. Essentially the team has control of the project. With
shared goals and scalable processes, Agile working enables teams to achieve
fewer defects, faster releases and sustainable activity without the team burning out. Agile, the 1990s management breakthrough, has enabled software
development teams systematically to achieve both disciplined execution and
continuous innovation, something that was impossible to accomplish within
traditional bureaucracy.[21] Agility's principles, as described in the IT sector's

'Agile Manifesto' are central to this. These include 'Individual and interactions over products and tools', 'Customer collaboration' and 'Responding to change over following a plan'.

Many organizations adopt the Scaled Agile Framework (SAFe) which is essentially a collection of agile methods. It creates a hierarchy (scrum of scrum of scrum of scrum of...) but also overlays all the support functions a team might need. Perhaps most importantly, SAFe ties together lean methods and the theory of constraints, helping larger delivery groups find and remove bottlenecks, which can be critical to accelerating value delivery.

## Project-based working

Project-based work is a growing feature of many workplaces, since in the world of transient advantages products and services need to be developed rapidly alongside business as usual. Project working is therefore a key plank of strategic execution, which can result in innovative breakthroughs, new products and services. Agile disciplines from the world of IT are being applied to project working and more broadly, becoming part of organizational culture or 'the way we do things around here'.

### The evolution of project management approaches

The origins of traditional project management were in planning and tracking large complex projects in areas such as construction. It reflects a systems engineering approach that involves centralized planning and, monitoring and decentralized execution. Its methods are highly disciplined and methodical, favouring logic, reason and planning. In earlier decades, project management was being applied to software development using the 'Big Bang' approach, so called because developers would be given a brief, develop a product, then have to wait until delivery to find out what might need amending or where the software failed to meet client expectations – an obviously risky and expensive process.

By the 1970s, a stage-based approach to software development was introduced known as the 'waterfall' model, so called because as each phase was completed it would lead on to another, making backwards moves to make corrections very difficult. With the waterfall model, projects need executive buy-in and funding at the start; teams are lined up, client requirements are gathered and there is an attempt to completely understand the whole project from the outset. The aim is for a perfect product, with testing applied until there are no 'bugs' in the system, then finally the product is demonstrated to the client. This method typically leads to both scope creep (since business needs might change during a long project, and developers might be asked to squeeze in 'one more thing') and limited flexibility, since once requirements have been predefined at the start of the project there is little room for manoeuvre. Moreover, the relatively slow feedback cycle in a fast-moving context, and limited client involvement throughout, means that customers may end up rejecting the finished product if their needs have moved on in the meantime.

These approaches work best in relatively predictable conditions when technical expertise is required over long project cycles, and when the material factors are known in advance and a central authority is in a position to ensure that all necessary actions are taken by the appropriate parties. In recent times it has been recognized that in fast-moving contexts, under conditions of uncertainty, predetermined solutions to problems can neither be reliably ascertained nor easily implemented, so executing traditional projects can be difficult. There can be too many project sponsors with conflicting needs; specifications often change and projects run out of funds before they are delivered. Nevertheless, these approaches are still very much favoured by large organizations who train employees in Prince 2 and other project–management-related methodologies and software.

## The development of agile project management

Software developers came to realize that, with rapid change as a backdrop, long stages of project development without feedback were doomed to failure. They saw that once products and services are launched they encounter competitors' products, regulators, suppliers, and customer responses that force costly revisions. Execution processes therefore must be both agile and lean. Thanks to the proliferation of web services, software today is being developed in smaller units that are easier to map to business processes. These enable frequent product releases and provide flexibility to deal with changes required in real time. Of course they must also be cost-effective, eliminating non-value-adding processes and management overheads.

### AGILE AS 'BEST OF BREED'

Agile project management is an iterative approach to delivering a project throughout its life cycle. One of its aims is to release benefits throughout the process rather than only at the end. Agile life cycles comprise several iterations or incremental steps towards the completion of a project. These steps are prioritized by the team in terms of importance. Agile teamwork is planned around two types of formal meetings, namely (a) daily short 'stand-up meetings' focusing on goal monitoring and re-prioritization, and (b) more extensive monthly 'retrospective meetings' focusing on learning and process improvement. Such meetings provide a means of iterative coordination for prioritizing among multiple goals in innovation.[22]

The agile project promotes collaborative working (and even co-creation), especially with the customer. The agile project team reflects, learns and adjusts at regular intervals to ensure that the customer is always satisfied and is provided with outcomes that result in benefits. The focus is on delivering maximum value against business priorities in the time and budget allowed, especially when the drive to deliver is greater than the risk.[23] At the core, agile projects should exhibit central values and behaviours of trust, flexibility, empowerment and collaboration.

In an agile project, the 'product owner' has a dual role, both as subject-matter expert and as liaison between clients and technical teams. They work with the client to agree the big picture needs, then translate these into units of work that are progressed in 'sprints'. 'Big picture' needs – for example 'as a division we want faster loan approvals so we can increase trading by 10 per cent rather than do safer loan approvals so we can lower defaults by 10 per cent' – are translated into a simple value story by the product owner with the client. Acceptance criteria are agreed and funding attached to the various units of work required. The larger the unit of measurement, the less accurate it will be, so the 'big picture' value story is broken down to the daily task level to make it easier for people to understand agreed-upon goals. This gives developers the right information to do the job and allows for traceability and accountability within the team.

Sprints have disciplined start and finish times of between one and four weeks and team members hold each other to account for completing the work during this time. At the start of each sprint, the product owner brings client information to the team's planning meeting. Using a big chart, and in daily short stand-up meetings, team members keep each other informed of progress and issues. Peer pressure forces delivery, as in weekly sessions the teams demonstrate their work to each other (and clients) and actively gather rapid feedback and ideas. Thus testing and integration are occurring simultaneously.

A series of sprints adds up to an 'iteration' at the end of which either a usable product is shipped to the customer or the next large milestone is set. At the end of each iteration there is a quick retrospective to gather learning and assess what has worked well or otherwise. In one sense, nothing is ever completely 'finished' though products are launched; rather each iteration in the development cycle 'learns' from the previous iteration. Thus Agile methodology is more flexible, efficient and customer- and team-oriented than any of the previous models.

Stakeholder prioritization is one of the fundamental building blocks of a successful project or organizational change strategy. A stakeholder is any individual or group of people who have a direct impact on the success of the project, or are affected by it. In designing projects and deciding which approach to take, it is vital to identify and involve the right stakeholders. Too often, though, project teams get the stakeholder prioritization step wrong based on the wrong assessment criteria or on input from too few people.

To identify relevant stakeholders it is useful to start with the project sponsor (the person with the idea) who has the funding, a vision of what the project should achieve and the political clout to help identify additional stakeholders. Early in the project the list of stakeholders based on this vision is usually vague. In finding out who other stakeholders might be, organization charts are often unhelpful if they are out of date, so it is better to create a current one from scratch. Then involve a wider pool of people likely to be involved in creating the solution – analysts, creators, testers, managers, etc – to brainstorm potential stakeholders. Special interest groups (SIGs) such as auditors, who have jurisdiction over what the project is allowed to change, should also be consulted. Most of all, end users (internal and external) should be involved. Circulating the stakeholder list to all the identified parties ensures that any important stakeholders missing from the list can be added. By identifying relevant stakeholders it is possible to get a good idea about what they want the project to deliver.

## Combining traditional and Agile approaches

A portfolio of business projects may require using a mix of Agile approaches alongside a more traditional process. What type of discipline, and how much structure, adaptability and flexibility are required? The answer will depend on what makes sense according to the company's life cycle stage, its structure and culture, with many companies preferring to rely on classic project-management approaches rather than on Agile or lean approaches.

Combining the two approaches is not easy and the challenge then is how to strike the right balance. A framework for determining whether or not a particular project should be agile could include:

- How well equipped is the organization's culture to deal with decentralized decision making? Or is it more attuned to top-down hierarchical planning?

- How complex is the project requirement? When there is a small number of complex major projects under way the discipline of traditional project management is a sensible choice. It allows for clarity about the work to be done, by whom and when.

- How stable are the requirements – how much will they change every month? The less stable the requirements, the more an Agile approach will be useful.

- What are the consequences of project failure? The greater the consequences, the more plan-driven the project tends to become.

- How large is the team? A team of 10 can be agile whereas a team of 500 cannot.

- What skills are required? Essentially, Agile involves managing people through a shared culture and having people with overlapping skill sets who are competent to make decisions themselves instead of through a hierarchy. Conversely, when teams are made up of specialists from different fields it can be more difficult to allocate work among the different disciplines.

- What are workers' skill levels? The lower the skills, the more supervision will be required and the less agile the team.

- What is the project's scope? The degree of decentralization will reflect the scope of the project – which might vary from short iterations to a deadline a year ahead.

When a hybrid of both traditional and Agile approaches is required, projects typically start off using traditional planned approaches before they become more agile. Tensions can arise that are reflective of different cultures. For instance, in large projects using traditional approaches, plans are broken down into chunks by centralized planners, predictable techniques used, progress monitored and deviations addressed. In contrast, Agile projects eschew detailed planning and estimating – it is about being able to re-plan as you go. This raises challenges such as:

- How to allocate budget between those projects that have detailed plans and budgets and those that do not.
- How to use adaptive planning techniques while still providing accurate progress status to traditional project manager counterparts.

There need to be clear demarcations between Agile and traditional approaches and the best of both applied. In traditional approaches, funding is allocated and increases over the project cycle. In hybrid approaches, funding is allocated within a series of sprints when results are already emerging. Similarly, major deadlines on large projects might be set centrally, while in stages between major deadlines teams can do the micro-scheduling themselves. Clear and frequent communications are needed within and between teams so that everyone knows what is going on and to build trust between users of Agile and traditional methodologies. Spotify, one of the pioneers in organizing for Agile, seeks to create an autonomous environment with just enough constraints to avoid chaos. One of these constraints is minimum viable agility. Spotify doesn't advocate any particular methodology, but it does have certain things it expects every team to do, such as visualize workflows and hold a retrospective at least every two weeks.

The skill sets for managing traditional and Agile projects differ; therefore, different kinds of project manager may be needed to run different projects. A traditionally trained project manager, who typically needs to have oversight of and control of the whole project, probably will not feel comfortable delegating decision making to the team and taking on the role of coach/facilitator/clearer of roadblocks for the team. Senior managers too may dislike not knowing in detail what is going on in all the projects. If managers will not relinquish control to the team, Agile will not work. HR can help managers to become 'bilingual' – to make the shift from top-down control approaches to more Agile – so that managers and teams can be on the same page.

## Experimenting – the routines of exploration

To succeed in today's fast-changing environment, strategies must become dynamic, redefined and reformulated on a rapid scale. Workforce innovation describes those working practices that enable people at all levels of an organization to react faster than in traditional hierarchies, and to use and develop their skills, knowledge and creativity to the fullest possible extent.[24] As we have discussed, these include self-organized team working, empowerment, weak internal organizational divisions and demarcations, inclusive improvement and innovation teams, management–union partnership, openness and transparency, and distributed leadership.

## Agile problem analysis

Being customer-centric is about meeting the customer where they're at, being empathetic to what they need. This means finding out what clients think about the issues they are facing, and therefore how firms can best help them, rather than simply selling solutions based on the firm's current capabilities. Considering the problem through the stakeholder lens allows you to reframe the problem before embarking on innovative solutions.

What the Center for Effective Organizations (CEO) calls *testing* and Plsek[25] refers to as experimentation is how an organization sets up, runs and learns from experiments. This requires some slack and '*pruning*' in resource capacity (people, time, money, etc) to allow space to experiment with new ideas.[26] Setting up problem solving as an experiment helps stakeholders to understand that solutions are unlikely to be generated until ideas have been tested. Related to Lean, agile problem analysis allows for accurate identification of real problems for which solutions can then be sought. It is important to separate symptoms from the real problem. As Hoverstadt points out, when managers find they are repeatedly taking decisions about the same operational issues, it is usually a sign that some sort of coordination mechanism is missing, resulting in problems being passed up to management to resolve.[27] One of the hardest tasks in designing an experiment is working out exactly what question to ask; and when you are asking for help in solving a problem, how much detail to give. When working with a team whose understanding of the problem ranges across a wide spectrum, it is useful to provide enough structure and detail so that the people who are unfamiliar with the issues can make a contribution.

First bring together a cross-functional team to distinguish between those issues that are real problems and those that are mere symptoms of the problem.[28] For example, a symptom presenting itself as a problem might be, 'it takes 40 minutes to complete an application form' – while the real problem is that the company is losing good applicants as a result of a cumbersome application process. The symptoms should be put on a list of irrelevant items and circulated, in case a real problem is lurking undetected. If the problem is beyond the authority of anyone to solve it, then it becomes beyond the scope of the project. It is essential to get a well-expressed problem statement quickly – to understand what problem your potential solution solves – and then create a project charter.

Design thinking with its three phases – immersion, ideation and prototyping – has changed the way many companies think of (and do) innovation and offers a methodology to make sense of and solve complex problems. Agility depends on focusing on one problem at a time – removing solved or false problems from the list as you go until you have identified the real problem and can rewrite the problem statement that provides the scope for the project. Problem-solving techniques such as this, which rely on frequent iterations, serve as catalysts for new ideas and increase the odds of success simply because there are more options available for consideration. If successful, what the project delivers becomes the new 'business as usual' (BAU).

### Involving people in problem solving and innovation

Innovation leaders are faced with addressing complex problems with no obvious answers so it is essential that they have the opportunity to tap into the diverse views, ideas, knowledge and insights of their workforces. After all, in the Web 2.0 age, employees ought to understand their market, the firm's technologies and their clients – and people expect to be involved. Tools such as crowdsourcing can be helpful in galvanizing people to find solutions to business challenges and dramatically increase the innovation capabilities of the company. The process works something like this:

1 Stakeholders brainstorm ideas for a problem to be solved.

2 A selected problem is launched company-wide as a challenge, often via a portal.

3 Staff, including experts, collaborate to find possible solutions.

4 The best contributions are rewarded with small cash prizes, gift certificates and/or accolades such as letters of appreciation from the organization's CEO or head of R&D.

For example, the French skincare company L'Oréal had a problem with its Active Cosmetics Division,[29] which was not performing as well in the UK as in other markets, due to cultural differences – for instance the British generally do not ask their pharmacists for skincare advice, nor do they generally visit dermatologists unless they have a serious problem. So the company was wondering how to improve matters. It had commissioned research into the mindset of British workers. This suggested that while many were keen to be more entrepreneurial at work, and more than one-quarter claimed to be sitting on a good idea, 9 out of 10 employees felt that their boss was uninspiring and were likely to look elsewhere for advice.

L'Oréal realized that its workers would be keen to help resolve the problem so the firm took its own advice and asked staff to become consultants with respect to the business challenge. They created an internal competition called 'The Next Fund' in which they invited employees to submit ideas about the underperforming division. The entries were judged by a top-level panel and a prize of £100,000 showed that the company intended to take the best ideas seriously.

The ability to utilize the diversity inherent within multidisciplinary teams has long been recognized as a key ingredient in creating a learning culture. One firm, for example, identified six business problems and, for each of the challenges they identified, they formed an expert team to look at any solutions submitted. The teams were made up of combinations of people who were currently working on the business problem and people who were new to the organization. This blend of experience turned out to be critical. While the design of the experiment was carefully structured, there was still plenty of scope for learning on the job.

The Virginia Mason Institute, operating in healthcare, uses its 3P (production, preparation, process) facilitation process with its clients. This provides directed ideation and guidance to enable a multidisciplinary group of stakeholders as participants to envision, simulate and create a future-state vision. Coaching sessions with stakeholder and user groups help them to reimagine their workflows, processes and use of space to create something new. These 3Ps can be used to design and create new products, processes and facilities, and they can be used when a software program must be expanded to accommodate more patients.

New forms of organization development (OD) are useful in the context of innovation. Large-scale engagements such as Open Space and Future Search conferences are examples of OD methods that enable conversations to take place involving large parts of the system. Hackathons are another example. These are used by start-ups and incumbents alike in developing ideas and projects of high value and novelty. 'Hackathons adhere to non-hierarchical and open ways of organizing, no clear process, structure or roles [are] defined.'[30] In the absence of traditional process, structure or roles that may stifle projects in hackathons, new organizing practices, like iterative coordination, may be necessary to manage innovation in the highly time-constrained setting of a hackathon.[31] Iterative coordination through frequent meetings such as 'stand-ups' could allow firms to inject necessary value into ideas, increasing their likelihood of being implemented as complete innovation projects since it allows firms to reprioritize their goals over time, enabling critical adjustments to be made regarding the degree of novelty that is acceptable to them over the course of their projects.[32]

## Innovation as everyone's job

For innovation to be socialized and become the 'way we do things around here', participative working and empowerment must become central features of the workplace. When this happens, anyone can generate ideas and emerging ideas are supported by disciplined processes. At Seattle-based Virginia Mason Medical Center innovation is everyone's job.[33] Each person in the organization – from the executives to the front-line staff – is encouraged to apply lean concepts and innovation to their day-to-day work. A true culture of innovation inspires staff to routinely try new things without fear of failure because it is about trying many ideas to find the one that will work best. Leaders encourage teams to break out of their mental valleys – or established patterns of thinking – so they can look at solutions in a different way. Virginia Mason uses four approaches to foster daily innovation:

1  *Everyday lean ideas (ELIs) system.* ELIs are small, quick-to-implement improvements tackled by staff in a local work unit, focused on improving safety, reducing defects, organizing materials or information, and saving time and money. An ELI immediately delivers small improvements while embedding lean thinking into staff who are potential future leaders. Ideas are fully tested and proven before they are implemented.

2  *Moonshine lab.* In early Japanese lean organizations, workers often stayed after hours to build new tools and fixtures that were added to the production line the following day. A moonshine lab is based on the idea of 'working while the moon shines' and creating prototypes to solve tasks at hand.

3 *Informatics in clinical daily work.* Virginia Mason also supports a small group of individuals who are constantly looking to leverage informatics to improve care.

4 *Innovation grants.* While ELIs nurture small ideas, innovation grants support breakthrough ideas that can help Virginia Mason to leapfrog important performance measures. Grants provide up to US $25,000 and ideas are expected to be tested within about 18 months.

Virginia Mason uses lean concepts such as 'jidoka' – or having the instructions and knowledge necessary to do one's job right first time – to mistake-proof primary care. One guiding principle has been to equip clinicians with vital patient information that they need to care for their patients at the point of care. One staff team used a lean process called '5S' to organize common areas, nursing stations and medication rooms. They sorted, simplified and standardized the areas so that everything is clean and in its proper location, so that clinicians can find what they need without delay. By arranging nursing zones into a U-shape, people have the shortest distance to walk; work enters and leaves at the same place; there is increased communication; and it is easier to balance the workload between people – they can flex between jobs and help each other.

It is often assumed that standardizing business processes acts as a restraint on innovation. At Virginia Mason the reverse is true. In practice, developing simple, standardized processes that are known, understood and effective has freed up staff to innovate and improve the service to be responsive to customers and the market. Therefore, innovation goes hand in hand with rigorous, repeatable and measurable processes that are known and available to everyone.

Building a customer-centric culture is about inculcating a vision and supporting it with operational processes and behavioural guardrails to enable employees to take judicious risks. Flexible bureaucracies are characterized by a shared leadership style as well as a higher level of accountability among followers that can contribute to the proliferation of creative ideas[34] as well as extra-role behaviours.[35] When people are fully aware of their company's high-level goals, individuals and organizational subunits can operate as communities of interest, sharing rather than hoarding data, self-scanning their actions, combining scarce resources peer to peer to provide coherent responses without going up the hierarchy. Then by applying lean or Agile project management methods (discussed earlier) people can minimize non-value-adding activities and methods, make best use of available resources and maximize client value.

As we shall discuss in Chapter 9, developing culture will involve combining various HR practices such as leadership development, individual training and development to communicate the *what* and *why* of customer-centric values, and to teach positive behaviours and practices. Leadership development should teach the importance of modelling customer-centric values in action, the practice of trusting, non-directive management, and coaching to build and embed competence. Goal-setting, reward and recognition initiatives need to reinforce and incentivize pro-customer practices, and communicate values (see the GE case study in Chapter 9).

---

CASE STUDY
*New revenue generation at UC Berkeley: 'You can't save your way to excellence!'*

I am grateful to Bill Reichle, Director of the Operational Excellence Program Office at UC Berkeley for the following case study. Bill also directs UC Berkeley's New Revenue Initiative. In this role, he partners with faculty, staff, students and alumni to identify and develop opportunities to create new, sustainable, revenue-generating programmes for the university.

A public university

The State of California developed a masterplan for higher education in 1960 to organize existing public universities into dedicated roles, to prevent public institutions competing with each other for resources or offering redundant programmes, and to optimize access to higher education for California's students. The plan envisioned a three-tier system of community colleges, state teaching universities and research universities. Today, the research tier, represented by the University of California (UC), has 10 campus locations with more than 250,000 students.

The 10 campuses of the UC system operate independently with policy guidance from a central UC Office of the President. UC Berkeley, the original campus founded in 1868, today hosts 29,000 undergraduate and 11,000 graduate students in 14 schools and colleges. Berkeley is recognized as one of the leading research universities in the world and for the breadth of its excellence. Berkeley's faculty has a distinguished history and has been awarded 22 Nobel prizes.

Culturally, the university is known for student protests against the Vietnam War in the 1960s and the birth of the Free Speech Movement in 1964. The legacy of free speech and protest is part of the fabric of Berkeley that carries on to this day.

Berkeley also prides itself in the number of students who are the first generation in their family to attend college, and the number of students from economically disadvantaged families. Of Berkeley undergraduate students, 32 per cent receive Federal Pell Grants, which represents more students than the eight Ivy League universities combined.

## The case for change

In recent years, UC Berkeley has experienced significant financial challenges caused largely by an ongoing and significant reduction in state funding for higher education. While state support was the primary source of revenue 15 years ago, today it is only the fourth largest behind tuition, research grants and philanthropy. Tuition, while traditionally kept low, has risen dramatically in the last 20 years as state funding has diminished. While revenues have grown from US $1.7 billion in 2006–07 to US $2.8 billion in 2017–18, expenses have outpaced revenues, rising from US $1.7 billion in 2006–07 to US $2.9 billion in 2017–18.

Berkeley operates within additional financial constraints that limit its options for managing its budget. Tuition rates are determined by the system-wide UC Office of the President. Berkeley also pays into state-wide systems with its fellow UC campuses, such as a new state-wide shared services centre. Also, the Berkeley campus sits on top of an active earthquake fault, requiring considerable resources to be allocated over the past 30 years to seismically retrofit ageing buildings.

By 2010, the financial challenges, and the need to bridge the shortfall in funding, had become the burning platform for change. As a public university, concern was mounting that tuition fees and expensive local accommodation may have outpaced students' ability to pay, meaning that only the wealthiest students could attend university or else would leave with very high levels of debt. As tuition fees increased, students expected to have more of a voice as well as higher expectations for a good student experience. Savings were therefore not sought on the student side – instead investments were made to improve the student experience (e.g. replacing the old slow system of using phones to register for classes with an Oracle-based registration system).

2010 was a propitious year to start grasping the financial challenge. There was aligned and committed campus leadership, momentum and energy on campus and a clear financial imperative to try something different. Denneen and Dretler argue that to create a more differentiated and financially sustainable institution, innovative college and university presidents are doing four things:

1  developing a clear strategy, focused on the core

2  reducing support and administrative costs

**3** freeing up capital in non-core assets

**4** strategically investing in innovative models.[36]

One of the ways UC Berkeley chose to respond to its financial challenges and to support its academic mission was to reduce costs by improving administrative efficiencies (the Operational Excellence programme).

## The New Revenue Initiative

The other main approach embraced by the university was to actively grow new revenue by creating strategic opportunities to monetize the intellectual and cultural assets of the university. The New Revenue Initiative solicits and evaluates ideas from campus and deploys a small team of market research, financial analysis and project management specialists to launch promising ventures. More generally, the programme aimed to build a culture of entrepreneurship on campus and create new, net revenue.

## Approach

It took six months to design and develop the initiative's structure, governance, processes, tools and forms. The guiding philosophy adopted was reflected in the campaign: 'Let 1,000 flowers bloom' – any and all ideas would be welcomed. Ideas were crowdsourced – online and at events. More than 1,000 ideas were submitted (Figure 6.1). These were assessed using an Initial Assessment Tool and ranked on a 10-point scale. Ideas that scored 5 or below went back to their originators, with suggestions for improvement, while ideas scoring more than 5 were assigned resources. Ideas scoring 9 or 10 on proof of concept were brought to senior leadership attention.

FIGURE 6.1  New revenue – idea pipeline

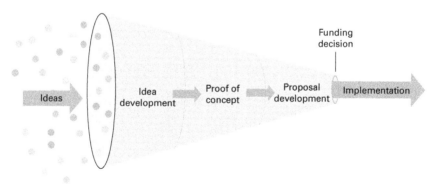

SOURCE © Bill Reichle

For the seven approved projects support was available to aid project design and implementation:

- Line of credit was established (US $30 million) – to provide start-up loans. Twelve proposals received loan funding and went into implementation. Some ideas sought support only – e.g. market research.
- Market research – a dedicated market researcher validated ideas through primary and secondary research.
- Project management – to ensure implementation.
- Alumni expertise in business and industry.

To date, the programme has evaluated more than 1,000 ideas and approved 12 of them with a combined projected annual revenue of US $13 million.

Lessons learned

- Good ideas are plentiful – execution is rare if the ideas are too esoteric or have no sponsor.
- Campus policies were developed in an era that never conceived of the need to develop external revenue.
- Higher education administration has a culture of risk aversion – need better personal and professional incentives to engage audiences.
- Crowdsourcing ideas meant creative submissions but the method depended on 'idea champions' advocating on behalf of their ideas and this did not materialize.
- Small ideas versus big ideas – small ideas that can scale and replicate are flowers that can bloom, though it can take as much work to get small ideas going as big ideas. While efficiency ideas tend to apply within departments and are easy to reward, by its nature, new revenue generation requires agile, cross-boundary working. Ideas that originate within departments that can be replicated in other departments require collaboration across campus.

---

## Spreading the learning from Agile

It is important to bring learning from lean work into the wider context of the traditional organization and export Agile practices – such as scrum, testing, rapid feedback and stand-up meetings – to create a gradual sea change in 'the way we do things around here'. For example, so fast is the pace of change in retailing that US retailer Gap has moved from a 'push' to a 'pull' model, listening intensely to what customers want and making all their processes lean to ensure rapid response. They and others are having to adjust and adapt their supply chains, building transparency into inventory systems, designing collaborative working within organizations and redesigning work processes.

Different functional groups, such as R&D departments and sales teams, have their own cultures, which differ from each other. By working out where different subcultures intersect, it is possible to find parts of the organization that can tolerate both Agile and traditional approaches. Then it is about finding ways to break down silos, encouraging people to move between disciplines, providing training, sharing with people the reasons why different approaches are needed at different times and what these involve.

Unilever has deliberately embraced agile working practices encompassing virtual working and has found it to be a total culture change in how work gets done. The firm has achieved many benefits from agile working, such as 30 per cent greater space utilization, multi-award-winning offices, including Singapore and Hamburg, and 60 per cent less waste and energy. In particular, employees are more productive and engaged.

## Designing work for agility and empowerment

Formal work design is usually decided top-down, i.e. CEOs make strategic decisions that affect work design for employees across the whole organization.[37] So leaders must take account of multi-level factors – the higher-level external context (global/international, national and occupational factors), the organizational context, the local work context (work group factors) and the people/individual factors.[38] Local managers make decisions that affect the work design of a smaller group of employees. At the human-technology interface managers must consider how tasks and projects are accomplished, not how 'jobs' are organized. Leaders and managers must become skilled at orchestrating a broad range of different resources – some human, some not; some employees, some not – to execute those tasks.

The problems affecting organizational performance often lie less at macro (organizational) design level than at work design level, an area which, from an HR and OE perspective, is often neglected. Creating a workplace fit for the future is not an easy task. Many of the challenges relate to 'softer' issues such as capability, employee turnover and engagement. Work design is increasingly the acid test of the relationship between employers and employees. As talent gains greater freedom to choose the most desirable projects and project leaders to work with, the relationship between managers and workers will increasingly become less hierarchical and high-quality work will be a key means of attracting and retaining effective employees. To produce more enriched work experiences, managers must explore how work can be designed to meet both the needs of the business and those of employees. This depends on managers' own work-design-related motivation, knowledge, skills and abilities (KSAs): 'Changing how teams connect and implement technology on a day-to-day basis, while also serving customers and clients in a new workforce structure, is difficult. Sometimes, it's easier for some leaders to just go back to old ways.'[39]

Even in digital environments, the human element is key to delivering what marketeers call 'moments of truth': those interactions where customer loyalty is earned or trust is lost, moments that are defined by the customer and are judged by an emotional, rather than rational, response. Recognizing this, many organizations now look for ways to 'empower' staff, particularly those in customer-facing roles to deliver the experience customers want. This places an emphasis on the skills, behaviours and attitudes of front-line employees and also on employees' levels of discretion and authority to act in service of the customer's needs. The implicit assumption is that empowerment involves sharing knowledge, skills and decision-making authority with employees so that they can benefit customers by using their own best judgement to solve service problems without having to escalate to senior decision makers. But empowerment is also more about an employee mindset or perception that combines three core factors:[40]

- a motivating belief in the intrinsic value and importance of the organization's customer service ethos

- a sense of competence in their role and ability to deal with problems

- a feeling of autonomy to exercise control and take self-determined decisions.

So as leaders focus on systems and initiatives that stimulate customer focus, idea generation and risk taking, they must also develop a culture that both considers individuals' emotional experiences at work and allays the fears that will hold their teams back. This is not easy to do. With the proliferation of flexible, remote and hybrid-working patterns, workplace culture and organizational structure may become out of synch with what is happening now and may need to be overhauled.

In large organizations, the challenge is to take advantage of scale in a way that still keeps important decisions close to the customer and wires together structure, work processes, new systems and people processes to be close to key customers so that they have an influence on decisions. To be truly agile, more fundamental moves are needed to embed an empowered mindset and produce the relevant individual and group behaviour, performance and organizational culture. This requires a systemic approach towards designing enriched work and a more enabling form of bureaucracy.

## Work design

Work that permits autonomy, demands problem solving, and meets other criteria for good design can bolster employees' cognitive skills and ongoing learning. According to Hackman and Oldham's Job Demands-Resources (JD-R) theory, favourable work design occurs when employees have ample job resources and limited excessive job demands and role stressors (especially hindrance demands). High-quality work design has high levels of resources in the form of role clarity, knowledge and social work characteristics (e.g. job autonomy, variety, opportunities for development and social support). Job resources emerge when employees collectively recognize their working conditions as effective for learning, goal achievement and wellbeing. Job resources may exist at the levels of task (e.g. job autonomy), organization of the job (e.g. role clarity), interpersonal and social relations (e.g. team climate) and the larger organization (e.g. organizational justice).[41] Hence, job resources refer to those aspects of work design that are conducive to wellbeing, learning and goal achievement. Job resources, in turn, promote work engagement, which has been defined as an affective-motivational state characterized by high levels of energy, enthusiasm and concentration.

Organizational factors can have a direct effect on work design (high job demands are uniquely related to job strain and burnout).[42] Aspects of bureaucracy such as centralization and formalization are negatively related to work characteristics like job autonomy, employee discretion, variety and task significance.[43] Similarly, lean tools can be counter-productive for instance when the removal of wasted time in lean production technologies reduces employee job autonomy.

Conversely, flexitime directly enhances autonomy over working hours. When work is designed so that it has motivating characteristics like job autonomy and social support, as well as reasonable levels of job demands, multiple positive individual and organizational outcomes arise. Work design can be a powerful vehicle for learning and development, for maintaining and enhancing employee wellbeing, positive work attitudes, job satisfaction and organizational commitment.[44] It leads to better job performance[45] and higher levels of innovation, a key ingredient of agility,[46] and it enables control and flexibility simultaneously (e.g. in the form of ambidexterity). All these outcomes are important given the challenges in today's workplaces.

Organizations must focus on improving their planning routines and work design if they wish to encourage proactive behaviour among employees and enable true organizational agility (e.g. intrapreneurship and job crafting). Ironically, operational uncertainty appears to enhance managers' opportunities to design enriched work because there are more decisions for employees to have autonomy over. This is the most effective way to manage unpredictable demands since such environments are harder for managers to control through standardized procedures and close supervision. A more dynamic and unpredictable operating context also appears to strengthen employees' motivation for autonomy because such work designs allow employees to manage stressful demands more effectively.[47]

## HR's role in promoting empowerment

Success in shifting towards agility, customer-centricity and innovation may require building (or acquiring) new knowledge, skills and abilities, working practices, redesigning roles and accountabilities, simplifying unnecessary 'red tape' and embedding new cultural norms to create a workforce that recognizes the importance of the customer and feels both capable and empowered to deliver.

This approach to organizing people and work embeds many HR and OD best practices – including self-management, direct and frank communication, individual change agency and team-based decision making – and places these qualities firmly in service of better outcomes for the end user, for business and for employee engagement. HR can also greatly contribute to organizational effectiveness by:

- Working out what cultural changes will be required and building (or acquiring) new capabilities and embedding new cultural norms. A systems diagnosis can help to identify what is going on and which problems to solve. Surveys and analytics can help to pinpoint things that are working well and those that are not. It is important to start at the strategy and operational performance level (macro) then look at how work itself is designed. It is about looking at organizational capabilities and the culture as a whole down to team and individual level. Each level needs attention from HR, especially the nature and functioning of teams, a relatively neglected area of focus for HR compared with individual capability.

- Demonstrating and supporting smart working aligned to strategy as characterized by:

  o A high degree of autonomy

  o A philosophy of empowerment

  o Concepts of virtuality in teams or work groups

  o Outcome-based indicators of achievement. For instance, at team level, is there shared understanding in the team about goals and objectives? Is the team integrated in the way they do their jobs? Are teams supported by the right technology? What levels of trust exist in the team?

- Introducing flexible work location and hours. These require a flexible physical work environment and conditions that support collaboration and high-trust working relationships.

- Ensuring leaders can lead these transitions to new ways of working appropriately. Leadership development is needed that teaches the importance of modelling customer-centric values in action, the practice of trusting, non-directive management, and coaching to build and embed competence.

- Goal setting, reward and recognition initiatives to reinforce and incentivize pro-customer practices and communicate values.

Sometimes a change in routine can produce beneficial results, without changing structure. If employees are to feel empowered, new routines must be established to reinforce employee freedom to innovate. Initiatives to support front-line empowerment are plentiful, for example giving contact centre employees budgetary freedom to offer discounts or surprise customers with loyalty gifts or offer compensation. One company provided mobile phones to front-line contact centre employees, way beneath the job grade normally allowed, so they could call customers directly to take feedback and improve service problems. Against the resistance of other staff and managers who saw this as a risk, the HR leader positioned this as an experiment, established trackable success measures and engaged resistant leaders in steering the project. The metrics proved a positive impact on customers and business outcomes, and there were unexpected improvements in employee engagement.[48]

Change can be achieved by adopting the experimental practices of more agile firms – work where you can, test and learn, fail fast and move forward, as the case studies in this chapter illustrate. In an agile environment, managers encourage knowledge sharing in teams – this emphasizes the importance of developing line managers as facilitators. Coaching styles are ideal for seeking employee input – and enabling employees to have a voice. Thus, managers directly impact on employees' feelings of support and sense of accomplishment at work. An employee-centric HR strategy is required to bring these practices to life.

In a more coercive context, HR can help managers to move towards empowerment one step at a time – again using a test-and-learn approach, for instance defining strategies and policies and putting in place the frameworks and the systems that enable managers to manage in new ways. By encouraging relevant work-based learning, HR can equip line managers with the requisite technical knowledge, as well as the 'soft' skills they need to support teams and manage and develop people effectively.

## Job crafting

If people are empowered they are more likely to proactively initiate changes to their own work design (bottom-up). Indeed, the term 'work design' is increasingly used instead of 'job design' to signal that work design not only includes assigned tasks and responsibilities but also activities that the individual or group might have self-selected or 'crafted', or that have emerged through experiments or through informal or social processes, such as role expectations from peers. This informal and emergent work design process influences employees' motivation, KSAs and opportunities.

Job crafting, a process developed by Dutton and Wrzesniewski, is one of the most popular 'bottom-up' forms of work design practice intended to make jobs more engaging and meaningful. Through this, employees change the task-related or social boundaries of their job to increase work meaning or decrease its stressful aspects.[49] In line with social exchange theory, employees can negotiate idiosyncratic deals (or i-deals) with their supervisor or manager about their employment and working conditions (e.g. new tasks, flexible hours), which benefit both employee and employer.[50] Various studies suggest that sociable and considerate leaders of work groups are open to negotiating i-deals.[51]

To proactively shape their own work designs, employees can engage in task crafting, which involves altering the type, scope, sequence and number of tasks that make up their job. For instance, employees might negotiate with their boss to take on additional duties thereby expanding their job variety. Next, they can relationally craft their job by altering whom they interact with in their work. For instance, employees might negotiate flexibility in their job because of a motivation to better balance home and work commitments. Finally, there is cognitive crafting, where employees modify the way they interpret the tasks and/or work they are doing, craft their job to match their KSAs, or take up the opportunities afforded by new technology to interact more with peers. Crafting is perhaps most important for improving work design when positive formal work organization solutions are lacking.[52]

## Conclusion: HR implications

As we shall discuss further in Chapter 10, an agile culture facilitates change within the context the organization faces. Agile organizations embed customer-centricity in their processes, delayering structures and empowering the organization, and bringing business and IT together. They have staff who are willing and able to give their best in a sustainable way; there is a learning mindset in the mainstream business; and underlying agile processes and routines drive innovation.

Many of this chapter's messages about agile implementation apply to the HR function itself. The HR implications of agile implementation are counter-intuitive in some respects and there is no 'one size fits all' to HR strategies. HR needs to embrace the strategic agility agenda – anticipating emerging business needs and their talent and culture implications. Workplace innovation and employee participation go hand in hand, together with the limitless possibilities for creative and rewarding entrepreneurship that these afford. By making better use of workforce talent, workplace innovation has a profound effect on employees' learning and development, health and wellbeing.

To model the way forward, HR should embrace and champion agile methodology, utilizing experimentation and incremental change to build people management solutions geared to supporting current and future business needs. HR should therefore:

- Act as innovation hub – collaborate with other disciplines to share knowledge, work on change programmes, etc.
- Design HR strategies 'outside in', i.e. working back from the needs of the client, and collaboratively.
- Support innovation hubs – design spaces, facilitate connections, provide training, etc.
- Simplify HR policies, especially performance management.
- Apply agile work practices and project management disciplines to HR delivery.
- Go mobile and social.
- Help to source and develop agile teams.
- Address key 'implementation gaps' – identify underpinning issues, remove barriers using agile problem analysis and team working.
- Develop reward and recognition schemes that reinforce innovation, teamwork and knowledge sharing.
- Recruit, develop and nurture agile managers/team leaders.

As we shall discuss in the next few chapters, leaders and HR need to create a workplace fit for the future, though the task won't be easy. HR can help to build agile people practices and a change-able high-performance work climate. Those who get the process right will reap the benefits.[53]

---

CHECKLIST

How knowledge-rich and innovative is your organization?

- Do people have clear parameters for experimentation? Do they know where innovation is needed?
- How much are employees involved in decision making? How much are their ideas invited, heard and responded to?
- How much are people expected to use their initiative to find customer-centred solutions?

- How widely are good ideas/good practice disseminated?

- How well does your organization manage for diversity?

- How does the current structure impede or facilitate work effectiveness/ strategy accomplishment?

- To what extent do people's roles provide 'line of sight' to mission, purpose and strategy?

- How effective is teamwork? What can be done to strengthen it?

## Notes

1  Boudreau, J (2014) From Now to Next, i4cp Executive Thinksheet, Institute for Corporate Productivity, October.

2  Worley, C, Williams, TD and Lawler, EE (2014) *The Agility Factor: Building adaptable organizations for superior performance*, Jossey-Bass, San Francisco.

3  Raisch, S and Birkinshaw, J (2008) Organizational ambidexterity: antecedents, outcomes, and moderators, *Journal of Management*, **34**, pp 375–409.

4  Duncan, R (1976) The ambidextrous organization: Designing dual structures for innovation, in RH Killman, LR Pondy and D Sleven (eds) *The Management of Organization*, North Holland, New York, pp 167–88.

5  March, JG (1991) Exploration and exploitation in organizational learning, *Organization Science*, **2**, pp 71–87.

6  Kelly, K (1995) *Out of Control: The new biology of machines, social systems, and the economic world*, Basic Books, New York.

7  Denning, S (2013) Why Agile can be a game changer for managing continuous innovation in many industries, *Strategy & Leadership*, **41** (2), pp 5–11, doi. org/10.1108/10878571311318187 (archived at https://perma.cc/N6ZJ-43XM).

8  Ulrich, D, Younger, J, Brockbank, W and Ulrich, M (2012) *HR from the Outside In: Six competencies for the future of human resources*, McGraw-Hill, New York.

9  Alberts, DS and Hayes, RE (2003) Power to the edge: Command... control... in the information age, *The Command and Control Research Program*, www. dodccrp.org/files/Alberts_Power.pdf (archived at https://perma.cc/NPE7-XU4H).

10  Mohrman, SA and Worley, CG (2010) The organizational sustainability journey [special issue], *Organization Dynamics*, **39** (4).

11  *Deloitte human capital trends 2016*, www2.deloitte.com/content/dam/Deloitte/ global/Documents/HumanCapital/gx-dup-global-human-capital-trends-2016.pdf (archived at https://perma.cc/D4J3-9BZ6).

**12** Rogers, EM (1995) *Diffusion of Innovations*, 4th edn, Free Press, New York.

**13** Harvard Business Review Analytic Services (2011) The reinvention of business: New operating models for the next-generation enterprise, www.hbr.org/resources/pdfs/tools/17360_HBR_Cognizant_Report_webview.pdf (archived at https://perma.cc/RME8-3LN4).

**14** Alberts, and Hayes, ibid.

**15** Agile Business Consortium (2016) Knowledge Sharing in a Large Agile Organisation, www.agileresearchnetwork.org/wp-content/uploads/2016/12/Knowledge-Sharing-White-Paper-Published.pdf (archived at https://perma.cc/4A3M-6FCY)

**16** Rotenstein, J. It's the culture, stupid! How Atlassian maintains an open information culture, *Management Information eXchange*, 15 June 2011, www.managementexchange.com/story/its-culture-stupid-how-permeating-information-culture-leads-corporate-success (archived at https://perma.cc/X677-V3KS).

**17** Olanrewaju, T, Smaje, K and Willmott, P (2014) The seven traits of effective digital enterprises, McKinsey & Company, www.mckinsey.com/business-functions/organization/our-insights/the-seven-traits-of-effective-digital-enterprises.

**18** McKinsey (2020) An operating model for the next normal: Lessons from agile organizations in the crisis, www.mckinsey.com/capabilities/people-and-organizational-performance/our-insights/an-operating-model-for-the-next-normal-lessons-from-agile-organizations-in-the-crisis (archived at https://perma.cc/X9N3-7CGN).

**19** Claridge, F and Deighton, R. NHS reset: A new direction for health and care, NHS Confederation, 29 September 2020, www.nhsconfed.org/resources/2020/09/nhs-reset-a-new-direction-for-health-and-care (archived at https://perma.cc/K7D3-UWUK).

**20** Takeuchi, H and Nonaka, I (1986) The new new product development, *Harvard Business Review*, January–February.

**21** Denning, ibid.

**22** Strode, D (2012) Coordination in co-located agile software development projects, *Journal of Systems and Software*, 85 (6), pp 1222–38; Sutherland, J (2014) *Scrum: The art of doing twice the work in half the time*, Crown Business, New York; Rigby DK, Sutherland, J and Takeuchi, H (2016) Embracing Agile, *Harvard Business Review*, May.

**23** APM (2022) What is agile project management?, www.apm.org.uk/resources/find-a-resource/agile-project-management/ (archived at https://perma.cc/RGA4-RVRZ).

**24** Totterdill, P (2013) *The Future We Want? Work and Organisation in 2020*, Advisory Board of the UK Work Organisation Network, Nottingham.

**25** Plsek, P. Complexity and the adoption of innovation in health care, Conference on Strategies to Speed the Diffusion of Evidence-based Innovations, 27–28 January 2003, www.nihcm.org/pdf/Plsek.pdf.

**26** Worley, Williams and Lawler, ibid.

**27** Hoverstadt, P (2008) *The Fractal Organization: Creating sustainable organizations with the viable systems model*, Wiley, Chichester.

**28** Dijoux, C. Bug fixing vs. problem solving: From agile to lean, 7 April 2014, www.infoq.com/articles/bug-fixing-problem-solving (archived at https://perma.cc/HX4J-WP58).

**29** Orton-Jones, C. Growth, innovation and business transformation, *Raconteur*, 14 May 2014, p 15.

**30** Puranam P, Alexy O, Reitzig M (2014) What's 'new' about new forms of organizing? *Acad. Management Rev*, **39** (2), pp 162–80.

**31** Meyer, MW and Lynne Zucker, L (1989) Permanently Failing Organizations, Sage, Newbury Park.

**32** Ghosh, S and Wu, A. Iterative coordination and innovation: prioritizing value over novelty, *Organization Science*, 11 October 2021, www.pubsonline.informs.org/doi/full/10.1287/orsc.2021.1499 (archived at https://perma.cc/PJV4-A2VE).

**33** Phillips, J, Hebish, LJ, Mann et al (2016) Engaging frontline leaders and staff in real-time improvement, *Jt Comm J Qual Patient Saf*, **42** (4), pp 170–83, www.ncbi.nlm.nih.gov/pubmed/27025577# (archived at https://perma.cc/9EH5-PZA7).

**34** Adler, PS and Borys, B (1996) Two types of bureaucracy: Enabling and coercive, *Administrative Science Quarterly*, **41** (1), pp 61–89.

**35** Saparito, PA and Coombs, JE (2013) Bureaucratic systems' facilitating and hindering influence on social capital, *Entrepreneurship: Theory and Practice*, **37** (3), pp 625–39.

**36** Denneen, J and Dretler, T (2012) The financially sustainable university, *Bain Brief*, Bain and Company, www.bain.com/publications/articles/financially-sustainable-university.aspx (archived at https://perma.cc/SG4S-JEWQ).

**37** Mumford, T, Campion, M and Morgeson, F (2007) The leadership skills strataplex leadership skill requirements across organizational levels, *Leadership Quarterly*, **18**, pp 154–66.

**38** Parker, SK, Van den Broeck, A and Holman, D (2017) Work design influences: A synthesis of multi-level factors that affect the design of jobs, *The Academy of Management Annals*, **11** (1), pp 267–308, www.researchgate.net/publication/314258855_ Work_Design_Influences_A_Synthesis_of_Multilevel_Factors_that_Affect_the_ Design_of_Jobs (archived at https://perma.cc/FFD8-7RTE).

**39** Tsedal Neeley in Christian, A. Why some employers won't give in to flexibility, BBC, 1 September 2022, www.bbc.com/worklife/article/20220831-why-some-employers-wont-give-in-to-flexibility (archived at https://perma.cc/7HRY-2ABZ).

**40** Peccei, R and Rosenthal, P (2001) Delivering customer-oriented behaviour through empowerment: An empirical test of HRM assumptions, *Journal of Management Studies*, **38** (6), p 839.

**41** Bakker, AB and Demerouti, E (2007) The job demands resources model: State of the art, *Journal of Managerial Psychology*, **22** (3), pp 309–28.

**42** Schaufeli, WB and Taris, TW (2014) A critical review of the job demands-resources model: Implications for improving work and health, in GF Bauer and O Hämmig (eds) *Bridging Occupational, Organizational and Public Health: A transdisciplinary approach*, Springer, New York and London, pp 43–68.

**43** Oldham, GR and Hackman, JR (1981) Relationships between organizational structure and employee reactions: Comparing alternative frameworks, *Administrative Science Quarterly*, **26** (1), pp 66–83.

**44** Thakray, M (2022) For roles to be meaningful to employees, they need more than just social events and volunteering opportunities, *People Management*, January.

**45** Humphrey, SE, Nahrgang, JD and Morgeson, FP (2007) Integrating motivational, social, and contextual work design features: A meta-analytic summary and theoretical extension of the work design literature, *Journal of Applied Psychology*, **92** (5), p 1332.

**46** Hammond, MM, Neff, NL, Farr, JL et al (2011) Predictors of individual-level innovation at work: A meta-analysis, *Psychology of Aesthetics, Creativity, and the Arts*, **5**, pp 90–105.

**47** Parker, SK and Sprigg, CA (1999) Minimizing strain and maximizing learning: The role of job demands, job control, and proactive personality, *Journal of Applied Psychology*, **84** (6), pp 925–39.

**48** Denning, ibid.

**49** Tims, M, Bakker, AB and Derks, D (2013) The impact of job crafting on job demands, job resources, and well-being, *Journal of Occupational Health Psychology*, **18** (2), pp 230–40; Wrzesniewski, A and Dutton, JE (2001) Crafting a job: Revisioning employees as active crafters of their work, *The Academy of Management Review*, **26** (2), pp 179–201.

**50** Liao, C, Wayne, SJ and Rousseau, DM (2016) Idiosyncratic deals in contemporary organizations: A qualitative and meta-analytical review, *Journal of Organizational Behavior*, **37**, pp S9–S29.

**51** Ibid.

**52** Dutton, JE and Wrzesniewski, A. What job crafting looks like, Harvard Business Review, 12 March 2020, www.hbr.org/2020/03/what-job-crafting-looks-like (archived at https://perma.cc/3H3M-KKXA).

**53** California Management Review (cmr.berkeley.edu), p 8; Parker, Van den Broeck and Holman, D, ibid.

# 07

# Agile people processes

In the last few chapters we have considered the 'what', why' and 'how' of resilient agility. We've looked at ways that organizations can strategize, implement strategy and create collaborative connections with delivery partners and other key stakeholders. We have considered some of the capabilities and routines that enable organizations to adapt and try new things. We have looked at how managers, leaders and HR can all play roles in developing agile organization designs and stimulating an organizational culture conducive to open innovation, learning and democratic knowledge practices. Running through the first three quadrants of the resiliently agile model is the focus of the fourth – the 'who' of agility: people.

While the organizational capabilities we have discussed so far are all important, equipping the organization for growth goes beyond simply investing in new IT and fancy kit or applying Agile methods and new project management practices. In knowledge-intensive and service-intensive work *people* are the source of production. It is people who are ultimately responsible for delivering the vision, ideas, products, services and day-to-day work that make a company successful. Having the right people focused on the right things is key to business success.

Over the next few chapters we explore what 'agile' means when applied to people and culture. Currently shortages of key talent are putting agility and productivity at risk. People are changing their expectations about what they want from employers. In this chapter we look at some of the challenges of attracting and developing a flexible workforce – in particular those deemed to be 'talent'. All too often these challenges are addressed piecemeal, with separate, short-term solutions where the temptation is to rush into action to 'fix' the problem. A more strategic approach based on facts is required in order to equip organizations with the people they need now and for the future. We look at the field of talent management and consider how processes such as strategic workforce planning and succession planning are gradually becoming more agile to reflect the changing context. We shall look at:

- a diverse workforce
- strategic workforce planning
- talent management
- finding the right people in the right place with the right skills
- build strategies – growing the talent pool
- agile succession planning
- developing customer-centric leaders.

Let's begin by considering what the term 'agile people' means.

## Agile people

Resiliently agile people are the lifeblood of high performance and an organization's true source of competitive advantage. At the same time, an agile organization requires flexibility to be built into the resourcing model. As a report for the UK's NHS recognized: 'All health services will need a flexible, agile workforce in the future. Whilst many have made recent investments in workforce reform, change is needed to develop a workforce that is sufficiently flexible, specialised and self-renewing to be properly responsive to changing stakeholder expectations.'[1]

Much is expected of a flexible workforce. Increasingly people work in organizations that are less hierarchically structured and have a fluid multiplicity of collaborations, with time and location-based work increasingly eroded. People have to embrace technology and new routines and ways of working. This requires new skills and capabilities such as scanning and working across the system; adapting; being resilient and innovating. Thus an agile workforce must be multiskilled and/or deep specialists; people who are able and willing to acquire new skills to meet changing needs. Such workers can rightly be described as 'talented'.

At the same time jobs are being disaggregated and becoming less secure, with organizations engaging workers through a variety of contractual relationships. Organizations have choices: in a fast-moving environment they can replace jobs by embracing automation that results in role redundancy, and/or they can create value-enhancing roles. To enable the latter, HR must adapt its levers (such as agile workforce planning, talent management, flexible resourcing, performance management, developing leaders, building capability) to ensure the organization has the right people to deliver agility outcomes. These incremental shifts produce learning and help to build the organizational adaptability required for success today and beyond.

## A diverse workforce

Currently there are acute skills shortages in many areas. One of the most challenging long-term issues facing the labour market is demographics. Since the pandemic many baby boomers have retired, taking their knowledge and skills with them. In the UK, finding and sourcing much-needed talent from abroad became harder since freedom of movement for EU workers ended and the rules for foreign workers coming to the UK became tougher. In Europe the workforce is ageing and UK employees can now anticipate longer working lives due in part to changes in pension arrangements and the ending of the default retirement age of 65 for men and 60 for women. As people work later in life, this is giving rise to the extended workforce in Europe (the '4G' workforce, in which there can be four generations of workforce employed simultaneously).[2] People who might once have retired at or before 60 will want new development opportunities rather than to retire and may need to move to other roles to allow younger workers to progress.

Today's talent market is increasingly global and, as the talent map loses its borders, workforces become highly diverse. Some in the HR community consider age diversity to be a problem.[3] They are concerned about how to create opportunities for career development for younger workers. They are also concerned that, with no obligation for people to leave their employer when they reach the previous retirement age, tougher performance management and severances may replace previously honourable exits at retirement for those no longer able to perform at former levels.

On the other hand, many companies see the rise of a multigenerational workforce as a bonus and as a potential source of innovation. For instance, DIY retailer B&Q considers that an age-diverse workforce brings a wealth of skills and experience. B&Q has operated without a default retirement age for over 20 years and aims to provide age-neutral benefits for its 32,000 employees. Its oldest employee is 96 and works on the checkouts. With 28 per cent of its workforce over the age of 50, it has many employees who are semi-retired. The firm recognizes that an ageing population comes with some physical restrictions, for example injuries, bad backs and people becoming frail, so it offers adjustments to utilize these people as well as it can.

## Changing expectations

With longer working lives, today's employees might expect at least five career changes during their working lives. Unlike the baby boomers (born 1943–60) and their predecessor generations who might have hoped to make their career in one organization, Generation X (born 1961–81), Generation Y or 'millennials' (born roughly 1982–1995) and certainly their successors, the 'Re-Generation' or Gen Z will have different aspirations and exacting expectations of their future employers.[4] There is an increase in non-linear 'portfolio' careers rather than 'careers for life'. This shift may lead to higher expectations of employers to make it easier for people to move in and out of roles and create more opportunities for non-linear progression.

The influx of millennials and Gen Z into the workforce has significant implications for workforce dynamics. The size of this group gives them not only a large 'vote' in the aggregate 'voice of the employee' but also significant influence on other generations about what to expect in a work environment (e.g. flexibility, rapid career movement, learning, transparency).[5] While the importance of salaries will never fade, employees are increasingly looking beyond just compensation when it comes to choosing an employer. Some 92 per cent of Gen Y see 'flexibility' as priority.[6] They are natural clients – they have intuition and they want to have impact. They have low tolerance for bureaucracy, hierarchies, process. ADP research in 2018 found that 56 per cent of Gen Y would prefer to work just four days a week, and 78 per cent would prefer to work longer on four days and retain the same level of salary.[7]

In the graduate recruitment sector, many major brand-leading companies, including international consultancies, are already finding that where once they would have had their pick of graduate recruits, they now struggle to attract potential candidates who may prefer bigger jobs in smaller, more fleet-of-foot organizations where they can rapidly acquire skills and experience.

Organizational values and purpose are seen as most important in attracting candidates, followed jointly by career development opportunities and pay and benefits. Upcoming generations of workers appear more interested in community, environmental and social endeavours (ESG) and careers such as teaching that offer the chance to do something worthwhile for others and the possibility of personal satisfaction. Stereotypically, millennials want to make the world a better place, to improve the environment in a broader sense, and are not driven by purely materialistic values. McKinsey research found that 82 per cent of employees believe it is important for their company to have a purpose.[8] Purpose can shape company strategy, engage customers and community, and steer choices at 'moments of truth'. It inspires employees: more than two-thirds say their sense of purpose is defined by their work. Also, once inspired by a company with credible purpose, 93 per cent of employees say they are likely to recommend that company to others.

The pandemic has produced many new conditions for people to work under, such as remote or hybrid working, and it also increases the pressure on employers. The impact of COVID-19 has shown that employees have needs and desires that companies may not have known about before, such as support for mental health and wellbeing. Gen Z employees tend to view career progression differently from previous cohorts. They typically have higher expectations around rapid promotions, salaries and job moves. They care deeply about a company's values on issues such as diversity, inclusion and the environment and expect a 'digital-first' approach to communications. Managers and HR at every level must respond to these changes and use them as an opportunity to transform the experience that people have at work.

Of course, things may change as time moves on, and there is already some evidence that as recession bites, record numbers of millennials are gravitating back towards large institutions and government agencies, seeking teamwork, protection against risk and solid work-life balance.[9] There is a new focus on upbeat messages and conventional big brands. However, if organizations are to retain these recruits, they may need to consider how to capture that sense of vocation and develop strongly value-driven employer brands that deliver their promise in reality.

## Strategic workforce planning

Given the confusing landscape, how can organizations predict what their workforce will look like in months or years to come? After all, the future is uncertain, workforce systems are complex, resources are limited, making mistakes can be costly and decisions have to be taken and justified. Talent management is built upon talent intelligence – the understanding businesses have of the skills, expertise and qualities of their people – that should be the basis of every people decision that companies make. Without it, decisions would be reduced to pure guesswork.

Therefore, strategic workforce planning, a long-neglected discipline, is becoming once again a key tool to enable organizations to get to grips with their future workforce requirements and to develop and implement agile workforce design. This follows a period when the old-style top-down 'manpower planning' approaches, which used detailed modelling and assumed a slowly changing context, fell by the wayside in the light of frequent changes and radical restructurings such as mergers and acquisitions, which made previous forecasts irrelevant.

'Hard' workforce planning is about numbers: predicting how many people and what skills are likely to be needed. Data need to be analysed and understood in context. 'Soft' (or strategic) workforce planning is about defining a strategy or developing a strategic framework within which information can be considered. With an increased emphasis on agility and responsiveness, there is a growing realization that good-quality management information set within such a planning framework is the key to identifying and maximizing the drivers of performance before reaching a stage where managers are forced into action by circumstance. It is as much art as science.

The aim of agile workforce planning is not to create an exact picture of the future workforce but instead to enable the organization to build capability and capacity for improvement, innovation, leadership, spread, scale-up and sustainability. In contrast to conventional workforce planning, agile approaches assume that the future is inherently unpredictable, so planning should be scenario-based and take into account longer-term megatrends and current trends. A megatrend is a large, technological, economic, environmental, political, social or ethical change that is slow to form – such as population growth and ageing populations – that contains the underlying forces that drive trends, possibly for decades. A trend is an emerging pattern of change likely to impact business and organizations and requires a response. As business changes, HR needs to future-proof the organization by monitoring both current and future trends with respect to skills and job roles, and by reviewing staffing strategies in the light of technological developments. Are more, or fewer, employees required? In estimating future workforce needs it is important to take a longer-term view, as far out as the next 10–20 years, identifying where gaps are likely to emerge and putting plans in place to deal with these before they become problematic. For instance, utility company National Grid takes a 10-year time frame that is revisited annually, with the focus kept on 'critical job families' that are core to the business.[10]

The main stages are:

- Understand the organization and the operating environment.
- Analyse the workforce.
- Determine future workforce needs.
- Identify gaps in the workforce.
- Develop an action plan that allows for functional, numerical and adaptational flexibility – an agile workforce that can adapt to change will contribute greatly to a change-ready organization which can proactively restructure as a result of progress.
- Monitor and evaluate action plans and solutions.

## Understanding the organization and its operating environment

Today, talent management and workforce analytics are increasingly integral elements of companies' future-readiness plans.

As the guardian of workforce data, HR needs to be able to spell out the implications of what the data are saying with respect to the organization's capability to deliver its business strategy and meet its obligations to shareholders. As Peter Cheese, CIPD chief executive, puts it: 'We (in HR) have to make the intangible tangible so we can demonstrate the value and importance of investing in people for the future success of organizations.'[11] This means answering questions such as:

- Are we losing our best talent?
- How many have we left?
- Are we improving month after month?
- Are we equipping people with the skills required for the changing business, e.g. digital capability?
- How many of our top performers have we promoted from within?
- What openings have been filled from within?

## Analysing the workforce and determining future workforce needs

Technology is a vital tool in getting to grips with the data you gather and already have in order to better understand your talent needs and recruitment, retention and deployment challenges. Increasingly, predictive intelligence can be leveraged to understand your company's skills needs now and over time – including the traits and behaviours of future leaders. A workforce platform should enable the organization to be reconfigured as business needs change, and talent to be reallocated quickly. Using relevant, comparable people data for greater transparency and open discussions, intelligent risk-taking and data-driven decision making are possible.

To gain a better understanding of where the critical gaps might be, it is important to identify critical workforce segments – those groups of workers who may be more crucial to delivering the future business strategy than others. These may be high-potential future leaders or hard-to-replace specialists or even part of the core workforce. That does not mean you can ignore the other segments, as different elements of the workforce deliver value in different ways. Some can help to upgrade core capabilities, while others have more potential to drive competitive differentiation. Choosing between improving core solutions and investing in innovation may not be necessary, as both may be needed.

Rather than getting into the detail of estimating the contours of the future workplace itself – which jobs stay, which jobs go – it is more useful to reflect on where the organization is in the evolutionary cycle of technology, and consequently how to prepare as it unfolds. For instance, HR Director Jacky Simmonds designed and led the 'Next Generation easyJet' programme that simultaneously dealt with current and future issues, reviewing changes to the working environment and implementing focused action plans in four key areas:

- customer service and operational excellence
- data and digital skills
- strategy and network
- cost.[12]

Inevitably a degree of risk is inherent in strategic workforce planning. Preparation benefits from anticipating future work demands earlier in the cycle. In many organizations, senior management and other key staff from the baby boomer generation may be considering leaving the organization or taking flexible retirement in the near future. It is important to find out not only who might be about to leave but also what vital knowledge they might take with them. Every effort must be made to transfer that knowledge quickly enough to prevent adverse impact on the organization. It is important to identify what levels of risk are acceptable and draw up a desired risk profile.

At the same time, planning needs to be tactical. What would happen, for instance, if entire teams were to suddenly and unexpectedly leave?

## Develop an action plan

In WEF research conducted in 2018 companies typically reported three future strategies to manage the skills gaps widened by the adoption of new technologies and other factors. They expect to hire wholly new permanent staff already possessing skills relevant to new technologies; or to automate the work tasks concerned completely; or to retrain employees. The most popular strategy is recruitment and two-thirds expect workers to simply adapt and pick up skills as their jobs change. Most are likely to turn to external contractors, temporary staff and freelancers to address skills gaps.[13]

More recently it is recognized that, with talent shortages, developing the existing workforce is the key solution. This requires a mix of upskilling, reskilling and unlearning. Doing things differently can require changing behaviour as much as skills. After all, the surest way to attract and retain the talent organizations need is to manage people in such a way that they want to stay and give their best.[14]

## Generate consensus on the plan

Once you have established insights into your current and future workforce needs and assessed the risks, it is a question of articulating the message confidently to relevant stakeholders and building a rigorous business case for any investment in talent. A collaborative approach is vital. Wide-ranging consultation with stakeholders should enable all parties to understand and agree the rationale for the actions being taken. Once agreement has been reached about what needs to happen next, ensure clear allocation and understanding of responsibilities: it is essential that all those involved are clear about what they are responsible for and what actions they need to take.

## Provide support for managers

HR may need to support line managers and others to fulfil their responsibilities and ensure they have the skills and understanding to fully participate in the planning process and act on the outcomes; for example, the skills to input and interpret data are essential. People professionals should intentionally help leaders and line managers to lead effectively for talent; understand the needs, expectations and aspirations of their teams; spot, develop and nurture talent at all levels.

### Review and capture learning

There should be clear and robust mechanisms to capture and review learning and feed this back into the process. Evaluation criteria will depend on the objectives. Essentially, workforce planning is about trying to predict the future to inform decision making so evaluation relates to the outcomes of those decisions and their consequences. Evaluation should be iterative – the more proficient organizations become at planning, the more likely they can identify relevant evaluation criteria and demonstrate their ability to make more accurate future predictions.

### Measurement for improvement and whole-system dashboard

HR metrics should be aligned with business goals, so it is important to get sponsorship from the top – the board needs to know what you are measuring and why. If a talent shortage looms, for example, why are you measuring absenteeism?

Organizations also need to be able to track continually their return on talent investment, so having the right measures and (access to) analytical capability is essential. A balanced scorecard can be helpful, working back from the desired outcomes of strategy to identify the talent 'lead' measures that matter such as the organization's capabilities relating to leadership, culture, alignment and learning.[15] Analytics can also be used to provide an evidence base for workforce productivity and bonus structures can be designed to reflect this. Some of the enablers of employee productivity include:

- better people management by managers
- appropriate HR policies and practices
- employee engagement
- improved resourcing and training
- good job design – autonomy and flexibility
- more effective communication and staff involvement
- leadership of change and role modelling
- knowledge sharing.

As with all aspects of workforce strategy, strategic workforce planning does not sit in isolation from other strategies. Unilever has put data analytics at the heart of its global HR strategy. The firm can now correlate employee engagement with attrition or career progression and identify factors that affect its talent pipeline. In a context of talent scarcity, with the potential for loss of knowledge, lack of innovation and decreasing shareholder value due to uncertainty, HR should help leaders to identify the talent gaps they are facing and explore options for closing them. At the very least it is worth looking ahead and deciding which are the top 20 roles needed for the future and develop a workforce development strategy for those top 20 roles. Break each role down into skills to understand which are going to change going forward and which ones you can reshape. A more sophisticated estimate of the minimum supply of skilled staff required will take account of how future productivity demands can be met without destroying people's work-life balance.

## A new 'war for talent'

The term 'talent management' dates roughly from the late 1990s, when McKinsey published 'The War for Talent' to highlight the underlying chronic shortages of what it called 'talent' in professional service firms and other highly skilled knowledge work.[16] It emphasized the need for employers to adopt new and more employee-centric means to attract and retain the 'talent' needed for success. It argued that talent management is about identifying talented people, finding out what they want and giving it to them – if not, your competitors will. This followed a period of 'anti-planning' with respect to the workforce and 'do-it-yourself' approaches to career management.

From this time onwards, talent management was increasingly recognized as a distinct aspect of strategic HR capability, competitive advantage and a driver of sustainable organizational performance. However, after the international financial crisis of 2008, talent management went into the doldrums and many companies mistakenly assumed that people would remain with their current employer due to the scarcity of good jobs. Those assumptions proved unfounded, leading to a mismatch between supply and demand. After all, the boundaryless careers that were predicted years ago are now a reality and these are 'the opposite of organizational careers – careers that unfold in a single employment setting'.[17]

As global competition for employees and customers intensifies, and the 'Great Resignation' phenomenon hits, employers in many industries are competing hard not just for market share but also to attract and source the best talent. When highly skilled talent is in short supply and employees have choice, 'key talent' can pick and choose who they work for. In the West only 18 per cent of firms say they have enough talent in place to meet future business needs,[18] and more than half report that their business is already being held back by a lack of leadership talent.[19]

Consequently, there is a renewed focus on talent management and on upgrading its related processes. Conventional talent processes reflect the top-down assumptions underpinning the old-style 'psychological contract' or 'old deal' – that the organization has the whip hand in the employment relationship. Psychological contracts are the unwritten set of expectations between employees and employers – and are how people understand the benefits of their job, whether monetary or social. The slow erosion of the 'old deal' has left today's employees with few illusions about remaining with their employer for life and, often, little loyalty. Today employees must look after their own careers, and even the best-laid plans for succession may be undermined by the sudden departure of a highly valued employee.

Therefore, in agile organizations there is a much stronger focus on designing talent processes to meet the needs of the 'talent'. Organizations try to develop enticing employer brands to differentiate themselves from the competition in order to attract the best. They offer 'onboarding' experiences to help new recruits quickly become productive – and then hope to retain them. However, as the labour market for knowledge and service work becomes more buoyant, and with loyalty to employers a thing of the past, retention is becoming a major challenge – hence the plethora of employee engagement and reward initiatives.

## Talent management: a debated topic

Finding, developing and making the most of talent becomes a strategic priority, especially for those organizations aspiring to build sustainable high performance. Given the importance of talent to business success, ultimate responsibility for talent and planning should lie with the CEO and the management line, while HR is responsible for managing the related processes to add value, including carrying out talent risk assessments, monitoring turnover data and drawing inferences, creating and implementing talent strategies to alleviate risk.

The term 'talent' conventionally applies to an exclusive cadre of high-potential employees who are groomed for future senior (leadership) roles and considered most valuable to organizations. Increasingly this exclusive approach to talent is being called into question and many organizations are adopting 'a very broad definition of talent management, taking a systems and strategic HRM viewpoint'.[20] This 'inclusive' view of talent management embraces the whole workforce. Partly that is because in today's fast-moving context it can be difficult to predict the organization's future workforce needs in the light of changing business models, so identifying which people and which roles will be most valuable is difficult.

Definitions of the term 'talent management' and its component elements continue to evolve, and a plethora of strategic perspectives exist. The emphasis in most is on the systematic effort to integrate the ways to attract, develop, deploy and retain the most productive and promotable people the organization needs, both now and in the future: 'Talent management is the systematic attraction, identification, development, engagement, retention and deployment of those individuals who are of particular value to an organization, either in view of their "high potential" for the future or because they are fulfilling business/operation-critical roles.'[21]

Talent management processes are often grouped into 'buy' or 'build' talent strategies. 'Buy' activities include attracting, sourcing, assessing, hiring and 'onboarding' new recruits. 'Build' processes include talent identification, engagement and retention, progression and development, including careers. Creating talent pools and career pathways are just some of the elements of a 'build' talent strategy.

Debates still rage as to where the emphasis should be put – on people or positions. Collings and Mellahi argue that strategic talent management involves 'the systematic identification of key positions which differentially contribute to the organization's sustainable competitive advantage, the development of a talent pool of high-potential and high-performing incumbents to fill these roles, and... filling these positions with competent incumbents and to ensure their continued commitment to the organization.'[22]

In contrast, Cappelli argues that 'it is more effective to develop talent within the broader context of the organization, rather than with a particular succession role in mind. This prevents developing employees to fit narrow, specialized roles but rather, once developed employees can be developed with broader competencies which would fit a range of roles.'[23] GSK uses the term 'talent' to cover both high potentials (those individuals who have the potential to move into broad leadership roles in the future) and high performers (those individuals who consistently deliver exceptional results). The high-performing category ensures that expert scientists as well as future leaders are seen as key to the business.

### Fresh approaches to talent management are needed

For agility, talent management approaches should no longer be restricted to the favoured few or simply follow the tired old formulas of 'fast-track' development and conventional succession planning. Innovations in talent strategies and solutions should have the potential to span the needs of multiple segments of the workforce – no matter where they are in the world. Systemic and open-source approaches to talent are needed that are relational and personalized in nature with informal networks often more effective than formal talent management processes in attracting and retaining talent. 'The key to workforce agility lies in a strategy that puts people first, enabled by technology. With an eye on business outcomes, leaders will develop talent strategies that help liberate human potential and help shape an agile workforce – one able to confidently face the changes ahead.'[24] As we shall explore in the next couple of chapters, engaging employees' discretionary effort – finding new ways to motivate people, unblocking barriers to employee motivation, providing fair reward and recognition – are just some of the underpinnings of a resiliently agile talent management strategy.

An emerging 'new deal' needs to be 'co-created' with employees the organization wants to attract and retain. Many companies today develop employee value propositions (EVPs) or employer brands to describe their commitments to workers. The company brand and other recruitment messaging should signal both what is on offer, and the kinds of behaviours (and culture) the company wants to encourage. Thus potential recruits are clear about what to expect and about the kinds of behaviours that will be expected of them. Understanding the needs, aspirations and motivations of key employee segments will be critical.

It is important to bear in mind the things that matter to people of all generations: recognition and respect, flexibility and choices, meaningful work, and balance – with life and with community. Deloitte's Millennial survey of 2014 found that over 80 per cent of candidates look beyond pay and benefits to other factors such as career prospects, the working environment, what an organization stands for and how it serves its clients.[25] At the same time, it is important to keep the differences in mind, too, and be prepared to flex the 'deal' to accommodate people's changing needs at different life stages and circumstances. Tailoring packages (often referred to as idiosyncratic or i-deals), including development, will increasingly be used both to source scarce talent and to create win-win opportunities for individuals and organizations. Generation Y, in particular, looks for opportunities for professional growth and generally prefers to learn in a mobile rather than static environment. Multiple employer brands targeted at different employee segments may need to co-exist.

Greater workforce diversity also has significant implications for how work will be delivered, and what future leaders look like. So who will tomorrow's leaders be? How will they be identified and developed? For instance, there are now more women than men in the UK workforce yet in most sectors women remain significantly under-represented in executive roles or on boards. Women also make up the majority of people in the UK workforce working flexibly. More flexible ways of working, combined with a growth in the virtual workplace and the growing priority given by individuals to work-life balance, mean that new models of management are needed that make the most of the talents of individuals not working in full-time roles. This is shifting the emphasis to the 'output' or quality of contribution made while working, rather than to the 'input' or the hours spent at work.

## Finding the right people in the right place with the right skills

Developing an agile workforce strategy is a holistic process and involves looking at how talent works throughout the organization. If the kinds of talent gap you are trying to close change in nature, you may need to change your employer branding or recruitment processes and reward strategies in order to continue to attract the 'right' people.

### Sourcing and recruiting talent

In a tighter labour market, the rise of remote working has enabled companies to spread their recruitment efforts globally across different time zones. Talent today is moving across international borders – engineering students from India, for instance.[26] Companies such as Google, Tata and Microsoft source talent globally, using intelligence sources to gain knowledge of where the best talent is to be found. Many organizations that need a steady stream of entry-level talent establish partnerships with universities that have high numbers of foreign nationals or a growing base of young people who thrive on international opportunities. For global sourcing of talent, employers will need a strong global technology platform that can be adapted to individual country needs so it has to be both scalable and flexible. Successful overseas candidates may need help to obtain the visas they need. Companies may have to support critical talent who want to work remotely – whether from home or elsewhere – so they will need to provide the communications technology, the collaboration tools and the systems to make work flow.

The challenge is to develop talents both inside and outside the organization that can be drawn upon to mobilize a response. Today employers are looking at their workforce as a much broader ecosystem than the people they directly employ. Many organizations are building talent pools through close links with universities and other potential sources of future recruits. Others are exploring digital talent platforms and expanding their talent ecosystem to include networks of freelancers and create access to potential opportunities. Designing new and existing roles to better meet changing needs is attractive to existing and future recruits.

Indeed, the pandemic has prompted new sourcing trends. Reshoring for instance is evident in many US firms, reclaiming jobs from places such as China and using machines to do jobs faster and more cheaply. Building a large contingent workforce is another talent management strategy being adopted by some companies where demand for their services fluctuates. These are non-permanent staff members including contractors and service providers. Building and maintaining a positive relationship with the contingent workforce pays dividends when there is competition for contractor services.

Technology is having a huge impact on talent acquisition, providing employers with a means to handle large volumes of applications. Potential recruits increasingly look for jobs online. A survey by Webrecruit (in 2014) found that 88 per cent of job searches now begin via Google, and 80 per cent of tablet users research job opportunities via their tablet at home after work.[27] Candidates tend to look at:

- first – job boards
- second – company careers sites
- third – recruitment agencies.

Conversely only 20 per cent of talent acquirers had a careers site – an area on a company's website dedicated to recruitment that is mobile optimized. That situation is changing fast, so organizations that seek to recruit using only conventional means, such as job advertisements in print media, may be missing out on pools of potential recruits. The latest generation of jobseekers have been engaging via social platforms for years and are likely to continue to do so. Many candidates carry out their own research into potential employers using sites such Glassdoor where current and former employees anonymously review companies. Social interaction via a firm's careers site can help build relationships with candidates, adding a personal element to the recruitment process.

Firms are starting to diversify their recruitment and do more to encourage applicants from underrepresented groups such as people with disabilities or from minority ethnic groups, for instance by using anonymous applications. Big Data analytics and other new methods are increasingly used to attempt to remove bias, for instance ageist hiring practices. Recruitment platform data on prospective candidates can help employers actively target priority groups and engage the people they want to hire, helping employers to better understand applicants and build a more diverse workforce, which Gen Z employees find attractive.[28] Companies need to be willing to look at candidates offering adjacent skills and experience rather than being a perfect fit.

For the following case study I am grateful to Robert Taffinder, formerly Senior Manager Resource Partnering, and Stephanie Tapner, Manager Resourcing and Case Management, at Nationwide Building Society.

---

CASE STUDY
*Agile recruitment at Nationwide*

Nationwide Building Society is rare among financial services organizations: it has emerged relatively unscathed from the 2008 financial crisis with its reputation intact. As a *mutual*, Nationwide is owned by and run for the benefit of its members (customers) with no shareholders to satisfy (in the way that banks do). However, in the wake of the 2008 financial crisis, in common with all financial service providers, Nationwide is subject to new regulatory requirements from the Financial Conduct Authority and Prudential Regulation Authority in order to avoid such crises being repeated.

In response to the changing context, Nationwide recognized the need to build up its first-, second- and third-line risk roles in order to retain its traditional focus on customer interest and to meet the new regulatory requirements. Similarly, new generations of customers expect to be able to transact 24/7, remotely, securely and conveniently, through tablets and other mobile technology. Nationwide's innovation strategy is simple: they are investing in technology, which makes life better for their members and their people. They are using digital innovations to better connect their people with their members and ensuring that members have access to their experts – anywhere and at any time.

However, Nationwide's recruitment practices were fairly traditional and relied on advertising on its careers site, posting vacancies on job boards or using recruitment agencies. Finding and recruiting such scarce talent would be a major challenge using conventional methods and in the face of the current 'war for talent'.

In response to these challenges the Resourcing Delivery team decided to build upon existing good practice and adopt a new way to attract potential candidates both cost-effectively and innovatively. The new approach began with research, listening closely to a wide range of people with different backgrounds, skills and capabilities, looking at emerging trends with respect to people's behaviour and perspectives on Nationwide's brand. Candidates' expectations were clearly starting to shift; lifestyle and balance appeared more important than salary. Social media was becoming a key means by which potential candidates now interact, so digital tools would be part of the solution. IT support would be needed to assist the recruitment team in using the careers site to advantage and in getting more candidates through the door.

The challenge was how to make Nationwide stand out as different in the jobs market. Ironically, though Nationwide has a good story to tell, the society's cultural modesty meant that many people did not know about it. So it was important to develop a strong and authentic story about Nationwide, about what being a mutual is all about, demonstrating what it stands for, sharing success stories. The aim was to surprise potential recruits, and one initiative – a video developed for internal recruitment purposes titled 'Haircut' – certainly caught people's imagination and was shortlisted for an external award.

In true agile style, a variety of other initiatives was developed through a three-phase approach that allowed for feedback and further development over a six-month period. Elements were added based on what the business was saying was great. So, for instance, the traditional careers site was made interactive, with an employee blog so that people can add their comments and their feedback can be acted on. A variant on the job website Glassdoor (like TripAdvisor for candidates, so that anyone can see reviews about an organization and what current employees say about it) was developed, allowing the team to respond to things that need improving with respect to recruitment processes and to learn from why people leave the organization.

The team itself has become agile and empowered and has come a long way in a short time. There is a great deal of collaborative working with other departmental functions such as Brand, Marketing and IT. Data analytics and reviews from the careers website provide useful intelligence, which resourcing consultants use to select the right kinds of attraction channels to reach specific types of skill set.

For the resourcing team, the challenge of success is that people expect more of you. It is important to manage expectations, look at internal platforms and what they can deliver, use data/evidence and communicate/renegotiate priorities on an ongoing basis, pushing back if necessary. The key to ultimate resourcing success is being clear what you stand for, as Robert Taffinder points out: 'If people are put off by that, it's not a bad thing. I'd rather have fewer candidates of higher calibre than have to deselect more people who would not operate well in our culture.'

---

## Onboarding

Having struggled to attract and recruit the best, many organizations often lose new hires within weeks. Turnover can be as high as 50 per cent in the first 18 months of employment.[29]

Organizations have traditionally offered new recruits induction training to introduce them to company-specific information, compliance requirements and ways of working. Onboarding, also known as 'organizational socialization', goes further than induction and refers to the whole range of ways in which new employees are personally welcomed into a firm and acquire the knowledge, skills and behaviours they need to become effective organizational members. Many companies begin the onboarding process during recruitment, before the new employee formally joins.

The ways that firms bring new staff in – and the environment they create for them – communicate, model and form the culture. Unless new employees are made to feel valued from the outset their motivation on arrival is likely to drop off dramatically. If new hires feel welcome and prepared for their new positions, they gain the confidence and resources to make an impact within the organization, and ultimately to help the company to continue carrying out its mission. The active involvement of line managers in onboarding is vital. Being introduced to new workmates in person and via social networks helps them to become culturally attuned to the company. 'Buddies' and mentors may be assigned to support the new arrival with relevant information and encouragement. These socialization techniques lead to positive outcomes for new employees such as higher job satisfaction, better job performance, greater organizational commitment, and reduction in occupational stress and intention to quit.[30]

There is also some evidence that employees with certain personality traits and experiences adjust to a new organization more quickly.[31] These traits include a 'proactive personality' – the tendency to take charge of situations and achieve control over one's environment. I refer elsewhere in this chapter to 'learning agility', a similar concept. Researchers have noted that role clarity,[32] self-efficacy, social acceptance and knowledge of organizational culture are particularly good indicators of well-adjusted new employees who have benefited from an effective onboarding system.

To improve the effectiveness of an onboarding programme it is helpful for one person to 'own' the onboarding process, oversee all departmental stakeholders,[33] and monitor and measure how well new recruits are adjusting to their new roles, responsibilities, peers, supervisors and the organization at large.

## Build strategies: growing the talent pool

Tapping into new sources of talent is a key priority as organizations gear up for growth. So it is important to combine internal development and external recruitment in filling talent pools.[34] Instead of hiring new people with a narrow skill set to meet a temporary need, leading companies strengthen existing people with additional skills to build a more agile workforce capable of responding to new competitive threats and capitalizing on new opportunities. This ensures that the organization has the requisite skill set required at a point in time.

For such employees a commitment-oriented HR system seems appropriate.[35] The emphasis for HR practices should be on building the motivation, commitment and development of those in the talent pool, shifting from a short-term 'transactional' psychological contract towards a more long-term 'relational' psychological contract.[36]

### Identifying high potential

In large talent pools the challenge is to distinguish between those with the ability to perform at the relevant level now and those who have future potential for more senior roles. Conventionally organizations have used variations on a 'nine-box grid' to assess performance and potential and to identify their current and future 'stars'. However, use of in-year appraisal ratings to define performance is risky given the instability of the measure. Moreover, 'potential' is often confused with 'ready for promotion', which begs the question of 'potential for what?' The process often ignores business-critical expertise and functional mastery. Increasingly firms are using psychometric tests to determine the nature of potential, rather than relying mainly on current performance assessments. Test provider SHL argues that three components that have proved to be robust in identifying true high-potential employees are: *aspiration* to rise to senior roles, *ability* to be effective in more responsible and senior roles and *engagement* to commit to the organization and remain in a challenging role.

## GE's future leaders

The way GE reviews its leadership talent is being revised. For decades, the annual organization-wide talent review process known as 'Session C' has taken place in April. Session C included an intense review of the business, mapping talent to strategy, assessing the performance of individuals and business units all the way up to the CEO. This involved a detailed and very candid analysis of the strengths and weaknesses of each of the GE organization's business leaders, including career development needs and depth of talent. To quantify people's performance, employees were then placed on a nine-box grid reflecting the two dimensions of achievement of stretch objectives and demonstration of company values.

Human resources owned the Session C agenda, but the business leaders controlled and conducted the actual reviews, with former CEO Jeff Immelt actively involved throughout. The process was time-consuming since lengthy, complex presentations on business results and meetings with union leaders were the norm. Now this process has been replaced by a monthly Pulse session, which is more of a conversation among leaders about talent that goes deeper into leadership and talent issues than the previous process. It provides the CEO with the chance to look at the business's talent pool as a whole. The key question for business leaders is: do we have the leaders we need to make the changes we need to make?

## Learning agility

To perform in this new environment, individuals will need greater resilience and agility than ever before and be able to reinvent themselves for future, as yet unknown, challenges. According to Miller, learning agility is gaining favour as a meaningful indicator of potential.[37] In assessing a person's learning agility HR can work with line managers to find out:

- What characteristics does a promising employee bring to challenges?
- How do they manage an unfamiliar situation? Do they get excited by matching their attributes against the demands of a task?
- What is the individual's likely career path – the type of position and highest level in the organization that they can attain?

Diversity of thinking is needed: leaders must be able to develop a corporate culture based on inclusion and a mindset of encouraging diverse viewpoints. Companies such as IBM look for a combination of cognitive, behavioural and attitudinal qualities that they expect to see in their leaders present and future. Leaders should:

- have depth and breadth in technical and global business knowledge
- be known as a true thought leader in their area of expertise
- be able to tackle difficult problems head-on and know when to seek input and guidance from others
- be a natural visionary who is not intimidated by taking calculated and informed risks
- be able to see the bigger picture without losing sight of the small but important things
- have multicultural and multilingual aptitude – able to deliver results and value to global clients and stakeholders from different locations
- be able to inspire self and others; instil a sense of meaning and purpose in others

And have:

- generational 'savvy' – able to bring out the best in an age-diverse workforce
- change management expertise
- comfort with ambiguity
- dilemma-flipping ability
- immersive learning and organizing skills.[38]

# Developing people

Macro forces like technology and climate change may cause many jobs to completely disappear. Without urgent and focused investment in reskilling for new jobs, millions of people may be unable to earn a basic living. The World Economic Forum's Future of Jobs Report (2020) estimates that by 2025 85 million jobs will be displaced by a shift in the division of labour between humans and machines.[39] But even more jobs – 97 million – may emerge that are more adapted to the new division of labour between humans, machines and algorithms. According to the Forum's report, the top 10 skills needed by employees of 2025 will be:

- analytical thinking and innovation
- active learning and learning strategies
- complex problem solving
- critical thinking and analysis
- creativity, originality and initiative
- leadership and social influence
- technology use, monitoring and control
- technology design and programming
- resilience, stress tolerance and flexibility
- reasoning, problem solving and ideation.

These fall into the skill categories of problem solving, self-management, working with people and technology use and development.

For organizations, when talent is scarce, developing people will prove much less costly than recruitment. Providing training and development has been regularly cited as one of the most important factors in creating a positive work environment, which ultimately affects employee performance and retention. Development gives staff a sense of progression within the workplace and is likely to lead to greater commitment and engagement. Upskilling to expand a person's capabilities is key to individual employability. The benefits are mutual: making employees more effective and productive through training helps to build organizational flexibility and resilience.

A continuous and agile approach to development and training is needed to keep pace with innovation and changing expectations. Aligning training and development activities with business strategy can accelerate significant improvements in individual, team and corporate performance in terms of output, speed and productivity. Such alignment requires a systematic analysis of the most important development needs, defining the gap between what exists and what is required to improve existing competencies. While holders of business-critical roles will still be given development support, the shift taking place is towards nurturing a broader spectrum of talent, finding talent in unexpected places, with exclusive and inclusive talent approaches existing side by side.

Learning and support must be easy to scale. A more flexible training offer is needed (such as modular training or 'earn while you learn' approaches), as well as increasing training in new areas. Accessibility needs to be just-in-time/on-demand/bite-size so that people can learn quickly and play their part in delivering the changes needed in their business units. In the digital age, where people and machines increasingly work together, employees and managers need digital literacy and competency. Managers need an understanding of what is possible through the use and deployment of digital technologies, and the ability to make decisions about which of the new technologies and services to adopt and when. Digital leaders must be able to work collaboratively and innovatively, with a focus on customers and customer-centric design.

In addition to 'hard' technical and digital skills, people at all levels, especially those tasked with management, need 'soft' skills, such as understanding what motivates people and how to pull teams together. Increasingly, too, training and development aims to increase people's self-awareness and ability to thrive in more fluid work environments. The popular focus in recent years on emotional intelligence is being complemented by insights from mindfulness and neuroscience. More broadly, some of the new skill sets and aptitudes required for new ways of working include:

- adaptability
- tolerance for complexity
- innovation and creativity
- resourcefulness
- learning agility
- entrepreneurial mindset
- resilience
- ability to manage ambiguity.

Reflecting the growing interest in the business relevance of learning, companies such as GE (at Crotonville), Deloitte and Apple have invested in corporate universities, which first appeared in the 1950s. These are often similar to a conventional learning and development function but increasingly are seen as more business-driven and technology-enabled. They send a clear message to employees that the organization wants to invest in their development. With a corporate university or academy it should be easy for any employee to see online what training opportunities are available on the job and in a classroom. Formal courses are increasingly geared towards skills not just knowledge acquisition, with participants selected based on their motivation to learn and managers' support in applying the learning. Unipart's corporate university, Unipart U, offers focused training and 'see-learn-do' problem-solving sessions in the work area of each business unit, rather than in traditional classrooms.[40] Staff use Unipart U's database to work out what they need to know, learn it in the morning and apply it immediately. Engineering is a key specialism and some of Unipart U's programmes lead to national vocational qualifications. It is expected that the corporate university will prove helpful when recruiting graduates.

Providing development opportunities – perhaps through cross-training, strategic project work or continuing education – helps people make progress even if promotion opportunities are few. By offering real-time development for everyone, for instance via online training, peer coaching and team learning, and investing in employees at junior levels, such as via apprenticeships or the chance to study for employer-based qualifications, HR can send strong positive signals to employees about the company's priorities and about how it values them. This requires taking a long-term view, building capabilities that can help people and organizations to improve and adapt to the changing needs of the business.

By forging creative collaborations with learning providers or other organizations keen to create shared learning opportunities for their workforce, firms can contain costs and increase the value of learning. Developing line managers as coaches, providing tools for self-assessment, holistic succession planning and innovative career management are just some of the tools in the new 'war for talent'.

## Agile succession planning

For many organizations the biggest risk factor relates to the organization's vulnerability after an unplanned departure of a top manager. Not surprisingly, succession planning for top roles forms part of corporate governance.

Despite this, very few organizations can mitigate the impact of valued people moving on. The Corporate Executive Board's 2011 survey of 33,000 corporate leaders in 23 countries revealed that almost half – 41 per cent – were struggling to find qualified executive leadership. More recent surveys confirm that the challenge remains acute.

Succession planning typically focuses on developing employees for certain types of roles – especially by expanding their career experience and functional skills – thus growing credible candidates for real jobs when they fall vacant. It also involves the longer-term development of talent pipelines to meet future business needs.[41] Akin to workforce planning, part of its developmental purpose is diagnostic – to identify where pipelines are weak and the specific skills, knowledge or experience lacking in the workforce. However, succession planning is not always fully integrated with other talent management initiatives – plans are often created in a vacuum, which leads to duplication of work. Succession plans should be closely integrated with high-potential talent assessment processes and leadership development to ensure leadership continuity – and make it work successfully.

Succession planning has itself been through something of a metamorphosis in recent years. Many organizations are moving towards integrating succession planning with broader talent management approaches. And although succession planning remains primarily focused on senior leadership and management roles, it is increasingly used for selected 'critical' roles at a range of levels where the organization is vulnerable. Planning for these selected roles should take place at appropriate levels of detail – often for groups of jobs, not single posts – and with relevant time frames. There should be a mix-and-match approach to filling vacancies, blending the open job market with managed career moves, identifying and using external as well as internal successors as appropriate. In particular, agile succession planning involves individuals in planning and delivering their own skill and career development.[42]

In global firms the corporate centre is usually directly responsible only for small numbers of very senior roles, but also ensures that appropriate devolved processes are in place within regions, divisions or functions. Succession or talent reviews, also called forums or succession committees, are becoming more strategic in scope and can enable job filling and development actions for succession candidates to help them gain specific skills or wider career experience – often in a different function, unit or location.

*A formal process*

In planning for succession a typical approach is as follows:

• First define the scope. What roles are critical to the organization? How far down should succession planning reach?

• Then define what current positions look like and what current competencies exist.

• Next define the future state. What competencies are needed? What gaps exist between the current talent pool and the future needs?

• Identify talent. Who are high-potential candidates? What is their level of readiness?

• Develop talent. Are development objectives aligned to meet succession requirements? What tools and resources are needed to implement development plans for individuals?

• Track development. How do you monitor and measure the success of an individual's development against their plan? Which external factors serve to impede or enhance individual success?

Succession planning must be integrated with other people management processes, especially assessment and actions for job filling and development.

*Towards a more 'agile' succession approach*

There are signs that a more 'agile' form of succession planning is emerging from the well-established 'developmental' approach. This approach assumes that change will happen. It draws heavily upon career planning and management to help create an informed, relevant and realistic view of succession. Rather than linking succession plans too strictly to organizational structure or specific roles that are subject to too much change, taking a person-based, pool-based approach is much more flexible.

At the same time it involves identifying successors for selected roles where the business is vulnerable – not just senior management – and planning for these selected roles at appropriate levels of detail, often for groups of jobs, not single posts, and with relevant time frames. So 'emergency' and 'ready now' successors are in primary focus in addition to those with short-term (one to two years) and longer-term (usually three to five years) potential. Every effort must be made to identify those hard-to-replace individuals whose knowledge and skills are vital to the organization and put in place strong engagement and retention plans. External as well as internal successors should be identified where appropriate, recognizing the long-term trend towards involving individuals in planning and delivering their own skills and career development. In an agile succession process, vacancies can be filled by combinations of managed career moves and the open job market.

Evaluating experience through the lens of learning agility adds a 'leading indicator' to the equation and yields better succession planning decisions. Properly applied, learning agility can help companies to develop a deep bench-strength of talent and an understanding of how best to use that talent.

## Increasing transparency

Today the very idea that organizations can manage talent may be an outdated conceit.[43] From the employee's point of view, agile succession planning must take account of their goals, aspirations and preferences. An agile process should be genuinely two-way and involve input from the chosen 'successor' and all relevant parties. Tools such as social media can help people to understand 'what's in it for me?' Focused career conversations between individuals and line managers or HR can help people to clarify their motivations and what they want from their work at this point in their lives, and help them to take stock of their personal appetite for learning. It is important to build talent dialogue into how you do business and use continuous feedback instead of intermittent spot checks. So get the facts – use multiple approaches such as surveys, coaching, exit data, focus groups – and analyse them.

Yet many managers are reluctant to talk about their talented employees in succession forums for fear they will be poached by other departments or, worse still, from outside the company.[44] Companies facing this problem need clear, unambiguous senior management endorsement that the talent pool is a company asset, not an individual executive's plaything. To help managers overcome their initial resistance, it is useful to train them to identify and develop talent, evaluate them on how well they do this and reward those who are most successful at developing and exporting talent. It is important to institutionalize these practices through KPIs and reporting, keeping the process 'live' by frequently updating executives on what is happening and communicating successes. People will support a succession plan much more enthusiastically if they can see that it works in reality. It is about building a talent management culture and mindset, developing a clear definition of 'successful leadership' for the future.

Succession planning should expose future leaders to opportunities to acquire a versatile set of skills and experiences; development opportunities should be meaningful and allow individuals scope to demonstrate their performance, potential and motivation. Such development opportunities might include short-term high-risk positions, rotational and global assignments, project roles, lateral moves or a 'temporary promotion', from which they can move on quickly, develop their skills further and apply their learning in the next experience. People can also grow in 'real jobs' and learn to handle problems, deliver and prove their worth.

## Developing customer-centric leaders

Building a connected and aligned leadership cadre is always critical to organizational goal success, but arguably it is even more important when the transformation required is a mindset shift from an internally focused product orientation to an outside-in perspective; from leadership styles reflective of a bureaucratic 'golden cage' to leadership for agility and empowerment. Of course, customer-centric strategies should be devised by people who believe in them. Yet in reality, what many leaders pay attention to sends quite a different message that is picked up by both customers and employees. A good rule of thumb is to look at how financial results are reported and the extent to which customers are mentioned. For instance ING Bank now presents its results in the context of its customer strategy.

As Peccei and Rosenthal point out, one of the most important influencers of pro-customer employee empowerment is management attention and role-modelling.[45] Although one visionary leader may promote a customer-centric strategy, if this is undermined by resistance or a lack of energy from their peers who prefer to cling on to their hierarchical domains and bureaucratic controls, not only will this delay and disrupt progress but it may destroy it entirely. Organizations committed to customer-centricity, such as ING, recognize this and give it conscious focus: 'We have spent an enormous amount of energy and leadership time trying to role-model the sort of behaviour – ownership, empowerment, customer-centricity – that is appropriate in an agile culture.'[46]

HR can design leadership development initiatives that challenge leaders' current mindsets, helping them to learn how to adapt and experiment, walk the talk on values, build capability in others and, in the process, embed the core skills of customer-centric leadership. Such development typically will:

- Teach active listening and questioning skills as a fundamental competence, reinforcing and giving this recognition in formal and informal ways.

- Embed customer-facing experiences in all new management hire induction processes, in key talent promotions and as part of customized development programmes. This is particularly important for 'back office' or functional leaders who have little natural front-line exposure.

- Bring senior leaders into regular contact with front-line workers in meaningful ways, for example in a hierarchical cross-slice or full process team workshop looking at service improvement, where all voices are equal.

- Expose leaders to customer-centric peers in other sectors to challenge mindsets and inspire, and then spending even more time unpacking the learning from this and its application potential.

- Reinforce practices that promote 'adult-to-adult' feedback and legitimize the naming and shaming of behaviours or activities that undermine values or ignore the customer.

As succession planning becomes more agile, it will become a key mechanism for managing business risk and for speeding up responses to shifting business demands and increasingly diverse employee aspirations.

## Conclusion

So the truth implicit in the old cliché 'people are our greatest asset' is becoming evident as companies compete to attract and retain the best people. Success depends entirely on people's skills, ability and willingness to give their best. Capable and often multiskilled knowledge workers can pick and choose who they work for, so assumptions behind old-style organizational processes such as workforce planning and succession planning, which are designed to protect the organization's longer-term interests, must now flex to accommodate the interests and aspirations of a more mobile and demanding workforce. This should reflect the changing nature of careers and be geared towards developing change-readiness in the form of employee agility and career resilience. The best calculations come to nothing if key people move on too quickly.

As we have discussed, in today's workplace:

- Definitions of 'talent' and 'high potential' are broadening beyond the select few future leaders.
- Recruitment and other strategies must be geared specifically to the target audience – and must be delivered if they are to retain people.
- People processes should be owned by the CEO and managed by HR.
- They must be developed with people, not done to them.
- One size does not fit all.
- Analytics can help to source people; relationships retain them.

HR can help to recruit and retain the best talent including from non-traditional backgrounds and develop the skills of the workforce and future leaders. Since it is unrealistic to expect to retain all the 'key talent' an organization requires, talent processes must become more open, transparent and inclusive, with development geared towards creating a wider talent pool and building transferable skill sets. A multigenerational workforce will look for new working arrangements, career routes and development opportunities. This will impact on all aspects of talent management including flexible working policies, styles of management, learning and development, career strategies and related career deals and so on. Developing capabilities, upskilling and reskilling the workforce, on-the-job and off-the-job, increases the possibility of being able to deploy and then redeploy resources, talent and skills. Developing agile and engaging managers and leaders at all levels who can communicate in 'human' ways and understand how staff will need to be managed to retain their motivation will increase retention and performance.

By investing in the workforce, organizations are more likely to reap the benefits of innovation and high performance.

In the next chapter we shall look at a key role for managers and for HR: nurturing employee resilience and engagement.

CHECKLIST

- To what extent are these new realities of work and organizations evident where you are? What are the implications for the way work is likely to evolve, for example the impact of automation and artificial intelligence for roles and skills?

- What kind of skills will your future workforce need? How might these differ from the skills needed today?

- What sort of 'talent' will you need?

- What forms of employment will be most appropriate – for the organization – for people? Permanent/temporary/flexible/freelance/contractor?

- How will team structures change? Will more people be working in teams, or alone?

- Where do you have gaps?

- Who 'owns' talent management in your organization?

- How strong is the commitment to diversity and inclusion? Have the competencies that are required for your industry changed – and have the human resource practices of your firm kept pace?

- Is there a good process for developing needed competencies and making sure people can have meaningful and developmental job experiences and career paths?

- How effectively do line managers hold career conversations?

- Is your firm developing the required leadership capability at all levels and the lateral leadership capabilities needed for success in a complex world?

- When opportunities are identified how are participants selected?

- In the last year, what feeder groups were available for each identified promotion?

- Of the promotions that occurred in the last year, were the selections reflective of the pool of eligible candidates?[47]

# Notes

1   Cornwell, J. The time to value our staff is now, Nuffield Trust comment, 24 March 2017, www.nuffieldtrust.org.uk/news-item/the-time-to-value-our-staff-is-now (archived at https://perma.cc/C48E-2LB4).

2   UKCES (2014) *The Future of Work*, UK Commission for Employment and Skills (UKCES), London.

3   CIPD (2014) *Managing An Age-Diverse Workforce*, CIPD, London.

4   Howe, N and Strauss, W (2007) The next 20 years: How customer and workforce attitudes will evolve, *Harvard Business Review*, July–August, pp 41–52.

5   AON Hewitt. 2014 trends in global employee engagement, www.aon.com/attachments/human-capital-consulting/2014-trends-in-globalemployee-engagement-report.pdf (archived at https://perma.cc/2B4L-ANJY).

6   CIPD (2019) Megatrends: flexible working, megatrends-report-flexible-working-1_tcm18-52769.pdf.

7   ADP (2018). *The Global Study of Engagement Research report*. https://www.adpri.org/assets/the-global-study-of-engagement/ (archived at https://perma.cc/P7X3-WA5Z).

8   McKinsey. Purpose: Shifting from why to how, McKinsey.com, 22 April 2020, www.mckinsey.com/capabilities/people-and-organizational-performance/our-insights/purpose-shifting-from-why-to-how (archived at https://perma.cc/U7MJ-XXGL).

9   Deloitte (2014) The Deloitte millennial survey, www.deloitte.com/assets/Dcom-Italy/Local%20Assets/Documents/Pubblicazioni/gx-dttl-2014-millennial-survey-report.pdf (archived at https://perma.cc/2DQY-ZEM6).

10  Business Case Studies. National Grid, n.d., businesscasestudies.co.uk/companies/#axzz37MJAn4W9.

11  Couzins, M. CIPD 2013 highlights: Unilever, Facebook and HMRC, *Personnel Today*, 2013, www.personneltoday.com/hr/cipd-2013-highlights-unilever-facebook-and-hmrc/ (archived at https://perma.cc/4WWB-FM84).

12  Ashridge Business School (2017) Making influential HR take off at easyJet, *HR Most Influential 2017*, www.hrmagazine.co.uk/hr-most-influential/profile/making-influential-hr-take-off-at-easyjet.

13  World Economic Forum. The future of jobs report 2018, www3.weforum.org/docs/WEF_Future_of_Jobs_2018.pdf (archived at https://perma.cc/3A25-XCTS).

14  Martin, JP (2018) Skills for the 21st Century: Findings and policy lessons from the OECD survey of adult skills, OECD Education Working Paper No. 166; CIPD. *Learning and Skills at Work 2020. Mind the gap: Time for learning in the UK*, CIPD, London.

15  Kaplan, RS and Norton, DP (2001) *The Strategy-Focused Organization: How balanced scorecard companies thrive in the new environment*, Harvard Business School Press, Boston.

**16** Chambers, EG et al (1998) The war for talent, *McKinsey Quarterly*, January, www.executivesondemand.net/manage mentsourcing/images/stories/artigos_pdf/gestao/The_war_for_talent.pdf.

**17** Arthur, MB and Rousseau, DM (1996) The boundaryless career as a new employment principle, in MG Arthur and DM Rousseau (eds) *The Boundaryless Career*, Oxford University Press, New York, p 5.

**18** Boatman, J and Wellins, RS (2011) *Global Leadership Forecast*, Development Dimensions International, Inc, Pittsburgh.

**19** Bersin & Associates (2011) *TalentWatch Q1: Global growth creates new war for talent*, Oakland, CA.

**20** Tansley, C et al (2007) *Talent: Strategy, management, measurement*, CIPD, London.

**21** CIPD (2012) *Resourcing and Talent Planning: Annual survey report 2012*, CIPD, London.

**22** Collings, DG and Mellahi, K (2009) Strategic talent management: A review and research agenda, *Human Resource Management Review*, **19** (4), pp 304–13.

**23** Cappelli, P (2008) *Talent on Demand*, Harvard Business School Press, Boston.

**24** Lyons, M, Biltz, M and Whittall, N (2017) Shaping the Agile workforce, Accenture, www.accenture.com/_acnmedia/PDF-60/AccentureStrategy-Shaping-Agile-Workforce-POV.pdf (archived at https://perma.cc/6R5F-3QKH).

**25** Deloitte (2014) Big demands and high expectations: The Deloitte Millennial Survey, www2.deloitte.com/al/en/pages/about-deloitte/articles/2014-millennial-survey-positive-impact.html (archived at https://perma.cc/PL2D-76QB).

**26** Deloitte (2018) The chemistry of talent, www.deloitte.com.mx/documents/mx(en-mx)TheChemistryTalent_24ago09.pdf (archived at https://perma.cc/ERS5-6ZMM).

**27** Webrecruit (2014) The Beginner's Guide to Careers Sites, www.webrecruit.co.uk/employer-blog/hr-professional/the-beginners-guide-to-careers-sites-free-download.

**28** Banerjee, R. What do generations Y and Z really want from work? Raconteur, 17 November 2022, what-do-gen-y-and-z-really-want-from-work.

**29** SHRM (2013) SHRM survey findings: Social networking websites and recruiting/selection, www.slideshare.net/shrm/social-networkingwebsitesrecruitingselectingjobcandidatesshrm2013final (archived at https://perma.cc/SG5Z-H2KX).

**30** Fisher, CD (1985) Social support and adjustment to work: A longitudinal study, *Journal of Management*, **11**, pp 39–53.

**31** Saks, AM and Ashforth, BE (1996) Proactive socialization and behavioral self-management, *Journal of Vocational Behavior*, **48**, pp 301–23.

**32** Adkins, CL (1995) Previous work experience and organizational socialization: A longitudinal examination, *Academy of Management Journal*, **38**, pp 839–62.

**33** PriceWaterhouseCoopers [accessed 30 August 2014] Best practices for retaining new employees: New approaches to effective onboarding, *PriceWaterhouseCoopers and Saratoga Global Best Practices*, docplayer. net/7390719-Saratoga-and-global-best-practices-best-practices-for-retaining-new-employees-new-approaches-to-effective-onboarding-introduction-1.html (archived at https://perma.cc/QX9F-VVLM).

**34** Cappelli, P (2008) *Talent on Demand*, Harvard Business School Press, Boston.

**35** Lepak, DP and Snell, SA (2002) Examining the human resource architecture: The relationships among human capital, employment, and human resource configurations, *Journal of Management*, 28 (4), pp 517–43.

**36** Boxall, P and Purcell, J (2008) *Strategy and Human Resource Management*, Palgrave Macmillan, Basingstoke.

**37** Miller, M (2012) Seeking the agile mind: Looking beyond experience to build succession plans, Avnet, Phoenix, AZ.

**38** I am grateful to Bob Johansen, Institute for the Future, for the last two bullet points in this list.

**39** World Economic Forum. The future of jobs report 2020, www.weforum.org/ reports/the-future-of-jobs-report-2020/ (archived at https://perma.cc/DSR2-3UEF).

**40** Chynoweth, C. Learn at 10 and do at 11: That's the Unipart Way, Business Section, *The Sunday Times*, 27 July 2014, p 10.

**41** Hirsh, W (2012) *Planning for Succession in Changing Times*, Corporate Research Centre, London.

**42** Ibid.

**43** Sparrow P, Otaye, L and Makramet, H (2014) How should we value talent management? University of Lancaster, www.lancaster.ac.uk/media/lancaster-university/content-assets/documents/lums/cphr/ WP14-01HowShouldWeValueTalentManagement.pdf (archived at https:// perma.cc/ZPM6-ZGJX).

**44** Porr, D. Agile succession: HR's toughest challenge, Human Resource Executive, 7–10 October 2014, www.hreonline.com/HRE/view/story. jhtml?id=534354896.

**45** Peccei, R and Rosenthal, P (2001) Delivering customer-oriented behaviour through empowerment: An empirical test of HRM assumptions, *Journal of Management Studies*, 38 (6), p 839.

**46** Mahadevan, D (2017) ING's agile transformation, *McKinsey Quarterly*, January, www.mckinsey.com/industries/financial-services/our-insights/ings-agile-transformation (archived at https://perma.cc/4NF8-GBVK).

**47** The global talent economy, Raconteur, *The Times*, 30 September 2022.

# 08

# Nurturing employee engagement and resilience

In Chapter 7 we looked at some of the challenges of attracting and developing the agile and resilient people organizations need. Today's economic outlook for many industries looks decidedly mixed so the emerging talent agenda needs to have some flexibility built into it. As we have seen, an agile workforce is a broader, more inclusive concept than focusing exclusively on future top talent.

As organizations struggle to sustain a competitive edge in this volatile context, many business leaders will need to set new strategies to increase productivity and innovation. But they cannot effectively execute what is required for future growth without the 'right' people focused on the 'right' things, motivated and 'engaged' with their organization; in other words, people who are willingly investing their 'discretionary effort' in the collective effort. How people feel about their work influences whether or not they release their discretionary effort and makes a difference to performance and innovation.

That is why I believe that especially in today's knowledge-intensive and service-intensive industries – where people are the main source of innovation, production and service excellence – employee engagement or 'the intellectual and emotional attachment that an employee has for his or her work'[1] becomes crucial to business success. Therefore, if leaders want their organizations to survive and thrive in today's challenging times, they must become intensely focused on improving employee engagement.

In this chapter we consider:

- the central link between employee engagement and performance, commitment and retention

- what employee engagement is
- getting to grips with employee engagement
- the 'engaged' model
- an emergent psychological contract
- team engagement
- how HR/OD can help to stimulate engagement and wellbeing.

We look at what is involved in creating a work context conducive to employee engagement and consider the roles played by executives, line managers, HR/OD and employees themselves.

## Links between employee engagement and performance

High-performance theory places employee engagement at the heart of performance and productivity – especially among knowledge workers – since when people are engaged with their work they are more productive, more service-oriented, less wasteful, more inclined to come up with good ideas, to take the initiative and generally do more to help organizations achieve their goals than people who are disengaged.

Research has correlated employee engagement with higher earnings per share, improved sickness absence, higher productivity and innovation – the potential business benefits go on and on. For instance, a Corporate Leadership Council (CLC) study found that companies with highly engaged employees grow twice as fast as peer companies. A three-year study by Towers Watson of 41 multinational organizations found that those with high engagement levels had 2–4 per cent improvement in operating margin and net profit margin, whereas those with low engagement scores showed a decline of about 1.5–2 per cent. Other studies suggest that highly engaged employees tend to support organizational change initiatives and are more resilient in the face of change.

In Britain's National Health Service (NHS), a meta-analysis of research into the links between patient health outcomes and employee engagement found that patient satisfaction was consistently higher in health organizations with better rates of staff health and wellbeing, and that there was a link between higher staff satisfaction and lower rates of mortality and hospital-acquired infection.[2] The study concluded that healthcare employers should try to accelerate increases in employee engagement scores as they appear to correlate strongly with patient outcomes.

Yet the UK is generally reported to suffer from a growing 'engagement deficit' relative to many other countries, including the United States.[3] A global engagement study by Aon Hewitt found that only just over half of UK employees saw a long-term path with their current company and fewer saw a compelling employee value proposition (EVP) to keep their talents with their current company.[4] Recruitment firms are aware of wide-scale, pent-up career frustration and, as employment opportunities become more abundant, significant employee turnover can be anticipated.[5] And as many organizations continue to downsize or implement other cost-reduction measures, employee engagement is likely to become a major casualty of change.

Retention is a major problem currently with consequences for organizational agility and performance. Immediately after the pandemic, many people left their jobs to look for more fulfilling work as reflected in the 'Great Resignation' or 'Great Attrition' trend with 47 million US workers voluntarily leaving their jobs in 2021 alone. Many older workers chose to leave work, citing reasons such as feeling undervalued, wanting early retirement or just not wanting to work any more. Yet older workers can be an untapped and potentially overlooked talent pool. In periods of worker shortage higher output is needed from a shrinking workforce to maintain productivity. This approach is likely to produce only short-term gains and may actually reduce productivity over time since it can undermine employees' health, wellbeing and engagement.

Lack of engagement and underperformance are other productivity factors that are symptomatic of psychological contract damage. While in periods of economic instability people usually choose to stay with their current employer for longer, Gallup's 2022 global workplace report estimated that at least half of the US workforce remain employed but have 'quietly quit' to some degree while only 9 per cent of UK workers reported being engaged or enthusiastic about their place of work.[6] The central premise of the term 'quiet quitting', first coined on TikTok, is that work should not be the central focus of our lives. Quiet quitters resist the expectation from their employers and fellow employees to put extra time and energy behind their work for the benefit of the business or in the hope of a promotion. Quiet quitting is about people upholding their wellbeing through the way they work and through rediscovering the relationship they have with work, rather than risk burnout by working excessive hours or by having only a work-based identity.[7]

So while attracting the talent needed for business performance can be challenging enough, revitalizing and retaining talent requires an understanding of the specific drivers of engagement for a given workforce and creating a context conducive to employee engagement.

## What is employee engagement?

Definitions of employee engagement abound. MacLeod and Clarke, while researching for their 2009 report 'Engaging for Success', found at least 50 different definitions of employee engagement.[8] Many make the association between engagement and high-performance work practices and other forms of human resource management (HRM).[9] Different definitions focus on employee behaviour (e.g. discretionary effort), on employee attitudes (e.g. commitment), on employee feelings (e.g. enthusiasm) and on the conditions of work and what the organization does (e.g. provides support).

Among the earliest definitions was the association of personal engagement with the 'needs-satisfying' approach to motivation by William Kahn in his 1990 article for the *Academy of Management* journal.[10] He defined personal engagement as the harnessing of organization members' selves to their work roles; when engaged, people employ and express themselves physically, cognitively and emotionally during role performances. Personal disengagement, on the other hand, is defined as the uncoupling of selves from work roles; people withdraw and defend themselves physically, cognitively or emotionally during role performances. Kahn and Heaphy later identified the importance of the 'relational context', which affects how people use varying degrees of their selves – physically, cognitively and emotionally – in work roles.[11]

The psychological concept of 'work engagement' developed by Schaufeli and Bakker is defined as 'a positive, fulfilling, work-related state of mind that is characterized by vigour, dedication, and absorption'.[12] Work engagement describes how workers experience their work: as stimulating and energetic, something to which they really want to devote time and effort (the vigour component); as a significant and meaningful pursuit (dedication); and as engrossing and something on which they are fully concentrated (absorption). The fully engaged employee:

- knows how their job contributes to the overall mission and goals of the organization
- has a job with enough variety to keep them challenged and engaged
- is able to use their talents and abilities effectively in their current position.

This form of employee engagement is closely associated with psychological 'flow', a sense of oneness with the activity being pursued.[13] In this emotional state employees feel passionate, energetic and committed to their work. This aspect of engagement is very intense and produces a sensation of 'being at one with the world', has the capacity to banish anxieties and concerns and makes one feel completely focused, satisfied and happy. This form of engagement is thought to produce the highest levels of performance in individuals.

According to social engagement theories, engagement does not exist because of the person or their environment – but in the relationship between the two. The key enabler of social engagement is commitment and trust between employers and employees. MacLeod and Clarke's chosen definition was that engagement is 'a workplace approach designed to ensure that employees are committed to their organization's goals and values, motivated to contribute to organizational success, and are able at the same time to enhance their own sense of well-being'.[14]

## Psychological contract

As we discussed in Chapters 1 and 7, with respect to white-collar work in particular, the psychological contract has been changing in nature and growing in complexity in recent years. Psychological contract theory is part of social exchange theory, according to which reciprocation is pivotal to the maintenance of a healthy contract. Since engagement is the point where business and employee interests coincide, employee engagement could be thought of as a barometer of the state of the employment relationship, manifesting the health of the psychological contract between employees and employers.

Since the mid-1990s many employers have moved away from employment relationships based on the old exchange: long-term job security and gradual career progression up a hierarchy for employees in exchange for loyalty and hard work for employers. Instead, a 'new deal' is supposed to have taken its place, according to which employers will expect employees to be flexible, high performing and committed while also managing their own careers and making themselves 'employable'.[15] The basis of this exchange is short-term agreements dependent on performance and mutual value.

Psychological contracts can be dynamic, to reflect changing circumstances and needs. For instance, companies aspiring to become agile now also want employees to show resilience, learning, adaptability and speed. However, if one party (the organization) in the exchange relationship fails to deliver, or unilaterally reneges on its part of the bargain without acknowledgement or renegotiation, the other party (employee) is likely to lose trust and respond by withdrawing discretionary effort or leaving the firm.

## A one-sided deal

In practice it could be argued that the mutuality implicit in the 'old' psychological contracts has been largely swept to one side and there is increasing polarization of employee treatment. For key talent, the unitarist assumptions behind the 'new deal' – that 'what is good for the business is good for the people' – seemingly hold true. For them, what Denise Rousseau et al call '*i*-deals' (or specialized idiosyncratic deals) will be struck.[16] Conversely, for employees with less-valuable skills the evolving employment relationship may be breaking down. The drive for organizational agility is often synonymous with cost-cutting. Now that 'more for less' has become the nature of business as usual, employees may suffer a reduced psychological contract in the form of work intensification, pressure and loss of job security. These conditions can lead to poor morale, exhaustion and the risk of 'burnout', which Maslach and Jackson consider to be the opposite pole of the engagement spectrum,[17] so employee wellbeing is likely to become a major casualty of change.

The consequences for organizations could be severe. First there is the medium-term challenge of retaining key people. The tougher the measures taken to keep organizations viable, the greater the risk of strained employee relations with 'survivor' employees simply 'hunkering down' and 'quietly quitting', doing the minimum necessary to get by. So at the very time when organizations most need employees to be engaged with their work and producing their best ideas, employee engagement and talent retention are at significant risk. Indeed, so concerned was the UK government about the 'engagement deficit' that the then Department for Business, Innovation and Skills (BIS) backed the 'Engaging for Success' inquiry (or the MacLeod Report[18]) to explore the assumed links between employee engagement, performance and productivity. The report's conclusion – that the business case for employee engagement is overwhelming – has been strongly reinforced since then as more research is published.

It is vital therefore that organizations reframe the 'deal' to maximize the value for both the firm and its employees over the next few years. In any case, demographic shifts and other factors may force a rebalancing. Findings from many consultancy reports and company engagement surveys suggest that what many employees (especially millennials) want from their employers may be different from what is on offer. The Aon Hewitt 2014 global engagement survey suggests that millennials – due to the sheer size and influence of this generational cohort – may be setting the organizational tone for employee engagement with only 12 per cent of employees reported to be highly engaged – and are likely to be shaping the perceptions of Generation X and baby boomer employees.[19]

So should business leaders be worried? Absolutely: arguably it is before talent shortages worsen that employee engagement should be recognized as a business priority.

## Key enablers of engagement

The MacLeod Report summarized four fundamental 'enablers' of any employee engagement strategy:

- Leadership that gives a 'strong strategic narrative about the organization, where it's come from and where it's going'
- Line managers who motivate, empower and support their employees
- Employee voice throughout the organization, to challenge or reinforce the status quo and involve employees in decision making
- 'Organizational integrity' where stated values are embedded into organizational culture; what we say is what we do.

The last of these, integrity, is in many ways the basis of trust – doing what you say, being ethically and morally bound, doing unto others as you would wish done unto yourself. Trust underpins the psychological contract and Kenexa's 2013 work-trends report points to integrity being the most important lever of trust, above benevolence or competence.[20] Purcell et al analysed the factors most strongly associated with organizational commitment, using the national UK Workplace Employment Relations Study (WERS) data.[21] The most important and influential factor, which applied to all types of employees, was trust in management.

### The roles of leaders and managers

The MacLeod Report found that 'engaging managers' and 'engaging leadership' are pivotal to creating work contexts conducive to engagement. Top leaders in particular have a multiplier effect on engagement, since their own approach is very visible and they have control over all the top engagement drivers. Yet it seems that, instead of seeking to understand how to maintain or enhance employee engagement, many UK top leaders simply ignore it, possibly because they are unaware of or do not understand its importance. The MacLeod Report puts it less charitably: 'The issue seems to lie in their unwillingness to "talk the talk" and truly relinquish command and control styles of leadership in favour of a relationship based on mutuality.'[22]

Line managers set the tone for employee engagement. Through their interactions with their teams on a day-to-day basis the organization's relationship with employees is made manifest. The defining contribution of great managers is that they boost the engagement levels of the people who work for them.[23] Yet managers are often unclear as to how to create an engaging context; they may lack the relevant skills or interest and there may be few consequences for doing nothing. Indeed, many managers consider engagement to be the job of HR.

## Getting to grips with engagement issues

So if managers and leaders are so crucial to employee engagement, how do great managers get the best out of their people? This is why Geoffrey Matthews and I wrote our book *Engaged* (2012).[24] We wanted to demystify this contested topic and provide practical guidance for managers and HR professionals who want to create a work context conducive to engagement.

Surveys are a conventional means of gathering data about what engages and disengages key segments of the workforce but it is essential to ask the right questions. Cattermole argues that surveys allow you to measure many different aspects of employee engagement, broadly divided into three main areas:

- Blockers – problems facing employees, e.g. inadequate IT systems or excessive workloads

- Drivers – motivating factors, e.g. recognition, good relationships with managers, opportunities to learn career-enhancing skills

- Outcomes – beneficial attitudes; employees' pride in their work and organization, willingness to recommend and desire to remain with their employer.[25]

The downside of surveys is that they can be expensive, overly cumbersome and may result in 'analysis paralysis'. There can be lack of management sponsorship and subsequent activity is often misaligned or irrelevant, so that energy is spread too thinly and efforts 'run out of steam'.

To avoid these risks, periodic pulse surveys can be used. The initial review of results should be checked and calibrated with relevant segments of employees, key lessons drawn, solutions generated with employees and appropriate focused action taken. Keeping everyone involved and informed is vital. Other sources of 'evidence' or clues – from exit interviews, performance reviews, HR business partners – can help create a broad picture of where the 'pain points' are. Improvements should be measured and initiatives concluded with a review of the additional learning gleaned as a result of the activity.

More generally, though, approaches to employee engagement should move away from being HR-owned, reactive, periodic and survey-focused towards being manager-led and HR supported. Engaging line managers focus on individuals and teams, proactively building a context in which engagement is a daily part of working life.

## What do employees want?

There is no 'one size fits all' when it comes to engaging individuals.

Many organizations have a diverse workforce, not least by age. There are said to be four or five generations in the workforce currently – traditionalists, baby boomers, Gen Xers, Gen Y/Millennials and Gen Z. Gen X is numerically the smallest generation. With a more educated workforce and different motivators by generational group, each cohort needs to be managed with an understanding of their specific needs and motivations, recognizing also that individuals within cohorts will differ in their needs. Each cohort needs to be managed with an understanding of their specific needs and motivations, recognizing also that individuals within cohorts will differ in their needs.

The 'Great Resignation' is neither a blip on the radar nor a one-time emergency for organizations. While businesses have had plenty to deal with throughout the pandemic, a fundamental shift has occurred – employees have gained accelerated influence over their working environment. These raised expectations are redefining the conversation completely. Given that engagement is a personal and individual phenomenon, is it then possible to generalize about what employees want from work and about how managers can influence engagement levels? As employee values change, there is a growing focus on flexibility, corporate social responsibility and the need to change organizational cultures, for instance to become more inclusive.

Many consultancy reports highlight the 'top 10 engagement drivers'. For instance, the 2014 Aon Hewitt survey found a number of shifts under way in what appears to connect Generation Y in particular to organizations, with the following increasing in importance:

- Changing career expectations – with the end of 'job for life' people do not expect to make their careers in one organization any more. Portfolio careers are increasingly common, in which people combine a range of paid and non-paid activities at any one time and progress between a number of careers in one working lifetime.
- Social media and connectivity in general are driving the democratization of work – people expect to be informed and to have a say.
- Desire for collaboration/co-creation/interaction with employer.
- The importance of empowerment/autonomy.
- Work environment.
- Ethos, brand and reputation.
- Quality of relationships, work-life balance.
- Opportunities to grow and develop.
- Management and leadership.
- Self-awareness.

The survey found that the top employee engagement drivers for all generations – and therefore potential elements of the evolving employment contract – centre on career opportunities, managing performance, pay and reputation, and communication. Employees want to work for companies with a solid employer reputation, reward for performance, career trajectories and a collaborative culture.

Similarly, Purcell et al's analysis of WERS data produced the following, often considered the classic building blocks of engagement:

- employee trust in management
- satisfaction with work and the job
- involvement in decision making at work
- climate of relationships between management and employees
- satisfaction with pay
- job challenge
- sense of achievement from work.

These insights offer a useful starting point for conversations with employees about how to create a more engaging context.

For leaders, acknowledging the problems is not enough – they must be seen to be acting on them. If people are to trust and believe in their leaders, they need to see that there is real commitment to their engagement and well-being.

## The 'engaged' model

In analysing many varied sources of employee data for our book *Engaged*, and recognizing the risk of generalization, Geoff Matthews and I categorized the main factors we believe to be present when people are engaged with their organization, not just their job, as set out below.

### Connection

Being agile has an ethical dimension as agility provides collective agency, which is the wellspring of action, and action always has a moral dimension. Many people want to work for organizations whose purposes and values they can embrace. This sense of higher purpose appears to be closely associated with motivation, commitment and ultimately the energy and effort workers are prepared to put in. They want to feel part of something worthwhile, that their work is meaningful and that the value it adds is clear since it links to important organizational outcomes. They want to feel that they belong (for a time at least) and have a sense of job security, affiliation and strong workplace relationships. Employees want to be valued for their contribution and to be dealt with in a fair and consistent manner.

As we discussed in Chapter 2, for people to engage with the organization, and not just with their own work, they need to connect with other people, including leaders, as well as having a chance to participate in strategizing. Flatter organizational structures don't solve the problem if the hierarchical mindset is still in place.

### Support

In engaging work contexts employees receive appropriate support from management and cooperation from others. The amount and nature of support they need may vary according to age, stage or circumstance; managers must be alert to what support individuals actually require. People may need development or exposure to new opportunities or help in managing complex workloads. With support, employees are able to do their best and they give it their all. Above all, being valued as individuals is crucial. While pay remains important, other forms of recognition and reward – such as flexibility – are also important.

### Voice

Given that the risk in the employment relationship is largely with employees, people want to know what is happening in their organization and to be able to influence matters that affect their working lives. In an engaging workplace, employees are involved, have opportunities to participate in what is happening and have their voices heard. They are also open to new thinking and embrace diversity and teamwork.

### Scope

People want work that is interesting and challenging and that offers meaning, stretch, enjoyment and satisfaction. They also want flexibility, autonomy, control and task discretion, the chance to develop their skills and careers, and opportunities for growth.

The blend and intensity of these different desires will vary according to individual preferences and career needs. Also what is happening in the broader organizational context can affect individuals and what they need from their organization. In challenging times for instance people may need more support and voice. They may (temporarily) prefer job security to career growth. Keeping alert to what people need is the essence of managing engagement.

## What does this look like in practice?

To respond to the engagement challenge of this new era we looked at examples of management practice in organizations where employee engagement levels remain high despite the challenging context.

The following are some examples of what we found.

## Creating connection

Engagement levels are higher when leadership styles have evolved beyond command and control towards more open, collaborative and participative approaches that act as the foundation for mutual trust and respect. Engaging leaders look beyond the current challenges, anticipate the big business issues and plot a way through to growth, taking short-term decisions with the longer term in mind. They reshape the work environment and culture to enhance performance and match their special basis of competitive advantage. Engaging leaders actively lead culture change, working to create a shared sense of higher purpose and a positive sense of the future; something to aim for that people can connect with and can really believe in. Purpose is a firm's vision for the value it seeks to create and how that value is created; it defines what the corporation is and docs, whom it serves and how it contributes to the wellbeing of society.

While the causal link from shared purpose to sustained high performance has yet to be proven definitively, there are various pieces of evidence that suggest such a connection. Analysis of survey data indicates that a strong sense of shared purpose leads to high levels of employee engagement.[26] Employees who share a sense of higher purpose are most concerned about how they can accomplish a goal that makes a difference to the purpose. It gives them a compelling reason to come to work. In turn high employee engagement drives sustainable high performance.[27] Bevan et al[28] and Buytendijk[29] found that high-performing organizations have a strong sense of purpose internally and with external stakeholders.

Some forms of organizational purpose appear more strongly linked to high performance than others. The shareholder value idea may have worked at one time, but it now appears outdated, does not fit well with the needs of the 21st century and may be harmful in some cases. While superficially clear and simple, the short-term nature of shareholder value purpose discourages executives from making investments that really might be good not only for business and society in the long run but even for the shareholders themselves. So shareholder value in general, and a relentless pursuit of that objective, can have negative social consequences.

Increasingly, there is a return to the historical relationship that holds the interests of society as paramount, and that corporations exist primarily to serve social needs, especially those of the customer. In 2002, Richard Ellsworth published data indicating that companies whose corporate purpose focuses on delivering value to customers are significantly more profitable over a 10-year period than companies aiming at maximizing shareholder value or those trying to balance the needs of all their stakeholders.[30] Springett also found that a customer-focused corporate purpose produces a strong sense of shared purpose among employees – suggesting that this might also be driving high organizational performance.[31] Part of the explanation seems to be that a customer-focused purpose leads to both a strategic focus and creative capability inside organizations.

As we have discussed previously, some leaders are increasingly advocating an employee-driven purpose as a means to improve both employee engagement and customer satisfaction. To be effective in inspiring people, such a purpose must be authentic and consistently applied. It would not work if, in order to keep prices low, employees are paid at, or close to, the minimum wage, receive few if any benefits, have no job security and are given only enough training needed to do basic jobs that have been designed to be simple and easy to learn. When workers at the bottom of these companies have no opportunities to make a good living or to do interesting work – much less to make a career in them – organizations should avoid declaring that people are their greatest asset.

So how do leaders inspire an authentic sense of shared purpose? Engaging leaders set and communicate a clear direction and priorities (developing what MacLeod and Clarke refer to as a 'strategic narrative') so that employees know what is required and feel empowered to deliver the right outputs without the need for micro-management. They develop self-awareness regarding their own core purpose, values and beliefs – the core that shapes their approach and by which they influence and take people with them when everyone is under pressure. They strive to role-model the values and use, and act on, 360-degree and other feedback to show commitment. They nurture leadership at every level.

For instance, William Rogers became CEO of UKRD in 2002 and oversaw its transformation into the UK's fourth-largest commercial radio group. In 2009, UKRD won a hostile takeover bid for the publicly quoted Local Radio Company PLC. Since then, further acquisitions have been made as the group builds its portfolio of local commercial licences. As William Rogers points out:

> We've tried to create a values-based culture and there are six words that set the parameters for the standards of behaviour we encourage: open; honest; fair; fun; professional and unconventional. It is one thing to introduce a values-based culture; the second thing is backing it up with cash and time. At UKRD

every single year, everyone has a full day out of the business talking about what these values mean to them in the workplace. It's also important that everybody understands that the values apply to everyone. All of the senior team takes part in workshops; they're not just there to make a speech. We also provide all of our teams with 'courageous conversations' training, which has led to a massive reduction in how much managers need to get involved in disputes between individual members of their teams. Between 90 per cent and 95 per cent of decisions in this company are made on the ground.[32]

Not surprisingly, UKRD came top of the 'Sunday Times Top 100 Best Companies to Work For' list for three consecutive years.

## Supporting people

Engaging managers get to know people as individuals, care for employees, create an open and positive work environment and build teams. They execute tasks in an enabling way, aiming to keep staff motivated and developing people's performance potential. They are versatile, able to judge when to involve employees and when to direct them. Engaging line managers set clear objectives so that people know what is required but allow staff to work out how to deliver them. They watch for signs of 'burnout' and aid people in managing workloads by being clear about what can be stopped as well as started. They support people best by designing interesting and worthwhile jobs and ensuring employees have the skills, authority and resources they need to deliver results that matter. They 'declutter' jobs of unnecessary bureaucracy so that people have a clear line of sight through their day job to the purpose, mission and goals of the organization.

Engaging managers strive to deliver on the employer brand and promise and ensure employees get a fair deal. In the current context, old-fashioned carrot-and-stick incentives to stimulate and reward performance are unlikely to be effective. While no organization can guarantee job security, engaging managers can help employees to cope with stress and anxiety during change. Providing meaningful support – even simply listening – not only shows employees whose jobs may be at risk that they are valued, it can also help survivor employees (those whose jobs remain after downsizing) to remain productively focused on their work.

It is about building trust and ensuring that companies honour their commitments to employees. For instance, in 2012 all staff at the UK firm JCB shared a £2.5 million bonus pot despite economic headwinds predicted in 2013. Chairman Sir Anthony Bamford said he wanted to reward the hard work and commitment of JCB's 5,000 workers.[33] Playing fair by staff and showing them that their efforts are recognized is a great way to build employee engagement and commitment.

Since some of the human reactions to change can be anticipated, HR can help managers to take actions to minimize the negative impact of change on people and build policies and initiatives that support people in managing their own wellbeing. Employee assistance programmes can help. Therefore managers need to develop more of a coaching style and be willing and able to involve staff in implementing change. When making change becomes part of every employee's job, it can become the spur to innovation and improvement.

## Voice

Engaging employers encourage and facilitate the kind of connections that employees want to make today. By doing so, they form communities of like-minded people collaborating on purposes that they share. Especially in tough times, frequent and honest communication is vital for (re)building employee trust, resilience and engagement. Engaging leaders and managers are visible, accessible and approachable; they communicate authentically and consistently about the bigger picture, strategy and direction. They are also willing to listen and act on what they hear.

Communication is not just top-down but also involves genuine dialogue at organization and team level and with unions and staff groups. Whether dealing with business problems or developing new ideas for growth, engaging leaders take a participative approach, building consensus between different groups and individuals within the business. They make sure that people can see clear signs of progress by marking milestones, celebrating successes, stabilizing what works and sharing the benefits of change.

## Scope

Scope is where individual motivation is at its highest. It is where people feel they have the opportunity to pursue their own sense of purpose through the work they do, and the possibility of growth and fulfilment. This is what Isles describes as 'Good Work'.[34] Career development matters to most people (see Chapter 9). For all its challenges, change can also open up opportunities for autonomy, development, and better work-life balance and to gain new skills, new networks and new responsibilities. The most successful businesses empower their employees to do their best work by encouraging learning, reskilling and growth, keeping people connected and informed and involving them in decision making.

Engaging managers work at improving the skills and competencies people really need, focusing in particular on people in new roles. They spot opportunities for employee development and actively coach their teams, involving them in working on real business issues, providing job shadowing and mentoring. And as we have discussed, engaging managers design rich and rewarding roles and clarify career tracks to enable internal (and external) mobility and enhanced experience for key groups and individuals. They champion employee interests and deliberately encourage people to change roles or re-energize themselves by moving between domestic and international divisions or from one country or department to another. This allows them to gain new experiences and helps develop different parts of the business – and is also a great motivator. After all, when people feel valued and have opportunities to grow, they are likely to perform well. Younger workers can be helped to build their careers in the organization and employees more generally can be upskilled for employability. While staff are responsible for their career development, HR can help them to understand how to go about planning their careers by:

- building career planning support based on a competency model
- apprenticeships and mentorship
- improving the skills for managers to support staff in career development
- making opportunities available.

Scope is also about people taking the initiative, managing their own contribution and development and embracing the philosophy of lifelong learning.

One international charity recognized that, while staff are responsible for their own career development, some organizational support should be available to help them understand how to go about planning their career. They developed career planning support tools based on their competency model that individuals can access and discuss with their line manager. Managers were given skills development to help them support staff with career development conversations and a pool of peer mentors was established so that colleagues can help each other to learn new skills and access new experiences. HR acts as facilitator of job and experience moves. In a context where the organization values the individual and the feeling is mutual, there is the possibility of a grown-up employment relationship.

HR can increase people's scope by helping line managers to design meaningful jobs and to coach and develop individuals and teams. They can also work with managers to develop career tracks so that people can grow their careers. In the John Lewis partnership, for instance, whose employees are vocal advocates of the company, people are developed on the job and have opportunities to expand their experience by moving around the organization. It is about upskilling people through new experiences, training and coaching, ensuring that the reward systems recognize team, as well as individual, contributions to overall performance. HR can work to improve employee communications and actively involve staff in change efforts. Even if rewards remain squeezed, HR can work with staff to develop other forms of reward and recognition and develop wellbeing policies that employees actually value.

## An emergent psychological contract

So a new, personalized psychological contract may be emerging at the heart of the employment relationship that is founded on equity between employers and employees. Elements of this emerging contract might include:

- Connection:
  - organizational affiliation
  - quality of relationships
- Voice:
  - information
  - involvement
  - co-creation
  - access to speaking truth to power
- Support:
  - peer support
  - mentoring by senior colleague
  - work-life balance
  - effective management
  - a positive work climate

- Scope:
  o self-awareness – with psychology-savvy talent coaches
  o autonomy and influence
  o real work – action learning, projects
  o careers and opportunities to grow.

Any organization that wishes to retain talent should be vigilant to how employees' needs are changing. Ultimately, though, employees are responsible for managing their own engagement. One people professional points out how her organization's culture respects people's autonomy. 'People want choice. It's such a significant part of our culture now. People having the ability to make a change [to] something as simple as the temperature in an office space really goes a long way for an employee to feel happy, feel appreciated, feel really engaged in their day-to-day work.'

Moreover, if staff genuinely do enjoy scope, receive the right level of support, have voice and feel connected with their organization, it is only to be expected that they can be trusted to get on with the job, be accountable for their performance and 'go the extra mile' for the organization.

## Team engagement

Beyond individual engagement, the level of team engagement will also affect performance. Creating an engaging workplace climate is usually a joint effort. The following case study tells how a partnership between a ward sister and an organization development (OD) specialist in a UK hospital helped a demoralized and underperforming ward team to become a well-motivated, healthier and high-performing team that genuinely does put patients at the heart of their work. I am grateful to Tracey Gray, formerly Head of Education at Doncaster and Bassetlaw Hospitals, NHS Foundation Trust, who was the OD practitioner in this short case study.

---

CASE STUDY
*Changing attitudes – improving outcomes*

These days the UK's NHS is subject to considerable media scrutiny and criticism over poor patient care. Naturally this negative press can be demoralizing for staff. At

Doncaster and Bassetlaw Hospitals NHS Foundation Trust serious concerns were raised by major stakeholders about the detrimental effect on patient experience due to the demotivation of staff on one of the wards. The regular metrics of patient care posted on the ward notice board (known as the 'wall of shame') showed an ever-downward spiral of staff morale, absence and patient care. The ward staff were feeling undervalued and had mostly come to believe that they were seen as 'problem children' and that this was how things would remain. The risk was that, if ignored, the situation could deteriorate and become another scandal of poor patient care.

An internal OD consultant, Tracey Gray, was commissioned to work with the ward sister to improve the situation. The work involved listening deeply to colleagues, whom it could have been easier to dismiss as part of the problem, and looking unflinchingly at some very challenging aspects of hospital life.

## Key elements and purpose of the intervention

Part of the challenge was how to get team members 'on board' with the idea of looking at their own practice and taking responsibility for improving patient care. Tracey had individual conversations with staff, based on which a four-phase behavioural and educational development programme was designed. Its aim was to improve the patient experience in this specific ward by changing the attitudes and behaviour of staff, resulting in measurable change for the better. The training programme focused on both individual and group values and interventions were chosen to emphasize teamworking and included individual coaching, action learning and workshops. Simulations were designed to vividly bring to life typical care issues and help staff to understand care needs from the perspective of vulnerable patients.

Everyone in the team received individual coaching from Tracey, who did not shy away from using the ugly data and demonstrated a passionate belief in the possibility that anyone can change. She listened closely to staff, using neurolinguistic programming (NLP) to understand how they perceived their role and to elicit people's values and beliefs, identifying differences in beliefs – which can lead to conflict. This raised staff awareness and helped people to get issues out and deal with them constructively and systematically, for instance in action learning sets, by using shadowing, and by giving team members new process skills to talk to each other. Thus as OD practitioner Tracey planted seeds of self-help within the team to ensure that potential future conflicts could be addressed positively. Throughout the programme, the emphasis was on helping staff to feel empowered to improve patient care.

The effects

Clear markers were established and there were many beneficial outcomes from these interventions, not least improved staff morale and satisfaction, patient safety and wellbeing. Simple and effective symbols were used to reinforce messages, such as reframing the 'wall of shame' as the 'wall of praise'. These helped to keep people focused and enable the team to measure visually the progress towards better patient care. As the programme progressed, a positive improvement in the ward's climate became evident. There was a significant reduction in staff sickness and absence, improved staff morale and fewer patient complaints. As the ward team grew in confidence, rather than seeing their situation as remedial, staff members started to feel proud of the special help they were receiving to become a high-performing ward team.

Significant changes were noted in the following months, such as the positive atmosphere on the ward, staff's improved awareness of patient needs and recognition of non-verbal signals, resulting in better patient care. The ward staff grew into a strong team, since they had increased understanding of each other and enhanced process skills. Nursing practice improved and all concerned were proud of what had been achieved: all of this within a short space of time and at low cost. Results were disseminated to the chairperson and executive board members, and the team who piloted the first event received certificates of completion and were rewarded with a celebratory buffet and presentation. This will no doubt have reminded the team members of how much they have achieved and just how much patient care on their ward has improved.

Spreading the learning

While the programme's interventions were both bespoke to and embedded within the ward in question, they also offer the potential for scaling into the wider organization, since champions are being developed within different areas who are being trained to become NLP master practitioners. Strong clinical leadership was a key element of the success of this initiative. Tracey worked closely with the ward sister, training her to support and embed initiatives in this ward and potentially others. The upskilling of clinical staff to apply such processes in their teams should help to spread and embed effective practice and behaviours across the organization. Thus not only has the programme had a beneficial impact on improving patients' experience but also the approach taken is very congruent with the humanistic principles and values of OD, which is about working *with* not *on* people to achieve renewal and growth.

## Links between employee engagement and wellbeing

In recent times, mental health and wellbeing issues have risen up many corporate agendas. Wellbeing and engagement interact with each other in powerful ways. MacLeod and Clarke define wellbeing as '... a state ... in which every individual realises his or her potential, can cope with the normal stresses of life, can work productively and fruitfully, and is able to make a contribution to his or her community'.[35] Wellbeing includes physical, emotional, moral and financial factors so a multifaceted approach to employee engagement is needed to ensure psychological safety and improve employee wellbeing. By so doing companies benefit from increased employee enthusiasm, motivation and productivity, without the burnout. When employees are engaged and thriving, they experience significantly less stress, anger and health problems.

Research suggests the picture today is far from rosy. Unfortunately, many employees remain disengaged at work. Gallup estimates that low engagement alone costs the global economy $7.8 trillion.[36] According to Deloitte's 2020 report, poor mental health costs UK employers up to £45 billion per year, a rise of 6 per cent since 2016.[37] The CIPD Good Work Index shows a significant level of work-related poor health among UK workers.[38] Change that is imposed and beyond an individual's control can lead to stress and depression. About one in four workers report that their job has a negative impact on their mental or physical health. One in five say that they always or often feel 'exhausted' at work, a similar proportion say they are under 'excessive pressure' and 1 in 10 say they are 'miserable'. The CIPD reports that the UK ranks 24th out of 25 for work-life balance compared with other 'comparator economies'. Three in five UK employees are working longer hours than they would like, even when considering their need to make a living. Some 32 per cent also report being given excessive workloads. Similarly Gartner's 2019 Modern Employee Experience survey found that only 21 per cent of highly engaged respondents reported having a 'high-quality work-life experience'.[39] Workforce burnout on the front-line is an urgent challenge that leaders must directly address so that they understand the root cause and impacts and the opportunities to address workforce fatigue and burnout.

The shift towards more remote and hybrid working is changing the landscape of work and brings different aspects of employee wellbeing into the spotlight. Instances of loneliness are reported to have risen sharply during the pandemic, with younger workers apparently suffering the most in a hybrid world. Most have left university and started jobs remotely, missing out on important social milestones. Social media has also exacerbated loneliness for many, offering a cycle of scroll and reward, creating a culture of instant gratification and competitive pressure. For some workers the time spent online has doubled as companies embrace hybrid and remote working. As screen time increases, workers around the world experience a lack of real connection and purpose. And with working days full of Zoom or other calls, the nature of work has become more transactional, eroding the casual social connections forged in the workplace.

Should employers care? Robertson Cooper argues that high psychological wellbeing leads to positive individual outcomes, such as commitment, morale and health, which in turn lead to improvements in organizational performance in areas such as productivity, customer satisfaction, attractiveness to recruits and lower turnover and sickness absence.[40]

Workers certainly care about wellbeing. A survey by Silicon Reef Life in 2022 found that 73 per cent of workers in the UK think employers should do more to address loneliness among staff who are working remotely.[41] In CareerBuilder's survey on stress in the workplace 31 per cent of respondents reported extremely high levels of stress at work and 61 per cent of employees reported being burned out on the job.[42] Those high stress levels were manifested in poor physical health (fatigue, aches and pains, weight gain) and compromised mental health (depression, anxiety, anger). These findings emphasize the links between wellness and engagement, and how stress undermines both. Where a combination of lack of recognition, increased workloads, poor management and lack of career opportunities exists, some people opt to voluntarily 'downshift', i.e. stepping off the career ladder in order to 'get a life'. Where the pressures on employees undermine their performance, the real impact of such stresses will be felt on business results. Offering people the chance to balance work and personal life therefore makes good business sense.

Research by Willis Towers Watson suggests that a growing number of employers are promoting wellbeing and defining workplace health as a central part of company culture and strategy.[43] HR has the challenge of reconciling organization demands for increased productivity and agility with enabling individual employee wellbeing and resilience.

A Glassdoor survey reports that employees are also looking for support in achieving balance in order to attend to the non-work areas of their lives. Some organizations are offering staff access to a mediation service for relationship issues including domestic abuse. Extra work pressures require employees to make sacrifices, particularly with respect to their home life and spending time with their children and many people work long hours in order to make career progress. In many surveys, employees report that truly flexible working is the main enabler of work-life balance as we shall explore in Chapter 9. Indeed the focus appears to be shifting away from a piecemeal approach to stress issues towards a holistic approach to employee wellbeing which means that wellness must permeate every aspect of an organization.

Stress can also arise from bullying, harassment or other form of 'moral injury.' People should feel free to speak up and have a formal mechanism to do so. Companies need to signpost people where to report and reassure people that if they do raise a complaint, it will be taken seriously. When an incident is reported, HR teams or senior leaders must ensure they have a clear plan in place for what happens next.

Many HR teams, knowing employees are feeling stressed, offer wellness programmes on improving work-life balance and stress management – usually through healthy eating, exercise or mindfulness. Developing employee-friendly policies is part of the solution, but such policies need to be owned by employees and senior managers if they are to become a reality. Some of the more interesting practices on this front come from the United States. For instance, years ago stressed-out employees of Boston City Council had an automated phone system that screened calls for depression. Callers listened to recorded descriptions of how they were feeling ranging from 'I get tired for no reason' to 'I feel others would be better off if I were dead.' They punched the appropriate number and could hear a recorded diagnosis that urged severe cases to seek counselling.[44]

Mental health tools have become more common, such as virtual yoga sessions, mental health support websites or expanded options for counselling through company employee assistance programmes (EAP). Many organizations implement initiatives or standards to reduce stress, develop health and wellbeing strategies, run occupational health roadshows and offer staff access to personal financial advice. A huge range of initiatives includes leave and workshops for women going through the menopause, discounted gym membership and health plans. Some employers have reshaped the physical environment to encourage healthy behaviour, for instance by adding healthy foods to break-room offerings and restaurant delivery menus, ergonomic workstations, appropriate lighting and subsidizing gym membership. The technology-driven wellbeing market has also exploded. More than 90,000 digital health apps were released as the pandemic took hold in 2020. The total figure now sits at more than 350,000, according to IQVIA, many of which are focused on wellbeing and mental health. However, if a company provides employees with apps, who owns the data that employees put into the app? There are potential moral, ethical and legal issues here that might be resolved if employers instead provide employees with the money to buy their own apps.

However, while workshops on stress management and resilience can contribute to a workforce that is healthier, more engaged and more productive, if the workplace remains a largely stressful environment, standalone wellness programmes tend to produce limited returns.

### Championing from the top

Employee wellbeing should be championed from the top. The need for inclusive leadership and an authentic focus on employee experience and wellbeing has never been more pressing. Leaders must anticipate and watch out for any dysfunctional reactions to change that employees may be demonstrating – and provide support as necessary. One group of NHS hospitals has a 'Wellbeing Guardian' at board level who provides active sponsorship of the staff wellbeing work. One trust set up small-scale 'think tanks' involving over 250 staff, each tasked with solving problems in specific areas, including sickness, use of data, retention and wellbeing. Since many front-line NHS staff were worn out caring for the pandemic's victims, HR teams trained mental health first-aiders, offered rest rooms and 'oasis spaces', set up wellbeing hubs, provided virtual wellbeing sessions and 'sleep hygiene' resources, and introduced psychological services for staff that provide one-to-one and team support on dealing with grief, stress, anxiety and depression.

The Saint-Gobain company believes there are clear links between staff engagement, wellbeing and business performance. The firm developed a programme 'Fit to Lead' that was aimed at senior leaders, some of whom were becoming burnt-out. The programme integrates leadership development with mental and physical wellbeing, the idea being that to inculcate a culture of wellbeing across the organization it was important to start at the top. As well as improving their wellbeing, the programme has also made the participants more effective at their jobs.[45]

## Role of line managers

Line managers shoulder the day-to-day challenge of supporting people and of maintaining or boosting employee morale. Research suggests an employee often quits if the quality of their relationship with their line manager is poor or if they feel undervalued. Conversely employees are less likely to quit if they feel their manager trusts them and cares about their wellbeing. HR should work with line managers to identify and actively address the root causes of employee disengagement. The aim should be to make employee engagement and wellbeing a daily focus for managers rather than simply an annual survey process. A holistic approach to combatting stress is needed, with wellbeing acting as a golden thread throughout the support on offer. Solutions should include ensuring appropriate workloads and implementing genuinely employee-centric wellbeing policies.

With remote working, managers can no longer rely on visual cues to gauge wellbeing, so managers need to quickly build rapport with their teams and build a work climate that resonates with employees wherever they are based so that people feel part of the workplace community. To ensure that remote workers can be heard employers can set up regular informal meetings for checking in and one-to-ones to help foster personal connections. Since the main stressors tend to be the work itself, work itself should be designed to enable the three psychological states identified by Hackman and Oldham as underscoring high engagement:

- Meaningfulness of work – namely that the work itself has meaning to you, is motivating and fundamental to intrinsic motivation. This consists of skill variety, task identity and task significance.

- Responsibility – that you have been given the opportunity to be a success or failure in your role because you have sufficient freedom or autonomy to take action.

- Knowledge of outcomes – important not only to be able to make changes as you undertake the work, but also to promote the idea that the work, including performance data, is yours to own (feedback).[46]

Some roles lend themselves more easily to certain aspects of the model than others, but a tweak in one or two of these areas can make a big difference to the level of engagement and satisfaction in the team.

Managers must be trained to understand how to manage employees working on hybrid arrangements. HR should work with front-line managers to monitor the level of demands they are placing on people and encourage a better balance between demands and resources, particularly during high-pressure periods, so that people can recover from the demands they experience through work. Managers must ensure that that a healthy level of pressure and challenge doesn't tip over into unmanageable workloads that make people feel anxious and overwhelmed. It is essential to communicate openly and regularly about what is expected, to provide support where needed, such as by building in some 'slack' in the form of time, as well as introducing protocols such as avoiding emailing people after hours, setting a norm that evenings, weekends and holidays are work-free so employees can maintain a healthy work-life balance. Managers can prevent employee burnout by (re)clarifying priorities, refocusing workloads onto priority areas and coaching their staff. Risk management and retention plans should be applied to key people and jobs where knowledge and skills are in short supply and when career opportunities may be limited.

In times of change, if people are to gain a sense of control over their destiny, managers must involve their teams as much as possible in planning, decision making and problem solving and keep people informed of developments. People are more likely to feel positive about change, and even be energized and excited by it, if they feel they are involved in creating the way forward. We shall return to the question of how change can be 'managed' in later chapters.

Line managers may themselves be under pressure from every angle, juggling both business-as-usual and change management. They too need to feel supported by top management and should be developed as leaders, given access to new tools, techniques and ideas. Managers and leaders need to be aware of the impact that their own management style may have on the team, especially during challenging times. For instance, managers who respond to pressure by taking more control may end up disempowering their team. Roffey Park proposes that leaders can manage their personal resilience when leading change by maintaining:

- Perspective – being able to take a step back from a challenging situation, and accept rather than deny its negative aspects while finding opportunity and meaning in the midst of adversity.

- Emotional intelligence – individuals not being overtaken by their emotions but allowing space and time to process them.

- Purpose – individuals holding a clear sense of their own values and moral compass to keep centred when all around there is change.

- Connections – leaders who are able to stay resilient in challenging times have a wide network of friends and colleagues to draw on, both to get things done and to provide support.

- Physical energy – individuals keeping physically fit, eating well and taking time away from work to engage in activities they enjoy enables them to maintain energy levels.[47]

Learning and development (L&D) professionals have a strong role to play in addressing wellbeing. The NHS provides mental health training for managers as part of the onboarding process. It also offers trauma-informed leadership training to help teams going through tough times. Some organizations are teaming up to provide peer-to-peer reciprocal mentoring at all levels with a special focus on wellbeing, diversity and inclusion and minimizing the negative impact of change on people.

So rather than addressing employee wellbeing as a silo initiative it must instead be accepted as everyone's responsibility. A well-crafted employee wellbeing strategy offers immediate support for employees while simultaneously taking long-term preventative approaches that deliver stability and wellbeing over time.

## Conclusion

Employee engagement, wellbeing and empowerment are key to agility and resilience. Getting the business case for improving engagement and workplace wellness taken seriously is central to success – helping executives understand that shifting the balance so that more people can be engaged more of the time will directly contribute to improving business performance. Effective wellbeing strategies can help people to make the transition to new working conditions and cope with the demands made of them and will also show staff that they are valued. To provide sustainable solutions, HR should proactively identify and address underlying issues that damage the employment relationship and undermine engagement. This is about creating the right climate and conditions where teams can thrive in the first place. As we have discussed, if people work in a constructive environment where they feel they are achieving something challenging and meaningful, they will be much better able to deal with change and the daily pressures of work. Pressure on employers for a more ethical and *win-win approach to the employment relationship* with employees is likely to increase as time goes by. Social connectivity and technological empowerment pose a real threat to old-style corporate models of organization. As employment patterns shift from life-time employment to lifetime employability, employers must interface with an emerging generation of younger workers whose attitudes, demands and expectations of employers may be very different from those only a genera-tion ago. Younger generations have seen the free market model fail and fail young people in particular. Unless something changes, employer and employee interests may be on a collision course.

This is not about HR promoting a new paternalism. At the end of the day, individuals engage or disengage themselves so employees too must take responsibility for managing their own engagement and for negotiating improvements to their context. Rather it is about HR aiming for win-win outcomes for both the organization and its employees. The outcome should be a change-able culture in which people can thrive, bring the best of them-selves in pursuit of a common purpose and renew themselves and the organization as they do so. Striking a better balance should bear fruit in terms of enhanced productivity, agility, employer reputation and the ability to attract and retain key staff.

So, as organizations plot their way to recovery and growth, today's chal-lenges could prove a blessing in disguise since they highlight that employers who focus on engagement and wellbeing can motivate and retain valued employees. However, rather than attempting to force engagement, it is healthier to encourage it by managing change with a human touch. After all, employees will welcome change if, as a result, they work in a positive envi-ronment, are part of a winning team, are more capable and empowered, have learned from their experiences and have the tools to be self-managing. Employers who are forward-looking, who *sustain their investment in people* and continue to develop the abilities of their workforce, are likely to main-tain their competitiveness and be well positioned for accelerated growth when the time comes.

This is the time, above all, where the *'values on the wall' need to work in practice*. So even if business leaders cannot provide job security, they can keep people informed and listen to what employees are telling them. While they cannot provide meaning for their employees, as this is individual and subjective, they can offer a clear purpose for their organizations. They can ensure that values-based behaviours are reflected in appraisals and promo-tion criteria, and that line managers are recognized for their efforts in engaging employees. They can demand that good intent, in the form of work-life balance, wellbeing or diversity policies, is translated into practice, and make every effort to close any 'say-do' gap of their own.

The engagement-performance potential is there – *delivering the results requires a joint effort*. Leaders, managers, HR and employees themselves have key roles to play since employee engagement flows up, down and across the organization. HR needs to focus on building the foundational context elements – building engaging leaders, delivering a compelling employee value proposition or 'deal' and working with line managers to create a culture of engagement. Employees need to step up to the plate, recognizing that in today's market economy they must continue to develop themselves and do a good job for their employers as they do so. Managers and executives need to focus on clarifying expectations, linking the work of their employees to important organizational results, making those linkages clear and providing support. They need to ensure necessary resources are available, and that employees have a say in what they do and how they do it. In short, managers and executives need to focus on helping their employees succeed. There are enough examples out there of firms making the high-engagement/high-performance connection to demonstrate that the real task for HR is to ensure a brighter future by equipping line managers with the tools and ambition to develop talent and build sustainable high performance through employee engagement. A positive goal that is really worth going for!

In the next chapter we consider further how employers can use HR processes to create a climate conducive to high performance.

---

CHECKLIST

How desirable is your organization as an employer?

- Connection:
  - Do employees feel a sense of belonging? Do they connect with the mission, values, and direction of the organization? With others? Their work?
  - Do managers act as credible leaders?
  - Are managers trusted? Do employees believe that the communication from managers is open and honest?
  - Do managers and leaders lead from a values base and create a strong sense of shared purpose?
  - Do employees understand how their work contributes to the organization's performance?

- o  Do employees find meaning and purpose in their jobs? Do they have clear line of sight to strategic purpose and the customer?

- o  Do people see positive and worthwhile outcomes from their work?

- Support:

  - o  Is there appropriate management support and coaching?

  - o  Do employees value their relationship with their manager?

  - o  Can people experience work-life balance? Are there regular workload reviews? Adequate resources and support systems?

- Do managers practise work-life balance and encourage others to do so?

  - o  Are flexible working policies available and utilized by people at all levels?

  - o  Is employee development equipping people for the changing world of work?

- Voice:

  - o  Are communications high quality and two-way? Are employees involved and able to participate in decision making?

  - o  Do employees feel part of the team?

  - o  Do people feel fairly treated? Is there a commitment to innovative diversity and work-life balance policies? Is there appropriate reward?

- Scope:

  - o  Do individuals and teams have the power to shape their work and environment to help them perform at their best?

  - o  Are employees stretched and challenged in ways that result in personal and professional growth and progress?

  - o  Are there clear career progression opportunities?

  - o  How well are different diversity groups aligned within the organization's career pathing process? Are individuals given sufficient career development, mentoring and support? Are there role models at higher levels of the organization? Are career coaches and mentors available?

# Notes

**1**  Heger, B (2007) Linking the employment value proposition (EVP) to employee engagement and business outcomes: Preliminary findings from a linkage research pilot study, *Organisation Development Journal*, 25 (2) pp 121–33.

**2**  The Point of Care Foundation Report on NHS Performance, 2014, www. engageforsuccess.org/the-point-of-care-foundation-report-on-nhs-performance/.

**3**  Murphy, N. Employee engagement survey 2011: Increased awareness, but falling levels, *IRS Employment Review*, 28 November.

**4**  Aon Hewitt. 2014 Trends in Global Employee Engagement, www.aon.com/-attachments/human-capital-consulting/2014-trends-in-employee-engagement-report.pdf.

**5**  CIPD and Success Factors (Feb 2013) *Labour Market Outlook*, CIPD, London.

**6**  Gallup. State of the global workplace report 2022, www.gallup.com/workplace/349484/state-of-the-global-workplace-2022-report.aspx (archived at https://perma.cc/2LCW-F2VQ).

**7**  Evans, J. A guide to combating quiet quitting, *Raconteur*, 4 October 2022, www.raconteur.net/workplace/how-to-combat-quiet-quitting/.

**8**  MacLeod D and Clarke N (2009) *Engaging for Success: Enhancing performance through employee engagement, a report to government*, Department for Business, Innovation and Skills, London, webarchive. nationalarchives.gov.uk/20121205082246/http://www.bis.gov.uk/files/file52215.pdf (archived at https://perma.cc/TTR6-ZMDP).

**9**  Truss, C et al (2013) Employee engagement, organisational performance and individual well-being: Exploring the evidence, developing the theory, *The International Journal of Human Resource Management*, 24 (14), Special issue: Employee Engagement.

**10**  Kahn, WA (1990) Psychological conditions of personal engagement and disengagement at work, *Academy of Management*, 33 (4), p 692.

**11**  Kahn, WA and Heaphy, ED (2013) Relational contexts of personal engagement at work, in C Truss et al (eds) *Employee Engagement in Theory and Practice*, Routledge, Abingdon/New York.

**12**  Schaufeli, WB and Bakker, AB (2004) Job demands, job resources, and their relationship with burnout and engagement: A multi-sample study, *Journal of Organizational Behavior*, 25, pp 293–315.

**13**  Csikszentmihalyi, M (1990) *Flow: The psychology of optimal experience*, Harper and Row, New York.

**14**  MacLeod and Clarke, ibid, p 9.

**15**  Herriot, P and Pemberton, C (1995) *New Deals: The revolution in managerial careers*, Wiley, Chichester.

**16** Rousseau, DM, Ho, VT and Greenberg, J (2006) I-Deals: Idiosyncratic terms in employment relationships, *The Academy of Management Review*, **31** (4), pp 977–94.

**17** Maslach, C and Jackson, SE (1981) The measurement of experienced burnout, *Journal of Occupational Behaviour*, **2**, pp 99–113.

**18** MacLeod and Clarke, ibid.

**19** Aon Hewitt, ibid.

**20** Kenexa (2012) Perception is reality: The importance of pay fairness to employees and organizations, a 2012/2013 Worktrends (Tm) report by Kenexa, an IBM Company, www.macaonline.org/Content/files/2013-5-16Perception-Is-Reality_WorkTrendsReport.pdf (archived at https://perma.cc/2E4G-RSRD).

**21** Purcell, J et al (2009) *People Management and Performance*, Routledge, London.

**22** MacLeod and Clarke, ibid.

**23** Michelman, P (2004) *Methodology: How great managers manage people*, Harvard Business School Publishing, Boston.

**24** Holbeche, L and Matthews, G (2012) *Engaged: Unleashing your organization's potential through employee engagement*, Wiley, Chichester; Jossey-Bass, San Francisco.

**25** Cattermole, G (2014) The future of employee surveys, in *The Future of Engagement*, Engage for Success Thought Leadership Series, Institute for Employment Studies and CIPD, London, pp 31–40.

**26** Brakely, H (2004) *The High-Performance Workforce Study 2004*, Research report, Accenture, London.

**27** Beslin, R and Reddin, C (2006) Trust in your organization's future, *Communication World*, January–February, pp 29–32.

**28** Bevan, S et al (2005) *Cracking the Performance Code*, Research report, The Work Foundation, London.

**29** Buytendijk, F (2006) The five keys to building a high-performance organization, *Business Performance Management*, February, pp 24–30.

**30** Ellsworth, RE (2002) *Leading with Purpose: The new corporate realities*, Stanford University Press, Stanford, CA.

**31** Springett, N (2004) The impact of corporate purpose on strategy, organisations and financial performance, *Human Resources and Employment Review*, **2** (2), pp 117–24.

**32** Quote from Faragher, J. Employee engagement: Secret of UKRD's success, *Personnel Today*, 3 May 2013, www.personneltoday.com/hr/employee-engagement-the-secret-of-ukrds-success/ (archived at https://perma.cc/4LLC-WQC8).

**33** Business Bites, *London Metro*, 19 December 2012.

**34** Isles, N (2010) *The Good Work Guide: How to make organizations fairer and more effective*, Routledge, Abingdon.

**35** MacLeod and Clarke, ibid.

**36** Gallup. State of the Global Workplace: 2022 Report, www.gallup.com/workplace/349484/state-of-the-global-workplace-2022-report.aspx (archived at https://perma.cc/V2VN-RAMN).

**37** Deloitte (2020) Mental health and employers: Refreshing the case for investment, January, www2.deloitte.com/uk/en/pages/consulting/articles/mental-health-and-employers-refreshing-the-case-for-investment.html (archived at https://perma.cc/HXF6-FKG5).

**38** Gifford, J. CIPD good work index 2020 UK working lives survey, CIPD, June 2020, www.cipd.co.uk/Images/good-work-index-full-report-2020-2_tcm18-79210.pdf (archived at https://perma.cc/ZP2E-E2YC).

**39** Gartner employee experience insights report, 2020, www.gartner.com/en/human-resources/insights/employee-experience (archived at https://perma.cc/MHL4-RSY2).

**40** In MacLeod, D and Clarke, N (2014) The evidence: Wellbeing and employee engagement, Engage for Success, May, engageforsuccess.org/wp-content/uploads/2015/09/wellbeing-and-engagement-04June2014-Final.pdf (archived at https://perma.cc/34FA-PEK6).

**41** Silicon Reef Life (2022) Combatting loneliness in the hybrid workplace, siliconreef.co.uk/blog/the-hybrid-workers-guide-to-combatting-loneliness/.

**42** Career Builder (2017) Do American Workers Need a Vacation? New CareerBuilder Data Shows Majority Are Burned Out at Work, While Some Are Highly Stressed or Both, https://press.careerbuilder.com/2017-05-23-Do-American-Workers-Need-a-Vacation-New-CareerBuilder-Data-Shows-Majority-Are-Burned-Out-at-Work-While-Some-Are-Highly-Stressed-or-Both (archived at https://perma.cc/62TC-JQT5).

**43** Willis Towers Watson (2020) Making an impact: Health and wellbeing guide, www.wtw-healthandbenefits.co.uk/hr-resources/health-and-wellbeing-guide (archived at https://perma.cc/Z8NW-YZWQ).

**44** *London Evening Standard*, May 1999.

**45** Calnan, M (2018)Why Saint-Gobain decided wellbeing should begin with healthier leaders, People Management, April, www.peoplemanagement.co.uk/article/1742257/saint-gobain-wellbeing-begins-healthier-leaders (archived at https://perma.cc/K6MU-4WQX).

**46** Hackman, JR and Oldham, GR (1976) Motivation through the design of work: Test of a theory, *Organizational Behavior and Human Performance*, **16** (2), pp 250–79.

**47** Lucy, D, Poorkavoos, M and Thompson, A (2014) *Building Resilience: Five key capabilities*, Roffey Park, Horsham.

# 09

# HR's role in building
# a high-performance work climate

Companies are always striving for better results and improving productivity is the focus of many organizational change efforts.

Productivity is broadly speaking the difference between the cost of input and the value of output. What seems clear is that productivity is slipping in the United States and the United Kingdom. In Chapter 6 we considered how operational improvements such as simplifying and improving processes, introducing new products and services, technology support, intelligent cost management, team-based work and increased cooperation and communication can make a difference to performance and increase potential for innovation. Investing more in technology and processes that boost productivity should mean that companies can afford to pay wages that keep up with the rising cost of living. This means embracing trends such as robotics and automation. While technology can help it is only part of the solution.

As we discussed in the previous chapter, there is a direct link between employee engagement and performance. It is people who make the difference between high and low productivity. Both talent shortages and employee disengagement are hampering productivity. During the pandemic, many people's psychological contracts with work were shattered – because their employer closed down and their job had suddenly gone. Much of the social side of work disappeared and was replaced by online meetings where the focus was often on the task in hand. Quiet quitting and the conscious disengagement from additional work beyond what is required appear symptomatic of a working culture that hasn't recognized or remunerated staff – rather than an outright rejection of the work itself. According to the Trades Union Congress, British workers put in two and a half weeks more work per year than the average European. However, this additional work is not translating into higher incomes or a better quality of life, with many millennials and Gen-Zers set to be worse off financially than their parents.[1]

Increasingly it is recognized that a high-performance work climate and high-performance work practices (HPWPs) are key to improving performance and productivity. These are defined as 'practices that can facilitate employee involvement, skill enhancement and motivation',[2] and as the sum of the processes, practices and policies put in place by employers to enable employees to perform to their full potential.[3] In this chapter we focus on some of the high-performance work practices that should flow through to job design and enhance business performance.

We also look at the joint effort involved in creating a 'change-able' work context without destroying the vital enabler of agility – people's engagement with the work they do and the organization they work for. By creating empowering work conditions, line managers can ensure that employees are engaged, motivated, productive and competent and aligned behind the business strategy. The HR function can use its 'levers' to contribute to building a climate of high engagement, performance and innovation. Yet a 2014 CIPD survey found that while many HR professionals focused attention on workforce planning (64 per cent) and training and development (54 per cent) to improve their organization's responsiveness to change, less attention was given to creating organizational environments that enable the agile workforce to thrive.[4] According to Peter Cheese, HR must step up to the plate: 'This means being efficient and effective – not just trying to force more out of the same resources, and not mistaking activity for productivity.'[5]

In particular we shall look at how HR strategies relating to flexible working, performance management, reward and benefits are changing to reflect context shifts and also specific organizational strategies:

- working flexibly
- virtual and hybrid working
- performance management
- recognition and reward
- career resilience.

## Working flexibly

So if organizations want to revitalize the workforce and achieve greater productivity they need to meet employees half-way, see what employees want and redesign their offers. In a world that is constantly changing there are still core things that people are looking for. Flexible working is one of them. Technology is enabling new flexible working arrangements that can benefit the employee, the employer or both. Smartphones and tablets enable people to stay in touch through emails and blogs and have made it much easier for people to work remotely. During and following the 2008 economic crisis many employers adopted practices that increased their flexibility, such as 'zero-hours' contracts that were potentially disadvantageous to workers. Similarly, during the pandemic in many organizations the entire workforce was working from home. As pandemic restrictions eased, many employers insisted that workers return to the workplace and these demands appear to be out of step with employee expectations.

Flexible options range from the informal, such as employees occasionally working from home, or 'hot-desking' in offices when their main work is in the field, to more formalized kinds of flexible working arrangement. For instance, before the pandemic, a report by Chess Media Group found that 87 per cent of modern workers were using flexiwork arrangements.[6] CIPD found that one in five employees worked from home at least once a week, and 1 in 10 spent most of their time at the location of a client or customer.[7]

Flexible working options typically fall into the following categories:

- *Functional* – here labour is allocated across traditional functional boundaries – for instance, through multiskilling, cross-functional working, task flexibility.

- *Numerical* – where there is variation in the number of employees or workers deployed in order to cope with peaks of work or occasional demands for specialist work – for instance, in various types of temporary work, seasonal, casual, agency, fixed-term workers, outsourcing, sharing resources, using contingent, contract or consulting talent.

- *Temporal* – this represents variability of working hours, either in a regular or irregular pattern – for instance part-time, annual hours, shifts, overtime, voluntary reduced hours, flexitime, zero-hours arrangements.

- *Locational* – this involves employees working outside the normal workplace, including transfers of work to back offices; for instance working at home, mobile, tele-/outworkers. Various forms of virtual working, such as telecommuting and remote working, involve moving the work to the worker instead of the worker to work.

The majority of workers who formally work on flexible arrangements are women. Research suggests that men rarely opt for these partly because of the stigma attached to, for instance, working part-time and partly because many people fear that opting to work flexibly will limit their career options and, in uncertain times, could make them expendable when budgets are being cut.

Increasingly though, flexible working is becoming employee-driven with people increasingly opting for flexible working as a lifestyle choice. While a decade ago the priority for most working people was career advancement, which meant doing what was necessary to move up the corporate ladder, today the priority is pursuing a better work-life balance. Given the ending of default retirement ages and the rise of the multigenerational workforce, especially in Europe, flexible working is about accommodating the needs of individuals and groups at different stages of their lives. It means allowing workers to manage their work schedule around their life, such as by allowing timetable flexibility for lunch breaks or childcare responsibilities. A US study by EY (formerly Ernst and Young) found that people are choosing job opportunities where employers offer flexible working arrangements.[8] Over one-third of employees in a CIPD survey said they would like to change their working arrangements and, of those, 43 per cent would most like to change the start or finish time of their day. Just under half (45 per cent) of employees take phone calls or respond to emails outside their working hours (with over one-third choosing to stay contactable rather than being pressured to do so). The CIPD predicts that a four-day working week will soon become the norm.

By enabling employees to have greater flexibility, organizations have a greater chance of employee engagement, a more productive workforce and stronger organizational performance. Yet CIPD research found that many organizations are struggling to embrace new ways of working that require judging people by their outputs and results, the opposite of micro-managing.[9] Lack of trust, cost considerations and misdirected investments are key factors preventing organizations from effectively implementing agile working practices. Culture change may be required to establish working solutions that are of value both to individuals and to the business.

## Virtual/remote working

Even before COVID-19 employers were realizing the benefits of introducing flexible and remote working options. During the pandemic virtual or remote working – a flexible working option – became a necessity in many industries and sectors. Physical space was no longer a boundary.

### The benefits

Employer benefits include the ability to attract and retain talent and reduced absenteeism. Various studies suggest that virtual employees are usually more productive than their traditional counterparts because they learn how to minimize downtime by performing routine tasks during the short pockets of time between other commitments throughout the day. Virtual teams reduce the scope for discrimination since, with visual stimuli removed, people focus more on output and less on the person generating it.[10] In many cases virtual working is introduced to save costs on real estate. In BT Retail, for instance, almost everyone at all levels of the hierarchy works from home. Employees also benefit – they save on commuting time and costs, can have a better work-life balance, greater ability to focus with fewer distractions, more time for family and friends, IT upskilling and higher levels of motivation.

Other potential benefits of virtual working, identified by Cascio, include:

- savings in time, travel and expenses
- greater and quicker access to subject experts
- opportunities to form teams without the need for physical proximity – therefore avoiding lengthy meetings and downtime
- expansion of potential labour markets.[11]

More generally, a virtual team – also known as a geographically dispersed team – is a group of individuals who collaborate across time, organizational and geographical boundaries. Virtual teams can be nimble and dynamic, shifting team membership to suit project needs with some employees assigned to multiple, concurrent teams. Virtual teams can shorten cycle time and increase innovation.[12] They tend to be more creative and can leverage learning better than conventional teams.

### The challenges

The challenges faced by virtual managers are somewhat different from their non-virtual counterparts. With matrix working, a virtual manager may not only be leading their own team but also be a resource for teams led by others. Perhaps the greatest challenge is building trust – a critical factor for effective virtual working yet harder to build when people don't meet physically. Because virtual managers cannot see their team members, some struggle to trust that people are working and may try to catch them out by phoning at different times of day to see if the person is available to speak to them. As a result, they undermine trust and working relationships.

At the same time, working from home can be stressful, and even more so when roles and operating models change. Virtual workers can become literally and psychologically distanced from their organization, so managers must deal with the team's feelings of isolation and communication difficulties. BT Retail has learned that virtual or teleworking does not suit everyone so the company also provides opportunities for teams to meet physically in different locations in order that both social and business needs can be met. Employers need to be intentional in creating space for the human as well as the business aspects of daily work life. It is important to make good use of any in-person time spent together, for instance having lunch with the team on those in-days. Those are the times to carry out more creative work that benefits from people being together.

One UK public body reduced the number of its offices from 100 to 40 across England over four years, moving 1,500 of 1,900 staff to be fully flexible. The organization provided all its social workers with 4G laptops, mobile devices and fully electronic case management systems. They ensured that online support and learning was also in place to reinforce the 'shift in culture'. In particular they paid attention to the social side of work, ensuring everyone attended the monthly team meeting, regardless of where they worked during the week. Agreements were made with partner organizations to have touchdown bases so that staff could meet with service users. They also introduced the Robertson Cooper 'Health & Wellbeing' tools so they could fully analyse the factors in high performance and pick up any issues with individuals who prefer working in 'offices'.

## THE ROLES OF VIRTUAL MANAGERS

Roffey Park researched the nature of virtual working, including the roles of the virtual manager and that of global teams.[13] It found that effective virtual managers are primarily builders of a collaborative culture that focuses on outcomes, supports worker autonomy and values diversity. Cultural barriers and differences can usually be addressed through proper team-building and cultural-assimiliation exercises. Team members knowing and understanding each other leads to less conflict, better anticipation and a sense of belonging, thus increasing the effectiveness and productivity of the team.

Clear rules, procedures and decision-making processes are needed to empower team members and speed up information sharing by defining the boundaries within which team members can operate. Effective virtual managers have a facilitative leadership style, are not micro-managers and are able to delegate effectively.

### Building trust

For virtual managers, not being co-located with their team members means they have to build relationships and trust – both remotely and face to face. Some use monitoring equipment software such as tracking the amount of time spent on billable tasks for clients and some believe it is acceptable to monitor email-sending behaviours, ostensibly to assess if an employee is at risk of burnout. Generally speaking, this is not a good idea as it undermines trust. Instead, managers should focus on getting to know their team. When visiting regional offices, for example, a virtual manager could deliberately bring together and spend extra time with remote teams, getting to know them individually and collectively, rather than simply getting on with their 'day job'.

### Communication

For remote working a culture of feedback, common purpose, informal social interaction and celebrating good work is essential to combatting loneliness. Communication can be twice as difficult when it is done by email, telephone, Skype, Teams, Slack, etc. Virtual managers need to be disciplined about making time for keeping in touch with the team, not just for formal projects or personal development communications but for everyday work issues. Effective managers understand their team members' communication preferences and use appropriate methods and channels accordingly, for instance picking up the phone for a chat instead of sending only instruction emails. At the same time, they need to watch out for signs of potential burn-out and be sensitive to reading between the lines.

### Results oriented

Similarly, effective virtual managers are focused and results oriented. They tend to be good at planning, coordinating and organizing tasks, and are able to multitask. They are skilled at managing performance from a distance, setting clear objectives and performance measures and, importantly, focusing on the outcomes and not the actual hours spent doing them. In assessing performance from a distance, without the usual non-verbal clues, they are still able to provide appropriate and timely feedback because they have regular planning and monitoring conversations where updating and reviewing progress takes place. They celebrate and acknowledge good performance. They also have good links within the wider organization, understand the organization's goals and have 'strategic vision', linking into the organization's political network. Thus they act as 'boundary spanners' and ambassadors for their teams. And while many of these skills and attributes are desirable for most managers, they are essential for virtual managers.

## Managing hybrid ways of working

After the widespread uptake of remote working during the COVID-19 pandemic, many organizations are grappling with employees' requests to have some sort of hybrid working arrangement, a combination of in-office and remote days, for instance coming into the office only a few days per month. This has led to distributed teams with different working arrangements and with different needs. At Weetabix, slogans are used to signal company policies. So there are 'Weetabix Wednesdays' – the one day a week where everyone is in the office and 'Choos-day Tuesdays' where people can choose remote or office work. Employee feedback is at the heart of every policy.

Hybrid working arrangements will make greater demands of managers and organizations than did the urgent shift to remote working during the pandemic. A small number of large employers are finding hybrid working arrangements so difficult to manage that – like Yelp and PayPal – they are going fully remote. Airbnb has stated that it will allow its employees to work from anywhere permanently in a bid to further improve flexibility. Other organizations have called for their employees to start spending at least some time back at their desks. Yet as workers reluctantly go back to the office they may find themselves hot-desking in new working environments and enduring high commuting costs once again while senior-level employees may continue with remote working, leading to complaints of double standards. Organizations that do not support flexible forms of working may risk increased employee turnover, reduced employee engagement and find their ability to attract talent in the future limited. Repeated surveys have found that employees are prepared to leave for greater flexible working opportunities if they are unable to access them in their current role.

For most organizations, hybrid working will require a significant culture shift as well as establishing new ways of working and associated policies and practices. For managers, HR and employees, it is a learning journey. All the Engaged model elements (connection, voice, support and scope) are essential to helping people succeed. The challenge is how to be collaborative, have very productive conversations and work in a creative way with your colleagues in a remote or hybrid environment. Alongside the skills and activities required for managing remote workers, hybrid is its own situation where you have to interact with some people in person and others remotely so it requires a different type of skillset in how you communicate and interact with each other. Managers must ensure fairness and inclusion, making sure that people are participating whether they are in the room or on camera. Scheduled informal virtual interactions are critically important to having the sorts of 'water cooler' conversations that remote workers would otherwise miss.

Key steps for successful hybrid working implementation should include the following.

**Agree an overall strategic position on hybrid** (and broader flexible) working for the organization.

The task is made more complicated if there is disagreement among the executive about which hybrid working approach to adopt, if any. Such conflict causes paralysis and delayed decision making. HR may be in no position to help, so managers may find themselves trapped between demanding senior executives and employees who are keen to work flexibly, and who may choose to leave if their needs are not met. So executives must align on their position and stick with it, while watching out for benefits and problems.

Policy and supporting guidance must reflect the chosen strategy. Most employers like the idea of people still interacting in person when it makes sense, so the nature and use of office space should be intentionally rethought so that when people come into the office it is for specific purposes, e.g. team building and creative problem solving, and the environment itself is set up for collaboration. When developing policies and procedures organizations should consider the following:

- Set out who (or which role types) is eligible for hybrid working.
- Explain how to request hybrid working – or clearly state that it is available to everyone.

- Clarify roles and responsibilities for hybrid workers and people managers.
- Explain how hybrid working intersects with other forms of flexible working.
- Review other related policies including, for example expenses, IT usage, homeworking and data protection.[14]

**Define hybrid working with regard to the specific organizational context.** This might include several different forms of hybrid working even within one organization, depending on role requirements. For example, in the new world of work, non-linear workdays can also fit seamlessly into hybrid and remote-working patterns. Employees in this arrangement can do their jobs outside the traditional rigid nine-to-five block, often whenever works best for them. While working asynchronously – keeping different hours from colleagues – workers can complete tasks in flexible, focused bursts scattered throughout their day. Thus employees can craft work schedules around their personal lives, rather than cram work into fixed, contracted hours. Non-linear workdays help shift work from being activity focused to being outcomes focused. Managers become responsible for setting the goals and the vision for employees, but they don't tell them how to get there.

However, for a non-linear model to succeed, McKinsey believes some framework generally must be in place: guideposts that ensure employees don't stray too far away from a workable schedule.[15] This could take the form of core collaborative hours, in which live, synchronous work can take place, such as meetings or brainstorms.[16]

**Provide training and ongoing development activity for people managers** to support successful hybrid management and leadership. This includes how to build a collaborative hybrid or virtual environment. According to Hult International Business School professor Debbie Bayntun-Lees, if hybrid arrangements are to succeed, leaders and managers must learn to interact in an 'intentional relational' manner.[17] Managers must enable an inclusive dialogue, in which everyone is given a voice, not least on how hybrid working might affect their team. The aim is to develop quality relationships and interactions and amplify employee voice so that both staff and managers feel known, valued and involved. This requires a willingness to learn, be visible, develop rapport, share power and responsibility and to collaborate with people.

Additionally, managers must support employee wellbeing, build trust and ensure psychological safety. This requires high levels of competence in 'soft' skills, such as self-awareness, empathy and emotional intelligence. These human-centric skills can help managers to understand individual situations and needs as they tune into people even on camera, interpret body language, and ask how people are doing or how they are feeling about their job and their performance. Managers must be deliberate in their use of genuine dialogue, allowing the time required for conversations to take place, picking up on non-verbal cues to ensure issues are fully aired.

Managers must also be intentional in taking advantage of learning resources. These include online learning but there has also been a rise in the focus on experiential learning, for instance on how to offer coaching and feedback whether in person or online and finding ways for employees to improve and upskill to be ready for new opportunities. Similarly, employers must provide employees with access – both in person and virtually – to skill development and real-time learning development resources.

**Plan for and respond to the organizational implications of hybrid working.** People also want their managers to be able to support them so need regular conversations to share plans, outcomes and feedback relating to hybrid working, including how the success of new ways of working will be assessed. During the pandemic people had to adjust to the blurring of lines between work and personal life in the remote and hybrid world. They have had to be more flexible about when they turn off work and how they balance their personal lives. Everyone needs skills like resilience, flexibility and adaptability and the ability to make decisions, especially with respect to hybrid working, if organizational guidelines do not yet exist. Managers and teams must jointly develop team agreements on acceptable behaviour and planning for more effective workflows so that people know what is going on. A good system will provide a fully automated way to record hours worked, maintain flexi-balances and manage planned and unplanned absences. With the use of self-service solutions, employees can easily organize and manage their own time, attendance, schedules, annual leave, absences and personal details.

**Support effective team building and cohesion in hybrid teams.** Leaders and managers become 'connectors', able to facilitate conversations to ensure employees are highly engaged with the organizational mission and work expectations that are also ideally connected to employees' aspirations and wellbeing. Addressing team power imbalances and potential conflict involves learning how to hold difficult conversations and managing employee expectations on issues such as flexible working options. At car finance specialist Zuto, management development programmes include modules on resilience and holding difficult conversations that are also open to interested employees. Beyond formal training, peer-to-peer learning, coaches, mentors and role models also have a part to play.

During the pandemic one company specifically amplified communications, offering people explicit support from former managers, new leaders, and specialist HR resources to help people with the transition journey to remote working. They offered learning (for example, self-paced learning on a digital platform as well as full-day virtual boot camps) and applied it in practice by together defining the purposes and objectives of the new team. High-quality videos and all-company virtual meetings effectively conveyed some of the key messages and built a sense of community.

For the CIPD, the most successful hybrid organizations today are those that view employees as their internal customers. They are dedicated to serving their needs and putting their employees in control. Thus, they foster a culture of empowered, engaged and motivated staff who are more satisfied, productive and committed.

## Towards agile performance management

Accountability is a key element of agility. Traditionally organizations hold people to account through the performance appraisal process. In the first edition of this book (2015) I commented on how various innovative consultancies and high-tech companies such as Adobe, Microsoft, Accenture and Deloitte were trailblazing a people management trend entirely consistent with the move toward agility – that of a new approach to performance management. These first-mover firms compete on the quality of their knowledge and work, and depend heavily on the quality of their talent for business success.

Typically, such firms were simplifying or replacing their 'old' annual performance review processes and formal rankings with frequent, informal performance conversations or 'check-ins' between managers and employees. Adobe, for instance, ended annual performance reviews in 2011–12. A crowdsource campaign came up with an alternative process designed and owned by staff. The company was already using the Agile method, which emphasizes principles such as collaboration, self-organization, self-direction and regular reflection on how to work more effectively, with the aim of experimenting and prototyping more quickly and responding in real time to customer feedback and changes in requirements. The approach to change was 'test and adapt'; projects were broken down into 'sprints' that were immediately followed by debriefing sessions. Thus, being able to respond rapidly to change became more important than sticking rigidly to a plan.

The notion of annual targets became largely irrelevant to the way Adobe's business operated.

These principles changed the conventional definition of effectiveness on the job – and they were in tension with the usual practice of cascading goals from the top down and assessing people against them once a year. Instead, Adobe explicitly brought the notion of constant assessment and feedback into performance management, with frequent check-ins replacing annual appraisals. HR provides workshops for managers on how to give effective feedback as well as tools and materials such as videos, webinars and online sessions. The statistics indicate that the new approach is working, with the culture that employees are creating leading to low voluntary attrition rates.

The idea soon spread, with companies like Juniper Systems, Dell, Microsoft, Accenture and Deloitte among the early adopters. A new focus on managing to strengths, not weaknesses, is emerging.[18] Such companies place significant emphasis on development to rapidly upskill staff. Therefore, frequent, meaningful feedback from supervisors immediately after client engagements becomes more important for developing people than relying simply on annual performance reviews to assess development needs. Regular check-ins allow managers to coach in a timely manner and subordinates to reflect and apply their learning more effectively.

US apparel retailer Gap uses performance management in a transformational way to increase speed and flexibility. Their GPS (Grow, Perform, Succeed) system involves managers and employees resetting objectives monthly in an iterative way – with the ultimate outcome for Gap being satisfied customers and shareholders as their 'north star'. They discuss how people are progressing against goals and how these need to be adjusted for the next few weeks. It is all about building a mindset of accountability. There are no ratings or reviews; this is more about working together collaboratively.

In this next case study, I describe how GE, perhaps the company most associated for decades with the conventional 'stack ranking' approach to performance management, is itself replacing the old system with one that encourages agility and employee growth. As a major corporation with significant influence, GE's move probably represents the real start of a new era with respect to people management. I am very grateful to John Wisdom, Senior Leader, Communications and Brand, GE Crotonville, for helping to develop this case study.

CASE STUDY
*A new performance development approach at GE*

First, let's consider the extent of the shift underway by looking back at how GE contributed to the development of what became the conventional way of appraising performance in many organizations. From the outset, the twin goals of performance management – those of holding people accountable and of encouraging development – are often in tension. As far back as the 1960s, General Electric led the way for companies to start splitting out appraisals into separate discussions about accountability and growth so that development would not be overshadowed.[19] By the 1980s the pressure was on to award pay more objectively, so for many organizations the goal of accountability became a higher priority than development. The challenge was that supervisors often failed to distinguish between different levels of performance, opting for 'average' assessments.

To address this problem, GE's then CEO, Jack Welch, championed the principle of meritocracy and the notion of performance differentiation. People were set stretch goals and were expected to succeed. Forced ranking was used to reward top performers, accommodate those in the middle and get rid of those at the bottom. This approach, known as the 'vitality curve' or 'stack ranking', was part of the Employee Management System (EMS) and hinged on the annual performance review.

For this, employees had to give an account of their own performance over the previous year within the constraint of a limited number of characters. Individual performance assessment was then reduced to a number on which employees were ranked against peers in a way that had consequences for their compensation and future in the company. Very few were in the top boxes as 'A' players, 'role model' or 'excellent' – these were the high potentials chosen to advance into senior positions for whom special development was reserved. Around 70 per cent were in the middle 'B' player 'strong contributor' category, who were to be accommodated. The bottom percentage of underperformers ('C' players – 10 per cent in GE's case) were dismissed. Not surprisingly, the system came to be referred to as 'rank and yank', and the annual review was dreaded by managers and employees alike.

Nevertheless, this more transactional view of performance, with performance appraisals and rankings used mainly to hold employees to account and to allocate rewards, became so well known and much copied that, by the early 2000s, appraisals after this model had become the conventional approach in organizations in almost every sector across the globe.

Why the move away from conventional performance management?

By the 2000s, pressure for a change of approach had been growing for some time. When rapid innovation is a source of competitive advantage, as it is now in many companies and industries, conventional performance appraisals have come to be viewed as a potential threat to growth through innovation and collaboration. Indeed, research suggests that such an approach to performance management is ineffective at boosting performance or growth.[20] In part, that is because the approach takes little account of some key aspects of human motivation.

To build an agile organization, employers need employees to be willing to be flexible in the work they do and to carry on learning new skills. Yet with their emphasis on the critical evaluation of last year's performance and focus on numerical ratings and financial rewards, conventional performance reviews typically induce a 'fight or flight' mindset in employees, rather than a growth mindset. Far from grooming talent for the future, which is critical for organizations' long-term survival, the conventional approach can act as a deterrent to people from undertaking the learning they need to improve current performance or to prepare for future roles.

Performance-related pay linked to the conventional approach is intended to be an incentive to higher performance. Yet, especially in public-sector bodies, the typically small budgets for wage increases have made appraisal-driven merit pay seem irrelevant. Moreover, performance assessments are often biased, resulting in employees becoming alienated. So, in many industries, as the labour market for talent tightens, the performance review process, often despised by managers and employees alike, was becoming a threat to retention.

There were also practical difficulties with the old approach arising from other changes in corporate life. As organizations embrace more agile organization designs, structures become flatter and supervisors' spans of control increase significantly, creating huge time demands on supervisors to both carry out appraisals and focus on employee growth. The move toward team-based project work is becoming widespread, bringing together as it does the best talent from across a business to work collaboratively on shared goals. Conventional appraisals and individual rewards based on individual targets can become a barrier to collaboration, knowledge sharing and innovation – key features of agility. Not surprisingly, as dissatisfaction with the traditional process has grown, and as the emphasis on accountability for past performance starts to dwindle, performance reviews have come to be considered a last-century practice.

Another key factor is the sheer pace of change in the business environment. Coming back to GE, future business needs are continually changing, so it becomes difficult to set annual goals that will still be meaningful 12 months later. As Susan Peters, GE's Head of Human Resources points out, 'Businesses no longer have clear annual cycles. Projects are short-term and tend to change along the way, so employees' goals and tasks can't be plotted out a year in advance with much accuracy.'[21] As a result, jobs are becoming more complex and can change rapidly.

Moreover, the old approach was no longer working for GE's younger workforce. Millennials and others wanted more real-time feedback. As Susan Peters puts it, 'Millennials are used to working and getting feedback which is more frequent, faster, mobile-enabled; so there were multiple drivers that said it's time to make this big change.'[22]

## Towards a new approach

GE has long been admired for its approach to connecting strategy, portfolio and talent in a strong HR culture. When one element changes, so must they all, though very few companies attempt to change all these strands at once. The quest for GE to develop a more agile culture (and the new approach to performance development) dates back several years and is reflected in the change of GE's management style under previous CEO Jeffrey Immelt who replaced Jack Welch in 2001. Since GE aims to become an agile organization, it has adopted a more experimental approach to developing strategy, culture, ways of working and talent – reviewing and adopting what works and learning from what does not.

With regard to strategy, portfolio and operations, GE is fundamentally restructuring to refocus on its high-tech and industrial businesses, emphasizing things like power and water infrastructure, advanced jet turbines and imaging equipment. This mirrors a broader business strategy shift towards innovation. With respect to operations, GE had previously proselytized and practised Six Sigma, a manufacturing quality protocol that aims to systematically boost quality control and eliminate mistakes. Today, GE's FastWorks platform for creating products and bringing them to market is a successor in many ways to Six Sigma and borrows from Agile techniques to a large extent. There is a focus on rapid and frequent experimentation, learning from the market, only funding projects that prove themselves, and acceptance and willingness to move on from failures.

GE routinely benchmarks itself against other organizations that are also involved with real-time project management. Learning from this resulted in a change to one of the primary operating processes, along with changes to operating principles – from growth to simplification. This meant reducing bureaucracy and silos, introducing new ways of working, getting close to the customer, and producing better, faster outcomes for customers.

The shift in how GE employees think about and track their performance mirrors these broader transitions underway at the company to substantially simplify its business. While the old style 'rank and yank' performance review process worked well for GE in times gone by, it is no longer deemed to deliver for the business. For growth through innovation, the business needs employees to collaborate, make quick and effective business decisions, and provide customers with superior products and services. Managers therefore need to cultivate empowered, collaborative, cross-functional teams, in which accountability is collective, and supervisors need to be capable of coaching and developing their subordinates.

## Transition to the new approach

The change was gradual at first. A few years after Jack Welch left GE, in 2005, the company got rid of formal forced ranking because it fostered internal competition and undermined collaboration. There was real support from the top for a change in the way people's performance was evaluated, and the role of leadership in providing the guiding principles to frame this shift was critical. Speaking to an audience of more than 2,000 emerging leaders on the Global New Directions programme in 2011, the then CEO Jeff Immelt told the group that it was his intention that GE would introduce a more personalized approach to benefits, along with more feedback. Jeff Immelt later committed GE to adopting a no-ratings approach, almost as a leap of faith.

In true Agile manner, GE launched a two-year pilot in 2015, with about 87,000 employees in groups of different sizes and from different industries. The HR group was one of the first to adopt it, including the experiment with no numerical ratings.

The philosophy of continuous improvement is reflected in the new approach to performance management. Annual goals have been replaced with shorter-term 'priorities'. Essentially, the approach depends on continuous dialogue and shared accountability. The goal is to promote frequent, informal conversations with employees (GE calls them 'touchpoints') about performance and development where they set or update priorities that are based on customer needs. Touchpoints allow managers and employees to discuss progress toward those goals and note what was discussed, committed to, and resolved. Two basic questions are revisited: 'What am I doing that I should keep doing?' and 'What am I doing that I should change?'

The aim is to facilitate more frequent, meaningful conversations between managers and employees, and among teams, with a focus on continuous improvement. The focus is on building the workforce the organization needs to be competitive both today and in the future.

Of course, very few managers find the process of giving constructive, critical feedback easy, and done badly, such feedback can damage both employee morale and relationships. To socialize in a more effective approach to giving and receiving feedback so that it becomes more acceptable, useful and actionable by the recipient, the language of feedback has been more intentionally connected to continuous improvement. For instance, rather than talking of 'strengths and weaknesses', which can follow an individual long past the point of applicability, managers are encouraged to use more 'free-form' feedback. The focus is on the behaviours employees may want to 'continue' doing and forward-looking actions, as well as on changes they may want to 'consider' making. With this new positive vocabulary, the emphasis is on development and coaching.

To support the new approach, a smartphone app, called 'PD@GE' for 'performance development at GE', developed internally, accepts voice and text inputs, attached documents, even handwritten notes. Since GE aims to work more horizontally, peers too are encouraged to give each other feedback on an ongoing basis, especially those working in self-directed teams. Employees can give or request feedback at any point through a feature called 'insights', which is not limited to their immediate manager, or even their division, but can come from anyone in an employee's network.

The focus is on contributions and impact within the context of current priorities. The app can provide summaries on command, through typed notes, photographs of a notepad or even voice recordings. The immediacy of the feedback makes it relevant and potentially actionable.

## Rethinking the role of the manager

Managers will still have an annual year-end summary conversation with employees where they look back at the year and set goals, but these are more meaningful and future-focused and less overloaded with expectations than the formal review the company is replacing because they are simply part of an ongoing dialogue. Thanks to the new performance development approach, the manager and employee can now draw upon a much richer set of data regarding an employee's unique contributions and impact throughout the year. A summary document, which both parties finalize and submit together, reflects on the impact achieved and provides a look ahead.

Of course, the new performance development approach makes it incumbent on managers to act as coach to their team members. GE recognizes that some managers may find making the shift to a more coaching and empowering style of management difficult. Consequently, a global training programme, piloted in 2017, has been rolled out to all 38,000 people managers in GE. This helps managers develop new skills needed to set a vision for the team and go forward together; run empowering team meetings and one-to-one sessions; know how to report up to their own managers; and break some old habits.

Rolling out the new approach

The success of the various trials in the pilot led to the decision to go without ratings across the entire salaried section of GE's 300,000 workforce in its various businesses and to roll out the new approach throughout the company, replacing the legacy Employee Management System.

One of the clear beneficial outcomes of these new approaches is increased organizational agility. Managers in the pilot groups have reported that moving away from forced ranking and from appraisals' focus on individual accountability makes it easier to foster teamwork. The new performance development system is promoting trust between managers and employees and within teams, and some business leaders in trial areas have noted a direct impact on business results. For instance, one business area involved in the pilot is now able to bring products to market sooner, while another has used the new approach to drive a five-fold productivity increase in just 12 months.

For employees, the more frequent, informal check-ins have led to more meaningful discussions, deeper insights and greater satisfaction. Employees are gaining access to more and different opportunities than when the only way to progress a career was up a ladder. As a result, they are growing their skills and experience in all directions. The new approach has been welcomed uniformly, and few long for the old system. As John Wisdom says, 'It's been quite a change and I don't see us going back on this.'

---

## Learning and development

Organizations that transform their performance management approaches typically are also rethinking employee management more broadly. GE is no exception and approaches to learning and development are changing to support the desired culture development. Raghu Krishnamoorthy, the GE executive in charge of Crotonville, GE's famous learning campus, considers the programmes he runs there as essential to enabling some of the culture shifts required for agility. He told a group of HR executives at a conference at the campus: 'In fact, we're repurposing the mission of Crotonville as a place where we inspire connection and develop people.'

People development is a key factor in supporting people's learning and establishing change, and this does not always have to involve the traditional learning interventions. To ensure that learning becomes continuous to meet the new challenges a much wider range of learning opportunities is now available than in the past – such as webinars, podcasts and books, as well as off-the-job courses – to support employees in finding new ways of thinking, working and growing in themselves.

## The challenge for HR

The challenge for HR is how to sustain a culture that keeps continuous feedback going without creating overly elaborate processes to ensure full participation. One area that many companies struggle with is how – without a formal performance measurement system – to create a fair, equitable and measurable system on which to base the distribution of pay. In some companies, there are 'shadow rankings', which means that people still do effectively the same thing as before, under the old appraisal system, but more informally, in the background. To address this issue Adobe, for instance, invested heavily in support and training for managers on how to make pay decisions without rankings.

Indeed, during the testing phase of its new approach, GE found that, in the absence of ratings, compensation was in danger of becoming a rating by proxy. While HR in GE is working on this challenge and does not claim yet to have found a magic solution to it, it seems likely that, since managers and employees are now having much richer performance discussions, managers will have more information to draw upon when making compensation decisions. As John Wisdom points out: 'After all, if the leader sees what you are doing, they have more flexibility for compensating you for that.'

While GE may not have invented stack ranking, it is the company most identified with it. The new performance development approach at GE encourages flexibility and agility: it is about building a culture of a better tomorrow, in keeping with the legacy of continuous improvement. Ideology at the top matters, and even with a change of leadership at GE, the new approach is unlikely to be a mere passing experiment because it is being driven by business needs, not imposed by HR. Given its corporate influence, GE may once again be in the vanguard of new people management practice that meets both the needs of the organization and its employees, fit this time for the 21st century.

# Reward strategy

Reward strategy is where employer and employee needs may be at opposite ends of a spectrum. While it may be true to say that money does not motivate everyone, nevertheless people need to feel that they have had a fair deal. Particularly when reward and performance management processes are being changed, people are likely to be suspicious that they will actually be worse off as a result, and in some cases this may prove to be the case. If the working environment is fractious, where it may not be easy to use pay increases as a way to alleviate staff discontent, traditional employee relations may be needed to avoid pay negotiations turning into disputes.

In hybrid environments with distributed workforces, some firms are setting a minimum global baseline linked to cost of living and industry-standard pay rates and using geographical pay differentials to establish compensation ranges. By undertaking regular reviews to ensure they are staying in line with market trends, employers can demonstrate that rewards are competitive.

## Linking reward to business strategy

Reward strategy should flow directly from business strategy. Its nature will therefore reflect the motivation of the business. For instance, some business strategies view people as costs to be cut. In contrast, other strategies recognize that 'people are the source of innovation and renewal, especially in knowledge-based organizations, and that the development of new markets, customers and revenue streams depends on the wise use of a firm's human assets'.[23] Therefore it is important to understand how employees perceive rewards, how these perceptions may vary by workforce segments and generations, how rewards affect behaviour and how behavioural changes affect business performance.

In the case of an innovation-led strategy, the reward emphasis must be strategic – looking at least to the medium term to grow the skills and approaches that should be rewarded. Reward should be integrated with other HR policies so that the 'right' employee behaviours are encouraged (see Table 9.1). The ethical dimension of organizations has emerged more clearly during the pandemic. For example, fashion retailer Boohoo has linked executives' bonuses to ESG goals, right down to including a sustainability strand in individual employees' performance discussions.

I am very grateful to Jon Sparkes, former HR Director of The Generics Group, for the following case study, which describes how reward strategy was developed in support of an explicitly innovation-led business strategy and how it also served as a recruitment, retention and culture-change vehicle.

TABLE 9.1  Strategy: innovation-led

| Employee role/behaviour | Reward policy thrust | Other HR policies |
|---|---|---|
| Creativity: seeking new solutions | Mix of individual and collective rewards | Broadly defined job roles |
| Risk-taking behaviour | Use of 'soft' performance measures, periodically monitored | Cross-functional career paths to encourage development of a broad range of skills |
| Medium-term focus | Emphasis on medium-term performance | Appraisal focusing on medium term and collective achievement |
| Collaborative and cooperative behaviour | Use of learning and personal growth opportunities as a 'soft' reward | High investment in learning and development |
| Concern for quality and continuous improvement | Broad-banded and flexible pay structure | Frequent use of teamworking |
| Equal concern for process and outcomes | High relative market pay | Promotion criteria reflect this |
| High tolerance of ambiguity and unpredictability | Strong element of basic pay and variable pay reflects own, team and organizational performance | Effective external and internal communications |
| Encouragement for learning and environmental scanning | Bonus reflects improved capability and contribution; managers rewarded for team and individual development | Self-nomination for learning events; open-access online learning materials; scenario-planning workshops |

SOURCE  Professor Stephen Bevan

CASE STUDY
*Generics Group AG*

Formed in 1986, Generics Group AG floated on the London Stock Exchange in 2000 at a valuation of £226 million; it employs approximately 500 staff in Cambridge (UK), Stockholm, Zurich, Baltimore and Boston. The focus of the business is the development and commercialization of technology, which it does through consulting in business and technology, licensing technology to partner companies, creating new 'spin-out' companies and investing in other companies. In other words, this company's core product is innovation.

For example, a lift manufacturer needed lifts to stop with greater accuracy so a Generics expert invented a new position-sensing technology. The intellectual property rights were determined and the technology was licensed in the North American automotive industry. Then a spin-out was created – Absolute Sensors Ltd (ASL) – to exploit the business opportunity. The Generics Group supported ASL for one year before selling its shares to Synaptics.

At the time of flotation the challenges for the business were to double consulting revenue in four years and increase innovation in order to generate greater licence revenues and business incubation returns. The firm wanted to increase the rate of business incubation and spin-out to produce growth in the investment portfolio. At the same time it wanted to maintain its creative and entrepreneurial culture and develop a prestigious reputation as the first port of call for business and technology solutions.

For the then HR Director Jon Sparkes, the challenge was to nearly double the headcount with no compromise on calibre. This was a difficult task since the firm's employees tend to be leading experts in their own fields and such people are regularly sought after by other high-technology businesses, so there is stiff competition for people with such skills. The strategy was to grow organically, achieving 15–20 per cent growth through recruitment and retention each year, and to acquire people through managing the integration of acquisitions. From the outset the firm had a flexible culture, with an open management style and the recruitment of entrepreneurial people. At the same time, post-2000 the firm had responsibilities as a listed company. The challenge was to reward employees for developing spin-outs and producing innovations, and to maintain the culture.

In its response HR had to recognize the firm's competitive market position. In East Anglia where it is based there was the highest salary inflation in the UK and house prices were increasing at the highest rate in the UK. The principles on which the reward strategy was based were:

- rewarding individual excellence *and* team performance
- rewarding innovators and entrepreneurs
- sharing in the capital growth of the business
- recognizing work-life balance and promoting the wellbeing of employees and their families
- promoting international culture.

## An integrated reward strategy

With respect to salary, individual salaries were market-tested quarterly and bonuses were based on company and team performance. Specific individual performance was incentivized with rewards for innovators and targeted sales incentives. There was also a recruitment bounty for those who helped to bring in new talent. Employees were also able to share in the capital growth since the share option scheme covers all employees and there are share offers for 5 per cent of each spin-out company.

## Maintaining culture

With respect to maintaining the flexible culture, various work-life balance initiatives were developed such as flexible working patterns, childcare information service membership, sabbaticals and extended leave. There was also a group pension scheme that was personal and portable, and access to an independent financial adviser. Various forms of private healthcare insurances were available and employees enjoyed enhanced maternity and paternity benefits.

To promote an international culture, on-site language training was available for all – German, Spanish, French, Swedish and English. There was a positive approach to recruiting outside the UK (there are generally staff of over 20 nationalities) and placements and assignments available outside the UK.

To stimulate innovation and new business incubation, staff were flexibly deployed on a continuum from 100 per cent consulting to 100 per cent exploitation – although a combination of the two was considered desirable as the consulting work kept the individual close to the market and helped in the development of relevant and valuable intellectual property.

Employees were encouraged to bring forward ideas to a peer review body. The firm provided assistance in building the business proposition and protecting the innovation. A £2 million internal fund was set up to ensure the integration of operating and innovating metrics. Staff could share in the profit from licensing or options in the spin-out – for example, a group of innovators inventing a technology that went on to generate licensing revenue would share in 10 per cent of the profit made from that intellectual property. If the exploitation route was a spin-out company then the innovators would share 10 per cent of the initial shares of the business (while their shareholding would later become diluted, they would benefit from the growth in the value of the business).

Over the years, many staff benefited from their participation in innovation. A small number went on to be founders and directors of spin-out companies in their own right, with one or two of those returning to Generics and building value for the company and themselves all over again.

In summary, there was no distinction between HR and the business. In nailing the fundamentals of recruitment, recognition and reward, Jon Sparkes was clear about the challenge and looked for solutions from both inside and outside the textbook. The focus was on the culture, recognizing that culture is as much a consequence as a cause of the strategies you put into effect.

Recognition

Often the motivator for hard work and loyalty is not money but recognition: a simple thank you for good work can offer as much, if not more than financial reward. For example, at Cambridge Consultants, which develops products such as the artificial pancreas, employees can nominate co-workers for a 'Nobel' prize for a job well done.[24] There is a small cash prize but, more importantly, the prize highlights the employee's talent and dedication. Annual reviews in which employees can gather feedback from anyone they choose (including the chief executive), plus a company magazine, quarterly 'togetherness' meetings, a free restaurant and tailor-made career plans are among the reasons why Cambridge Consultants enjoys a low staff turnover rate of 6 per cent coupled with 10 per cent year-on-year growth.

# Benefits

In hybrid settings, rewards should include benefits that are not location-specific. It means ensuring that employees in different geographies have access to locally relevant benefits: what an employee needs in the United States will differ from one in Switzerland. Previously sought-after perks such as onsite gyms, subsidized travel costs or company cars are not necessary for remote staff. Offering a flexible benefits programme tells people that you, as a company, believe in autonomy and personalization, such as by offering childcare vouchers for new parents or discounted commuting for those returning to the office. Employees are far more likely to use and value benefits available to them if they have been actively involved in designing them.

Travel and insurance firm Saga, whose focus is to be 'champion of age in the workplace' demonstrates this by holding listening groups, introducing age training and improving flexibility. It has also introduced new policies such as its grandparents' leave policy, which gives staff one week of paid leave when a grandchild is born. As a result, Saga has avoided an exodus of older skilled workers.

## Career resilience

Career development is another form of benefit that needs a joint commitment to make it work. The nature of careers is changing. In the past people were expected to be loyal to one company; today people are likely to pursue their professional objectives and personal goals through multiple companies. Of course, organizations must accept that many people will move on – but they need to mitigate the risk of loss of key talent. Consequently, some turnover of staff, including those with business-critical skills, should be expected.

Even pre-pandemic with a tightening labour market, to fill skills gaps in the workforce employers were already looking internally and developing their employees and workers. Companies were also investing in career development, given impetus by the surge of the millennial generation and Gen Z into the market with potentially different needs and demands from older workers. The form such support took was typically ad-hoc in-person onsite career discussions. As we discussed previously, employee engagement and retention are intimately linked to people having the opportunity to develop and grow at an organization. If people cannot make progress, they are likely to go elsewhere.

While organizations want employees to be willing to adapt, embrace change and take greater ownership of managing their careers, few appear to have recognized the link between equipping people to manage their careers and organizational agility. Flexible career paths are simple and easy to provide when the business understands the business benefits of offering these options. Immediately post-pandemic the phenomenon of the Great Resignation struck, with many people leaving their organizations. For leaders it was a challenge to recruit in the external workforce and now they were losing their internal workforce as well.

Benefits are a key part of reward strategy. Offering career opportunities is a major benefit. In the Generics case study just presented, to attract and retain stellar staff, Jon Sparkes carried out analysis of the career development paths of successful people and an assessment of the psychometric profile of proven innovators. He used this when recruiting staff in the UK and internationally, making no compromise on calibre. This allowed him to distinguish between generalists with wide breadth of skill, specialists with depth of skill in one area and polymaths who had deep skills in several areas – this last group being recognized as driving innovation, so opportunities were tailored to them. This enabled the firm to successfully recruit the right calibre and mix of people.

## Mobilizing talent

Equipping employees to manage their careers by providing career support should be an explicit part of organizational strategy. Yet traditionally companies are reluctant to articulate a longer-term view of careers, and career support has declined in real terms.

One company recently found that many young working parents were leaving, joining a competitor offering a more family-friendly working and career environment. Ironically, if you train people and set them up with contracts, making them more employable and giving them the flexibility to move, they tend to stay. So, many leaders now recognize that it is in the best interest of the business to invest in their people if they want to retain them. This has brought a real focus on understanding what kind of development employees want or need, how that aligns with what the organization needs and where firms should they be investing in development for their employees.

Setting up an internal mobility programme requires deliberate effort to identify the pathways to mobility so that you can communicate where the opportunities are. Career growth is not always about moving upwards – it can also entail a sideways move, such as temporary job swaps or involving employees in part-time projects, that can help people to gain valuable new skills, experiences and insights. Job requirements can be defined in ways that enable people to undertake a realistic self-assessment and competencies can help to ensure a good match between opportunity and the potential candidate. This way, a data bank of people requiring specific forms of development can be matched against available options that may include job swaps and secondments. Corporate structures that block internal mobility and talent hoarding managers must be unblocked – team members must feel free to consider internal moves without the risk of penalty. The increased mobility of staff can also be assisted by greater awareness of the roles of different business groups, often gained from briefings hosted by different business groups at their place of work. Where this is combined with an open job posting scheme, 'surprising' moves can prove very successful for all concerned.

Mobilizing internal talent is beneficial. Research from Glassdoor suggests that articulating a prosperous career path and maintaining a positive culture are the most important ways to ensure worker satisfaction. As the road to internal promotion is rarely clear, companies must be more creative when thinking about the nature of the road and the destination. Exploring if there is potential for current low to mid-level employees to move up into higher-level positions will only benefit how you look in the eyes of your employees. Career-pathing and internal-mobility software can help to systematize the process, increase the visibility of opportunities and make it easier to identify and grow internal talent.

Some organizations at least are starting to feel the need to articulate a clearer 'career deal' and better information about career paths. NHS Property Services for instance aims to see 70 per cent of promotions filled internally. Formal training is seen as part of the answer and mandatory training compliance has gone up and the leadership team has completed a leadership development programme.

Career pathing is about finding the sweet spot between worker aspirations and capabilities and the goals of the firm. The British Council offers sessions for staff on 'my career and aspirations conversations' and one for managers on how to lead these in an open, honest and balanced way: setting it up, preparation, rapport, listening, questioning, coaching, action planning, etc. To be most effective, career pathing should be integrated into a company's overall talent management strategy. By aligning talent management processes and providing linkage between job roles, desired competencies, and key experiences, career paths can lead to a well-rounded, highly trained workforce that is agile and equipped to deal with future challenges.

Cao and Thomas outline the following:

1  Create a career road map.
2  Build position profiles.

**3** Identify core competencies and expected behaviours.

**4** Incorporate training and development.

**5** Establish accountability.

**6** Measure internal hiring success.[25]

One UK local authority had difficulties recruiting and retaining junior staff working in customer call centres. Many employees wanted to stay working locally but the work offered no chance for progression. HR and OD, working with an external consultant, led a process to identify with stakeholders a number of career paths to other parts of the local authority. Career centre staff were involved in the process and their needs and motivations were fully taken into account. Supervisors were trained to hold career conversations with staff, many of whom have subsequently made lateral moves and gained promotions in other parts of the council. The call centre is now seen as a desirable place to work and acts as a talent pool for the whole organization.

---

CASE STUDY
*Career self-management in GE*

In a vast organization, such as GE, that is aiming to become agile, enabling career mobility is one way a boundaryless organization functions for its employees. GE has a rich bench-strength of talent. Given the more horizontal way GE operates, how do people now develop their careers? Lateral rather than vertical career progression will become the norm for many employees. The new, more personalized approach to people management includes opportunities such as stretch or 'bubble' assignments, flexible working and additional benefits.

People are also encouraged to move roles and, in a company as large as GE, which is made up of a number of companies, they can work in different industries while remaining a GE employee. Anyone working in any division of GE can learn about opportunities available in the other business units and how to move into those units, if so desired. Career-minded individuals are usually willing to be self-directed with regard to career development but often struggle to find out about job opportunities across the various GE businesses. In the past, even recognizing what a new job might entail could be difficult. Similarly, managers seeking to fill roles experienced difficulties finding people internally with the right skills. For instance, when the GE Digital organization was created, there was a need for programmers and program architects. These existed across the company but were hard to identify among the 18,000 job titles!

Accordingly, in true Agile manner, trial work is underway to simplify job titles. In another trial, technology will be used to put people more in control of their own development and learning. A set of algorithms will connect data and analytics in a way that will allow people to access job and learning opportunities. The same technology will also help managers to find the talent they need within the company more easily.

---

## Career management in hybrid contexts is in transition

In the strange new hybrid world the spontaneous informal career network-ing 'water cooler' opportunities are missing for remote workers. Organizations are grappling with questions such as: how do we make sure that people don't get sidetracked and that career growth doesn't get stunted? How can employees continue their personal and professional development? What's missing from the remote work experience and how might this impact career development? How can we have a fair assessment of skills and move people through career development when 'out of sight is out of mind'?

People are aware that, whether in person or virtually, they must acquire a new skill set to get to that next level and what many hybrid workers want is real-time access to learning and development resources. Arla Foods launched a Learning Week in 2017 that has been extended with a recurring Wednesday @ One project. This features a varied learning experience with team members from different departments and external speakers, which helps workers to leverage each other's knowledge and skills on a range of topics. The initiative also gives staff permission to prioritize their learning with dedicated time to build on their industry knowledge.

People also want their managers to be able to support them. Managers must learn to give people feedback, coach and guide them in remote settings and ensure skill development so that people can be ready for that next move. What is needed is transparency and visibility about people's readiness for that next move. This means deliberately setting up formal and informal meetings to ensure people feel valued and motivated and have opportunities to develop. The widespread adoption by companies of technology-based learning resources has mostly moved skill development from in-classroom learning to online, and there has also been a rise in experiential learning with a shift to more rotational work, gig work projects, and other types of experiential learning but adjusted to a hybrid workplace.

### What steps should employees take to be noticed and demonstrate their capabilities in a hybrid world?

But career resilience is not simply about relying on line manager guidance. To take advantage of potential opportunities, a continuous learning mindset is critical in today's world because things are changing so rapidly people should continue to reskill and upskill ready for those next opportunities. People need to become aware of their own skills, capabilities, strengths and interests and show that they are ready by getting coaching and feedback and demonstrating enhanced capabilities.

However, even if you are upskilling yourself, if people above you are unaware of it you will miss out, so it is important to share your growing skills profile clearly (as for LinkedIn) with your manager and also in any way you can within the organization. That way, employers can see not only what a person's next role might be but if there are also other future roles for which they may be a good fit. Before hybrid working, people who sang their own praises were viewed negatively, but now individuals must break through on their own. So while the manager is there to support and guide them and to provide information about what might be available and perhaps remove barriers to that next step, in a hybrid world the manager has less visibility of how people are performing their job – both the what and the how they are going about it – so they have to rely on information from peers, customers/clients and even from the work itself to round out that picture.

It is really the individual's responsibility to advance their own career. This requires initiative on the part of the employee to make sure that they are getting feedback and visibility from many sources so the organization can see how they are doing their job and what they are accomplishing. If people want to learn more about something that is very different from what they do today they need to initiate deliberate dialogue and ask for feedback from their managers – 'How am I doing? Do you have any suggestions?' – and express their point of view – 'I'd like you to know...' (not in an abrasive way) 'that I want to move ahead', or 'I'd like to do this, I'm thinking about this what do you think? Here's something I feel comfortable that I could do / something that I'm curious about. I feel like I have related skills that could benefit the organization but I'm not sure I want to leave my current role yet.

If there's an opportunity for me to spend part of the time over in that area to try out a project / work with a larger team. Gigs, rotations or project work could work well.' Dialogue back and forth is very necessary in a hybrid world. People should connect with self-help networks but it is important for employers to target career advice to encourage, advise and support those from different and diverse backgrounds.

In a hybrid world, some additional skill sets have become prominent. Communication, interpersonal skills and collaboration skills may have been taken for granted before. When meeting in person people tend to rely on verbal communication skills; in a more hybrid or remote environment people are writing more emails, more chats, more text and more documents. Some people have stronger verbal than written skills. Stereotypically extroverts may be very comfortable engaging verbally in dialogue and networking, talking to their bosses, interacting with people on camera on Zoom or Teams. Introverts are typically more comfortable in a written world where they can take time to compose their thoughts before committing them to writing. The skill sets of both stereotypes are needed in a hybrid world where non-verbal cues may be lacking.

Career development in a hybrid world requires you to work with your manager or leader and also to take some responsibility to work on these skills that are not necessarily in your sweet spot in order to create opportunities for yourself. Organizational leaders should look to see how they can support employees and managers in continuing to make this transition.

## Conclusion

As HR professionals adapt their own performance management system (PMS) and reward strategies to today's context and to their organization's needs, it is right to focus effort on improving the things that matter in the short term. After all, it is tough out there, with increasing economic pressures on employers and employees in many cases. However, it is important to avoid the temptation of simply going for the quick win by tightening up the PMS to get 'more for less' out of the workforce, squeezing the lemon until the pips squeak. As the cases in this chapter demonstrate, really successful performance management is about achieving a better balance of employer and employee needs – and is about building trust, performance and capacity to drive the organization forward in the years to come.

We have considered:

- Performance management practices and reward strategies can *enable or inhibit high performance.*

- *Workforce strategies should flow from the business strategy* – and take employee needs and context into account too.

- Reward, recognition and benefits should be *integrated* with other HR policies so that the 'right' employee behaviours are encouraged, developed and rewarded.

- Career development is a *joint enterprise.*

- Strategies *influence not only individual behaviour but also company culture* – so it is important to recognize the effects of what you propose.

HR can help to improve line manager skills by training managers in high-performance methods and coaching. HR can help people to manage their own development by providing tools for self-assessment and career tracks. Training and development should be complemented by organizational structures, policies and cultures that support flexible working, adaptable skill application and better leadership and ownership of tasks at all levels.

Ensuring mutual benefits (as well as risks) for both organizations and employees is potentially the most sustainable and honest basis for an employment relationship better suited to the demands of today's volatile global economy and more fluid work arrangements. Organizations that do this should reap the rewards of a grown-up relationship with their staff, who will want to invest their discretionary effort in helping their organizations succeed.

---

CHECKLIST

- How is performance managed in your organization?

- How empowered are people?

- Are managers trained to delegate, coach and provide feedback?

- Do managers keep fingers on the pulse, create a shared sense of direction, clearly communicate expectations?

- How constructively is conflict dealt with?

- How clear are standards? And are employees involved in raising the bar?

- There may be policies for flexible working – if not, why not – what is the reality? Is it career limiting to be a working parent or to work on anything but a full-time contract?

- Are roles appropriately designed to provide stretch, yet be doable?

- Are people provided with the skills, time and resources to do the job for which they are responsible? Is there any 'slack' in the system?

- How much do systems help or hinder people in doing their jobs? How simple can procedures become while maintaining safeguards?

- How clear is everyone's line of sight to the customer?

- How well do managers recognize and reward individuals and teams?

- How does the typical career path of today differ from the career path of the future, given the organization's strategic direction?

- Flexible career options: does the organization have lateral or cross-functional moves available, or could employees even move into a new role with less responsibility to learn a new area but not risk future promotion opportunities within the organization?

# Notes

1 TUC. British workers putting in longest hours in the EU, TUC analysis finds, 17 April 2019, www.tuc.org.uk/news/british-workers-putting-longest-hours-eu-tuc-analysis-finds (archived at https://perma.cc/PY8M-VLRW).

2 Applebaum, E, Bailey, T and Berg, P (2000) *Manufacturing Advantage: Why high-performance work systems pay off*, Cornell University Press, New York.

3 Combs, J, Liu, Y and Hall, A (2006) How much do high-performance work practices matter? A meta-analysis of their effects on organizational-performance, *Personnel Psychology*, 59 (3), pp 501–28.

4 CIPD (2014) HR: Getting smart about agile working, www.cipd.co.uk/hr-resources/research/hr-smart-agile-working.aspx (archived at https://perma.cc/JDC3-HGN8).

5 Cheese, P (2022) Living in interesting times, *People Management*, Oct/Nov 2022.

6 Morgan, J (2014) *The Future of Work: Attract new talent, build better leaders, and create a competitive organization*, Wiley, Chichester.

7 CIPD, ibid.

8 Ernst & Young (2014) The manager's guide to leading teams under flexible work arrangements, www.cio.co.uk/whitepapers/leadership/the-managers-guide-to-leading-teams/ (archived at https://perma.cc/L4XR-DJ6P).

9 CIPD, ibid.

10 Wilmore, J (2000) Managing virtual teams, *Training Journal*, February, pp 18–19.

**11**  Cascio, W (2002) Strategies for responsible restructuring, Academy of Management Perspectives, 1 August, **16** (8), pp 80–91.

**12**  Lipnack, J and Stamps, J (2000) *Virtual Teams: People working across boundaries with technology*, John Wiley and Sons, Chichester.

**13**  Smith, A and Sinclair, A (2003) *The Role of the Virtual Manager*, Roffey Park, Horsham.

**14**  CIPD. Planning for hybrid working, 4 August 2022, www.cipd.co.uk/knowledge/fundamentals/relations/flexible-working/planning-hybrid-working (archived at https://perma.cc/ZTP9-SFYW).

**15**  McKinsey (2022) *The American Opportunity Survey*, June, McKinsey Global Institute.

**16**  Christian, A. The non-linear workdays changing the shape of productivity, *BBC The Toolbox*, 4 October 2022.

**17**  Debbie Bayntun-Lees in Everett, C. Managing the new remote workforce, Raconteur.net, 30 September 2022.

**18**  Deloitte. Global human capital trends 2015, www2.deloitte.com/insights/us/en/focus/human-capital-trends/2015.html (archived at https://perma.cc/5D7Y-M5QZ).

**19**  Cappelli, P and Tavis, A (2016) The performance management revolution, *Harvard Business Review*, October, hbr.org/2016/10/the-performance-management-revolution (archived at https://perma.cc/S69S-6FWV).

**20**  Barry, L, Garr, S and Liakopoulos, A. Performance management is broken: Replace 'rank and yank' with coaching and development, *Deloitte Insights*, 4 March 2014, www2.deloitte.com/insights/us/en/focus/human-capital-trends/2014/hc-trends-2014-performance-management.html (archived at https://perma.cc/6WXY-NFPC).

**21**  Nisen, M (2015) Why GE had to kill its annual performance reviews after more than three decades, *Quartz*, qz.com/428813/ge-performance-review-strategy-shift/ (archived at https://perma.cc/997J-CLTS).

**22**  Ibid.

**23**  Cascio, W (2002) Strategies for responsible restructuring, *Academy of Management Perspectives*, **16** (8), pp 80–91.

**24**  Orton-Jones, C. Growth, innovation and business transformation, *Raconteur*, 14 May 2014, p 3.

**25**  Cao, J and Thomas, D (2013) When developing a career path, what are the key elements to include?, Cornell University, ILR School, digitalcommons.ilr.cornell.edu/student/43/ (archived at https://perma.cc/5WTH-NTQR).

# 10

# Building a change-able culture

As we have discussed throughout this book, nothing is more constant or pervasive than change. So these days the leader's job is less about designing a change programme and more about building a change-able culture – one that allows anyone to initiate change, recruit co-workers, suggest solutions and launch experiments. We have considered how company-wide conversations can amplify weak signals and support the complex problem solving required to address core management challenges.

In Chapter 2 we looked at some features of a 'change-able' culture required for agility. This is akin to the 'learning organization' concept defined by Senge and others, since experimentation, innovation and learning are characteristic of a change-able culture too.[1] We also have previously considered the importance of the 'receptive context' in which a particular group or organization 'naturally' takes on change and new ideas. Organizations with a high receptive context are those with the capacity to continually change and adapt throughout the organization; they can quickly adopt innovative concepts in order to meet the challenges they experience. Change is built into the core processes of the organization. In a dynamically stable, change-able culture, people are ready and willing to embrace change as the norm; to innovate, learn and produce high performance even while things are changing around them.

In this chapter we consider if, and how, a change-able culture can be built. We look at:

- Can culture be 'changed'?
- Taking stock of culture
- Defining what 'good' looks like
- Building emotional energy for change

- Building a social movement
- Aligning management and leadership
- Delivering the brand reality of diversity and inclusion.

## Can culture be 'changed'?

There is much debate about whether organizations *have* a culture, or *are* cultures. I would argue that organizations both *have* and *are* cultures, often made up of many subcultures – such as functional, gender or age-based. Cultural shifts can and do emerge over time as part of the 'natural' process of adaption, especially within subgroups and networks. Writers from the Human Dynamics Group, who view change through the lens of complex adaptive systems, consider that individuals and organizations identify and shape emerging patterns in their relationships, behaviours and interactions. These practices are transmitted by people working within the culture to others who become acculturated to see things the same way.

Of course, cultural shifts can be prompted by many things – the arrival of a new CEO, external demands and dramatic events such as the failure of a business model or the pandemic. Organizations as complex adaptive systems are embedded within other systems within the broader external context and co-evolve with them, which requires constant adaptation, experimenting and pruning.

There are many debates about whether or not it is possible to deliberately change organizational culture and I have written extensively elsewhere on this subject.[2] When thinking about changing culture it is tempting to think about changing behaviour, yet behaviour is always partly conditioned by the values, processes, structures, systems and routines that surround it. According to chaos theory, culture is reducible to two simple concepts: patterns and rules. Simple rules are spoken or unspoken guides for behaviours across a complex adaptive system.

And while there is a fixed and definable set of rules for pattern formulation, any small change in initial conditions can result in huge changes in resulting behaviour. Even tinkering with just one aspect of culture can be enough to send a ripple effect through other parts of the system. Under certain conditions, ordered, regular patterns of behaviours or events can be seen to arise out of seemingly random, erratic and turbulent processes. Some complex systems exhibit features that are referred to as 'self-organization' or 'emergence'.

I would argue that culture change can be effected deliberately, to some extent at least, but traditional change management is unlikely to be effective in producing lasting shifts in 'hearts and minds', behaviour, attitude, norms, working practices and other aspects of culture. Any cultural shift, no matter how well intended, will not take root unless it is accepted by the people who operate it. Chaos and complexity theories suggest that people operating within the system are free agents who influence each other. In practice, any change among and between individuals and their patterns of connections and interpretations changes the culture. Power dynamics can change and new villains, heroes and heroines can become the focus of stories around the grapevine teaching people what is new, and what success and failure look like. In that sense culture change cannot be imposed from above.

The most powerful processes of change occur at the individual and group level, an area that traditional bureaucratic structures often struggle with. Quade and Holladay talk of 'dynamical change' that is unpredictable, characterized by 'multiple forces acting in unpredictable ways, generating surprising outcomes'.[3] For this type of change the concern is to engage people in a new way and build adaptive capacity within the system. Dynamical leaders can see and influence patterns in their systems, understand the dynamics at play, utilize differences for maximum capacity building and move towards sustainable outcomes. They actively work with adaptive alignment to give sufficient structure and stability and build generative interconnections throughout the system – what Kelly calls 'swarmware' – so that local leaders can freely exchange knowledge and resources to make things happen.[4]

For instance, one organization uses a 'wiki' social networking site to encourage people to contribute ideas while others use workshops, focus groups, interviews and large group events aimed at engaging people in strengthening organizational competitiveness. Increasingly, therefore, there are debates about whether the notion of 'managing' culture change should be replaced by providing a 'platform' for change.

## The Star Model™

Arguably, too, 'culture' can be shifted to some extent by altering organizational artefacts such as policies, routines and structures, what Kelly calls 'clockware'. The Galbraith Star Model™ suggests some key 'levers' that managers can control that can affect employee behaviour. Indeed, according to the Star Model™, culture and behaviours are the result of 'design policies' in five specific categories.[5] The first is strategy, which determines direction. The second is structure, which determines the location of decision-making power. Third, management and work processes have to do with the flow of information and resources. Fourth, rewards provide motivation and incentives for desired behaviour. The fifth category of the model is made up of policies relating to people (human resource policies), which influence employees' mindsets and skills. The selection and development of the 'right' people – in alignment with the other policies – allows the organization to operate at maximum efficiency. The assumption is that by aligning all parts of the system, managers can influence the organization's performance as well as its culture.

However, efforts to innovate within the formal system (involving hierarchies) can be aided or undermined by interactions within the 'swarm-ware' – informal or 'shadow system' involving friends and colleagues.[6] The shadow system includes many 'opinion formers' at all levels who are usually well networked and are often more influential than top management. In the corporate ecosystem, power is typically assumed to reside largely with the board and executive team and cascade down – the converse of what is needed if a highly mobile and distributed work style is required. Moreover, organizations are usually rife with micropolitics and interests vested in maintaining the status quo. Successfully shifting culture is largely a factor of how willing people are to change their own behaviours and how they influence others.

Let's assume that you are seeking to create a culture more conducive to innovation. Any attempt to shift cultural practice and build new, more useful habits and routines needs to take account of, and embrace, the social nature of innovation and change. What Facebook, Google, Netflix, Spotify and Uber all have in common is a particular way of working and a distinctive people culture. They work in small teams that are united in a common purpose, follow an Agile 'manifesto', interact closely with customers, and are constantly able to reshape what they are working on. After all, a brilliant new product is not usually the property of a single individual or 'skunkwork' group who may have generated the original idea; further creative development and enhancement of the idea also occurs during local implementation and as the idea spreads within the organization.[7] As the proliferation of ideas and learning via social media illustrates, this capacity for creative thought via connections is an inherent ability that we all possess.[8]

The culture shifts through the conversations people have, the stories they tell and the new routines that emerge. Enabling the right conversations in the right forums also builds the right organization habits and rituals that underpin the organization culture. The way failures are handled, learnings applied, and leaders role-modelling certain behaviours are all critical symbols and rituals in the broader development of agility. Employees are quick to spot inconsistencies and say-do gaps, for example when leaders continue to demand perfection (in meetings and documents) and yet seemingly want to encourage experimentation and learning. Changing culture is likely to require creating favourable conditions for new behaviour and practices to emerge. It is important to lead from the edge, working with 'clockware' and 'swarmware' in tandem. It is about paying attention to, and seeking to influence, both formal and informal systems, going for multiple actions at the fringes and letting direction arise. Thus new sources of value are created through generative relations.

## Taking stock

Before you embark on any attempt at cultural transformation it is important to understand something of how networks and influence operate in practice and to put as much effort into understanding your employees as you do into understanding your customers. It is about listening to the shadow system, uncovering and working with paradox and tension. Treat interviews, social media, surveys and suggestion boxes as valuable sources of information. Combine the input you receive with customer satisfaction scores, business metrics and employee turnover rates to isolate the issues that matter most to your employees and your business. It can be helpful to use one of the many frameworks for understanding cultural elements to enable conversations and the sharing of perceptions about how things are.

### The cultural web

Among the best-known frameworks for taking stock of an organization's culture is the *cultural web* of Johnson and Scholes.[9] This identifies six interrelated elements that make up what Johnson and Scholes call the 'paradigm' – the pattern or model – of the work environment. The six elements are:

- *Stories* – the past events and people talked about inside and outside the company. Who and what the company chooses to immortalize says a great deal about what it values, and perceives as the 'right' behaviour.

- *Rituals and routines* – the daily behaviour and practices of people that signal acceptable behaviour. This determines what is expected to happen in given situations, and what is valued by management.
- *Symbols* – the visual representations of the company including logos, reception areas and the formal or informal dress codes.
- *Organizational structure* – this includes both the structure defined by the organization chart and the unwritten lines of power and influence that indicate whose contributions are most valued.
- *Control systems* – the ways that the organization is controlled such as via financial systems, quality systems and rewards (including the way they are measured and distributed within the organization).
- *Power structures* – the pockets of real power in the company. The key is that these people have the greatest amount of influence on decisions, operations and strategic direction.

By analysing the factors in each, you can begin to see the bigger picture of your culture: what is working, what isn't working and what needs to be changed. Indeed, from an organization design perspective it can be helpful to map these factors against the Star Model™ elements – strategy, work processes, management processes, reward, systems and structure – to explore their interrelationships.

Surveys and focus groups are often used to initiate constructive conversations about the organization's baseline ('as is') culture – its key cultural strengths and weaknesses that may have a high impact on business strategy. Typical questions to explore include:

- What are we doing well and should do more of?
- What do we do poorly and should stop doing?
- What do our customers want?
- What should our employees expect from the organization and vice versa?

Yet as we considered in the previous chapter, in attempting to mobilize people for new ways of working, it is important to recognize that mechanistic approaches to culture change are of limited effectiveness in a complex system. One will not find much energy for change by assuming that 'culture A' (defined by patterns of behaviour, of thinking and deciding) needs to be replaced by 'culture B', or by overlooking the fact that people have strong emotional ties to the existing culture. Deficit or 'push' approaches to shifting culture should be replaced by 'pull' or attractor approaches.

## 'Pull': defining what 'good' looks like

Throughout this book I have highlighted the importance of shared purpose as the 'glue' that holds the organization together. Helping people to see if and how their own purpose aligns with that of their organization is crucial to gaining engagement. It is about encouraging employees to care intensely about executing strategic objectives because they matter.

### Developing shared purpose

Engaging leaders actively lead culture change, working to create shared purpose and a positive sense of the future: something to aim for that people can connect with. A common cause is essential, with an aligned strategy that people – both customers and employees – can sign up to. According to research by Accenture the majority of consumers want to interact with businesses whose values and purpose reflect their own personal beliefs.[10] This conscious consumerism level of identification can translate into a 'purpose premium', where consumers demonstrate increased levels of brand loyalty. Conversely, more than half of consumers who are disappointed by a brand's words or actions on social issues will complain about it.[11]

The nature of the organization's purpose may have a differentiating effect on levels of engagement. Research by myself and Nigel Springett into how people experience meaning at work found that an organizational purpose that focuses intensely on customers is more likely to engage staff than purposes focused on shareholders, profits or a mix of stakeholder needs.[12] In recent times, many employees and customers are calling for companies to embrace purposes that have environmental, social and governance (ESG) aspirations. Professor Colin Mayer, academic lead for the research 'The Future of the Corporation', proposes that profits do not equate to purpose.[13] Instead purpose is about: 'Profitably solving the problems of people and planet, and not profiting from creating problems.'

Purpose and brand values must be well communicated, but the most powerfully engaging visions and values are not developed as a top-down exercise since two-way approaches are more likely to lead to effective engagement. It is essential that there is a clear line of sight to this purpose in people's day jobs if the motivational effect is to be achieved. Deloitte has a 'Chief People and Purpose' officer to ensure this happens. Values that are truly 'lived' and translated into meaningful experiences for customers and employees alike provide parameters for people's actions since aligned values and behaviours create trust. Any gap between these creates distrust and cynicism.

Clarifying the organization's purpose involves asking:

- Why does this organization exist?
- In whose name are all our efforts made?
- How do our origins and original purpose impinge on who we are today?
- What is our 'story'? How important is it to us? When do we tell it?
- What elements of our history and our story have the ability to enrich and inspire us today? What gets in the way of what is needed today?
- What core values do we seek to live, work and be known by?
- What is the great passion for in our organization?

Working with purpose should be an inclusive process. Narrative techniques such as storytelling, in which everyone describes their experience of the organization and what it means to them, can be powerful in surfacing the beliefs and values, key players, symbols, rituals and practices that matter most to people. The big strategic stories are made up of these many smaller stories of personal experience of, for instance, helping the customer. It is about introducing vocabularies that help people to say things in new ways and thus be able to talk about this new way of working. The role of the leader is to listen, be open and connect rather than attempt to control the conversation. As a result, managers are likely to have a better understanding of staff, while staff are likely to feel heard and understood and be prepared to put in the effort required to make the difference.

## A 'critical few' shifts...

Defining a common purpose is one thing; living it, however, is another. Purpose must be made concrete through a set of quality standards: priorities that will guide front-line staff in delivering the desired customer experience.

So it is important to define a critical few patterns of behaviour and thinking that will be essential to the success of the desired change-able/innovation culture. Various studies highlight attitudinal and behavioural elements of a receptive context such as openness to change; collaboration and teamwork; good relationships; involvement; learning by experimentation; employees feeling valued and fairly treated. These are practices that help people to become skilful and effective at, for instance, communication, innovation, adaptive planning and iterative product delivery. Firms such as GE make desired behaviours clear through a well-articulated set of 'Beliefs'.

Success criteria should be defined by the broadest groups possible. Criteria might include visionary elements or tangible behavioural shifts or both, so that people understand what shift is required and why. For instance, one group seeking to develop a more innovative culture might propose that, in five years from now it should be commonplace that:

- Staff at all levels feel encouraged to think creatively.
- We have moved beyond 'change as a project' and have established a pervasive 'habit for change'.
- We can boast of hundreds of locally generated innovations that have led to service and/or product breakthroughs.
- Innovative ideas that delight customers are generated anywhere in the organization; they spread through the entire system at a speed that rivals cannot match.
- Other organizations look at what we do for examples of best practices in the area of innovation and change.[14]

Whichever criteria are selected, it is vital that leaders are 100 per cent on board with leading or supporting the desired direction of travel. Without their sustained commitment, communication and implementation will soon break down.

## A receptive context for agility: mobilising people for change

Understanding what needs to change is one thing: mobilizing people to want to make the changes needed for business success is quite another. Apart from technology there is much less knowledge of agility and its benefits, and there is no expectation that it should be adopted. To that end you do have to work that little bit harder to persuade people to give it a go.

Any attempt to shift cultural practice and build new, more useful habits and routines needs to take account of, and embrace, the 'swarmware' or social nature of innovation and change.[15] That is because organizations, as complex adaptive systems, are essentially collections of individual free agents who act in ways that are not always totally predictable and whose actions are inter-connected such that one agent's actions change the context for other agents. Employees' collective values and opinions guide behaviour and will to a large extent determine how 'change-able' organizations can become.

One company seeking to become more agile ran listening sessions, involving people across the organization. The objective of these sessions was to understand both the healthy and the less-healthy elements of the culture. From that it could begin to determine a set of company values that were widely supported and could drive behaviours that would improve the culture. An inclusive approach to developing the values meant they were more likely to be supported and embraced by the organization. The company trained up a number of voluntary culture champions, thereby creating a network of people that could promote the values and culture across the business.

Having run the listening sessions and started developing the values, a company offsite was used to involve the wider organization in identifying specific initiatives that could be run to embed the culture and values. The culture champions ran workshops with groups of people across the organization to brainstorm ideas that they could then take back and develop.

Viewed this way, change is a group and individual process. Through discourse participants construct the happenings of everyday life, along with roles and relationships, norms, expectations and obligations that define membership of the group. Thus change comes about through conversation. Ideas developed within a group context become a cultural resource for the group as well as for individuals.

In hybrid and remote working environments, technology can help with the challenge of engaging people with software services enabling asynchronous online meetings that allow people working in different time zones to join in. People can be engaged before, during and after the event itself. 'Campfires' and 'lunch-rooms' that people can choose to go to allow deeper conversations to happen. For instance, Selina Millstam, who heads up talent management and culture change at the Swedish communications technology company Ericsson, wanted to have a company-wide conversation that would encourage people to share and coordinate their beliefs about what values and behaviours would be crucial to the long-term success of the business. The moderated conversation took place over 72 hours, with more than 95,000 employees across 180 counties invited to participate. The shared time allowed people in different time zones to connect, with each participant encouraged to re-engage with the exchange in an asynchronous way over the three days, thus building a strong sense of community across the global workforce.[16]

So HR teams should re-evaluate communications tools for how well they serve community building – for instance using consistent channels such as Teams Chat – and encourage more frequent, regular check-ins. A question could be posed before the Chat to encourage discussion. Meetings should ideally start with space for people to discuss how are feeling that day, at that moment, so that they can be open about their concerns. Managers need to show a growth mindset and empathy: putting themselves in other people's shoes and humanizing communication at every point.

## Stimulating learning practices

Willingness to learn and share good practice is a characteristic of an agile innovative culture. Technology platforms can make sharing knowledge easy and quick. To build a culture of lifelong learning you need people first to understand the benefits of learning and developing a growth mindset, so it is important to encourage learners to adopt the discipline of sharing knowledge in 'psychologically safe' environments such as a training programme where they can reflect and engage in dialogue on issues that matter to them. Getting people talking about what they have learned is a good way to embed new routines and spread fresh ideas. Then people need time to learn. Agile and lean working practices provide a way of working at a sustainable pace. A healthy system of work will have some 'slack' that provides space for self-learning. In addition, introducing the concept of continuous improvement and adopting an experimental approach helps to challenge the fixed mind-set. At this point you can accelerate learning initiatives.

The strategic response to complexity and uncertainty is to create choices, generate lots of options through experiments or small bets that need to be safe-to-fail, and keep options open to see what works. Dave Snowden offers a helpful set of guidelines for safe-to-fail experimentation:

- Have several of them running in parallel so that you can be gathering information about the system in several different ways simultaneously.

- Snowden argues that experiments should be designed with failure in mind. We often learn more from failure than success anyway, and this is research as well as intervention. We want to create an environment in which success is not privileged over failure in the early stages of dealing with complex issues.

- Design experiments that are finely grained, pragmatic and short term in their experimental phase. Cheap is good too. These experiments should be crisp and clear so that everyone knows what is expected.

- Some of the experiments should be at the edges of the problem rather than at the centre.

- Draw on 'naive capability'. These are people with deep expertise in a related field that might give new insight (like bringing in a script writer to help solve a community engagement issue).

- Think what success and failure might look like. What stories will be told about successes? Which ones about failures? Have plans in place in advance for amplifying successes and dampening failures.[17]

## Building emotional energy for change

Mobilizing people requires more than rational cognition; it also requires significant emotional energy – those strong positive emotions that drive the movement forward.[18] People tend to be highly motivated when they focus first on their strengths and not their problems. Organization development interventions using strengths-based approaches such as appreciative inquiry (AI) can be helpful for individual, group and whole-system engagement (see Figure 10.1).

FIGURE 10.1  Appreciative inquiry (AI)

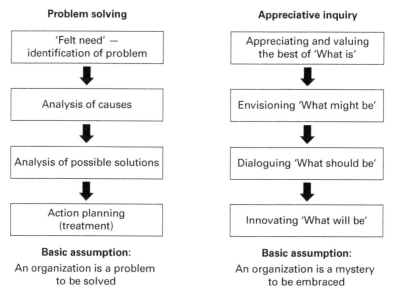

AI tends to generate many ideas and much enthusiasm for change. The ideas are typically processed and reviewed by an influential project group that can suggest a way ahead to senior management, for instance in the form of a new set of values, plans for operationalizing these or at least a route map of the actions required to bring about the shifts towards the desired culture.

CASE STUDY
*Agile HR and culture change within SNC-Lavalin's Atkins business*

The leadership team of SNC-Lavalin's Atkins business in the UK and Europe region recognized the need to shift the culture – likened to a slow-moving, risk-averse supertanker of an organization – to become more agile. HR worked closely with the regional leadership to create a more inclusive business that values good ideas wherever they come from. Helen Gebhard, Recruitment Partner – Service Excellence notes that: 'The leadership team don't believe they have all the answers – with a workforce of 9,000 in Europe, there is huge capability to tap into. This means being quite brave when it comes to developing strategic initiatives and genuinely empowering employees.' Empowerment is made real in a number of ways. People can volunteer and get involved in strategic projects, regardless of their job level. Principles such as 'fail fast' mean that projects that are not going to work are swiftly stood down, freeing up resource to focus on those that will work. Vitally, the fear of failure *is not seen as a reason not to try something new.*

High-level operating principles and 'Our Story'

Central to culture change was creating shared understanding of the shifts underway as the organization was reshaped. High-level operating principles such as 'everyone sells' and 'knowledge shared is power' were rolled out at workshops for all staff to help people understand the behavioural changes required. Leadership played a significant role by sponsoring and role-modelling the desired direction of travel. Culture change requires constantly listening, sending and reinforcing the message. In one communication drive, senior leadership team members were asked to visit a business area unfamiliar to them (known as a Director Engagement Tour) to find out what people were experiencing. This highlighted a gap between what was intended and what was actually happening on the ground and enabled it to be addressed. As Sharron Pamplin, formerly HR Director UK and Europe, comments: 'On the one hand, it's encouraging that people are hearing the messages about what we are trying to achieve; on the other, the problem is how to live it.'

Another key element was the development of 'Our Story' – about the company's history and how it is evolving as a business. Components included the changing business landscape, the risk of becoming irrelevant, what the business challenges were and how to face them. The key message from 'Our Story' is what to do differently to ensure that the Atkins business is still relevant tomorrow, next week and into the future. To develop the storyline, professional storytellers met with the UK and Europe leadership team and in two hours had worked out seven outline chapters of 'Our Story'. The content was then co-created by the top 300 senior managers in a workshop that others joined via Skype. Divisions developed their own chapters of the story, bringing to life the special elements and creating a diversity of views. Creating the first draft of the story involved only 10 per cent of staff. Now 80 per cent have helped to co-create the story.

One year on from the creation of the story, a special Yammer focus within the HR team, #Keepthefeeling, produced many positive stories of change. In July 2017, Atkins was acquired by Canadian firm SNC-Lavalin. This story was also used to tell new colleagues from SNC-Lavalin about the Atkins business.

HR is targeting effort at the middle management population. While these colleagues understand the ambition of the company, they also have the day-to-day business to run, so change can seem like an interference. Some may lack the skills and behaviours to lead in the way now required. Therefore, a line manager app is being developed to educate managers about the shift, defining the roles of the line manager and project manager with respect to people management responsibility. There are eight areas of focus on the app, together with videos, 'how to' guides, links and TED talks. The Line Manager Essentials training programme is also being updated.

## Decision making

When organizations flatten their structures, the cultural and mindset shifts required for people to be effective are significant. Decision-making authority in particular is often contested and, if left unresolved, can become a real blocker of speed and agility. As discussed in Chapter 5, the aim of the organizational redesign within SNC-Lavalin's Atkins business in the UK and Europe region under the leadership of Nick Roberts was to break down silos and increase collaboration across the organization. One of the perverse consequences of removing P&Ls from a large group of directors was that most decisions were now being pushed up to the small group of MDs, who were the only people left with P&L responsibilities. Directors were feeling disempowered while MDs were sinking under the weight of decisions to be taken. The problem was recognized, and dialogue began, which unlocked what was becoming a big issue. Similarly, in one of HR's own team calls, the topic of decision making within HR – who to go to for which decisions and who comes to see you – was discussed. The decision-making connections – between HR operations, HR business partners, Reward, L&D, Recruitment and Talent – were mapped out visually. This highlighted that Sharron Pamplin, the HR Director, was at the heart of all these connections and may inadvertently have been blocking decisions due to the many demands on her time. Once aware of this, Sharron pushed back decisions to the team, asking, 'do I really need to be involved?'

## Building a social movement

Real culture change occurs through conversation. Communication is integral to building community and breaking down silos. Essentially, shifting culture is about building a social movement committed to doing something better. Therefore it may sometimes be necessary to go slow in order to go fast. It is usually when people are exposed to new thinking, participate in the conversation and have time to take on board new ideas that they are willing to embrace new ways of working and adopt new behaviours.

So, engaging leaders deliberately adopt a collaborative decision-making style and set key principles and parameters that empower others: 'Managers/ leaders must leverage the power of shared values and aspirations while loosening the straight-jacket of rules and strictures.'[19] They strive to role-model the values; they use and act on 360-degree and other feedback to show commitment. They grow tomorrow's leaders and nurture leadership at every level, using language that is less about 'I' and more about 'we'. They build people's confidence to use their initiative to deliver what is required without the need for micro-management.

Leaders build trust by being transparent in their dealings, asking for help and encouraging involvement. So it is important to widen the circle of involvement, connect people to each other, create communities for action and promote fairness. One of the most important metaphors in culture change is that of a 'learning space', used to convey the notion of a community coming together to concentrate, co-create and learn together. Learning spaces not only provide the opportunity for people – in particular the frontline people – to emotionally engage with the intended change, they can also add value to the thinking and the experiences made along the way.

Learning spaces bring together groups of people whose power may be more informal and is often related to their expertise, to the breadth of their network or their personal qualities. These are the opinion formers within the shadow system who are enthusiastic about the change, who have ideas about how to make it work within some specific organizational segment, and who have the capacity to influence others. Meyerson refers to such people as 'tempered radicals'.[20] The leader's task is to identify and engage these potential catalysts for culture change. Leaders must demonstrate empathy and maintain or enhance the self-esteem of the people they are interacting with. They must listen to employees and ensure there are effective formal mechanisms for employees to express their concerns, either at regular open meetings, through anonymous channels such as internal surveys, or via an ombudsman.

Whatever modes and channels of communication are used, consistency and transparency are key to their effective use. After all, you cannot sit in an ivory tower if you wish to connect. When one CEO first sent out a monthly note to staff asking for their input and then responded to emails, staff were shocked that he had actually bothered to read them. As he persevered with this new discipline, staff came to enjoy the regular and personal interaction with the CEO and knew that he had listened to them. Many CEOs now regularly blog and respond to employee commentary and feedback. This opens up a 'skip level' space for dialogue that allows issues to be aired. It also allows provocateurs and mavericks who might otherwise be suppressed to air different perspectives. Old rules and controls can be challenged or relaxed. And during the pandemic many executives managed to connect with the workforce via platforms and showed their concern and their 'human face', which employees appreciated.

## Build cohesiveness

Once a community of people who are 'up' for change has come together they can create some new 'traditions' that build cohesiveness. For instance, Covey and Crawley suggest:

- Do some 'city planning' – define borders and boundaries. Determine who you are and who you are not. Have welcome signs, reception areas, a distinctive logo, recreation and meeting rooms, and a master plan for five years.

- Focus on what you share in common. Share knowledge and information; unite people by focusing them on common causes and concerns.

- Celebrate success. Be positive, focus on the strengths of individuals to make their weaknesses irrelevant.

- Take pride in new products and services. Build traditions by having ceremonies and annual events.

- Have fun at work. Play and socialize together.

- Build meaning into work. Be passionate about some shared vision or mission. Tie every new venture to the mission and seek alignment of personal interests behind the vision.

- Take care of your own. When members of the community feel cared for they will be more willing to care for others. Inspire people to give back to the community.[21]

## Build in peer support

Of course, there is a limit to how many people any single leader can have a one-on-one conversation with, but it is vitally important to keep track of the pulse of the organization to find out if messages are getting through to the front line. One local government body in the north of England has established a change advocates programme. These are volunteers who represent every part of the organization at the front line and at middle manager levels. After some training their role is to help mediate change, and to work closely with the people affected, encouraging employee engagement. The change advocates meet in monthly network sessions where they can learn more about change processes, share problem areas and exchange ideas. They have also established action learning sets in which trust and other sensitive issues can be safely discussed. As a result, there are multiple opportunities for both formal and informal employee voice.

The culture shifts through the conversations people have, the stories they tell and the new routines that emerge. Once the constructive conversations are concluded, the ideas and insights are documented so that the input can be reviewed, prioritized and acted upon at the functional and leadership levels. But conversation alone will not maintain a social movement for change and innovation for long. People are likely to be motivated to join, take part or stay according to what they perceive as feasible and desirable. This calculation is likely to be based upon what they see is available by way of tangible (money, knowledge, time) and intangible (support, help, endorsement) resources. While the vision is what inspires people for change, it is resources that actually get them moving.

---

CASE STUDY
*Culture change in GE*

I am grateful to Janice Semper, Leader, GE Culture and Manager of Executive Development in GE Corporate for the following case study. She and her small Culture Team sit within GE's HR function where Janice also leads on the company-wide Talent Management Strategy.

Towards greater agility

In today's fast-changing world, where levels of uncertainty are rising thanks to political and economic volatility and technological advance, the nature of work is changing, and everything needs to be done faster. Organizations therefore need to be more agile, adaptive and customer-driven. GE is no exception.

With 300,000 employees, and having long been a global leader in its various industries, GE is reinventing itself; becoming a digital industry organization. GE's smart machines are designed to help solve complex problems for customers using integrated software and data analytics. This shift in strategic orientation means that new ways of working and new skill sets are needed. For instance, GE employees need to understand the company's customers in a deeper way than ever before in order to provide the right bespoke solutions.

For such a huge, complex organization as GE, the cultural challenge of agility appears immense. To use an old analogy, a small yacht can turn more quickly than a supertanker. Given the company's size and scale, it can be difficult for people to focus on the things that matter most when things are changing fast. Also, given that the complex problems the company deals with can take time to solve, it is easy to get bogged down in detail that slows things down. A more nimble, entrepreneurial approach was needed that 'requires us to work in a different way', as Janice Semper points out.

Implementing culture change

GE has a strong tradition of linking HR provision to business strategy. Over the past few years, there has been a strategic focus on simplifying the work environment that encompasses lean management, speed and competitiveness, commercial intensity and digital capability. Implementing lean management involves removing layers, increasing spans of control, and reducing the number of checks and approvals needed to get things done. Wherever there is complexity and duplication, shared services are being created. The company is also making work easier by implementing new digital technologies that make employees more productive wherever possible.

Simplification represents a cultural as well as a structural transformation. GE's cultural focus on simplification is helping the company to operate faster, compete more vigorously, reduce costs and improve quality.[22] Janice Semper's challenge is to continue to 'rewire the ecosystem' to streamline work, reduce administrative burdens and simplify complex processes so that people know what is needed and are empowered to provide the right client solutions in an agile way.

To help translate company strategy into behaviours and practices that support the strategy, GE is in the process of implementing three Cultural Pillars:

**1  FastWorks**
FastWorks is being implemented across GE's businesses and is helping teams move faster. Based on the lean start-up methodology, FastWorks provides a set of tools and

principles/frameworks that help people to work in an agile way. This new way of working involves an intensified focus on – and understanding of – customer needs. It is bringing GE closer to customers, so that a high level of customer input and involvement across the product life cycle is maintained. Key phases of the approach are Discovery – knowing what is important to the customer – and Experimentation – to create solutions in an agile manner that add value or create value.

2  **GE Beliefs**

Through a crowdsourcing process, GE has articulated a set of Beliefs that reflect the nature of the changes taking place within this huge company. These act as a central reference point and hub for new behaviours and mindsets. Essentially, the GE Beliefs help leaders and employees to operationalize the strategy since they bring simplification to life. These are expressed in five clear statements focused on reducing complexity and delivering fast, better solutions to customers:

- o   Customers determine our success.

- o   Stay lean to go fast.

- o   Learn and adapt to win.

- o   Empower and inspire each other.

- o   Deliver results in an uncertain world.

The GE Beliefs are helping to create a new culture within GE. They act as the North Star, guiding people's behaviour. They play a large role in leadership development and are also used to change how GE recruits, manages and leads, and how its people are evaluated and developed.

3  **Performance Development (PD)**

As described in Chapter 9, the performance management approach for which GE has long been well known has been redesigned to support FastWorks and help people to live the GE Beliefs. The emphasis is on agility, continuous discussions and customer outcomes. Today, rather than targeting goals, managers emphasize priorities, helping employees continuously adapt and channel their efforts to the most important customer needs.

These Cultural Pillars act as anchor points while other aspects of the company's ecosystem – all the things that influence culture – are gradually rewired for agility. For instance, one key work-stream is looking at how to reimagine the reward system.

## Stimulating emergent change

Janice Semper sees the Culture Team's role as being to stimulate emergent change through influencing, rather than imposing change. Janice works closely with other key change agents. For instance, Janice works in a strong partnership with Viv Goldstein who heads up the Business Innovation Team. Together Janice and Viv were co-founders of FastWorks, the business innovation process incorporating lean methodologies that forms the first of GE's three Cultural Pillars. This dynamic partnership brings valuable complementary skills and influence to bear in providing the infrastructure for change to emerge. Thus culture, people management and business innovation are seen to be mutually supportive, interdependent and valuable.

Since this is new territory, a large part of the job is to experiment, in line with company strategy and FastWorks practice. So, the Culture Team is learning how to iterate, 'trying to connect the dots as we literally rewire the ecosystem, learning as we go'. However, Janice acknowledges that for her and the Culture Team, bringing about change in such a huge organization can be very challenging and at times 'flipping so many things on their heads can be overwhelming'. Their job is to stay true to the direction of travel as they continue to align the company systemically.

Janice highlights the importance of senior leaders setting the tone but argues that emergent change requires ongoing, open and transparent dialogue at local level. The conventional corporate top-down cascade of information can be too slow to stimulate the changes needed. People need to hear the messaging from their immediate leaders and peers, so a range of 'Practical Tips' on how to communicate simply and effectively is available for people leaders, based on feedback and suggestions from employees. The role of the corporate team behind the scenes is simply to help facilitate a different kind of conversation.

Storytelling is proving effective at showing people what is possible when they engage in dialogue, and the company's intranet hosts a site, 'MyGE Story', which enables the sharing of stories of change across the organization. These tend to be gritty, honest, local stories that people can relate to. For instance, a group of four very experienced welders based at GE's manufacturing solutions locomotive plant in Fort Worth, Texas, made the switch to computer programming in order to program welding robots. The welders took themselves through a two-week crash course in the complex coding necessary to program the robots. Their work has proved groundbreaking. Previously, the welders had competed against each other to make the best-looking weld or to weld the fastest. Now they were competing together against their own prior work, training machines to weld as well as, or better, than they could.

But the group also helped one another. To begin with, the welders programmed their machines according to their own preferences, but they soon began sharing information, helping one another to master the complex welds needed for a locomotive platform. Thanks to the breakthroughs achieved, the welders are helping to produce the most competitive locomotive in North America. As one of the welders reflects: 'This not only opens up opportunities for the business but offers employees a chance to be a part of something bigger than themselves.'[23]

Another means of stimulating change involved engaging 25 leaders at all levels in a coalition for change. These were people who had been identified as already demonstrating the desired behaviours of the new approach to leadership. Historically managers were expected to command and control in their approach. Now, in the digital era, managers are expected to be people leaders who can inspire and empower their teams. Janice and her team invited these individuals to play an active role in influencing their peers and modelling new practice, for instance simply by walking along with peers having informal one-to-one chats. Coalition members were asked to build their own coalitions for change that could both spread the word and connect with each other. The message was, 'We love what you're doing. Are you willing to help others get there? We can supply you with additional tools to help spread the word.' These included social media-enabled 'coffee room' dialogues. The positive impact of these coalitions is already being felt.

Janice recognizes that the context will in any case drive certain changes. The dynamic nature of GE means that there will always be new business models and new people coming along, such as the influx of digital talent, who will help other employees to 'morph' and adopt new tools and approaches.

## The Learning and Development contribution

One element of ecosystem rewiring involves the Learning and Development (L&D) function, which is being redesigned to better support the changing company strategy and reinforce the behavioural and skill shifts taking place in the organization. A set of 12 behaviours has been articulated relating to team, environment, work and growth. All the leadership curriculum content has been redesigned to support the Beliefs.

Similarly, management training is now deliberately geared towards reinforcing the behavioural shifts that underpin the new Personal Development (PD) approach. This means managers learn how to have dialogues with team members, coaching them and helping teams take accountability for their work. One of the change work-streams is exploring how to upskill and build coaching competency within the population of 38,000 people leaders, many of whom have long service histories within GE. Some people leaders will have to unlearn certain behaviours so that they can become coaches who can effectively engage in dialogue with their teams, and, of course, not all managers will be able to make the shift from managing tasks to becoming an empowering leader. The intention is to help such managers move to roles where they can become instead great individual contributors. With the fluidity possible in GE, there are many opportunities for talented people to find their niche, work on things they feel passionate about and thrive in the right roles.

More generally, given the wider context of changes relating to the future of work and to careers, this fluidity represents a real opportunity for GE to make the most of talent. Of course, given GE's size and scale, and the complexity of its multiple industries and locations, facilitating such moves in a semblance of order is a big challenge. However, scaling is also historically a core competency of the organization, so GE is well placed to maximize this opportunity to benefit the company and its employees. Work is underway to simplify job titles and provide technology to help people better understand the range of jobs available in GE and to locate jobs to which their talents may best be suited, while also enabling managers to find the right talent available within the business.

## The HR function and change

Most of the change is delivered by the line, for the line. However, in developing the behind-the-scenes infrastructure and support for change, the tiny Culture Team works closely with HR colleagues to help move change forward.

The HR function itself is undergoing a shift in orientation. Traditionally HR's role required practitioners to have competencies in process compliance and monitoring. Though this was a significant role in the past, it is now recognized that today HR could make a greater contribution through developing HR competencies such as being a 'credible activist' and 'culture and change champion'.[24] This is about coaching people around behaviour change, helping employees adapt. However, many HR team members are still grappling with complex systems and heavy workloads that mean they have little time to devote to the potentially time-consuming activity of coaching.

For HR practitioners, the bigger shift required – as Janice observes, 'it's really more about mindset than anything else' – is to focus on outcomes. So, rather than producing tools for employees to use and training them how to use them, for example in a Performance Development (PD) conversation, a more useful activity for HR is to help people understand the outcomes that could be achieved. This would require not just different HR skills but also, if the success of the PD process is assessed on impact rather than activity, new measures of success. Instead of seeking to know whether a PD conversation has taken place between people leaders and their team members, the HR team should be interested in whether people feel they have been fairly treated and have had a great dialogue with their people leader. This shift may be challenging for some HR practitioners, yet developing an outcomes-focused mindset will potentially enhance HR's contribution in the digital era.

How do we know what's working?

Janice believes that her team has the right tools, processes and frameworks to support emergent change, though she observes that a change process involving localized dialogues can be 'messy' and result in different levels of adoption, with some pockets of the organization moving faster than others. This can make the measurement of success more complicated.

In conventional top-down, linear change processes, setting measures to gauge progress towards the desired goal is relatively straightforward. Given the emergent nature of the change process underway in GE, Janice and her team are using multiple methods to understand 'where we are at'. For instance, they are using Pulse surveys in various ways, redesigning measures in quantitative surveys to reflect desired outcomes. The quantitative data are combined with qualitative data gathered from various sources including the HR team, and employees themselves, especially those attending sessions at the company's L&D headquarters in Crotonville. The Culture Team works with data scientists to examine these multiple data streams, looking for patterns.

How sustainable is change?

In 2017, Jeff Immelt was replaced by John L Flannery as GE's CEO. So, will the move towards a more agile culture be maintained in the new era? This seems highly likely, not only because John has been with the company for 30 years and is very aligned to the messaging around *customer* and *learning*, but he is also passionate about culture, the core infrastructure of agility. His high-level support is already setting the tone and providing the platform for even more change.

More generally, agility requires the development of change capability through continuous learning, experimentation and reflection. As Janice reflects, if these practices become part of the organization's DNA, they build resilience and innovation, offering hope of sustainability whatever the future holds. Since change is likely to be ongoing, there is much value to be gained from being an active participant in the process: 'It's been an incredible journey that we're all still on, and it's been a great privilege to be part of it.'

## Aligning management and leadership

Strong leadership is a consistent feature of most studies of high-performance working and cultural change. With respect to culture, the leader's role is to facilitate the development of a culture of deeply shared meaning. Edgar Schein considers that leaders are well equipped to transmit and embed culture since they control most of the 'primary' and 'secondary' embedding mechanisms of culture (see Table 10.1).[25]

People are highly influenced by what their leaders say, do, prioritize and reward – so what leaders systematically pay attention to communicates major beliefs. Leaders should recognize their impact as role models, teaching people what behaviour is really acceptable. There cannot be one set of rules for senior management and another set for everyone else. Employees will build up trust in real and sustainable change only when they see it happening at the top of the company. So if leaders want to ensure that their workers are motivated, they must make sure that their own personal values are aligned with those of their employer – and that the organization acts on those values. There needs to be a collective form of organizational leadership with regard to the development of an innovation culture, with leaders held to account, individually and collectively, for how well and how positively they do this. For example, to encourage innovation 3M Corporation holds senior managers accountable for generating one-third of their division's annual revenues from products that did not exist three years previously;

TABLE 10.1  Schein's culture-embedding mechanisms

| Primary embedding mechanisms | Secondary articulation and reinforcement mechanisms |
| --- | --- |
| What leaders pay attention to, measure and control on a regular basis | Organization design and structure |
| How leaders react to critical incidents and organizational crises | Organizational systems and procedures |
| Observed criteria by which leaders allocate scarce resources | Organizational rites and rituals |
| Deliberate role modelling, teaching, and coaching | Design of physical space, facades and buildings |
| Observed criteria by which leaders allocate rewards and status | Stories, legends, and myths about people and events |
| Observed criteria by which leaders recruit, select, promote, retire and excommunicate organizational members | Formal statements of organizational philosophy, values and creed |

Source  Schein, E (2004) *Organizational Culture and Leadership*, 3rd edn, Jossey-Bass, San Francisco, pp 1–2 this creates an emphasis on encouraging and nurturing creative ideas from all employees.

McKinsey research suggests that leaders wanting to build a thriving culture of innovation must be systematic and intentional.[26] The world's 50 most innovative public companies hold innovation as a central value three times as often as the rest of the S&P 500 and cascade those values into the on-the-ground experience of employees. It is up to the CEO to build optimism and consistently encourage risk-taking by championing innovation as fundamental to the organization's success. Leading innovators use symbols that have great power – whether physical, verbal or action oriented – to reinforce the primacy of innovation, such as the CEO frequently visiting the sites where innovators work. They make innovation the norm by establishing rituals and routines such as innovation days, hackathons and so on. They shield and empower innovators by building a sense of belonging and safety through a shared commitment to innovation. Leaders destigmatize failure and make it OK to experiment, ask questions and provide feedback. They also reward learning – from failure as well as success.

## Leaders and purpose

One business leader who does recognize the power of corporate purpose is Paul Polman, previously CEO of consumer goods multinational Unilever. As a leader, Polman suggests:

> You have to be driven by something. Leadership is not just about giving energy but it's unleashing other people's energy, which comes from buying into that sense of purpose. But if that purpose isn't strong enough in a company, if the top doesn't walk the talk, then the rest will not last long. The key thing for CEOs is to make that a part of your operating model.[27]

Polman is considered by many to be the leading light in the corporate sustainability movement. He recognizes the power of partnerships as well as of greater diversity and inclusiveness in driving change in today's VUCA (volatile, uncertain, complex and ambiguous) environment. For Polman, the task of leaders is to take this complexity, distil it in simplicity and drive that to action. 'That's a skill that you have to learn.'

To avoid getting overwhelmed by the problems facing the world 'you need to have an enormous discipline to stay focused on the things where you as your business, who you ultimately represent, can make the biggest impact'. So, for Unilever, it is focusing on issues like food security, sanitation and deforestation where Unilever can provide solutions. This produces social and environmental benefits as well as profitability.

> If it's hygiene, then we have a Lifebuoy hand wash, if it's women's self-esteem we have Dove, so every brand becomes a cause, a social movement in that sense. But I think the main thing is to have a firm belief about the core responsibility of solving these challenges, and not delegating that to someone else.

For Polman, if you want to prepare the company for the future you must take a long-term view. One important symbol of this was when Unilever abolished the quarterly profit reporting in order 'to send a clear signal that we are going to do well all the time'.[28]

In the wake of the pandemic, the issue of corporate purpose has become ever more prominent. Charlie Mayfield, chairman of Be the Business and formerly John Lewis Partnership chairman argues that the pandemic forced leaders to think hard about their organization's overarching purpose and contribution to society, because they were less likely to be 'consumed' by day-to-day operations and the forward plans they had made before. 'As a leader you've got to think about how you can develop yourself so that you can make some of these crucial decisions for the future,' he said.[29] Social purpose arguably is going to be of huge importance to many more people. The lockdowns gave many employees time to consider their role, its purpose and whether the career they had chosen or the organization they work for was sustainable. After all, work is the place where people get on in life. It is not just about money – people achieve life goals through it.

And purpose is ever more central to the ability to attract and retain talent. Andy Briggs, CEO at insurance provider Phoenix Group, said business leaders should 'stay close' to what their employees wanted and needed from work. Understanding what is important is vital. 'One size won't fit all and different things work for different people.' However, purpose has become ever more important to most people. Briggs suggested there would be a shift in the way success was measured, with employees and job candidates likely to judge a business based on its contribution to society, the environment or the satisfaction of its people, rather than its profitability. 'The businesses that don't seek to embrace and be leaders around sustainability – people won't want to work for them,' he said. '[This] covers customer dimensions, sustainable investments, environment, contribution to the community. Covid-19 has been a horrific time for the world.' But this commitment needs to be authentic not just rhetorical or for PR spin. The acid test is how you really measure success: at the end of the year, do you judge the performance of your teams and your business based solely on the financials, or do you judge it on the customer experience, colleague engagement or on the contribution to sustainability?[30]

## Delivering the brand reality of diversity and inclusion

Every company should have a mission but if the values underpinning this are not practised, the whole exercise lacks meaning. Today society expects more of employers on issues of inequalities and social justice. Increasingly, diversity impacts on customer expectations and the business reputation and brand, and not least what society expects from a modern employer. Culture again comes to the fore: customers expect companies to be ethical and fair employers, including across their supply chain. Just consider the market backlash against Nike's supply chain crisis in 2005, when shocking working conditions including child workers were revealed in some of its supply companies. More recently various protest and campaigning groups such as Black Lives Matter have raised public awareness of how far society still has to travel to become inclusive of everyone in terms of respect and opportunity.

It seems that today society places a high value on sustainability and diversity and calls for a more transparent workplace where new generations of employees have much higher expectations of companies. Glassdoor found that 67 per cent of job seekers in 2021 consider workplace diversity an important factor when considering employment opportunities. Not surprisingly workplace diversity issues are under a public microscope. One example is the staff protests at Google in 2019 over diversity issues, with demonstrations outside and inside the offices challenging Google as to whether it was truly fulfilling its public commitment to diversity.

Enriching workplace diversity is not only integral to the success of the organization, it also produces a positive employee experience. A Forbes Insights report claims that companies with greater gender and ethnic diversity consistently outperform the competition since they more accurately reflect the diversity of society and reach more potential customers.[31] They also invite more people to the table, incorporating a broader range of perspectives into their decision making – a win-win for everyone.

While it is commonplace to talk about diversity and inclusion (D&I), what does the reality on the ground look like? Creating diversity initiatives that encourage and support different groups of employees who may feel marginalized and isolated has been a 'Cinderella' area in some sectors.

When recruiting many large employers describe themselves as offering an outstandingly positive career space where everyone is welcome and all will thrive. However, this welcome often is diluted once someone joins the company, due to a lack of diversity within. And while many companies are implementing a hybrid or fully remote working setup, during the pandemic many employees feared that remote working would favour some people more than others. So it is also necessary to promote a more inclusive digital workspace.

In all this debate over diversity and inclusion, the role of HR departments can be a game changer. When HR 'leans in' to champion diversity this turns rhetoric into reality. Many different strategies can include:

- Conducting an audit to see where current bottlenecks and friction are located
- Rewording and refocusing current hiring efforts to use more neutrally inclusive language
- Implementing new unbiased candidate screening and shortlisting protocols
- Training designed to target some of the most common issues in a workplace
- Promoting anti-discrimination in the workplace.

To create an inclusive and bias-free environment where employees feel a sense of belonging despite the differences, a shift in organization culture may be required. To create diversity-friendly workplaces that are a better fit for the 21st century HR must drive stronger and more rigorous diversity action and find ways to support, advise and encourage firms to go beyond legal minimum requirements. Indeed, at breakfast cereal manufacturer Weetabix, inclusion is a key element of the people and cultural strategy. Responsibility sits with the head of R&D, not the HR team.

The following examples of innovative and creative diversity in action were initiatives designed to deliver long-term results. Each programme aims to alter attitudes and behaviour in the workplace and to provide the best support and encouragement for those in minority groups. The intention is also to ensure that those in the majority (or in the leadership team) understand the work experience of those from diverse backgrounds (e.g. because of sexual orientation) or groups where discrimination has occurred over years (such as for gender and race).

## Walk a mile in my shoes

This is a mentoring scheme to transfer diversity knowledge and work experience between senior leaders and employees from a range of diverse backgrounds. But the senior leader is not the mentor (as might be expected); instead, it is the person with a minority background. Considered by the company to be both innovative and imaginative, it was also seen as risky but an important step forward to transfer learning between these two rather distant groups and thereby help to build inclusive leadership skills and knowledge. It was so successful that a second mentoring programme was quickly established with a new wave of senior leaders being mentored.

## Integrating diversity into leadership

This initiative is a leadership 'twin' as it runs alongside a flagship leadership programme, providing minority ethnic participants with key skills, experiences and structured support and encouragement to specifically address diversity issues.

Rather than a separate leadership programme, this initiative aims to provide employees from minority backgrounds – who have won their place on merit – with support, coaching and, if required, an added injection of confidence or cultural knowledge to ensure they can take on a more senior leadership role.

Both initiatives were designed to create an inclusive environment, and a level playing field, rather than one that would make the participants feel that they were being offered remedial training or support. The support on offer is carefully tailored to ensure their life experiences and current workplace needs are respected. It is an important distinction. People in varied diversity groups often say that they do not wish to be targeted for 'special' treatment or to be labelled as needing 'extra' support. Such an approach may feel patronizing and instead creates resentment and an unwillingness to participate as people may not wish to be singled out in this way. Some companies unfortunately only discover this after introducing a well-meant initiative. As one person said after a cool response to a diversity event, 'It was not a partnership and we were hardly consulted about what we would find useful in such a network or whether we wished to be publicly identified in this way. Some of us did, some certainly did not. Not everybody felt comfortable with that.'[32]

Improving diversity in the workplace is no easy task. Both initiatives described were tailor-made with consultation and discussions to engage all stakeholders across the business. As one of those involved in the design process explained:

> There was no point in anything other than tailor-made approaches for diversity. What would work in our organization has to 'fit' the business needs. Otherwise, there will be no buy-in from the individuals we are seeking to help nor from our managers as to why they need to support and promote diversity.

HR and managers can make a real difference to furthering the D&I agenda, not just because it is the 'right thing' to do but because it can make a real difference to business results. Invariably, in pace-setter companies such as those with the initiatives just discussed there is a talented HR team that provides leadership and insight and attempts to embed diversity throughout the business.

The opportunities to take part in executive education and leadership development are also critical parts of the diversity jigsaw. Every leadership process and practice including executive education, informal development and key assignments that count for so much in promotion and succession planning need close examination, to be shaped through the lens of diversity and inclusion. When every HR director and every business school can say the same then diversity will have come a lot further on its journey towards becoming mainstream.

## Reinforcement

Once the desired cultural shifts have started to happen, they should be reinforced through the formal structures and processes associated with the creative generation of improvement ideas. After aligning on a common purpose, this can be made concrete through a set of values-based 'guardrails', quality standards and priorities that guide the practice of front-line staff. Through practice, new habits become the norm.

To embed the 'new' practices in the organizational system a supportive infrastructure – technology, processes, rewards, structures, etc – should be developed to be consistent with the desired culture change. Empowerment is a common thread running through a change-able culture. When people are trusted to do their job and are given clear expectations rather than an instruction manual, they feel more valued and empowered – qualities that cannot help but show in the customer experience and innovative outcomes they provide. Practices that create transparency and visibility and remove obstacles to desired behaviours ease the flow of information and smooth inter-action. These include clear, simple goals, structures to facilitate learning and knowledge sharing; strong administrative support; information support systems; and development-focused performance management systems. As we discussed in Chapter 9, performance management and reward systems that place a higher premium on the behaviour that leads to agility and innovation can help to shape new group norms and build a receptive context for change and innovation. For example, Google is renowned for providing employees with a day per week to focus on creative projects of their own choice.

To help the changes stick set metrics to track how the culture is developing and intervene when necessary. A systematic reinforcement programme will combine training, coaching and 360-degree feedback mechanisms. Seeing leaders acting in new ways encourages employees to follow suit and makes common purpose a living reality within the organization. Helping people to develop the right skills enables them to do their jobs well; giving them respon-sibility for managing their own development can lead to greater agility and resilience. Training and coaching should evolve over time as the needs of employees and the organization change.

## Conclusion

To enable organizations to thrive in an environment of constant change and complexity, their cultures need to be 'change-able', i.e. ready and able to change deliberately as well as organically as they adjust to changing circum-stances. We have considered the key roles of shared purpose and customer empathy in building an innovative, change-able and inclusive culture. Developing such a culture involves 'heart' and 'head', formal and informal approaches to shifting behaviours, for instance by setting new standards, allocating rewards (financial and non-financial), providing follow-up and feedback. It is where Kelly's 'clockware' and 'swarmware' coincide. For all its challenges, change can also open up new possibilities – for development, better work-life balance and growth as people gain new skills, new networks and new responsibilities. Even tough challenges can be opportunities for individuals and teams to learn from and become more resilient, if people face these together and in a positive spirit. People need space to make sense of the new and adjust their behaviours. Through ongoing dialogue and opportunities for collective reflection people can take stock and start to co-create the new 'way we do things around here'.

The key to building a change-able culture is *employee empowerment and a fair deal*. If a business wants its staff to participate in the process of change and innovation and also improve productivity, it is unreasonable to expect them to be working 'flat out' all the time. Senior leaders need to develop and communicate clear priorities and accept that it is important to free people up by stopping doing some things – so a formal process to review and communicate what will be deprioritized may be needed. HR can help by developing effective work-life balance policies and flexible working opportunities. They can coach managers in how to ensure that workloads are manageable and help managers to create time for people to learn.

At the end of the day, culture change needs to trickle down, up and across the organization if it is to last. In the next chapter we look at the significant role of leaders in building this culture and at how 'values-based' leadership can be developed and embedded as a cultural capability.

In summary, to build a change-able culture and maximize engagement and performance:

- Connect people to the organization – develop values bottom-up – clearly articulate values in behavioural terms and incorporate them into organizational life.

- Connect the organization's purpose and strategy with individual goals and objectives; hold people to account on both performance and values; signal what is valued and work hard to retain your best people.

- Break down silos; build a climate of trust around a higher shared purpose.

- Ensure adequate support – develop engaging managers and values-based leaders.

- Work with top leaders to provide a climate of psychological safety – 'fail fast', no blame culture.

- Increase voice – actively involve people in change.

- Help people transition to new ways of working, including embracing life-long learning.

- Prepare people for new roles – arrange cross-organizational attachments, for instance.

- Ensure people can access information and skill development so they can be accountable for decisions.

- Build trust by treating people fairly.
- Work to enable and embed learning in organization practice – act as knowledge hub; encourage collaborations.
- Encourage knowledge sharing among networks – continuous corporate and personal renewal.
- Focus on employee wellbeing.
- Develop capabilities and skills – provide growth opportunities; develop in/out/in career tracks.
- Develop career tracks that offer real growth.
- Ensure performance and reward processes are fair.
- Offer working options.
- Implement effective diversity policies.

---

CHECKLIST

How change-able is your organization?

- How would you describe your culture? What elements of your culture help or hinder you today?
- How well aligned is your culture with achieving your corporate purpose?
- How clear are people about the purpose, strategy and the rationale for change?
- What kinds of communication can help to strengthen employee engagement, performance, resilience and agility?
- Do people have the skills, authority, information and resources to be empowered? What needs to happen to increase employee empowerment?
- Do you have well-defined teams that regularly review how they are doing and get to know each other?
- Which communities of practice thrive in your environment?
- Are coherent goals set for quality, innovation, safety, etc?
- Are values articulated in a way that shows how they translate into behaviour?
- Are line managers trained in people management skills, including coaching and feedback?

- Are roles designed to provide stretch, be do-able and have line of sight to the customer/purpose?
- Are staff involved in creating new standards and raising the bar?
- Is space created for staff to reflect on customer challenges?
- What do you want your employees' experience of working for you to be in five years' time?
- What do you want your customers', partners' and suppliers' experience of working with you to be in five years' time?
- Do you act on staff feedback – and are staff allowed to make the improvements they identify?
- Do you use hard and soft intelligence about staff experience and morale to seek out problems and target support for solving them?
- What measures, incentives, sticks and carrots exist to ensure there are diversity key performance indicators (KPIs) at every level of the business from team leader through to the C-suite?
- Similarly, who is the diversity champion at the most senior level of the organization? No leadership invariably equals limited or no progress on diversity.
- Is unnecessary bureaucracy eliminated?
- How clear are staff about what work needs to stop, start, continue? Have rewards and recognition been realigned to reinforce desired behaviours, such as collaboration, and customer-centric outcomes?

# Notes

1  Senge, PM (1990) *The Fifth Discipline: The art and practice of the learning organization*, Doubleday, New York.
2  Holbeche, LS (2005) *The High Performance Organization*, Butterworth-Heinemann, Oxford; Holbeche, LS (2005) *Understanding Change*, Butterworth-Heinemann, Oxford.
3  Quade, K and Holladay, R (2010) *Dynamical Leadership: Building adaptive capacity for uncertain times*, CreateSpace independent publishing platform.
4  Kelly, K (1995) *Out of Control: The new biology of machines, social systems, and the economic world*, Basic Books, New York.
5  Galbraith, J (1995) *Designing Organizations*, Jossey-Bass, San Francisco.

6  Stacey, RD (1996) *Complexity and Creativity in Organizations*, Berrett-Koehler, San Francisco.

7  Amabile, TM (1996) *Creativity in Context*, Westview Press, Boulder, Colorado.

8  Weisberg RW(1993) *Creativity: Beyond the myth of genius*, WH Freeman, New York.

9  Johnson, G, Whittington, R and Scholes, K (2012) *Fundamentals of Strategy*, Pearson Education, Harlow.

10 Accenture UK (2018) UK consumers buying from companies that take a stand on issues they care about and ditching those that don't, Accenture study finds, https://newsroom.accenture.co.uk/english-uk/news/uk-consumers-buying-from-companies-that-take-stand-on-issues-they-care-about-and-ditching-those-that-dont.htm (archived at https://perma.cc/NTH3-STMX).

11 Accenture Strategy (2018) To affinity and beyond: From me to we, the ruse of purpose-led brand, https://www.accenture.com/t20181205T121039Z__w__/us-en/_acnmedia/Thought-Leadership-Assets/PDF/Accenture-CompetitiveAgility-GCPR-POV.pdf#zoom=50 (archived at https://perma.cc/DNL2-MTV5).

12 Holbeche, LS and Springett, N (2005) *In Search of Meaning at Work*, Roffey Park, Horsham.

13 Mayer, C (2021) *Policy & Practice for Purposeful Business*, The British Academy, London.

14 Based on Plsek, PE (1997) *Creativity, Innovations and Quality*, Irwin Professional Publishing, New York.

15 Kelly, ibid.

16 Gratton, L. Four principles to ensure hybrid work is productive work, *MIT Sloan Management Review*, 9 November 2020.

17 Johnston, K, Coughlin, C and Garvey Berger, J (2014) Leading in complexity, May, www.cultivatingleadership.com/site/uploads/Leading-in-Complexity-CC-JGB-KJ-2014-4.pdf (archived at https://perma.cc/T2RR-ZM7N).

18 Huy, QN (1999) Emotional capability, emotional intelligence and radical change, *Academy of Management Review*, 24 (2), pp 325–45.

19 Hamel, G (2009) Moon shots for management, *Harvard Business Review*, February, hbr.org/2009/02/moon-shots-for-management.

20 Meyerson, DE (2003) *Tempered Radicals: How everyday leaders inspire change at work*, Harvard Business School Press, Boston.

21 Covey, SR and Crawley, JD (2004) Leading corporate communities, *Executive Excellence*, June, p 6.

22 Source: Janice Semper. Also: Agarwal, D, van Berkel, A and Rea, B (2015) Simplification of work: The coming revolution, *Global Human Capital Trends 2015: Leading in the new world of work*, Deloitte University Press, New York, pp 90–91.

**23** Watson, B (2017) The wingmen: GE welders band together in new career as robot programmers, GE Reports, www.ge.com/reports/wingmen-ge-welders-band-together-new-career-robot-programmers/ (archived at https://perma.cc/LS8N-4A7S).

**24** Ulrich, D, Kryscynski, D, Ulrich, M and Brockbank, W (2017) *Victory Through Organization: Why the war for talent is failing your company and what you can do about it*, McGraw Hill, New York.

**25** Schein, E (2004) *Organizational Culture and Leadership*, 3rd edn, Jossey-Bass, San Francisco, pp 1–2.

**26** Furstenthal, L, Morris, A and Roth, E. Fear factor: Overcoming human barriers to innovation, McKinsey & Company, 3 June 2022, www.mckinsey.com/capabilities/strategy-and-corporate-finance/our-insights/fear-factor-overcoming-human-barriers-to-innovation (archived at https://perma.cc/B5YP-CK7B).

**27** Cofino, J. (2013). Interview: Unilever's Paul Polman on diversity, purpose and profits, *The Guardian*, theguardian.com, Wednesday 2 October.

**28** Polman, P. and Winston, A. (2021) *Net Positive: How Courageous Companies Thrive by Giving More Than They Take,* Harvard Business Review Press.

**29** Sir Charlie Mayfield keynote: "Productivity in a post-pandemic UK - how to go from here to there?" Youtube.

**30** Webber, A. 'Purposeful' work essential to attracting talent post-Covid, *Personnel Today*, 11 Jun 2020, www.personneltoday.com/hr/purposeful-work-essential-to-attracting-talent-post-covid/ (archived at https://perma.cc/ZK49-BU48).

**31** Forbes Insights (2017) Diversity & inclusion: Unlocking global potential global diversity rankings by country, sector and occupation, global_diversity_rankings_2012.pdf.

**32** Holton, V. and Holbeche, L.S. (2020) Diversity, rhetoric and reality: how HR can be a game-changer, EFMD Global Focus Magazine, Issue 1, Vol. 14 pp 52–55.

# 11

# Agile leadership

In this chapter we focus on the nature of leadership required for agility. In leading the changes necessary to implement a strategy, all leaders must operate effectively in three domains:

> There's a strategic domain, which is all about tomorrow. There's the operational domain, which is all about today… about Gantt charts, goals and budgets. And then there's the interpersonal domain, because irrespective of where you are working or what timescale you're working on, the key thing is to bring out the best in people.[1]

Throughout this book we have considered all three leadership domains, but in the face of rapid technological change, of Web 2.0 technologies and the emergence of Web 3.0, which will be characterized by decentralization and artificial intelligence, leading for agility requires specific kinds of leadership.

We shall consider two aspects of leadership theory that are key to pulling together a resiliently agile organization. First, values-based leadership stands out since employees need to be led by authentic, ethical leaders they can trust. Trust and mutuality are the foundations on which organizational agility and resilience are built. After all, as various well-known company disasters teach us, even the most brilliant structures and control mechanisms have proved useless when individual and organizational values have not been aligned. Values-based leaders lead by making shared purpose and values the 'glue' binding organizations together.

The second key theme is shared or distributed leadership. Given the complexity of the business environment, it is unrealistic to expect that top leaders will have all the answers, especially in knowledge-based organizations, and old-style hierarchical approaches are of limited use. When speed is of the essence, conventional structures that drive decisions towards the centre run the risk of decision making becoming gridlocked. This type of shared leadership is frequently referred to as 'horizontal', 'distributed', 'collective' or 'complexity' leadership, and I use several of these terms in this chapter. The task of top leadership is to build shared leadership and accountability across the organization. We shall look in more detail at the changing demands on individual leaders and how they can help to build a culture of leadership across organizations. In particular we look at:

- Why values-based leadership?
- How can agile leadership be developed?
- From 'I' to 'we' – building shared leadership.

## Why values-based leadership?

Management literature is awash with theories about the kinds of leadership required for today's conditions of complexity and ambiguity. Charles Handy wrote that a corporation should be thought of as a community of citizens remaining together to pursue a common purpose.[2] Demands for participation are growing from new generations who see the world very differently from their predecessors. As we have seen throughout this book, 'traditional and hierarchical modes of leadership are yielding to a different way of working – one based on *teamwork* and *community*, one that seeks to involve others in decision making, one strongly based in ethical and caring behaviour'.[3] This emerging approach to leadership and service began with Robert Greenleaf and his concept of 'servant leadership'.[4] Since senior leaders symbolically represent the collective identity, what they believe and how they act influences the organization around them.

In an ever-changing world, agile leaders need to shape organizational culture and communities that employees want to be part of. The global pandemic, a divisive political environment and protests against racial and gender injustice are reflected within organizations as employee concerns for safety and wellbeing and a desire for a diverse and inclusive workplace. The Qualtrics 2021 Employee Experience Trends Report found that, during the pandemic, having a sense of belonging to an organization emerged as the most important driver of engagement.[5] Staff want employers to stand for certain values and will agitate when necessary, with many younger employees valuing purpose above pay.[6] Of course this requires that people trust what leaders say. As we have discussed, today there are widespread 'trust deficits' between leaders and 'followers' in many walks of life. To be trustworthy, leaders must 'walk' the 'talk' on values.

## Leaders and values

To respond to the engagement challenge in this new era, the importance of values-based leadership cannot be overstated. Discussion about the values of leaders goes back to earlier leadership theories. In 1978, for example, when Burns talked of 'moral leadership' he distinguished between two types of leadership – transformational and transactional.[7] Transactional leadership involves developing and maintaining task structures and plans, information management and control systems. It works on a 'give and take' basis where a leader provides a reward or punishment in return for the work (or its lack) that the subordinate is doing. Transformational leadership is meant to bring about big changes in the lives of followers, thereby making their lives better and more fruitful and improving the society in which the organization operates. In both cases, values-based leaders build a sense of shared purpose and community by never changing their fundamental principles and values, only their approach or strategy in a given situation.

Contemporary theories talk of 'authentic' leadership, 'post-heroic', 'credible' leadership and others. Knowing oneself and being true to oneself are essential qualities of authentic leadership. May et al, for example, argue that authentic leadership involves: 'the leader knowing him- or herself, and being transparent in linking inner desires, expectations, and values to the way the leader behaves, in each and every interaction'.[8] Similarly, Goffee and Jones argue that leadership demands the expression of an authentic self.[9] People want to be led by someone real. People associate authenticity with sincerity, honesty and integrity. For Norman, Luthans and Luthans, the authentic leader has confidence, hope, optimism and resilience and also a moral/ethical transparency orientation.[10] Thus values-based management behaviour is consistent with the organization's core values: what leaders say is exactly what they mean.

If leaders and managers want to earn trust and build a more resilient employment relationship with employees, they need to win respect by being open and honest, leading in such a way that the dignity and rights of others are respected. Engagement means far more than having an engagement strategy; mechanistic approaches that lack sincerity will soon be found out. This relationship focus requires social leadership and emotional intelligence, the ability to improve interpersonal dealings within a group, acknowledging and working through historically dysfunctional relationships to create a more collaborative, whole-system approach for the future.

In particular there must be a cohesive leadership team at the top since the management team is the most important 'great group' – which now must also be heterogeneous because of multiple stakeholders. They must bring key stakeholders on board and create alignment. As John Brock, formerly chairman of Coca-Cola Enterprises notes, leaders today must work with a wide range of stakeholders, such as shareholders, community representatives, customers and employees:

> I think the role of a business leader today is much more challenging because you've got so many other constituencies out there that you didn't have before. You've got to engage with these multiple constituencies and make decisions in a more consensual way. And that requires a real skill.[11]

Ratan Tata and Mark Wallenberg argue that we should learn from large, enduring firms who have survived many periods of upheaval.[12] Organizations that are in it for the long term choose their leaders according to the challenge at hand; some may have appropriate skills for a restructuring, but different leaders will be needed when expansion is called for. As we have considered in this book, leaders must play many roles including master strategist, relationship/network builder, culture developer, change manager and talent developer. While it is unlikely that any individual can play all of these roles, a cohesive management team can.

Leadership styles must evolve beyond command and control towards building a firmer foundation for mutual trust and respect. Of course, if top teams are consumed with politics with which their boards may collude, silo-based behaviour is likely lower down the hierarchy that will impede agility. Executives need to show visible leadership, build trust – 'walk the talk' – and create energy around mission and vision. The top team must model the way forward with respect to values; surface and address political issues that impede collaboration; be open and transparent in sharing relevant information and avoid promoting 'sharks' who achieve business results at the expense of others. As Heifetz and Laurie argue, rather than quelling conflict leaders need to draw out issues and let people feel the sting of reality.[13] With respect to defining and rewarding success, the *how* should matter as well as the *what*.

## Ethics and purpose

Increasingly in public debates the primacy of shareholder value is being challenged and businesses are being prompted to address social issues. Leaders are now expected to be transparent in their dealings, accountable for the ethical practice of their organizations and supply chains. Firms well known for their ethical stance such as Ben & Jerry's, The Body Shop and many others focus on a 'triple bottom line' – 'people, profit, planet' – i.e. aiming to benefit their communities, the environment, customers and staff as well as investors. The assumption is that companies that do good do well and vice versa. For instance, in the travel industry, ethical travel matters now. At one time people went on safari without caring much about the welfare of the local people. Now they want to see that their money is funding worthwhile causes: orphanages, schools, research centres. They want to feel they are doing good while having a good – and expensive – time.[14]

A TMI study found that leadership was what made the greatest difference to navigating complex strategic initiatives and crises.[15] And the good news is that staff in many sectors say their leaders responded well to the coronavirus pandemic and to resolving problems of social justice, according to a 2020 poll by Weber Shandwick.[16] This both underlines the level of trust placed in employers and serves as a potential source of criticism if companies fall short.

Collins and Porras highlight the shareholder value paradox, drawing distinctions between long-lived successful 'visionary' companies who take a longer-term view and take stakeholder perspectives into account, and companies driven purely by short-term shareholder value considerations: Paradoxically, the visionary companies make more money than the more profit-driven companies.[17]

It is possible that this paradox occurs because of what John Kay calls the obliquity principle: by focusing in a direction that matters to employees (such as delighting the customer), the organization obliquely also makes more money than if the focus was directly on shareholder value, which would drive a different set of values and behaviours. 'Obliquity gives rise to the profit-seeking paradox: the most profitable companies are not the most profit-oriented.'[18]

These shifts are reflected in a Roffey Park study on the differential effects of different kinds of corporate purpose on business performance and on employee motivation.[19] Firms with a customer-focused purpose outperformed those with a shareholder purpose or a mix of purposes. Employees of customer-oriented firms tended to experience:

- their leaders as more trustworthy and able
- the culture as more creative
- their contribution as better recognized and rewarded
- more commitment to and from the organization
- their work as more meaningful
- less stress arising from their work
- a stronger sense of purpose.

## Putting employees first

Interestingly, while putting customers at the heart of company purpose is a powerful and motivating approach, today there is increasing emphasis on putting employees first since it is only when staff are happy that customers will feel the real benefits of dealing with a firm. For instance, the Disney Corporation, renowned for its customer experience, believes that creating great customer experience comes down to having great people and treating them well. Looking after your people makes them feel more engaged with your organization and more committed to your service goals.

The role of managers and management should be to enthuse and encourage employees so that they can create a different shared value: enhancing employees first and customers second. Vineet Nayar, the CEO who led giant IT services company HCL Technologies through a profound reinvention, emphasizes the importance of creating an environment of trust where employees believe what you are saying and are willing to follow you because purpose is made real in company practice. In HCL, all the enabling functions such as HR, Finance and the office of the CEO are as accountable to the employees as the employees are accountable to them. This commitment is made real in tangible ways. For instance, HCL created an electronic 'trouble ticketing' system where an employee can open a trouble ticket on any of these functions, which must then resolve these issues within a certain period of time. The ticket is only closed by the employees. Similarly, management and managers are as accountable to the employees as the employees are to them. This accountability is evident since the CEO's 360-degree feedback is done by 80,000 employees across the world and the results are published on the web for all to see. This culture unlocks a huge amount of energy in the corporation.

In one organization it was recognized that, moving into hybrid working, a combination of travel restrictions and turnover across the organization contributed to colleagues feeling detached from senior leaders and the discussions happening at senior management team and supervisor levels, leading to a sense of disconnect. To counter this and reconnect senior leaders (directors) with colleagues across the organization, they consciously started a series of visits and communication forums (both in-person and virtual over MS teams) to raise visibility and transparency about their roles, the work and the decisions that were being made as well as creating spaces and opportunities for them to engage in listening exercises with teams both within and across their departments/divisions. The impact of these activities can already be seen in the high level of engagement (both in numbers and in the qualitative contributions) in organizational townhalls and in various Yammer communications. The focus on building and maintaining relationships across departments and teams will be monitored within future staff engagement surveys.

## How can agile leadership be developed?

New leadership configurations and leadership competencies will be required to lead organizations for agility into the future so how we select and develop them must change too. Agility fundamentally changes the way organizations operate – teams and working practices are different and the culture and behaviours required are different. The role of agile business leaders changes too. Leaders must take the long view, balance current reality and optimism and keep faith with employees, giving people confidence about the future and creating a climate for change. In a context where simplistic either/or solutions may not be appropriate, resiliently agile leaders must reconcile the leadership dilemma, being both:

- short-term *and* long-term focused
- congruent *and* flexible
- supportive *and* directive
- task *and* people focused
- business as usual *and* innovation
- helicopter view *and* feet on the ground.

## Leaders as learners

Senior managers have usually spent many years developing rules of thumb, instincts, crisis management models and metrics that have made them successful in traditional ways of working. Top teams often prefer to hold on to what they have done in the past even if this means they act as operational managers rather than strategic leaders. Indeed, Arthur Koestler highlights how difficult unlearning old ways of thinking can be:

> Of all forms of mental activity, the most difficult to induce even in the minds of the young, who may be presumed not to have lost their flexibility, is the art of handling the same bundle of data as before but placing them in a new system of relations with one another.[20]

As we have discussed, agile leaders must be able to lead in complexity, take evidence-based decisions, be a relationship/network builder, culture developer, change manager, talent developer and enabler of shared leadership. Some leaders, therefore, may need to develop new skills, open their minds to new approaches to leadership, learn new techniques, receive 'fresh knowledge' from outside their system and step out of their comfort zone.

As Marcel Proust points out: 'The only real voyage of discovery consists not in seeking new landscapes but in having new eyes.'[21]

## Look outside

Top leaders must develop systemic understanding and gain insights into the 'zeitgeist' and its implications in order to identify what Heifetz and Laurie call the 'adaptive challenge'.[22] Mayo and Nohria argue that the ability to understand the zeitgeist and pursue the unique opportunities it presents for each company is what separates the truly great leaders from the merely competent.[23] These authors found that a lack of sensitivity to contextual factors can trip up even the most brilliant of executives. Without this, a leader's personality and skill are but temporal strengths. Without foresight and insight, leaders will not be able to plan for the future or inspire and guide the organization. They need to look back from the future and act now.

To develop systemic understanding many senior managers go on study trips and make benchmarking visits to companies in other geographies, which may offer fresh insights into key strategic challenges. Some companies send senior and high-potential managers to large business or management conferences, accompanied by a learning facilitator who helps the leadership groups to process their learning at the end of each day. Organizations like IBM, HSBC, Lend Lease, IMC Group and others are structuring their leadership development activities to create opportunities for their current and future senior leaders to have personal, first-hand experiences of developing relationships with people who are experiencing some of the world's most pressing challenges, and also of working directly with people to help address these challenges. Through such powerful experiential learning senior executives have the chance to engage with new ideas and help to make sense of the demands of this new business context – like ecology, complexity, systems thinking and social constructionism – and how these link with business language through new concepts like 'shared value', 'brand substance', 'closed-loop manufacturing' and 'integrated reporting'. These firms value these kinds of experiences when making decisions about recruitment, career development and succession planning, and make sure they are embedded in the HR processes that underpin them.

While leadership roles will come and go, increasingly leadership is viewed as a function, not a role. For agility, leadership will be all around, with different people leading initiatives. The task of hierarchy is to build self-managing teams and to make sure initiatives are happening in the right places. Clear strategies and direction setting will be needed, including the expectation of continual adjustment, because self-management in teams depends on clarity. Looking to the future, leaders will probably be partnered with machines. They will need digital dexterity and systems thinking to see how the social and technical fit together. When machines and people start to work together, comfort with, and skills in, risk taking will be needed throughout the organization. David Welbourn and colleagues of the Bayes Business School advise leaders hoping to influence systems to:

- Have an open, enquiring mind.
- Embrace uncertainty and be positive about change.
- Draw on as many perspectives as possible.
- Ensure leadership and decision making are distributed throughout the system.
- Promote the importance of values – invest as much energy in relationships and behaviours as in delivery.[24]

Organizations are also increasingly running large-scale scenario-planning sessions that involve many staff members and managers, opening up minds and garnering collective wisdom on perceived trends and challenges. The creation of an alert, informed and engaged cohort of practitioners is key to the development of a more shared sense of leadership. One medium-sized firm involved its senior managers and high-potential employees below board level in carrying out collaborative inquiry – researching aspects of the business, its environment, opportunities and threats. The firm has since implemented many of the findings to great advantage enhancing both its business results, the capability of leaders and its reputation as an employer.

## Look inside

Whole generations of senior leaders have reached executive positions based on their technical and business prowess. Today's challenges require them to use themselves as instruments of change to help their organizations thrive in the new environment. What sets outstanding leaders apart, according to the Work Foundation, is that they think systemically and act long term; bring meaning to life; apply the spirit rather than the letter of the law; grow people through performance; are self-aware and authentic, putting leadership first, their own needs second; understand that talk is work; give time and space to others and put 'we' before 'me'. Agile leaders are able to engender trust by being honest.

Many of the skills associated with agility have long been identified with psychological and change-management studies. Given the importance of relationships, leaders need to be emotionally intelligent and have effective negotiating, influencing and conflict resolution skills. Key qualities of values-based leaders that emerge from various studies include self-reflection, balance, self-confidence, courage and humility.[25] For instance, Collins highlighted humility as a quality of 'Level 5' leaders of 'great' organizations.[26] Such leaders have learned to get in touch with what they consider important and have developed their own set of beliefs. For Paul Polman:

> As a leader you've got to think about how you can develop yourself so that you can make some of these crucial decisions for the future. First of all, you need to feel comfortable about who you are. So a good leader, I think, is a good human being in the first place. Too often we are being programmed by the environment around us to behave differently. But I think a true leader is an authentic person, who feels good about who he is. I don't have a problem crying when I need to cry. There's nothing wrong with that and showing that you care because it's the same in any organization; if you show that you care, others will care for you, 100%.[27]

How should such skills and 'awarenesses' be developed?

For Quinn, leaders learn how to handle uncertainty by reflective conversations;[28] Badaracco also argues that change is brought into being through dialogue.[29] Productive deliberation is a chaotic process of zigzagging between feelings, thoughts, facts and analysis, resisting the temptation to grasp hold of a single grand principle or allow it to tyrannize all other considerations. As leaders wrestle with their own development they need to find sources of advice they can trust such as peers, coaches, mentors or colleagues at all levels.

Action learning sets and peer networks provide spaces for leaders to hone their thinking. Unilever found that the technical skills of some executives were not keeping pace with the ways in which social and other media can now be used to communicate more widely with employees and other stakeholders; it was therefore unable to plug into new developments and trends. Unilever established 'reverse mentoring' whereby graduate recruits coach and mentor executives in how to use modern media to connect with the workforce. Standard Chartered Bank has experimented with leadership development that provides leaders with space to reflect and engage in dialogue on complex issues that have no easy answers. Similarly, the University of Hertfordshire involves a leading expert on complexity – Professor Ralph Stacey – in leadership development for senior academics and professional services managers based on reflection and dialogue.

In identifying the next generation of leaders it will be important to look beyond the conventional talent pool for leadership, developing a process that scouts internally and externally for people with the potential for leading successfully in conditions of accelerated complexity. This search should be a cross-organizational effort, involving stakeholders in its development.

## Developing future leaders

In developing future leaders it will be important to ensure that roles are broad and meaningful 'real jobs' in which people will have a chance to experience and grow through the challenges, develop change management and other key skills and acquire prowess at designing environments conducive to agility, engagement, resilience and great results.

One traditional manufacturing company wanted to encourage leadership at the front line but there was concern that there could be too much power distance between those at the top and the front-line workers. The top team had recently clarified the organization's new customer-centric values, but some high-potential managers recognized that if current senior leaders were to remain remote from the daily realities of the organization, they were unlikely to be effective or inspirational people managers. Their recommendations to top management were as follows:

- Involve high potentials and senior managers in stepping up to play a more active role in running and developing the business – usually a role held by top management – so that top management can be more externally focused and strategic.

- If senior managers/leaders become disconnected from customer experience they should go 'back to the floor' – to understand more specifically the customer experience – not only in induction.

- Managers should lead the customer-centric change agenda and engage with the people who make front-line decisions. Managers should learn how to delegate effectively and develop teams that can work across boundaries, expose them to new thinking (especially in the light of changing channels), help them become aware of decision-making bias, etc.

- Hold managers accountable for how they are developing people and managing change.

- Don't force technical experts to manage people as the only way to get on – develop other career possibilities.

- Longer term, recruit in or build the management capability we want (people with diverse experience).

- Reinforce customer-centricity through offering a leading people experience to staff.

- Create an employee life-cycle map and assess the quality of people experience at each stage and identify relevant improvement processes.

- Take a fresh look at the competencies required over the next three years, e.g. change leadership, also taking new values into account.

- Review the whole approach to managing performance to align with new values; focus on behaviours and contribution – including how managers develop people – and hold people to account for their contribution in customer outcomes.

While top teams may not always like what they hear, they must be open to messages from below and not 'shoot the messenger'. And by institutionalizing new practices, behaviour should start to change at all levels, including at the top.

One unexpected benefit of the COVID-19 pandemic is that many CEOs have been able to identify who their future leaders might be. They have seen who can make decisions and execute rapidly; who is able to take on new challenges and lead in the face of uncertainty; and who has the courage to persevere. In many cases leaders have found emerging talent two to three layers down; people who rose to the occasion and helped to lead crisis-response and plan-ahead strategies. Not only have CEOs gained insight into who the future leaders are but they have also seen the value of rapidly deploying top talent to the most important work. Organizations that do both things – find future leaders and redeploy talent skilfully – will be able to move faster.[30]

## From 'I' to 'we': building shared leadership

To strengthen the potential agility and resilience of organizations leaders need to build a culture of shared leadership with trust as its foundation. In fast-changing times it becomes even more critical to distribute the leadership load. A more collaborative approach to leadership is needed, with leaders who can motivate and coordinate a team-based approach. This will certainly require getting more people involved in strategic work. Vineet Nayar argues that it is essential to invert the pyramid, distribute the work of leadership, enlist the front line and change the DNA of an entrenched organization.[31]

Raelin argues that traditionally organizations have been thought of as machines and leadership as serial, individual, controlling and dispassionate.[32] Instead, human organizations should be thought of as democratic communities. While conventional models of leadership concern themselves primarily with the attributes and behaviours of individual 'leaders' (e.g. trait, situational, style and transformational theories) in agile organizations the concept of shared or 'distributed leadership' (among free agents) is perhaps as, or more relevant.

Flexible bureaucracies with a shared leadership style are characterized by two main properties – emergence and interdependence – that are constantly being renegotiated according to the changing needs of the organization. The most crucial test of an agile organization is how well its members make the right decisions at the right time to produce the results needed. There is a higher level of accountability among followers that can contribute to the proliferation of creative ideas and extra-role behaviours.[33] So for agility the shift taking place is away from leader-follower relations to a shared leadership model that depends on the collective efficacy of formal and informal networks, where expertise is the driver of change, and leadership is broadly distributed such that people within a team and organization lead each other. Collaborative working is undertaken between individuals who trust and respect each other's contribution and are jointly responsible for leading the organization. *How* leadership is distributed is more important than *whether* leadership is distributed.

Embracing distributed leadership will require mindset shifts for people at all levels but especially for top teams who may need to rewire their own mental models for adaptability and complexity. Agile leadership is less about telling others what to do and more about creating the conditions to empower and enable others to make the right decisions that generate results. Whereas the mindset needed to make decisions in the complicated space is one of confidence that the right answer can and will be known (and therefore certainty is of high value), in the complex space, because there is no knowable or 'right' solution, uncertainty, curiosity and openness are more useful.[34] For Keith Grint,[35] the leader's role with a complex or a 'wicked' problem, therefore, is to acknowledge that they do not have the answer to the wicked problem and to engage the community to address the problem. As Paul Polman found:

> Working together on solving something requires a high level of humility and a high level of self-awareness. When we launched the Unilever Sustainable Living Plan, people inside the company were very worried about exposing ourselves. But I did something there that I didn't realise at the time, but that actually made a big difference, by just saying publicly I don't have all the answers on how to do this and I can't do it alone.[36]

Leaders must ask the right *questions* rather than provide the right *answers* because the answers may not be self-evident and will require a collaborative process to make any kind of progress. This approach is particularly important to 'wicked' problems because they are not susceptible to individual resolution but demand the collective responses typical of systems not individuals. It is the community that must take responsibility and not displace it upon the leader.[37] As Polman relates: 'Often people ask me what my job is and I say honestly it is to make others successful, and the more you do that the more you will see that you create prosperity.'[38]

## On the journey towards shared leadership

To create what Raelin describes as 'leaderful' organizations, senior leaders have four critical processes: (1) set the mission (purpose), (2) actualize goals, (3) sustain commitment and (4) respond to challenges. In 'leaderful' organizations, leadership is concurrent, collective, collaborative and compassionate. This inspires genuineness among its community members so that they can bring their 'whole person' to work. Top leadership must design and actively champion the distributed model based on a shared vision that should be reflected in formal and informal aspects of organization. The task for leaders is building relationships with employees, management, boards, suppliers and partners, creating coalitions of support, countering resistance to change and communicating the vision to staff and wider stakeholders. This requires communication across the organization – lots of it – and sense making, arming decision makers and employees with the tools to find, filter and focus the information they need.

To embed shared leadership the ability to move quickly to apply solutions is essential.[39] People may require new skills, or at least a different skills emphasis, if they are required to act in new ways. 'T'-shaped skills are needed – where people have depth in some areas and also broad horizontal skills such as communication and collaboration. After a transition period, the top leader – or a top leadership team – still steps in from time to time to make key decisions that keep the firm aligned with external demands. Centralized leadership also weighs in when lots of local decisions are getting in the way of economies of scope and scale, or when time constraints require a short circuiting of more consensus-based decision making. In short, top-level formal leaders still play a key role, but their responsibilities are changing.

Successfully introducing shared leadership in organizations within a traditional command-and-control structure will depend on the degree to which senior leaders are willing to 'let go' of their overarching control and embark on their own transformation journey (as we discuss in this chapter). One hospital had a strategic imperative of making quality improvements. Though some directors were initially reluctant to 'let go', introducing peer-to-peer learning helped to build a community of people who have gone on to create a real quality improvement movement within the hospital. The process helped to build leadership in a core group of 30 people at all levels of the organization and built rapport between directorates. This helped to facilitate conversations about the importance of creating the right infrastructure for quality improvement. Directorates reported that participating in this process had captured the energy and imagination of many clinicians. As a result of the process, participants accepted the need to do some new things, to review what had worked, to drop some activities that didn't add value and to do some things differently. Participants were surprised at the levels of duplication they uncovered in the quality-improvement work going on across the trust. As a result directorates were able to reduce the number of active projects (more than 300) by 50 per cent.

As distributed leadership becomes the norm, people at all levels are likely to engage in collaborative action, accepting leadership in their particular areas of expertise. For instance, at Disney, the purpose of 'We create happiness' is embedded in the first day of training for each new recruit and is brought to life through real-life stories of how staff have put the purpose into practice, so helping to create an organizational mindset. Purpose is also made concrete through a set of quality standards that guide front-line staff in delivering the desired customer service, striking a good balance between standards and freedom, and by the promotion of high-performing individuals. Providing guiding principles ensures that the protective functions of alignment, control and risk mitigation are also distributed. Giving front-line employees responsibility and autonomy creates a sense of ownership that inspires them to do everything they can to improve the customer experience. When they see a problem, they fix it without waiting to be asked. Customer insights from front-line staff are fed upwards through the hierarchy via robust channels to leaders who can act on them. Bringing in people who are 'up for' distributed leadership helps to mobilize other people, so hiring for attitude as well as aptitude is important.

Shared leadership may also be a more fluid feature of organizations, in which leadership is based on relevant expertise. If leadership is to emerge 'bottom-up', for instance through networks, an open culture is needed within and across the organization, where groups agree how they will work together and team relationships are built on trust, mutual encouragement, support and protection. In such cases both formal and informal leaders may need to develop clear parameters for the team effort, blurring the distinction between 'leaders' and 'followers'.[40]

Shared leadership is facilitated by collaborative environments and empowerment mechanisms such as participation and delegation, which encourage the sharing of functions and result in the development of leadership capacity to sustain improvements.[41] Shared purpose, common goals, values and beliefs act as parameters for empowerment. When team members have similar understandings of their team's main objectives they are more inclined to both speak up and invest themselves in providing leadership to the team and respond to the leadership of others towards collective goals.

## Supporting teams

Shared leadership can also be institutionalized through formal team structures. The use of self-managed teams (SMTs) – for instance quality circles, task forces, communications teams, new venture teams and business brand teams – appears to be increasing since these are most effective at resolving difficult and complex problems, increasing productivity and heightening creativity in work settings. Widely used in large companies such as Google, HP, Walmart and PepsiCo as well as among many smaller firms, they have been credited with achieving conceptual breakthroughs and introducing unparalleled numbers of new products. Shared leadership enables team members to express their different abilities, thus allowing different types of leadership behaviour to be exhibited in a single team.[42]

Teams need *voice* – with team members having input into how the team carries out its purpose.[43] Successful distributed leadership companies work to increase the voice of front-line workers and also to inject more lateral and external voices into the generation, vetting and selection of ideas.[44] Procter & Gamble (P&G), for instance, augments its internal R&D with its 'connect and develop' programme, which invites suggestions from networks outside the company to boost innovation and find new markets. Similarly, collaboration is not left to the preferences of individuals but built into structures, reward systems and HR practices. At Cisco, cross-functional councils and boards were created to quickly make strategic decisions and respond to new opportunities. Senior managers must act as role models – a significant portion of their compensation is based upon peer ratings of how well they collaborate.

Teams need social support – the extent to which team members actively provide emotional and psychological strength to one another. When team members feel recognized and supported within their team they are more willing to share responsibility, cooperate and commit to the team's collective effort. Effective teams generally have found practical ways to surface and resolve conflict. Teams may also need help from senior management. On the journey towards shared leadership, teams will face impediments, not least fear. After all, taking an initiative and learning something new can be scary, triggering the 'fight or flight' instinct. If management leaves teams floundering, teams will be discouraged. Leaders need to provide support without removing responsibility, in order to build ownership, for instance helping people to work through their fears in 'safe' contexts such as focus groups and 'brown bag' lunches; removing practical barriers to shared ownership; building an internal support system; encouraging communities of practice where like-minded people get together and support each other.

External team coaching can help teams to make coordinated and task-appropriate use of their collective resources in accomplishing the team's task. Coaching can foster independence and a sense of self-competence among team members, nurture collective commitment to the team and its objectives, and increase the possibility that team members will demonstrate leadership and personal initiative. Researchers distinguish between two particularly useful types of team coaching: those that reinforce shared leadership (supportive coaching), and those that focus on identifying team problems through task interventions (functional coaching). Functional coaching is needed when teams lack a strong shared purpose. The role of an external team leader is to do whatever is not being adequately managed by the team itself.

---

CASE STUDY

*Team effectiveness and business performance*

Many studies have found a positive relationship between shared leadership and team effectiveness and performance. One company with a long-standing history of innovative business practice and a progressive management model is WL Gore, founded by Bill Gore in 1958. Best known for its Gore-Tex range of high-performance fabrics, it makes over 1,000 products and employs 9,000 people in 50 locations. When Bill Gore started the company he wanted it to bring innovative products to the market. He sought to understand the human element in innovation and many of the company's current practices derive from his insights. For instance, the company operates as a lattice or a network, not a hierarchy, and associates (staff) can go directly to anyone in the organization to get what they need to be successful. There are no job titles, since this would imply that some people have authority to command others in the organization. Associates are all owners in the company; they are free to decide what they want to work on, since WL Gore works on the principle that this is where they can make the greatest contribution. But once associates have made their commitment they are expected to deliver on their promises.

Go slow to go fast

At WL Gore some of the most impactful decisions are made by small teams. Teams are encouraged to take a lot of time to come together, to build relationships and trust. The firm invests in making sure that teams are effective; as a result, people know they have the authority to make decisions and are responsible for the outcomes. There are 'rules of engagement' – the norms of behaviour and guidelines everybody must follow. Every associate understands how critical these values are, so when leaders make decisions, they must sell the 'why?' in order to get the organization to move. The company believes it is better to spend more time up front ensuring that associates are fully bought-in and committed to achieving the outcome. So it is less a problem of alignment as one of involvement, since associates are owners and they feel responsible for business outcomes.

---

WL Gore adopts a predominantly 'grow your own' talent philosophy in order to create a robust and loyal culture. At Gore, leaders emerge and are appointed to positions of authority because they have followers. The voice of the organization determines who is really qualified to be a leader, based on the willingness of others to follow. They use a peer review process to identify the individuals who are growing into leadership roles. Who are associates listening to? Who do they want on their leadership team? They also selectively and judiciously bring in external hires. Once leaders are in a leadership role they understand that their job is to bring out the strengths of their teams and to make their colleagues successful. Leaders know that their 'followership' comes from their peers, and that they can easily lose this if they don't live up to the company's values.[45]

A similar philosophy is reflected in 'holacracy'(see Chapter 5), a distributed authority system that has been implemented at Zappos. In contrast to a conventional management model this is a radical 'self-governing' operating system where there are no job titles and no managers. Instead of a top-down hierarchy there is a flatter 'holarchy' that distributes power more evenly across a hierarchy of circles, which are to be run according to detailed democratic procedures. Employees can have any number of roles within those circles. A set of 'rules of the game' provides an infrastructure for building empowerment into the core of the organization so that everyone becomes a leader of their own roles and a follower of others', processing tensions with real authority and real responsibility through dynamic governance and transparent operations.

## What happens to top leadership?

What are the implications of embracing shared leadership for people in formal leadership roles? Gone is the heroic leadership model with a monopoly on the vision; it is replaced by a commitment to building shared visions with a range of stakeholders. This leadership model is about stimulating teamwork, which is far more achievable in complex times where a leader being seen as the source of all wisdom will often end in failure. This brings many benefits – it exploits the diversity of perspectives and experiences, draws on strengths and builds potential in the organization.

Building distributed leadership requires active support from the top leaders – without that, initiatives from the floor tend to be ignored and people may give up trying to make a difference. For many leaders, of course, adopting this approach is challenging because of the risk involved and for the shift in skill requirements and power structures it represents, which some may find uncomfortable. Instead of direct control it is about exercising influence. Rogers and Tierney argue that this is particularly the case with leaders of professional service firms, where many organizations are less orderly than they were, with minimal job descriptions and blurred lines of authority, and leaders face a day-to-day struggle to define and implement strategy.[46] They are held accountable for matters beyond their control.

Employees too may feel uncomfortable with a shift towards shared leadership. Some may continue to expect senior management to 'lead' and be unhappy about taking on more responsibility; others may expect that 'anything goes' and that all their ideas will be acted on even if they are irrelevant to the organization's needs. To avoid chaos, at any point along the journey leaders need to exercise the 'loose-tight' approach – managing both the expansion of thoughts that gives rise to potentially creative alternatives and the honing of a viable option. Looseness usually dominates the early stages of the innovation process; in the later stages, tightening becomes more important to scrutinize the concepts and bring the selected ones to the market. A balanced approach and clear signalling about when the balance is shifting – and why – avoids confusion.

---

CASE STUDY

*SNC-Lavalin's Atkins business*

In earlier chapters we discussed how SNC-Lavalin's Atkins UK and Europe business was becoming agile, and how HR was applying agile principles to transform the HR service. Here we consider the leadership philosophy of the CEO driving that culture change, Nick Roberts.

To recap, during his time as UK and Europe CEO, Nick instituted substantial change at Atkins – both structural and more specifically cultural. Nick believed that change was necessary; that companies that stand still end up going backwards. While some changes were already underway before Nick became CEO, such as the behavioural change work being done by Caroline Brown in the Nuclear Business (see first edition), the pace and scale accelerated.

## New approach to leadership

At SNC-Lavalin's Atkins business, UK and Europe, it was clear that the kind of leadership style required for agility was very different from the stereotypical 'hero', command-and-control kinds of leadership approaches of the past when managers were expected to issue orders for people to execute. The previous style of leadership had spawned a social system in which managers were expected to have all the answers. In certain types of client work – for instance, in nuclear projects with high degrees of technical work – this kind of approach is still important. More generally though, CEO Nick Roberts considered the old style of leadership a limitation for the company. Now a manager's job is to give, or help to clarify, direction; create the environment in which other people can implement rapidly and 'fail fast'. It is all about making a move, moving and impacting. Leaders at all levels now must be willing to be visible, 'naked', to state what they do and do not know.

But to institute such a change of leadership approach is not easy, and Nick argues that the top leader must be prepared to be directive and tough if they believe strongly in what they are trying to do.

## Approach to strategizing

Previously, SNC-Lavalin's Atkins business adopted a classical approach to strategy making, with a central strategy team providing process and guidance. In the rapidly evolving environment the company found itself in, Nick felt it was important to move to a more empowered, agile approach to emergent strategy outside the annual review process. If people sense that there is a potential major change underway in the competitive environment, the top team instigates a 'lock down' in which they explore the challenge with a team of experts. These provide all the information needed for the top team to agree an immediate response to that move in the form of a proposition, which is then further explored by others and kept under continual review. This sensing, intelligence-led approach to strategy is a deliberate attempt to adopt Learning Organization principles and practices.[47]

As leader, Nick Roberts is very aware of his responsibility to act as role model to the organization – and is also aware that he and many other people are on a steep learning curve. For Nick, leaders do not need to have all the answers: 'You should be humble enough to say that to the organization.' His view is that it is about being honest and asking people what is the best way to get there.

In one example, Nick recounted listening with great interest to a technical innovation being described by a specialist colleague, Phil, in one of the weekly Operations and Intelligence calls. Nick then commented to the audience:

> Whenever I hear from Phil, I feel empowered and inspired by the potential of this idea, but I'm not confident that I know enough about it to be able to represent it well to clients. I could really do with something that tells me how to describe the possibilities and to be able to say that what you want to do about that is A, B, C, etc. I could do with help with the language – just three or four questions – that open up the discussion in the right way for clients.

The reaction Nick got following that call was unprecedented, with hundreds of callers agreeing with Nick about the challenge, and many suggestions about ways of tackling the problem that were harnessed through the video-enabled infrastructure.

How sustainable is organizational agility?

In these and other ways, SNC-Lavalin's Atkins business moved very quickly in the direction of greater agility while also producing solid results. The question is, what happens next and how sustainable will organizational agility prove to be as the context continues to change? Nick's hope is that, whatever the future holds, the agile capability has become embedded and that the language and behavioural change will endure because people now see the reason why it is important. In future, he believes, when people have a problem they will say, 'we need to have an O&I call on this – we've got to collaborate on the solution.' As he says, by taking a values-based approach to change, 'what we've built is a level of resilience in the organization.'

As for Nick himself, learning is a continual process that is key to both personal growth and organizational agility in our fast-changing world. He reflects: 'It's been an interesting journey. One day I'll stand back and might feel proud about it. Let's say that I'm pleased with what's been achieved in two and a half years.'

## Towards a shared leadership culture

To shift towards a distributed leadership model requires strong conviction from senior leaders and a willingness to make fundamental changes within their organizations. Leaders need to be able to inspire a movement and ignite a passion for change. Long-standing practices may need to be revisited and the current values of leaders and managers put under the spotlight. Other system elements must be reconsidered:

- What is rewarded within the organization?
- How are leaders selected?
- What consequences are there for leaders who don't live up to the desired values?

This journey will not be an easy one, and there will be many forces that will fight the change. And yet the potential benefits of this approach are significant, as the following case study illustrates. It describes how one CEO stimulated the journey towards a positive culture of shared leadership and accountability. For the study I am indebted to Andrew Lycett, former CEO of RCT Homes, and to Sarah-Ellen Stacey, formerly HR and OD Director.

---

CASE STUDY
*RCT Homes*

RCT Homes became Wales's largest housing organization when it took over the ownership and management of Rhondda Cynon Taf Council's entire housing stock in December 2007. This followed a successful vote by tenants to transfer their homes to a new independent organization in order to drive investment and service improvement. As well as almost 11,000 homes, RCT Homes also inherited 290 staff from the local authority, with a further 60 new staff recruited.

RCT Homes is a new type of housing organization – a community mutual – whereby tenants can take part in operational decision making, determining how resources are allocated and how services are delivered. From its inception RCT Homes was charged with 'supporting the social and economic regeneration of the communities it serves'.[48] This brought with it a need to transform the culture that most of the workforce had been used to and to create an environment where staff could flourish and be empowered to achieve excellence while, at all times, putting their tenants first.

Andrew Lycett, RCT Homes's CEO for eight years, said: 'I recognized from the outset that we needed to think differently if we were to achieve a paradigm shift in the way staff and tenants were to be empowered.'

Signals of change

The approach to bring about these shifts was both planned and emergent. From the outset, for staff who were transferring to the new organization there were clear signals of change. The original aspiration of the tenants was captured in 90 separate 'promises' that had been made in the Transfer Offer document. This was used to set change agendas for every aspect of the business and required everyone to be involved in delivering change. All teams were expected to involve tenants in service reviews and standard setting, and in appointing staff for customer-facing roles. For staff used to dealing with tenants only over transactional issues, such as rent payments and arrears, this was a very different approach.

Plans were put in place for a series of organizational development interventions to give momentum and clear direction to the cultural transformation that would be required within the new organization. Key activities in the first six months built the foundation for conscious change.

The first significant action was to bring together staff, board members and tenants in four half-day workshops to develop RCT Homes's vision and values. The list of promises provided the why or the reason that RCT Homes had been established. This process of establishing RCT Homes's vision – 'To provide the best services, designed and delivered with our communities' – defined what it aimed to achieve. Six values – empowering, trustworthy, proud, enjoyable, bold and excellent – outlined *how* the organization would do it. This purpose gave clarity to staff, tenants and other stakeholders about the journey ahead.

Setting the baseline

Having set out its goal and aspirations, RCT Homes wanted to understand its starting position. What was it like to work at RCT Homes in the early days? How far would it need to travel to achieve the vision and values?

The organizational development (OD) team spent the first six months really getting under the skin of the organization in order to understand this, drawing invaluable information from feedback from focus groups, the vision and values workshops, a newly formed staff forum and an inaugural staff survey, conducted in April 2008. The weight of the findings showed that, while staff were proud to work for RCT Homes, a number of sizeable obstacles needed to be overcome. These included:

- managers not listening to their staff
- lack of fun and recognition for work well done
- a culture of blame and mistrust
- 'silo working'

- staff feeling disempowered
- instability and insecurity
- poor customer and performance focus.

Many of these themes were also reflected in the results of a comprehensive customer survey that was conducted concurrently, being returned by almost one-quarter of all tenants, enabling a clear causal relationship to be drawn between organizational culture and outcomes for customers. So with this clear 'evidence' everybody understood the need for change. This was the first time that either survey had been conducted within housing services, increasing its power in terms of raising understanding of the starting point for the journey ahead.

## Developing the organization

It was clear that OD interventions were needed in order to turn around each of the obstacles listed. This was not a one-off cultural change programme that had a start and finish date, nor was it about exhorting staff to work harder. Change towards great performance, customer service and empowerment was promoted on multiple levels using a range of initiatives, actions and events. Key organizational messages were layered through everything, providing consistency and reinforcement, incrementally building momentum towards changing the organization.

## Employee communications

Employee communications were pivotal in reinforcing the clarity of direction and a sense of progress. RCT Homes worked with an external consultancy that specialized in employer branding, marketing and communication. A new way of communicating was developed under the theme of 'We're better together'. As well as the strapline 'promoting partnership: higher performance and trust', the 'tone of voice' and language used in all communication became more informal and conversational. RCT Homes consciously avoided 'corporate speak' and formal language. For instance, what had formerly been 'the staff handbook' became 'Nuts and Bolts' and an infrequent staff newsletter became *Update*, a regular colour publication with a popular magazine style and contributions directly from staff. Launched in 2008, it includes regular features such as interviews with winners of RCT Homes's 'Esteem' staff recognition scheme, a spotlight on a team or function, celebrations of customer service excellence and a 'You said – We did' section explaining how staff suggestions have been used to implement service improvements. A bright-yellow plus sign (chosen to depict both positivity and togetherness) is used in office signage and merchandise created to promote the values of the organization. The connections between the different OD activities, initiatives and events were underlined by the use of similar titles such as the 'Leading Better Together' management development programme and the 'Performing Better Together' appraisal system.

Within its first year, RCT Homes launched a number of groups, schemes and initiatives to directly address issues around voice – staff recognition, empowerment and customer-driven performance. See Table 11.1 for some examples.

Thus a positive common language was forged that helped employees to see how these different processes contributed towards achieving the vision. OD activities continued to reinforce progress towards the vision. RCT Homes's annual conference for all staff acted as a tool to transform the organization, share business success and promote continual improvement. This event had team involvement each year, which enabled teams to report back on their successes and see their part in the bigger picture. It proved to be a real touchstone of progress within the organization as a whole.

Developing leadership

Improving management and leadership was key to moving things forward. RCT Homes's executive management team recognized very early on that managers were

TABLE 11.1  Voice schemes and initiatives

| Scheme/ Event/Group | What is it? | To tackle... |
| --- | --- | --- |
| Esteem | Recognition scheme where staff nominate colleagues who have gone the extra mile to exemplify RCT Homes's values | Appreciation and celebration of great performance. Further embeds the values of the organization |
| Staff forum | Group of staff representing different parts of the organization – seeking input to decisions and testing ideas | Empowerment. Seeks views beyond the manager-staff relationship |
| Voice | Suggestion scheme for staff to put forward their ideas for service and business improvement | Staff empowerment and enabling managers to listen |
| Job well done | A team reward scheme for meeting targets over a quarter. Rewards could include anything from a night of ten-pin bowling to a fish-and-chip supper | Raising awareness of performance targets, while encouraging fun at work |
| Additions | Range of discount benefits, including childcare vouchers and cycle-to-work scheme | Recognition and reward for staff |

not aware of what was expected of them. Low confidence was evident in the first staff survey when managers themselves rated the organization's management lower than did any other staff group. The findings indicated that many line managers did not recognize themselves as being managers or leaders – that was widely viewed as someone else's responsibility further up the chain. Some difficult decisions had been made, including making changes to the executive team along the way. The organization needed to invest heavily in equipping line managers with the skills, knowledge and behaviours to enable them to lead their teams effectively. So began the 'Leading Better Together' programme for all leaders and related activities. First, leadership behaviours were aligned with RCT Homes's values and shared with everyone. They were brought to life in 360-degree feedback and in the organization's 'Performing Better Together' appraisal system. Managers began to discuss with their own line managers not just what they had been doing but how they had led their team.

RCT Homes also considered what could be done to sustain and embed learning. Bimonthly 'Leading Better Together' events bring together all managers – from team leaders to the chief executive – for a half-day session. These events enabled the executive management team to add the why in relation to strategic business direction and decision making. The agenda involved managers in decision making, reinforced key business messages and got managers working together. The events proved invaluable in sharing business performance and celebrating success.

Another activity that helped to sustain and embed improvements in leadership was the development, in-house, of a 'How to...' toolkit for managers. The range of guides covers communicating effectively, conducting a 'Performing Better Together' review, involving teams in service development plans, managing stress, holding effective meetings and much more. The language is user-friendly and the toolkit offers real case studies from internal teams offering very practical lessons on how to excel.

## Customer service

The 'blame culture' identified in RCT Homes's initial staff survey proved a particularly challenging hurdle. RCT Homes wanted to encourage more open and effective conversations and actions in the area of high performance and customer service excellence, but staff were concerned about the consequences both of being honest about their own development needs and of taking different approaches from the norm. When teams saw benchmarking data for the first time, comparing RCT Homes's performance against other similar organizations, conversations began to change.

A great deal of OD activity remained focused on continuous improvement. All staff went through a customer service learning programme, 'Being the Best', developed by Mary Gober International Ltd. This tackles service excellence not just in terms of skills but also in terms of an individual's mindset, language and demeanour. Staff are encouraged to welcome complaints as 'real gold' and emphasis is put on a 'can do' mindset.

Again, mobilizing people for improvement is one thing, embedding new practices is another. RCT Homes made the intangible tangible. The drive for customer service excellence was supported by the modernization and restructuring of RCT Homes's customer services centre, new service-level agreements, the introduction of regular customer satisfaction surveys and a range of new performance information that managers are encouraged to share with their teams. Service development plans identify key performance targets and 'Check and Challenge' events bring together staff from different teams to discuss progress against key shared goals. Individuals discuss performance and customer service in their 'Performing Better Together' sessions and in team meetings.

A positive working environment

The personality and working environment of RCT Homes changed considerably over its first five years. The 2008 staff survey revealed that staff were very loyal and had a strong sense of being part of the 'RCT Homes family', but there was little sense of fun or enjoyment in the workplace. Group activities such as local community volunteering, charity fundraising, sport and leisure activities proved to be key to creating a more relaxed and open working environment. Not only did they bring together individuals from completely different areas of the organization, they also provided opportunities for staff at different levels to work together and build trust in less-pressurized environments. They also encouraged the establishment of a more empathetic relationship with customers.

Every year RCT Homes supports Business in the Community's 'Give and Gain Day' by offering the whole organization the opportunity to contribute a day's voluntary work to local community projects. The sense of teamwork, pride in the local community and simple fun is evident throughout the day. Team-building and development events often include an element of volunteering on RCT Homes's estates and every year one of the 'Leading Better Together' sessions is a volunteering opportunity. Teams right across RCT Homes have put real energy and effort into myriad charity and fundraising events, including Children in Need, Comic Relief and numerous local causes. In total, RCT Homes staff have contributed more than 3,500 hours of voluntary work in the local community and in 2012 their volunteering took them even further afield when a team of tradespeople from RCT Homes's repairs service raised thousands of pounds to fund a trip to Uganda, where they led pupils from Pontypridd High School in the building of a hostel for rural schoolgirls.

The vast majority of voluntary activities come from ideas generated by staff themselves – and the effect on their loyalty and pride in their impact on local communities has been palpable. In 2012, RCT Homes became the first housing organization ever to be named 'Responsible Business of the Year' by Business in the Community in Wales.

## Health and wellbeing

An emphasis on health and wellbeing has also been a vehicle of organizational change. RCT Homes encouraged individuals to start sports or social teams and many of the charitable events included sporting achievements or endurance events, such as taking part in Wales's Four Peaks Challenge and a 24-hour sponsored cycling event. Healthshield – a health plan providing contributions towards dental, optical or medical treatment – was introduced for all staff during 2010. Staff sickness levels reduced from an average of 14 days per employee per year to less than eight – a saving to the company of more than £150,000 a year. Determined not to rest on its laurels, RCT Homes is working towards the Welsh Government's Corporate Health Standard.

## Results and benefits

The benefits are substantial.

RCT Homes's staff surveys have provided evidence of significant change in the workplace. Overall staff satisfaction figures increased by an average of 25 per cent since RCT Homes began operations. When it was awarded Investors in People Bronze status in 2012, the assessors highlighted quotes from staff including:

- 'There is a faster pace to things now. You don't have all the answers yourself so you have to collaborate with others in order to get things done.'
- 'We are encouraged to see ourselves as one team working for our tenants.'
- 'It feels different to what it used to – the attitude is more caring; I feel proud to be part of the organization.'
- 'It's a great place to work.'

RCT Homes's investment in community regeneration and training opportunities has had a major impact on many lives. Jason, a trainee in facilities management, said: 'I wouldn't be where I am now. I would be unemployed without the confidence and qualifications.' Most importantly, the changes have been felt by RCT Homes's tenants and customer satisfaction increased significantly – all this during a period of unprecedented growth when RCT Homes's annual turnover increased from less than £10 million in 2008 to nearly £49 million in 2012 and its breadth of operations grew to incorporate four subsidiary companies delivering a very diverse range of technical, charitable, development and social enterprise activities.

As this case study suggests, top leadership working from a strong sense of purpose and values, supported by a capable OD specialist, can help to develop a culture of shared leadership focused on doing the right things for the tenant/customer.

---

## Conclusion

A VUCA world doesn't render the rules and the discipline of leadership irrelevant; it raises the bar on the discipline required to succeed with vision, understanding, clarity and agility. We have learned that during the pandemic many leaders took the opportunity to adapt their organization to become more agile and resilient. They sensed and adapted to a VUCA environment, created innovations and helped their organizations to prevail.

Increasingly, leadership and leadership development are seen as inherently *collaborative, social and relational processes.*

Especially in fast-moving times, leadership will be understood as the *collective capacity of all members of an organization* to accomplish such critical tasks as setting direction, creating alignment and gaining commitment. For agile leaders the shift taking place is towards *exercising influence rather than directive control.* Taking this next step will require leaders at the top to gain deeper understanding of the role of organizational systems and culture and how they can be an 'instrument' of change.

In developing communities of leaders the main task for senior leaders is to *create the conditions* that produce and reinforce collaboration, shared leadership, ownership and accountability at all levels. This will require great communications, strategic conversations and the *creation of cross-organizational networks* united by shared purpose.

HR can help leaders to strengthen connection by coaching them on how to develop a strong shared purpose and strategic narrative, and on how to become authentic role models of company values, challenging management behaviour that is not in line with company values. Such leaders will need to remove obstacles to empowerment, and design structures that facilitate the flow of information, ease interaction and create transparency. This is about creating a foundation of trust on which a new, more mutual employment relationship can be built.

Perhaps the ultimate test of a leader is growing the next generation of leaders, creating a common language and set of leadership concepts that everyone understands and can relate to. 'In every organisation, you've got processes, you've got strategy, you've got structures, you've got people... but leadership is the ingredient which gets the best out of all the other ingredients.'[49]

---

CHECKLIST

As an HR/OD consultant:

How effective are leaders at taking the lead on:

- External scanning (regular assessment of the environment)?
- Providing direction, setting strategy to achieve our vision / mission?
- Involving people in strategizing and change?
- Aligning culture and policies to deliver strategy (mission, goals, intent)? Do the elements support each other?
- Role modelling - walking the talk on purpose, values and learning?

How do our leaders impact our culture?

- Holding on to the old or championing the new?
- Do our leadership qualities, styles and mindsets bring out the best in us?
- What do we do to build future leaders?
- How willing and capable are our middle managers in building an effective work unit climate? What type of support/ tool/programme will help this group do this?
- What is working well and what may need to change?
- What do you need to do to close gaps?

As a leader:

- Are we sufficiently externally sensitive – so that we can stay ahead of the environmental challenges? How can we get better at scanning the environment - building and using our external antennae?

- Are we deploying the organization's strengths and weaknesses well against environmental opportunities and threats?
- Do we have a unified purpose, vision and mission – that appeals to ourselves and our staff at a deep level (and unites us for action and change)?
- How aligned are our culture and vision/strategy? Do they support each other or cancel out each other?
- Do I really believe that agility is the right way forward for my organisation? Does the top team agree?
- How can we create and transmit values that bind the organisation together?
- What are the right skills to drive my organisation forward?
- How do we engage the people you need to deliver success?
- How do we speed up processes?
- How will tomorrow's leaders need to be different from today's leaders?
- How do we create collective leadership?
- How does customer focus become embedded in the organisation's DNA?
- How do we create a culture of performance and innovation?
- How can we manage change effectively and not 'throw the baby out with the bathwater'?
- How do we maintain trust and keep people motivated through change?
- How does our leadership help or hinder the organisation's ability to adapt at speed?
- What behavioural changes might be needed in me/the leadership team to tackle the challenges our organisation faces?
- What do I/we need to learn as leader(s) and what's the best way to go about this?

## Notes

1  Steve Radcliffe in Russell, J (2022) The incomplete leader, *RSA Journal*, Issue 3, pp 42–45.
2  Handy, C (2002) What's a business for? *Harvard Business Review*, 80 (12), pp 49–56.

3  Spears, L. The 10 gifts of a servant leader, DailyGood Robert K. Greenleaf
   Center for Servant-Leadership, 4 June 2013, www.dailygood.org/story/447/
   the-10-gifts-of-a-servant-leader-larry-spears/ (archived at https://perma.
   cc/2F57-J833).

4  Spears, LC (2004) Practising servant-leadership, *Leader to Leader*, Fall,
   pp 7–11.

5  Qualtrics. The 4 things your people need you to know, The Qualtrics Employee
   Experience Report, 2022, www.qualtrics.com/ebooks-guides/employee-
   experience-trends-2022/ (archived at https://perma.cc/9BVC-FGEP).

6  Williams-Alvarez, J. Employees step up pressure for corporate reform,
   *Financial Times*, 7 December 2020.

7  Burns, JM (2012) *Leadership*, Open Road Media, New York.

8  May, DR et al (2003) Developing the moral component of authentic
   leadership, *Organizational Dynamics*, **32** (3), pp 247–60.

9  Goffee, R and Jones, G (2005) Managing authenticity, the paradox of great
   leadership, *Harvard Business Review*, December.

10  Norman, S, Luthans, B and Luthans, K (2005) The proposed contagion effect
    of hopeful leaders on the resiliency of employees and organizations, *Journal of
    Leadership and Organizational Studies*, **12** (2), pp 55–64.

11  Gitsham, M. The changing role of global leaders, *Harvard Business Review
    Blog Network*, 14 February 2012, hbr.org/2012/02/what-it-takes-now-to-lead-
    a-bu (archived at https://perma.cc/9PZF-LGAV).

12  Tata, R and Wallenberg, M (2014) The power of enduring companies,
    *McKinsey Quarterly*, September.

13  Heifetz, R and Laurie, DL (2001) The work of leadership, *Best of HBR*,
    September.

14  Morris, W. Towards a new luxury, *The Sunday Times*, 21 September 2014.

15  Temin, D. The Role of Boards in Crises: 10 Steps For Directors Before, During
    And After Crisis, Forbes blogs, 8 October 2014, www.forbes.com/sites/
    daviatemin/2014/10/08/the-role-of-boards-in-crisis-10-steps-for-directors-
    before-during-and-after-crisis/?sh=6cc0e5aa2ba4 (archived at https://perma.cc/
    UCC4-9PYK).

16  Weber Shandwick and KRC Research (2020) Home country as stakeholder,
    webershandwick.co.uk/wp-content/uploads/2021/11/EMEA-Report_
    FINAL_29-OCT.pdf (archived at https://perma.cc/82PU-KRKP).

17  Collins, JC and Porras, JI (2005) *Built to Last: Successful habits of visionary
    companies*, Random House, London.

18  Kay, J. Forget how the crow flies, *Financial Times*, 17 January 2004, p 21.

19  Springett, N (2005) *Shared Purpose*, Roffey Park, Horsham.

20  Koestler, A. AZQuotes.com, n.d., www.azquotes.com/quote/1092786 (archived
    at https://perma.cc/5HF6-YCTF).

**21** Proust, M. *Remembrance of Things Past*, Vol. 5 – The Prisoner (originally published in French in 1923, and first translated into English by CK Moncrief).

**22** Heifetz, RA and Laurie, DL (2001) The work of leadership, *Harvard Business Review*, **79** (11), pp 131–40.

**23** Mayo, AJ and Nohria, AN (2005) *In Their Time: The greatest business leaders of the 20th century*, Harvard Business School Press, Boston.

**24** Welbourn, D et al (2012) *Leadership of Whole Systems*, The Kings Fund, London.

**25** Kramer, HJ Jr (2011) *From Values to Action: The four principles of values-based leadership*, Wiley, San Francisco.

**26** Collins, J (2001) *Good to Great*, Random House, London.

**27** Polman, P. Former Unilever CEO Paul Polman says aiming for sustainability isn't good enough: The goal is much higher, *Harvard Business Review*, 19 November 2021.

**28** Anding, JM (2005) An interview with Robert E. Quinn entering the fundamental state of leadership: reflections on the path to transformational teaching, *Academy of Management Learning and Education*, **4** (4), pp 487–95.

**29** Badaracco, JL Jr (2006) Leadership in literature, *Harvard Business Review*, March.

**30** McKinsey & Company. Ready, set, go: Reinventing the organization for speed in the post-COVID-19 era, 26 June 2020, www.mckinsey.com/capabilities/people-and-organizational-performance/our-insights/ready-set-go-reinventing-the-organization-for-speed-in-the-post-covid-19-era (archived at https://perma.cc/W9XC-LQ9G).

**31** Nayar, V, in K Moore (ed) *Employees First, Customers Second: Why it really works in the market*, Forbes Leadership, 14 May 2012, www.forbes.com/sites/karlmoore/ 2012/05/14/employees-first-customers-second-why-it-really-works-in-the-market/ (archived at https://perma.cc/ZR9C-ZWDG).

**32** Raelin, JA (2005) We the leaders: In order to form a leaderful organization, *Journal of Leadership and Organizational Studies*, **12** (2), pp 18–30.

**33** Adler, PS and Borys, B (1996) Two types of bureaucracy: Enabling and coercive, *Administrative Science Quarterly*, **41** (1), pp 61–89; also Saparito, PA and Coombs, JE (2013) Bureaucratic systems' facilitating and hindering influence on social capital, *Entrepreneurship: Theory and Practice*, **37** (3), pp 625–39.

**34** Johnston, K, Coughlin, C and Garvey Berger, J (2014) Leading in complexity, Cultivating Leadership, May, www.cultivatingleadership.com/site/uploads/Leading-in-Complexity-CC-JGB-KJ-2014-4.pdf (archived at https://perma.cc/J3ZG-8EF6).

**35** Grint, K (2005) Problems, problems, problems: The social construction of leadership, *Human Relations*, **58** (11), pp 1467–94.

**36** Cofino, J. Paul Polman talks about authenticity, transparency, a sense of purpose in business and why profit warnings don't worry him, theguardian.com, 2 October 2013.

**37** Heifetz, RA (1994) *Leadership Without Easy Answers*, Harvard University Press, Cambridge, MA.

**38** Cofino, ibid.

**39** Kinsinger, P and Walch, K (2012) Living and leading in a VUCA world, *Thunderbird University*, www.forevueinternational.com/Content/sites/forevue/pages/1482/4_1__Living_and_Leading_in_a_VUCA_World_Thunderbird_School.PDF.

**40** Silva, DY, Gimbert, B and Nolan, J (2000) Sliding the doors: Locking and unlocking possibilities for teacher leadership, *Teachers College Record*, **102** (4), pp 779–804.

**41** Bowerman, KD and Van Wart, M (2011) *The Business of Leadership: An introduction*, Routledge, Abingdon, p 333.

**42** Bergman, JZ et al (2012) The shared leadership process in decision-making teams, *The Journal of Social Psychology*, **152** (1), pp 17–42.

**43** Ancona, D and Backman, E. It's not all about you, *Harvard Business Review Blog Network*, 26 April 2010, blogs.hbr.org/2010/04/its-not-all-about-me-its-all-a/ (archived at https://perma.cc/WM9A-HNQ2).

**44** Carson, JB, Tesluk, PE and Marrone, JA (2007) Shared leadership in teams: an investigation of antecedent conditions and performance, *Academy of Management Journal*, **50** (5), pp 1217–34.

**45** Hamel, G. Lessons from a management revolutionary, Gary Hamel's management 2.0, 18 March 2010, blogs.wsj.com/management/2010/03/18/wl-gore-lessons-from-a-management-revolutionary/ (archived at https://perma.cc/S2B4-NV6Q).

**46** Rogers, P and Tierney, T (2004) Leadership without control, *European Business Journal*, **16** (2) pp 78–82.

**47** Senge, PM, Kleiner, A, Roberts, C et al (1994) *The Fifth Discipline Fieldbook*, Currency Doubleday, New York.

**48** Taken from RCT Homes's marketing material.

**49** Steve Radcliffe in Russell, ibid.

# Conclusion

As the pace of transformations in the business environment continues to accelerate many organizations will struggle to keep up, become too slow to respond to what the marketplace now demands and may ultimately go under. Symptoms of organizational atrophy – internal focus, rigid thinking, slow decision making, risk aversion, command-and-control management styles, organizational politics – are everywhere. We have discussed why the systematic adoption of Lean and other Agile tools across a whole management system remains rare and organizational agility is in short supply. There are many barriers to success, yet in this book we have considered how this gloomy failure scenario can be avoided.

By now I hope it is clear that I believe organizational agility to be more than just a set of tools and activities: it is a state of being. As with all living systems, organizations need to be change-able in order to thrive. They need to be aware of the bigger picture, sense the right time to move, find new propitious spaces in which to thrive, experiment and learn from what works and what does not. Like living organisms, organizations must find new sources of nourishment and keep fit (literally and metaphorically) in order to gain the suppleness required for responsiveness and free movement. Organizational systems need to develop and practise new routines that allow the unfamiliar to be 'managed' in such a way that leaves scope for specific innovative responses to exceptional situations.

Here is a brief summary of the key themes we have examined that suggest how greater agility and resilience can be built, where there is a will to do so.

In previous chapters we have looked at various aspects of organizational agility and resilience. We have considered agile approaches to developing and implementing sound strategies. This requires a clear and unambiguous focus on customers – existing and potential – and the development of customer relationships that allow for some co-creation. We have seen that these strategic processes – strategizing, scanning and implementing – require collective awareness and informed effort, an ongoing proactive search of the environment for opportunities that can be capitalized on and threats that must be mitigated.

In recent times the very role, purpose, nature and legitimacy of organizations, professions and institutions are coming into question. Organizations are more obviously than in the past accountable to, and part of, their communities and society as a whole. Today there are rising public expectations that companies – including across their supply chains – should act in more ethical and more financially, socially and environmentally responsible ways as corporate citizens. So organizations must become responsive and proactive with respect to their communities, and demonstrate in all aspects of their operations their responsibility towards the environment and to other stakeholders such as customers, suppliers, employees and shareholders. Whether the organization is for profit or not for profit, people want to give their best to organizations serving a worthwhile cause. As the RCT Homes case illustrates, when organizations voluntarily extend their efforts beyond their statutory obligations and take further steps to improve the quality of life for employees and their families, as well as for the local community and society at large, their corporate social performance and reputation are likely to improve.

We have looked at Agile principles, values, methods and working practices such as teamwork, short iterations and feedback cycles that allow for responsiveness and innovation to meet changing customer needs. We have seen how the principle of simplicity rather than complexity applies, particularly with respect to finding solutions that are fit for purpose rather than over-sophisticated, aligning work with appropriate funding. We have discussed how waste and duplication should be removed and core processes refined around the customer journey. Teams and individuals should be empowered and accountable, with clear decision-making rights, aided by high-quality regular communications and development. Standards should be set so that everyone knows what is expected of them. These Agile principles and methods should arguably be spread across the organization to become 'the way we do things around here'. Even the grand 'set-piece' change programme methodologies must adapt to ensure greater relevance and adaptability.

Leaders should ensure the design of organizational elements supports agility. These include lateral enablers such as:

- Bringing together cross-functional teams. Identify the key capabilities that need to come together to solve the customer problem (whether technology, product, sales, operations, etc), and then look at how they can collaborate better.

- Creating horizontal networks. Once you know the capabilities you need to bring together, consider whether this can be done through formal or informal networks. Does it require structural changes or are there things (such as KPIs, skills, leadership priorities, etc) that can be modified to enable collaboration?

- Funding. Understanding the flow of money and how capital is allocated and how that helps or hinders your approach to cross-functional, customer-driven agile working can help accelerate the adoption of Agile.

- Data and analytics. Identifying how data should be gathered, stored, analysed and used to generate insights. This should inform the choices around how to best leverage the potential of data and analytics to build the required capabilities.

And while these tools, methods, structures and practical/technical issues are important, the more important enablers of organizational agility relate to people and culture, all of which will undergo change to become resiliently agile. In this transformation, senior leaders play a very significant role.

## Situation counts

I have argued that, if organizations are to survive and thrive in this fast-changing environment, leaders must embrace agility and be committed to building their organization's resilience and ability to adapt. True agility seamlessly blends adaptability, speed, improvement, innovation, resilience and renewal. However, there is no 'one size fits all' for agility as the nature and degree of agility required by different organizations will vary according to their situation. What is common to all is the need to collectively and actively keep focused on external context trends, anticipate how these will affect the business and its customers and to proactively put in place actions to capitalize on opportunities and mitigate threats. This external focus must percolate throughout the organization, and channels for pooling and sifting the collective intelligence must be found.

In this changing business landscape, agile organizations are dynamically connected with partners across increasingly porous organizational boundaries, internal and external. To work well with partners and create effective connections that bridge silos and enable organizational flexibility, people must navigate complexity. They need sophisticated relationship and trust-building skills. They must be supported on this learning journey as they attempt to take judicious risks. Company policies too must become culturally sensitive and adapt to ensure they are aligned to different geographical, cultural and business contexts.

## Customer comes first

In agility, the customer is monarch. To optimize company performance over time, organizations need to be ambidextrous, effective both now and in the future. Using agility simply to pursue short-term cost savings and efficiencies tends to undermine organizational resilience and suboptimizes the speed and innovation potential of agility. To build agility into an organization's DNA requires both living by the customer-centric values that underpin agility and a focus on resilience, to create a culture conducive to experimentation and learning. A shared purpose around the customer provides the 'north star' for everyone's efforts if the mission is lived out for real and in particular is reflected in leadership priorities and behaviours. Whether the customer is the end user, or intermediaries, local communities or the planet, people must have line of sight to the customer in their day job for the motivating effect to be impactful.

Similarly, sustainability, like agility, is key to delivering all sorts of value. To make the organization more resilient and equip it for a sustainable future, leaders should clarify what 'agility' means for the organization and look beyond the short term to achieve more meaningful gain. Executives and boards must be aligned to this ambition. New definitions of success must be found that weigh quarterly results and investor dividends in the balance with potentially more important outcomes for a wider set of stakeholders. To deliver outcomes for customers and wider stakeholder groups new capabilities, routines and practices may be required. The composition of the organization, and its partners, should reflect the customers they serve, with diversity and inclusion a central facet of a resiliently agile organization.

So the quest for improvement and risk management in the here and now must be deliberately balanced by the pursuit of longer-term value generation, innovation and multiple transient advantages. Whether innovations are required in products, services, technical capabilities or ways of working, innovating in one area may lead to innovations in other areas and unlock the potential for a step change in capability.

## Agility = mindset

Today's global business environments are fast-paced and operate 24/7. In such a complex environment the notion of centralized decision making is becoming increasingly anachronistic and impractical. Ensuring people are empowered to make decisions at the right level makes sense. Given the growing demands for employee participation, and the need to gather collective intelligence, more democratic approaches to management and leadership are required. Leadership styles must evolve beyond command and control towards more collaborative, participative approaches based on mutual trust and respect. To build shared leadership employees too must be willing to step up and play a proactive role in furthering their organization's goals. However, if the change of leadership approach is not authentic and if the hierarchical mindset remains in place, employees will soon learn not to trust management. Shifts in management approach must therefore be authentic and values-based. Developing disciplines around what must remain 'tight' (i.e. under top-down controls), and what can be 'loose' to allow for employee participation and task discretion, and communicating why, avoids confusion and enables the right blend of innovation and risk management.

Everyone needs an agile mindset that is open to learning, alert and flexible, that reframes change as dynamic stability, as an inevitable part of the organization's life journey so that agility can be embraced as the new norm. Leaders in particular must embrace agile leadership approaches that will lead the way for others to follow since they have a disproportionate impact on the success or failure of their organizations. This may require leaders to develop new skills – and, since nothing is certain – the ability to live with ambiguity and make good decisions fast.

## An enabling context

Agility thrives in a conducive context, underpinned by shared purpose, values and guiding principles that are collectively held and shared. In open, agile and high-performing cultures, empowerment and innovation go hand in hand. Managers play a crucial role in setting the tone, building a climate where people feel safe to raise concerns and learn. In addition to providing resources, structures, systems and processes and especially clarity about goals and roles so that people know what they are doing, leaders must create an enabling context for change and innovation, including a safe psychological space for experimenting. When trust exists, there is greater accountability and less need for direct control. Without it, people are likely to be cautious, slow to respond, unwilling to share their best ideas and defensive when change is needed. Leaders must set parameters for experimentation, including shared purpose, so that risk can be managed and people are empowered to make change where it is needed. Leaders should reinforce the desired direction using communications, recognition and rewards and inject a sense of urgency that keeps people motivated.

Policies such as performance management and management development should be reviewed from the position of being customer-focused and values-driven, enabling learning, autonomy and responsibility. The focus should be on measuring outcomes, mapping achievement rather than time worked, especially when people are working remotely. With respect to performance management, perhaps the most important part is not only people having the conversation around performance but also a conversation about their careers leading somewhere. Coaching, career development, leadership development and skill building can all accelerate the management capability of agility. HR should proactively identify and remove barriers to adoption and ensure there are effective processes for evaluation.

## Culture building

I agree with Hamman and Spayd that the task for leaders is 'Fundamentally… as much about the interior – of individuals, of organizations – as it is about the exterior. It is as much about developing people as it is about building systems. It is as much about creating an agile culture as it is about adapting structures and processes.'[1]

Culture building becomes central to the agile leader's task and requires top-level commitment and stability as a key enabler of transformation. Deliberately attempting to align values across the organization can take time. CEOs who want to lead transformations must be engaged and stick with the goal over time. Having too much to do is no excuse for losing attention. So if leaders really want to reduce waste, to focus on things that matter and increase the organization's capacity for this work, they must lead from the front, start to tear down the barriers and take a systematic approach to building more agile ways of working. Executives who do not support the direction should move on. Of course, if people grasp the methods early, and they trust their employer, that enables greater traction sooner. In such a context the organization becomes a change-able community of leadership at all levels united in a common effort. This is about creating a social movement where change and innovation can be initiated by anyone, not simply at the top.

To stimulate culture change leaders must raise awareness of the need for change, promote dialogue, connect people with each other, create communities for action and widen the circle of involvement so that agility and resilience spread throughout the organization. We have looked at how communications and tools such as social media can be used to enable connections to be made. Leaders can prepare the ground by creating a new vision that is fully 'bought in' to by the executive and board and can become well understood within the organization. Whether or not a formal change programme is required will depend on the circumstances, but if a change programme is necessary, it should be bespoke, branded and 'owned' by the organization. Experienced advisers and coaches can be helpful, especially in challenging and guiding senior management on the change journey.

The leader's task is to be authentic and curious, to listen more and provide a sense of coherence. Leaders should use themselves as instruments to model learning. Rather than solving problems in the conventional way, leaders should frame the problems as questions for others to solve, for instance inviting thoughts from the workforce on 'waste reduction' or on 'how to put the customer at the centre of what we do'. Look for reinforcing mechanisms (often by using listening techniques) and existing organizational symbols and routines (leadership messaging, meeting agendas, leadership townhalls, company celebrations, employee awards, etc) to build new habits and routines. These are powerful ways to build an atmosphere of trust which is the bedrock of agility. Some executives hold a weekly 'stand-up' to hear about what improvement has been carried out that week. This shift from the 'transmit' to the 'receive' mode of leadership marks the end of so-called 'super-hero' leadership to be replaced by something people recognize as being more powerful and effective.

Organization development and training programmes can help to build the capabilities of leaders at all levels and encourage them to demonstrate commitment and consistency in their messaging and support of others. One firm offered monthly follow-on 'report-out' meetings for leaders after training in which initially they typically talked about the successes in their business units. Over time leaders started to share stories about where they and their units were struggling, which allowed much deeper and more helpful conversations to take place, which then aided leaders on their own transition journeys.

Above all, senior managers must recognize that their attitudes, behaviour, language and priorities teach people what is really valued. They must recognize that they have a responsibility to reinforce the organizational values and new practices so that rather than 'do as I say' they model 'do as I do'. They should act as champions to support and enable people with their new ways of working, removing barriers that get in the way. They should seek help from coaches and peers in developing these new approaches to leadership. The aim should be to bring consistency and strengthen what works – while everything around that can change. Constancy of support from the most senior management is the key to scalability. The test of leadership success is if agility is so embedded that when the leaders move on, the organization remains agile.

## Leading change

Some traditional organizations, such as ING, make top-down agile digital transformations. Others, such as Moderna, embrace digital as their modus operandi from the outset. Many organizations attempt to acquire digital and other capabilities through mergers and acquisitions. Whatever the approach, the challenge is to manage the human aspects of change. Leaders must be able to bring people with them through change, remain true to values and lead from a basis of shared purpose. And although technical capabilities are important, leaders can only lead improvement if they understand change and connectedness and can create unprecedented employee engagement.

In conventional large organizations introducing Agile as a major change programme may seem just another management fad. It is important therefore to socialize the idea of what agility is and what it is trying to achieve – such as serving the client faster – before launching any large-scale change programme. Just as, or more, effective is to use data gathered from business-led surveys to identify barriers to being customer-driven and have intensive dialogue about possible solutions, prototyping the best ideas. For example, one pharmaceutical company found that the main barriers to scaling up agility via digital and analytics were typically found in regulatory restrictions, structures and risk-averse managers. Similarly, the firm's employee experience survey found that governance and decision making were perceived to be very rigid and time-consuming; the hierarchical nature of the organization meant that employees generally were unwilling to speak up; people generally did not feel empowered by their managers. Systems, processes and tools did not always work as designed causing frustration and hindering agility. In true Agile manner, rather than try to address all these issues in one change programme the firm began a series of sprints, which led first to improvements in processes so that people could do their jobs better. They also introduced the discipline of weekly conversations within teams to discuss the work and what could be done to unpick blockages. Management development helped managers to understand the transition in their own roles and commit to different practice. In short, one thing soon led to another, and before long, large pockets of the organization were starting to act with greater agility, though there is still a long way to go. The point of this story is that change does not always have to come in set-piece programmes but can emerge given the right stimulus and spread organically across the organization.

Perhaps one of the most powerful change stimuli is when people see executives acting differently. All executives should see themselves as agile digital leaders, empowered, proud and responsible for leading this transformation. OD specialists can facilitate large-scale processes for engaging the whole organization in a positive change journey.

## Agile people

People are the bedrock of organizational agility. We have looked at the importance – and challenge – of flexible resourcing, of bringing in, developing and retaining agile (and mobile) 'talent'. We have seen how HR processes relating to talent management are becoming more agile as organizations struggle with talent shortages, varied fields of operation and more diverse workforces. We have seen how important it is to link the personal and professional from the outset of a staff member's journey as they join an organization.

We have discussed the vital importance of employee engagement and wellbeing and the need to be employee-centric. Today's working conditions can be highly pressurized for employees who are often beset with multiple demands – for dynamic ideas, customer service, innovation – and required to do 'more for less'. When this happens, people's engagement (and health) may suffer and personal and organizational resilience may be undermined.

As we have noted, some leaders are increasingly coming to the view that employees should be seen as the primary stakeholder, since when they are engaged in shared purpose they produce better outcomes for customers and their employer.

HR, managers and employees themselves all have key roles to play in ensuring that a better balance is struck that enables employee engagement, health and wellbeing. The employment deal on offer must feel mutual and the emerging employment relationship must be two-way: what does the organization expect from you, and what do you expect from the organization? Trust is the vital determinant of the employment relationship. However, trust is based on whether organizations act in principled ways. For instance, the values of organizations will increasingly be put to the test on the fairness of their treatment of 'gig economy' workers. HR policies should be designed around engagement principles, geared to ensuring fairness, employee involvement in decision making at work, employee development, satisfaction with pay, job challenge and a sense of achievement from work.[2] People may need flexible working arrangements at different ages and stages of their lives. Wherever possible, the organization should seek to accommodate rather than deny employees this flexibility. With respect to hybrid working, attention must be paid to ensuring that managers and employees are prepared for these more complex working arrangements and that potential risks are mitigated. People may need support with their development needs and career aspirations. So organizations should look creatively at shaping opportunities for people, for instance helping staff to move around the organization by putting a greater emphasis on capability and competency rather than experience in a particular area.

So in order to strengthen resilience, organizations must pay careful attention to employee needs and seek to achieve win-win outcomes for employees and the business.

## Take action

In summary, however daunting the task of building organizational agility, there is reason to be hopeful, since even small steps in the direction of agility and resilience can bear fruit as many organizations that are on the agility journey will attest. It is worth focusing action on unblocking barriers to organizational health and on building the foundations for greater agility to come. Such foundational work can include:

- Learning as key to innovation:
  - Work to build a **climate of trust** around a higher common purpose – tackle the real barriers to organizational health; use values and standards as guardrails for performance.
  - Connect the organization's **purpose and strategy** with individual goals and objectives and hold people accountable – drill these down into daily reality to produce outcomes for people.
  - Work to enable and embed **learning** in organizational practice.
- Inspire people to get, and keep going:
  - Recruit and develop managers and leaders who 'get' agility and can **empower** people.
  - **Harvest ideas**: provide processes for this to happen and ensure that action is taken to follow up.
  - **Celebrate** small successes and learn from 'fabulous failures'.
- Build a mutual and fair employment relationship:
  - **Develop** people (including teams and managers).
  - Create high performance **climates**.
  - Create **meaningful** roles.

When all else changes, purpose and values act as glue.

As I have said throughout, drawing lessons from long-lived organizations and from many of the case studies featured in this book, shared purpose and values are key to organizational agility and resilience. They not only provide coherence and legitimacy, they act as a mainspring for renewal, improvement, change and learning. They provide people with a real line of sight to the point of it all that is motivating and uplifting. They act as the foundation of trust, the vital enabler, on which agility and resilience can be built. When the purpose is uplifting and provides worthwhile benefits to stakeholders, including the community, it can galvanize employee energy, enthusiasm and high performance. Being true to purpose and values is particularly important when leading employees through periods of major change. When this happens, resilience and agility – i.e. change-ability – become part of the DNA, flowing through every aspect of the organization, acting as the mainspring for sustainable performance, innovation, renewal and health. That way, agility and resilience become the 'gift that keeps on giving' – to everyone's benefit!

# Notes

1  Hamman, M and Spayd, MK (2014) Being an agile leader, a White Paper, Agile Coaching Institute, www.agilecoachinginstitute.com/wp-content/uploads/2014/05/Being-an-Agile-Leader-ACI-White-Paper-Mar-2014.pdf. (archived at https://perma.cc/GG9M-F9PW).

2  Hamman, M and Spayd, MK (2015) The agile leader, a White Paper, Agile Coaching Institute, agilecoachinginstitute.com/wp-content/uploads/2015/03/whitePaper-ACI-The-Agile-Leader-Jan-2015.pdf.

# INDEX

Note: Page numbers in *italics* refer to tables or figures